Sing with Understanding

AN INTRODUCTION TO CHRISTIAN HYMNOLOGY

Second Edition, Revised and Expanded

HARRY ESKEW ❖ HUGH T. MCELRATH

with drawings by Charles Massey, Jr.

*"I will sing with the spirit,
and I will sing with
the understanding also."*

1 CORINTHIANS 14:15

CHURCH STREET PRESS
NASHVILLE, TENNESSEE

Second Edition, Revised and Expanded
© Copyright 1995 • CHURCH STREET PRESS
Original Edition © Copyright 1980 • BROADMAN PRESS
All rights reserved.
3020-02

ISBN 0-8054-9825-7
Dewey Decimal Classification: 782.27
Subject Headings: HYMNODY

Printed in the United States of America

Church Leadership Services Division
The Sunday School Board of the Southern Baptist Convention
127 Ninth Avenue, North
Nashville, Tennessee 37234

PRODUCTION STAFF

Jere V. Adams, *editor*
Deborah Hickerson, Connie Powell, *textual editing*
O. Dixon Waters, *artist designer*
M. Lester McCullough, *manager*
Mark Blankenship, *director*
MUSIC DEPARTMENT OF THE CHURCH LEADERSHIP SERVICES DIVISION

To

Margaret & Ruth

ACKNOWLEDGMENTS

*S*ing *with Understanding* has grown out of a lifetime of nurture in churches, educational institutions, and professional organizations. Our roles as teachers of hymnology have served as the stimulus for the development of this textbook. The contributions of teachers, students, and colleagues permeate its pages. We express our appreciation to our respective institutions—New Orleans Baptist Theological Seminary and The Southern Baptist Theological Seminary—for secretarial support. We extend a special word of thanks to Christopher Jenkins of New Orleans Seminary who typed and verified the "Selected Bibliography."

In preparation for this revised edition, we wish to acknowledge our debt to at least some of those who have assisted us in various ways. Once again we express our thanks to Dr. Carlton R. Young, professor emeritus of Emory University, who has written a new Foreword for this edition. We also thank Professor Charles Massey, Jr., of the art faculty of Ohio State University, who has added several illustrations to those he provided for our first edition. Our thanks also to Margaret Routley, who supplied the photograph used for the drawing of her husband, Erik Routley (1917-82).

We are grateful to several publishers and individuals who have permitted their copyrighted hymns to be reprinted. These are acknowledged on the pages on which they appear. Those who have given permission free of charge are indicated with an asterisk [*].

We also are indebted to individuals who have assisted in reviewing or providing information for certain sections of this new edition: Alan Bartel and George Black (recent Canadian hymnody), Emily Brink (metrical psalmody), Victor Gebauer and Carl Schalk (the Lutheran chorale), Robert Harman (cultural perspectives), I-to Loh (Chinese hymnody), Alan Luff (Welsh hymnody), Mary Oyer (African hymnody), Paul Richardson (the Epilogue), and Linda Shipley (The Hymn and Music).

In addition to these persons and hymnological scholars of earlier generations, we need to acknowledge our indebtedness to many of our colleagues of today who have taught us and inspired us at conferences of the Hymn Society in the United States and Canada, the Hymn Society of Great Britain and Ireland, and the International Arbeitsgemeinschaft für Hymnologie (International Fellowship for Research in Hymnology). These include hymnologists and hymn writers as well. Thanks to them, we are able to write from the perspective of firsthand encounters with many of those who have contributed to the exciting new expressions of today's church song.

Finally, we want to express our heartfelt thanks to all who have made use of our first edition in colleges, universities, and seminaries, especially those who have contributed suggestions for improvement in this revised and expanded second edition.

Harry Eskew
Hugh T. McElrath

FOREWORD

This revised edition of *Sing with Understanding* sustains the witness of Harry Eskew's and Hugh T. McElrath's remarkable first edition. It remains the only reliable one-volume work to combine the history and practice of Christian song. The writers expertly and succinctly cover the gamut from New Testament song to today's mesmerizing Taizé choruses, Scripture songs, ethnic global praise, and the compelling songs of the Wild Goose Worship (Music) Group. In addition, they provide a thoroughgoing examination and pedagogy of religious song in practical settings.

The authors' chronicle of the past decade of hymnal publishing in the United States is the first comprehensive examination of the impact of the recent British hymnic explosion. This explosion gave rise to the unprecedented outpouring of religious verse born in Albert Bayly's last hymns and elaborated and matured in the work of Erik Routley, John Wilson, Fred Pratt Green, Fred Kaan, Brian Wren, and Timothy Dudley-Smith. It also spawned a third generation of poets and composers in the United States. Some of these poets are Gracia Grindal, Carl Daw, Jaroslav Vajda, Ruth Duck, and Thomas H. Troeger. A few of the composers are Carol Doran, Jane Marshall, and Carl Schalk.

It is not easy to *Sing with Understanding*—with a sense of purpose, or with good humor—when hymnal committees and their editors (who ought to know better), expressing political correctness, ineptly alter hymns old and new. In doing so they inflict the church's song and its singers with ill-will, indigestion, and heartburn—a neo-Puritanism that suppresses the humor and joy that each generation since Ambrose has found in singing Jesus Christ's gospel of the changed heart, employing a variety of metaphors, musical styles, and performance practices.

It is not easy to *Sing with Understanding* when vital congregational song is replaced by religious jingles—bits and pieces of songs and hymns strung together in subliterate choruses of key evangelical or scriptural words, or by choirs belting out two-part mixed choral products wedded to sound tracks, the progeny of oleaginous publishers seldom rising above trifling disposable pop-folk-rock sound bites—reconstituted from slick, disingenuous fusions of minimal music with stale fragrances of vital religious rhetoric.

To all this, and more, the writers' sure scholarship provides perspective and blessed assurance that since St. Paul it has seldom been easy to *Sing with Understanding*. With this revised edition, Harry Eskew and Hugh T. McElrath continue to hearten and strengthen the hymnological enterprise with valuable and unique contributions to the bibliography and pedagogy of congregational song.

Carlton R. Young,
Professor of Church Music, Emeritus
Emory University
Atlanta, Georgia

LIST OF DRAWINGS

Ambrose of Milan 86

Francis of Assisi 94

Martin Luther 98

Paul Gerhardt 103

John Calvin...115

Timothy Dwight 125

Isaac Watts 132

John Wesley 136

Reginald Heber 147

Frances Ridley Havergal 151

Erik Routley 176

William Walker..182

John Greenleaf Whittier 193

William Batchelder Bradbury 196

Ira David Sankey 201

ABOUT THE ARTIST

Charles Massey, Jr., has been a faculty member in the Department of Art at The Ohio State University since 1974. He was Chairperson of that department from 1982 to 1988. He received the OSU Alumni Award for Distinguished Teaching in 1981.

His work in printmaking, primarily lithography, and drawing is "a personal, intense realism which involves itself with a positive vision, inherent in the soul of a simple, yet sophisticated world that is often taken for granted."

Professor Massey has exhibited internationally, nationally, and regionally in more than 550 exhibits since 1971. He has received over 160 awards and is included in more than 70 public collections, including the Library of Congress, The Art Institute of Chicago, and the Pushkin Museum in Moscow.

CONTENTS

Acknowledgments iv
Foreword v
List of Drawings vi
The Hymn in History: Suggested Readings for Supplementary Study
   Sources to Which Abbreviations Refer viii
Introduction ix

PART I: THE HYMN IN PERSPECTIVE

1. The Hymn and Literature 14
2. The Hymn and Music 29
3. The Hymn and Scripture 49
4. The Hymn and Theology 63

PART II: THE HYMN IN HISTORY AND CULTURE

5. Early Church and Pre-Reformation Traditions 78
6. Reformation Traditions 98
7. British Traditions 127
8. American Traditions 178
9. Cultural Perspectives 219

PART III: THE HYMN IN PRACTICE

10. The Hymn in Proclamation 238
11. The Hymn in Worship 249
12. The Hymn in Education 277
13. The Hymn in Ministry 295

EPILOGUE

14. Trends and Issues in Hymnody 312

Appendix 1: A Service of Worship in Song 326
Appendix 2: Hymn Analysis Checklist 329
Selected Bibliography 331
Indexes...360-400
   General...360
   Biblical Reference 379
   Hymn Title and First Line 382
   Hymn Tune 395
The Hymn in History: Suggested Readings for Supplementary Study ......insert

The Hymn in History: Suggested Readings for Supplementary Study

(SEE INSERT IN BACK OF BOOK)

Sources to Which Abbreviations Refer

BAILEY– Bailey, Albert Edward. *The Gospel in Hymns*. New York: Charles Scribner's Sons, 1950.

BENSON-E– Benson, Louis F. *The English Hymn*. Richmond: John Knox Press, 1962. (Reprint of the 1915 ed. of George H. Doran Co., New York)

BENSON-H– ———. *The Hymnody of the Christian Church*. Richmond: John Knox Press, 1956. (Reprint of the original 1927 ed. of George H. Doran Co.)

BLUME–Blume, Friedrich, (ed). *Protestant Church Music*. New York: W. W. Norton & Co., 1974.

CHASE–Chase, Gilbert. *America's Music*. Rev. 3rd ed. New York: McGraw-Hill, 1987.

DAVIDSON–Davidson, James R. *A Dictionary of Protestant Church Music*. Metuchen, NJ: The Scarecrow Press, 1975.

FOOTE–Foote, Henry W. *Three Centuries of American Hymnody*. Hamden, CT: The Shoe String Press, 1961. (Reprint of the original 1940 ed. of Harvard University Press, Cambridge, MA)

JULIAN–Julian, John. *A Dictionary of Hymnology*. 2 vols. Grand Rapids, MI: Kregel Publications, 1985. (Reprint of 2nd rev. ed., 1907, a republication of John Knox Press, 1962.)

PATRICK–Patrick, Millar. *The Story of the Church's Song*. Rev. ed. by James R. Syndor. Richmond: John Knox Pres, 1962. (Republication of original 1927 ed. of The Church of Scotland Committee on Publications.)

REYNOLDS–Reynolds, William J. and Milburn Price. *A Survey of Christian Hymnody*. 3rd ed. Carol Stream, IL: Hope Publishing Co., 1987.

ROUTLEY-H–Routley, Erik. *Hymns and Human Life*. London: John Murray, 1952.

ROUTLEY-M– ———. *The Music of Christian Hymns*. Chicago: G.I.A. Publications, 1981.

RYDEN–Ryden, E. E. *The Story of Christian Hymnody*. Rock Island, IL: Augustana Press, 1959.

SCHALK–Schalk, Carl (ed.) *Key Words in Church Music*. St. Louis: Concordia Publishing House, 1978.

STEVENSON-PA–Stevenson, Robert. *Patterns of Protestant Church Music*. Durham, NC: Duke University Press, 1953.

STEVENSON-PR– ———. *Protestant Church Music in America*. New York: W. W. Norton & Co., 1966.

INTRODUCTION

The basic purpose of *Sing with Understanding* is to encourage more meaningful congregational singing of hymns. It seeks to address the needs of those who lead in corporate worship—clergy and musicians—and also attempts to bring others, including lay persons, to a greater appreciation of their hymnals and the fascinating heritage of church song. Its primary use, however, is as a textbook for college and seminary classes in hymnology and related areas. Along with increased understanding, it is hoped that this book will contribute to helping persons "sing with the spirit" with true inspiration and enthusiasm.

Singing with the spirit and the understanding implies some acquaintance with the nature of the vehicle used—the hymn itself. The word *hymn* in present-day understanding is a generic term for any kind of song suited to congregational expression in worship. Its treatment throughout this volume assumes a Christian context and content, yet historically, the Christian hymn has not been subject to narrow definition.

In a now-famous commentary on Psalm 148, Augustine of Hippo set forth his conception of the hymn as "praises to God with singing." It is an excellent definition, but it is incomplete. Not all hymns used today are concerned with praise, nor are they all addressed to God. The apostle Paul refers to "speaking *to one another*" as well as to "making melody ...*to the Lord*" in hymns (Ephesians 5:19, NASB), thus recognizing for singing a social as well as a divine direction. Hymns may therefore be expressions of prayer, belief, personal experience, and exhortation to one another, as well as praise to God.

To serve adequately these various functions, good hymns possess certain qualities. Some of these desirable qualities have been included in an "official" definition by the Hymn Society in the United States and Canada:

> A Christian Hymn is a lyric poem, reverently and devotionally conceived, which is designed to be sung and which expresses the worshipper's attitude toward God or God's purposes in human life. It should be simple and metrical in form, genuinely emotional, poetic and literary in style, spiritual in quality, and in its ideas so direct and so immediately apparent as to unify a congregation while singing it.[1]

The chapters that follow seek to examine the implications of these hymnic characteristics. The one incontestable facet of Augustine's earlier

---

[1]Carl F. Price, *What Is a Hymn?* Paper VI of the Hymn Society of America, 1937, 8.

definition is that a hymn is to be sung. Realizing that the definition of the hymn claiming the least best defines it, the Hymn Society, through an action of its research committee, concluded "that for a working definition, the hymn may be regarded as a congregational song."[2]

Hymnody is the collective term for all this song literature. It is the subject matter for our study. The term is also used to refer to specific branches of the total hymnic corpus (for example, German hymnody, Methodist hymnody).

Hymnology is the comprehensive study of this hymnody. It is concerned not only with the origins and development of hymns, but also with their appreciation and use. As An Introduction to Christian Hymnology, this volume seeks to introduce a complete study of hymns, viewing them from several perspectives.

PART I: THE HYMN IN PERSPECTIVE (Chapters 1-4) examines hymns as poetry, music, biblical truth, and theology.

PART II: THE HYMN IN HISTORY AND CULTURE (Chapters 5-9) is a chronological survey, concentrating attention on hymn texts and tunes available and currently used. It is particularly concerned with those hymns that may be found in five widely used American hymnals:

- *The Baptist Hymnal*, 1991,
- *The Hymnal 1982* (Episcopal, published in 1985),
- *Lutheran Book of Worship*, 1978,
- *The United Methodist Hymnal*, 1989, and
- *The Presbyterian Hymnal*, 1990.

Hymns mentioned in the text are keyed to these five hymnals using the letters B, E, L, M, and P, respectively.

The historical survey focuses attention on the texts and tunes. Biographical information is minimal since each of the five major hymnals have companion volumes[3] which can provide background data for the hymns and information about their authors and composers.

- *Handbook to The Baptist Hymnal*,
- *Companion to The Hymnal 1982*,

---

[2]*The Hymn*, the quarterly publication of the Hymn Society in the United States and Canada, 29, 1 (January 1978), 37. Information on this organization is available from the Hymn Society, National Headquarters, Texas Christian University, Fort Worth, TX 76129.

[3]*Handbook to The Baptist Hymnal*, ed. Jere V. Adams (Nashville: Convention Press, 1992); *Companion to The Hymnal 1982*, 3 vols., ed. Raymond F. Glover (New York: Church Hymnal Corporation, 1990); Marilyn Kay Stulken, *Hymnal Companion to the Lutheran Book of Worship* (Philadelphia: Fortress Press, 1981); Carlton R. Young, *Companion to the United Methodist Hymnal* (Nashville: Abingdon Press, 1993); LindaJo H. McKim, *The Presbyterian Hymnal Companion* (Louisville: Westminster/John Knox Press, 1993).

- *Hymnal Companion to the Lutheran Book of Worship*
- *Companion to the United Methodist Hymnal*
- *The Presbyterian Hymnal Companion*

The reader is encouraged to supplement the study of this book with suggestioned readings found in the "The Hymn in History" on the insert at the end of this book.

One's understanding of hymns is enhanced by moving beyond the mere consideration of words and music to a consideration of cultural and historic contexts. Chapter 9 seeks to explore the cultural diversity which characterizes congregational song.

PART III: THE HYMN IN PRACTICE (Chapters 10-13) explores the practical uses of hymns in the mission of the church: *Proclamation* and the sharing of the good news; *Worship* and the hymn's place in corporate devotion; *Education* and the teaching values of hymns; and *Ministry* and the hymn as a medium of social service.

The questions for thought and discussion at the close of most of the chapters are given as aids for study and teaching. Also suggested are some projects for action. In addition, a "Selected Bibliography" by chapter (plus general works and sources for American denominational hymnody) is provided for more extensive study.

This revised edition has provided the opportunity to update the bibliography. Because of the large number of new publications in hymnology, the bibliography is selective rather than comprehensive. In addition to updating each of the original chapters, this edition concludes with an EPI-LOGUE that focuses on trends and issues in hymnody in the 1980s and 1990s, especially in Britain and America. Another significant change in this revision is the expansion to referencing hymns from five major recent hymnals. This provides a broader coverage of song available to American congregations in the closing decade of this century.

Hymnology is a rewarding field of investigation. It has captivated the interest of numerous Christians who want to know more about the hymns they sing and also want to learn more of the content of their hymnals. It is our hope that readers of this volume will also find hymnology a discipline that brings an increased understanding of the purpose of hymns and an enthusiasm to work for more vital and meaningful congregational singing wherever they may worship and serve.

PART I:
THE HYMN IN PERSPECTIVE

1
THE HYMN AND LITERATURE

Prominent hymnologist Jeremiah Bascom Reeves has remarked that "the hymn is the most popular kind of English poetry."[1] He is one of many who has brilliantly focused attention on the wide interest in hymns among all classes of folk in contrast to the comparatively limited appreciation for other kinds of poetry. The significant point in the above statement is not the great popularity of hymns, for this is self-evident, but the fact that they, in a very real and technical sense, are *poems*.

Mention the word *hymn* to almost anyone and the first image that comes to mind is a hymn tune. It is quite natural for the concept *hymn* to conjure up some kind of music because hymns are for singing. Hymnologically speaking, however, the *hymn* as a term refers to the text. The point to be emphasized is that the text of a hymn possesses certain qualities and characteristics associated with poetry.

FORM AND STRUCTURE

One of the most obvious characteristics of a poem, unless it is in blank verse, is that it is organized into sections of equal and regular structure usually known as stanzas. A stanza is a division of a hymn consisting of a series of lines arranged together in a recurring pattern of meter and rhyme.

Stanza, as a technical term, is often confused with *verse*. Possibly this is because *verse*, when one has the Bible in mind, does indeed refer to one of the short divisions into which the Scriptures are traditionally divided. However, although one of the secondary definitions of *verse* makes it synonymous with *stanza*, its first and more precise meaning is that of *one line of poetry*.

One of the reasons the idea of the hymn as a poem is overlooked may be

[1] Jeremiah Bascom Reeves, *The Hymn in History and Literature* (New York: The Century Company, 1924), 3.

the usual interlining of the words with the musical notation found in most American hymnals. This kind of arrangement made in the interest of facilitating the matching of words to music for singing is a comparatively recent development in the history of hymnbook publishing. In most hymnals published even today outside the United States, words and music are separated.[2]

In earlier times a hymnal looked like most other collections of poetry, with the words neatly placed in stanzas on the pages. If there were any references to tunes, they would simply consist of the listing of the names of suitable tunes that could be found elsewhere. In the 18th and 19th centuries, small pocket-sized hymnals were in vogue; they were personally owned and brought by individuals to worship, just like small Bibles or Testaments. The music for hymns was published separately in tunebooks that often would supply only one stanza of hymn text for each tune.

Hymn stanzas are usually found with either 4, 6, or 8 lines each. Occasionally a hymn can be seen with 5, 10, or various other numbers of lines. The varieties of stanza length can be surveyed by looking at the number of digits in a hymnal's metrical index, which, in reality, is a list of stanza forms.[3]

RHYME SCHEME

One of the most obvious features of poetry is the use of rhyme scheme. **Rhyme** pertains to the terminal sounds of poetic lines. There must be a correspondence in the sound of the last word or syllable of each poetic line for rhyme to be present. The coupling of rhyme and meter enables poetry to be remembered more easily than prose.

Rhyming patterns may be quite varied. In hymnody they tend to be comparatively simple. In four-line hymns many poets use rhyming in pairs (rhyming couplets):

> "Holy Spirit, Truth *divine*,...a
> Dawn upon this soul of *mine*; ....a
> Word of God, and inward *light*, ...b
> Wake my spirit, clear my *sight*." ....b
> (M465, P321, Samuel Longfellow)

---

[2] See Erik Routley, "On the Display of Hymn Texts," *The Hymn*, 30, 1 (January 1979): 16-20.
[3] Refer to the metrical index of tunes in the five hymnals referenced in this text. See Introduction.

More often, an alternating pattern known as **cross rhyme** is found:

> "The head that once was crowned with *thorns* ....a
> Is crowned with glory *now;* ....b
> A royal diadem *adorns* ....a
> The mighty victor's *brow.*" ....b
> (E483, L173, M326, P149, Thomas Kelly)

Some hymnists do not choose to rhyme all lines:

> "Just as I am, without one *plea,* ....a
> But that thy blood was shed for *me,* ....a
> And that thou bidst me come to *thee,* ....a
> O Lamb of God, I come." ....b
> (B307, E693, M357, P370, Charlotte Elliott)

> "There's a wideness in God's *mercy,* ....a
> Like the wideness of the *sea;* ....a
> There's a kindness in God's justice, ...b
> Which is more than *liberty.*" ....a
> (B25, E470, L290, M121, P298, Frederick W. Faber)

Stanzas with five and six lines can have a variety of rhyme schemes:

> "Dear Lord and Father of man*kind* ....a
> Forgive our foolish *ways;* ....b
> Reclothe us in our rightful *mind;* ....a
> In purer lives Thy service *find,* ....a
> In deeper reverence, *praise.*" ....b
> (B267, E652, L506, M358, P345, John G. Whittier)

> "Ask ye what great thing I *know* ....a
> That delights and stirs me *so?* ....a
> What the high reward I *win?* ....b
> Whose the name I glory *in?* ....b
> Jesus Christ, the crucified." c
> (B538, M163, Johnann C. Schwedler; tr. Benjamin H. Kennedy)

"Lord (Great) God, your love has called us here, ...a
As we, by love, for love were made. ....b
Your living likeness still we bear, ...a
Though marred, dishonored, disobeyed. ....b
We come, with all our heart and mind c
Your call to hear, your love to find." c

(M579, P353, Brian Wren, © 1977 by Hope Publishing Co., Carol
Stream, IL 60188. All rights reserved. Used by permission.)

A study of the various rhyming possibilities in hymns of 7, 8, 10, and more lines would reveal that there is an amazing variety. The best known hymns, however, are comparatively simple in their rhyme patterns, thereby making them more memorable.

METRICAL PATTERNS

A somewhat less obvious feature of poetry is its meter. Meter refers to a systematically measured rhythm of accent in verse (that is, rhythm that consistently repeats a single basic pattern). Like all verse, hymns are organized into poetic "feet." Each "foot" consists of either two or three syllables, only one of which is accented.

We have inherited our poetic nomenclature from the ancient Greeks. In Greek classical poetry, the most common metrical unit is the *iambic* foot; it consists of an unaccented or unstressed syllable (upbeat) followed by an accented one (downbeat). A line of verse having four of this kind of foot is known as *iambic tetrameter*. (Tetra means four; a three-foot line of poetry is designated *tri*meter, and so forth.)

In hymnals, the number of syllables of a line of poetry is counted rather than the number of feet. *Hymn meter* is therefore indicated in the group of numbers denoting the number of syllables in the lines of a stanza. A four-line stanza in which each line has the iambic tetrameter arrangement is indicated as 8.8.8.8. This is commonly known as Long Meter (LM). The familiar "Doxology" has this pattern; therefore, in hymnological parlance it is known as Thomas Ken's Long Meter Doxology (B5, 27, 253, 449; E11, 43, 380; L564, 565; M94, 95; P591, 592, 593).

The iambic foot is the basis for the three most used meters in English hymnody. Besides Long Meter (LM), there is Common Meter (CM), 8.6.8.6. and Short Meter (SM), 6.6.8.6. It is important to note the above abbreviations. An added D indicates "Double" or repetition of the pattern for hymns having eight-line stanzas.

Rhyming patterns are also indicated by the grouping and punctuating of numerals. For example, the aabb rhyme scheme of "Immortal, invisible, God only wise" (B6, E423, L526, M103, P263) would be indicated thusly: 11 11.11 11 for its ST. DENIO tune.

Consult the metrical index of a hymnal to find familiar examples of hymns in these meters.[4] It is obvious that, apart from musical meter, the term "meter" is applied to hymn tunes, as will be explained elsewhere.[5] Great care must be taken to mate tunes with texts that bear the correct number of lines and syllables and have the appropriate kind of poetic feet.

In addition to *iambic*, a frequently used pattern is the *trochaic* (the reverse of the *iambic*), with first an accent and then a weaker pulse. This meter is more direct and exciting than the more stately *iambic*. Hymn meter indications generally do not specify the kind of poetic feet into which a hymn is arranged. Two hymns, therefore, can have identical hymn meter (for example, 7.6.7.6.D., meaning stanzas of eight lines which alternate in number of syllables between seven and six), but one hymn could be in *iambic* and the other in *trochaic* accentual pattern. Compare the first two lines of the following two hymns, both of which are in 76.76 D meter:

> "**Come**, ye *faithful, **raise** the **strain** 7
> **Of** tri*u*mphant **glad**ness;" 6
> (Trochaic)(E199, 200; L132, M315, P114, 115)

> "Lead **on**, O **King** eternal, ...7
> The **day** of **march** has **come**;" 6
> (Iambic)(B621, E555, L495, M580, P447, 448)

It is clear that one 76.76 D tune could not be used with both hymns. To illustrate this, try to sing LANCASHIRE to "Come, ye faithful, raise the strain"!

When matching hymns to tunes, great caution must be taken to ensure that the musical and textual accents agree, even when both are in the same hymn meter. Study of a metrical index of tunes will reveal many other hymn patterns.[6] It can be a fascinating study!

---

[4]Note, for example: LM—"When I survey the wondrous cross" (B144, E474, L482, M298, 299; P100, 101); CM—"God moves (O God) in a mysterious way" (B73, E677, L483, P270); SM—"I love Thy (Your) kingdom, Lord" (B354, E524, L368, M540, P441); LMD—"Sweet hour of prayer" (B445, M496); CMD—"America the Beautiful" (B630, E719, M696, P564) and SMD—"Crown Him with many crowns" (B161, E494, L170, M327, P151).
[5]See Chapter 2 of this textbook, "The Hymn and Music."
[6]For a treatment of other meters, see Chapter IV and V of Austin C. Lovelace, *The Anatomy of Hymnody* (Nashville: Abingdon Press, 1965; repr. G.I.A. Publications, 1982).

CONTENT AND EXPRESSION

In addition to outward structure and form, a hymn may be considered a poem by its inner content and expression. The great poet Milton said that the content of poetry must be *simple, sensuous,* and *passionate.* The hymn as a poem should possess something of all these qualities.

Ideally, a hymn is written in clear, unambiguous language that is as obvious to the mind of a child as to that of an adult. It deals with profound thoughts but states them simply and directly. *Simplicity,* the servant of clarity, is a prime characteristic of hymnic expression.

The hymn as poetry is also *sensuous*—it appeals to the senses. It draws its themes from the commonplace materials of life, and it conjures up images familiar to ordinary folk because it comes from what people see, feel, touch, and eat in everyday experience.

A hymn is charged with *feeling.* It appeals to the heart, emotions, and mind. A hymn stirs the emotions and lifts the soul—comforting, challenging, making joyful or sorrowful, exalting sentiment, and quickening genuine feeling. Hymns are inherently *passionate.*

Often the finest hymnists are not known as outstanding poets. Conversely, great poets are seldom known for their hymn writing. It was the poet Alfred Lord Tennyson who said, "A good hymn is the most difficult thing in the world to write."[7] He proved his statement by giving the world only one genuine hymn ("Sunset and evening star" entitled by the poet "Crossing the Bar"), which was not written until his 81st year.

But a few outstanding literary figures have produced hymns that would qualify as fine poetry. Look, for example, at this stanza from George Herbert:

> "Come, my Way, my Truth, my Life:
>   Such a way as gives us breath,
> Such a truth as ends all strife,
>   Such a life as killeth death."
> (E487, L513, M164)

This profound and sincere petition is a model of simplicity, sensuousness, and impassioned feeling.

Another example of vivid simplicity, contemporary imagery, and powerful feeling is this stanza by Gilbert K. Chesterton:

---

[7]Hallam Tennyson, *Tennyson: A Memoir* (London: Macmillan, 1897), Vol, II, 401.

"O God of earth and altar,
  Bow down and hear our cry;
Our earthly rulers falter,
  Our people drift and die;
The walls of gold entomb us,
  The swords of scorn divide;
Take not Thy (Your) thunder from us,
  But take away our pride."
(E591, L428, P291)

POETIC DEVICES

Hymns also make frequent use of rhetorical devices and figures of speech that are part and parcel of classical poetry. For example, many hymns use **allegory** which enables a vignette of history to carry a spiritual idea. This is seen in "Guide me, O Thou great Jehovah" (B56, L343, M127) wherein the pilgrimage of the Israelites becomes a picture of the singer's life and hope beyond death. The use of allegory is shown in the hymn with the references to manna (bread of heaven), the pillar of fire, and crossing over Jordan (the river of death) onto "Canaan's side" (heaven—the promised land).

Alliteration—the repetition of the same first sound in consecutive words—is sometimes used in hymn writing. Note, for instance, the use of the "s" sound in this line from Whittier's "Dear Lord and Father of mankind" (B267, L506, M358):

"Take from our souls the strain and stress"

Note the "sh" and "l" sounds in this line from an unpublished contemporary hymn:

"Shaping lives for sharing love" [8]

A much less used device sometimes found in hymns is **anadiplosis** (an-a-di-plo´sis)—using words or ideas ending one stanza as the start of the next. A fine example is found in Charles Wesley's "O for a thousand tongues to sing" (B216, E493, L559, M57, P466).

---

[8]From "To God we lift our voices," an unpublished hymn by M. M. Pace, the pen name of its author who has given permission but prefers to remain anonymous.)

End of stanza 1: "The triumphs of his *grace!*"
Start of stanza 2: "My *gracious* Master and my God"

End of stanza 2: "The honors of thy *name.*"
Start of stanza 3: "Jesus, the *name* that calms my fears"

It is not an accident that many of these devices are found in Charles Wesley's hymns since he had a thorough training in classical poetry. In his hymns we also find the use of **anaphora** (a-náf-o-ra)—the repetition of the same word at the beginning of successive lines for rhetorical purposes. This is seen with the word "born" in "Hark, the herald angels sing" (Stanza 3, B88, E87, L60, M240, P31, 32) and "Come, Thou long expected Jesus" (Stanza 2, B77, E66, L30, M196, P1, 2).

Another literary artifice skillfully used by Wesley was the **chiasmus** (ki-áz-mus, from the Greek ch= cross—the crossing of lines of clauses). A prime example of this is from "Jesus, lover of my soul":

A = "The holy Savior"
B = "The sinful singer"

"Just and holy is Thy name, ...a
  I am all unrighteousness; ....b
False and full of sin I am, ...b
  Thou art full of truth and grace." ....a
(B180, E699, M479, P303)

Here are two persons in bold contrast—the holy Savior and the sinful singer. Wesley starts with the Savior (a), then moves to two lines on the unrighteousness of the singer (bb), and finally refers to the Savior again (a). This device can be an apt vehicle for setting forth the paradoxes of the Christian faith.

Paradox—a statement that is seemingly contradictory but nevertheless true—may appropriately be found at times in hymnic expression because it can dramatically set forth the paradoxical truths of Christian doctrine.

Perhaps the best hymn to illustrate the use of *paradox* is George Matheson's "Make me a captive, Lord":

"Make me a captive, Lord,
  And then I shall be free;
Force me to render up my sword,
  And I shall conqueror be."
(B278, M421, P378)

Closely akin to paradox is **antithesis** (an-tí-the-sis)—sharply contrasted ideas set in juxtaposition. This device is used in hymns formulated according to what is often called the Hebrew pattern, involving the three-fold plan: thesis, antithesis, synthesis.[9]

Hyperbole (hy-pér-bo-lee)—a figure making use of exaggeration—is common to all poetry and is often found effectively used in hymns. For example:

"O for a thousand tongues to sing"
(B216, E493, L559, M57, P466, Charles Wesley)

"In the cross of Christ I glory,
  Tow'ring o'er the wrecks of time"
(B554, E441, 442; L104, M295, P84, John Bowring)

Personification—the representation of a thing or abstraction as a person or by the physical form—is often used in hymns for imaginative effect:

"Put unfailing arms around you"
(Stanza 3, "God be with you till we meet again," M672, 673; P540,
  Jeremiah E. Rankin)

"My faith looks up to thee"
(B416, E691, L479, M452, P383, Ray Palmer)

"Leaning on the everlasting arms"
(B333, M133, Elisha A. Hoffman)

Metaphor—the figure of speech using a word or phrase denoting one kind of idea or object in the place of another to suggest likeness or analogy between them—is found in hymnic lines:

---

[9]See Chapter 4 of this textbook, "The Hymn and Theology."

"Prayer is the soul's sincere desire,
    Unuttered or expressed,
The motion of a hidden fire
    That trembles in the breast."
(M492, James Montgomery)

"My heart an altar, and thy love the flame."
(Stanza 4, "Spirit of God, descend upon my heart," B245, L486,
    M500, P326, George Croly)

Simile (sím-i-lee)–comparing unlike objects in one aspect–is used in hymnic poetry:

"Like a river glorious is God's perfect peace"
(B58, Frances R. Havergal)

"Like the murmur of the dove's song,
    Like the challenge of her flight,
Like the vigor of the wind's rush,
    Like the new flame's eager might:
Come, Holy Spirit, come."
(M544, P314, Carl P. Daw. Jr., © 1982 by Hope Publishing Co., Car-
    ol Stream, IL 60188. All rights reserved. Used by permission.)

Tautology—the repetition of the same thought in a slightly different way—is frequent in hymns:

"Jesus, thou art all compassion,
    Pure, unbounded love thou art;"
(Stanza 1, "Love divine, all loves excelling," B208, E657, L315,
    M384, P376, Charles Wesley)

This kind of literary device reflects the synonymous parallelism of the Hebrew psalms and should be expected frequently in metrical paraphrases of the Psalms:

"God of mercy, God of grace,
    Show the brightness of your face;
Shine upon us, Savior, shine,
    Fill us with your light divine."
(Psalm 67, E538, P203, Henry F. Lyte)

"He comes with succor (rescue) speedy
  To those who suffer wrong;
To help the poor and needy,
  And bid the weak be strong;"
(Psalm 72, E616, L87, M203, James Montgomery)

Apostrophe—addressing inanimate objects or concepts—lends itself to effective devotional use in hymns:

"O Zion, haste, thy mission high fulfilling,"
(B583, E539, M573, Mary Ann Thomson)

"O perfect love, all human thought transcending,"
(B512, L287, M645, P533, Dorothy Frances Blomfield Gurney)

Climax—the arrangement of ideas in ascending order of intensity—lends drive and heightened emotion to meaningful hymn singing:

"Ours the cross, the grave, the skies,"
(Final stanza, "Christ the Lord is ris'n today," B159, E188, 189;
  M302, P113, Charles Wesley)

"Demands my soul, my life, my all."
(Final stanza, "When I survey the wondrous cross," B144, E474,
  L482, M298, 299; P100, 101, Isaac Watts)

"Our Maker, Defender, Redeemer, and Friend."
(Final stanza, "O (Oh) worship the king," B16, E388, L548, M73,
  P476, Robert Grant)

All of these and other poetic devices[10] may not be noticed by the ordinary worshiper, but will become apparent when one seeks the secret of the expressive power of good hymns. The presence of poetic devices is evidence of the true literary quality of many of the most memorable songs of devotion and praise.

---

[10]See Lovelace, *The Anatomy of Hymnody*, Chapter 4. Many other poetic devices often found in hymns are identified in this work, including *epanadiplosis* (repetition of a word at the beginning and end of a phrase), *epizeuxis* (immediate repetition of a word or phrase), and *synecdoche* (a part used rather than the whole).

LITERARY PATTERNS

In addition to the use of figures of speech, hymns are fine pieces of crafted verse in the organized plan and symmetry of their thought structure. Note the following literary designs:

Itemization is employed by hymnists to furnish thematic unity and progression. This is apparent in the plan of the following examples:

1. "O praise *the gracious power* That tumbles walls of fear,"
2. "O praise *persistent truth* That opens fisted minds,"
3. "O praise *inclusive love*, Encircling every race,"
(First three stanzas, "O praise the gracious power," B226, P471, Thomas H. Troeger. Copyright and reproduction by permission of Oxford University Press, Inc.)

1. "O *Love* that wilt not let me go,"
2. "O *Light* that followest all my way,"
3. "O *Joy* that seekest me through pain,"
4. "O *Cross* that liftest up my head,"
("O Love That Wilt Not Let Me Go," B292, L324, M480, P384, George Matheson)

1. "Open my *eyes*, that I may *see*"
2. "Open my *ears*, that I may *hear*"
3. "Open my *mouth*, and let me *bear*"
("Open my eyes, that I may see," B502, M454, P324, Clara H. Scott)

Dialogue is the structure of question-answer hymns. Consider the conversational style of these hymns:

"Am I a soldier of the cross"
(B481, M511)

"Ask ye what great thing I know"
(B538)

"Watchman, tell us of the night,"
(E640, P20)

"What child is this,"
(B118, E115, L40, M219, P53)

"Who is He in yonder stall,"
(B124, M190)

Litany is an effective and useful literary pattern. It is found most often in petition or praise hymns in which the thought is completed by using the same short refrain or response in each stanza. For example, "Let us with a gladsome mind," based on the litany in Psalm 136, has this affirmation in each stanza:

> "For his (God's) mercies shall endure,
>   Ever faithful, ever sure."
> (E389, L521, P244, John Milton)

"For the beauty of the earth" is climaxed in each stanza with the ascription of praise:

> "Lord of all, to thee we raise
>   This our hymn of grateful (sacrifice of) praise."
> (B44, E416, L561, M92, P473, Folliott S. Pierpoint)

Call and Response is a pattern frequently found in spirituals and folk songs:

> "Lord, I want to be a Christian (Call)
>   *In my heart*," (Response)
> (B489, M402, P372)

> "They crucified my Lord, (Call)
>   *And he never said a mumbalin' word*;" (Response)
> (M291, P95)

Sometimes this response is referred to as the "tag line" or "interlinear refrain," as in gospel songs:

> "O for a thousand tongues to sing,
>   *Blessed be the name of the Lord!*
> The glories of my God and King,
>   *Blessed be the name of the Lord!*"
> (B206, Charles Wesley)

There are various other ways songs and hymns make use of repetition to supply interest and cohesion.

THE HYMN—A DISTINCT LITERARY FORM

Tennyson's statement (page 19) concerning the difficulty of writing a good hymn highlights the nature of the hymn as one of the most rigorously limited types of literature. Its first limitation is that it must possess qualities of lyric poetry: it must sing! But its strictures are even greater since it must also express religious truth. Furthermore, when it must be a medium of concerted action and feeling simple enough to be performed congregationally, its restraints are compounded and multiplied.

Therefore, in the final analysis, the hymn represents a unique form of literary art, sustaining a relationship to poetry somewhat akin to that of prayer to prose. It is a type of poetry existing of and by itself, having qualities that are distinctly its own.

Some would go so far as to affirm that the hymn *per se* is not to be considered a subdivision of lyrical poetry at all. Rather, they claim that it is so distinct that it fits into categories neither of poetry nor of prose. Hymns are, after all, *sui generis*—the products of an art having its own qualities and requirements. They may indeed be poetry-like; however, they do not have to be true poems to achieve status as true hymns.[11]

Be that as it may, the purely artistic appreciation of hymns as poems has a legitimate place in worship and devotion. The capacity to discern and appreciate the highest good and artistic best can and should be cultivated by those seeking through hymns and their singing to glorify God, the author of all art and beauty. Though hymns do not have to exhibit all the characteristics considered above to qualify as poems, they have both religious and aesthetic value when they do. The literarily informed critical faculty is not the opponent but, rather, the friend of true religion.

[11]See "Hymns and Poetry—A Personal Reflection" in Dudley-Smith, *Lift Every Heart* (Carol Stream: Hope Publishing Company, 1984), 12-294; and by the same publisher, "Poet and Hymn Writer" in Pratt Green, *Later Hymns and Ballads and Fifty Poems* (1989), xiii-xxiv.

QUESTIONS FOR THOUGHT AND DISCUSSION

1. What percentage of the hymns sung by your congregation are of lyrical quality?

2. Is there a relationship between literary quality and spiritual effectiveness in "Love divine, all loves excelling" (B208, E657, L315, M384, P376) or "When I survey the wondrous cross" (B144, E474, L482, M298, P100, 101)?

3. What hymns by outstanding poets in British and/or American literature are represented in your hymnal?

4. Which of these poetic and literary devices or patterns are found in the following hymns? apostrophe, alliteration, anaphora, hyperbole, climax, paradox, Hebrew pattern, itemization

"O for a thousand tongues to sing" (B216, E493, L559, M57, P466)

"Make me a captive, Lord" (B278, M421, P378)

"Go to dark Gethsemane" (B150, E171, L109, M290, P97)

"O (Our) God, our help in ages past" (B74, E680, L320, M117, P210)

"How sweet the name of Jesus sounds" (B453, E644, L345)

"O Love that wilt not let me go" (B292, L324, M480, P384)

2

THE HYMN AND MUSIC

To become a congregational song, a hymn text must be set to music. The musical setting of the hymn—even though it is usually harmonized for part-singing or accompaniment—is known as a tune, a hymn tune. The appropriate joining of a hymn and tune is often linked to a successful marriage where husband and wife must be compatible.

A hymn tune can be studied as melody, harmony, rhythm and meter, texture and form.[1]

MELODY

In most hymnals, the melody is usually the highest of the four voice parts. The other voices—alto, tenor, and bass—are subordinate to, and generally lack the same melodic interest of, the soprano.

Melody consists of *pitch* and *duration* and rhythm. Pitch may be thought of as "high-low" and duration as "long-short" and may be referred to as motion and rhythm; each melody may be illustrated as a motion skeleton and rhythm skeleton,[2] as in the following example from the hymn tune ANTIOCH (B87, E100, L39, M246, P40, "Joy to the world! the Lord is come"):

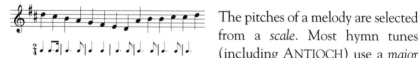

The pitches of a melody are selected from a *scale*. Most hymn tunes (including ANTIOCH) use a *major scale*. A relatively small percentage of tunes in current hymnals use a *minor scale*. Two hymn tunes in minor are KIRKEN (B351, L365, "Built on the (a)

---

[1]A basic knowledge of the rudiments of music is necessary for a clear understanding of much of the material treated in this chapter. It is recommended that readers who encounter terms that may be unfamiliar utilize a good dictionary of musical terms, such as the *New Harvard Dictionary of Music*, ed. Don Michael Randal (Cambridge, MA: Belknap Press of Harvard University Press, 1985).

[2]"Melody," *Harvard Dictionary of Music*, ed. Willi Apel, 2nd ed. rev. (Cambridge, MA: Belknap Press of Harvard University Press, 1969).

Rock the church doth stand") and EBENEZER (M108, "God hath spoken by the prophets"; M586, " 'Let my people seek their freedom' "; E381, L233, "Thy strong word did cleave the darkness"; E527, "Singing songs of expectation"; P129, "Come, O Spirit, dwell among us"). A few hymn tune melodies are *modal*, being based on the medieval church modes. One example of a modal hymn melody is KING'S WESTON (B396, M592, "When the church of Jesus"; E435, L179, M168, "At the name of Jesus"), in the Dorian mode (D to D on the white keys). Another example is the plainsong-based melody, VENI EMMANUEL or VENI, VENI, EMMANUEL (B76, E56, L34, M211, P9, "O come, O come, Emmanuel"), in the Aeolian mode or natural minor.

Most hymn melodies are *diatonic*, using the normal whole and half steps of their scales. The most common chromatic alteration in hymn tunes is the raised fourth modulating to the dominant in major keys, as found in ST. MAGNUS (E483, L173, M326, P149, "The head that once was crowned"; E447, "The Christ who died but rose again").

Some hymn tunes use the five-note or *pentatonic* scale, often found in folk music and music of Africa and the Orient. One familiar form of the pentatonic scale omits the fourth and seventh degrees:

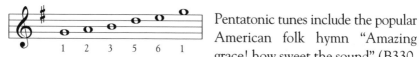

Pentatonic tunes include the popular American folk hymn "Amazing grace! how sweet the sound" (B330, E671, L448, M378, P280), the African-American spiritual, "Lord, I want to be a Christian" (B489, M402, P372), the Chinese SHENG EN (M633, "The bread of life for all is broken!"; E342, "O Bread of life, for sinners broken"), and the Indian ASSAM (B305, "I have decided to follow Jesus"). Although the melodies of pentatonic hymn tunes use only five notes, the harmonies generally make use of the full diatonic scale.

In order to be sung by an ordinary congregation, hymn tunes generally are limited in range, falling within an octave or an octave plus an additional scale step. The general range of most tunes—the *tessitura*—is moderate. Hymn tunes with high and low tessituras respectively are LASST UNS ERFREUEN (B27, E400, L527, M62, "All creatures of our God and King"; E618, M90, "Ye watchers and ye holy ones"; M94, "Praise God, from whom all blessings flow") and HAMBURG (B144, M298, P101, "When I survey the wondrous cross"; B374, "Your supper, Lord, before us spread").

Early in this century there was an increased emphasis on unison tunes to accommodate the average congregation. The general range of hymn melodies is from C¹ (middle c) up to E♭, occasionally extended from B♭ (below middle C) to F.

Most melodies move by step or skip, by scalar or triadic movement. The first phrase of ANTIOCH (B87, E100, L39, M246, P40, "Joy to the world! the Lord is come") is a descending full octave of the major scale. OLD 100TH (B5, E377, 378; L245, M75, P220, "All people that on earth do dwell"; B253, E380, L564, M95, P591, 592, "Praise God, from whom all blessings flow;" E380, L550, "From all that dwell below the skies"; L531, "Before Jehovah's awesome throne"; M621, "Be present at our table, Lord") begins with a scale-wise progression descending from the tonic to the dominant. NICAEA (B2, E362, L165, M64, P138, "Holy, holy, holy! Lord God Almighty!") begins with an ascending triadic movement spelling out the tonic triad. As with most melodies, hymn tunes generally combine scalar and triadic movement, both ascending and descending, to achieve a balance of melodic movement.

The melodies of hymns may develop by sequential repetition, as in the following third brace Of ST. GEORGE'S WINDSOR (B637, E290, L407, M694, P551, "Come, ye (you) thankful people, come"):

Note that these two melodic phrases are identical; the second one simply begins a fourth higher.

More of these interesting relationships can be discovered from the study of melodic construction in hymn tunes. Another aspect of melody—phrase repetitions—deals with form in hymn tunes, which will be discussed later.

HARMONY

Hymn tunes are generally set in the harmonic style of the so-called "common practice period" in wide use from the time of Bach through the era of the Romantic composers. Relatively few hymn tunes have distinctive 20th-century harmonies. The conservative style of hymn-tune harmonies can be attributed to at least two factors. First, congregational music is for untrained singers who need singable melodies unencumbered by elaborate harmonies. Second, congregational music—"people's music"—embodies harmonic sounds which untrained singers can identify and express their faith in song.

Most hymn tunes in current hymnals are harmonized in a simple, straight-forward style with relatively few passing tones, suspensions, and other nonharmonic tones which are associated with Bach chorale harmonizations. Note the first brace of the chorale LOBE DEN HERREN (B14, E390, L543, M139, P482):

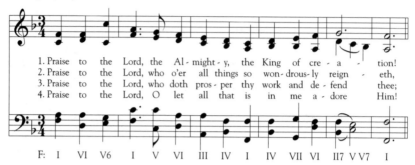

LOBE DEN HERREN uses a large variety of chords. Its harmonic rhythm is fast: the chords change every beat until the final chord at the cadence. A simpler harmonization is the early American tune CORONATION (B202, E450, L328, M154, P142):

This first brace of CORONATION consists of only the tonic (I), dominant (V), dominant seventh (V7), submediant (VI), and the tonic second-inversion ($I_{6/4}$) chords. Furthermore, the harmonic rhythm of this excerpt is somewhat slower because the first full measure consists solely of the tonic (I) chord. Among the simplest harmonizations of hymns in American use are those of Lowell Mason and several of his contemporaries, such as Thomas Hastings and William B. Bradbury. This simplicity is also illustrated in the latter 19th-century gospel hymns, such as PROMISES (B335, M374):

The harmonies of these four measures consist basically of the tonic (I) and subdominant (IV) chords. The harmonic rhythm is quite slow because the same harmonies are retained for one or two entire measures. In PROMISES, the harmonies are utterly subordinate to the driving march-like rhythms.

Most harmonizations of hymn tunes consist of the basic chords, as illustrated by the following two braces of BEECHER (B208, M384, "Love divine, all loves excelling"; B248, "God, our Father, we adore Thee"; B470, "Once to ev'ry man and nation"; E470, "There's a wideness in God's mercy"; P343, "Called as partners in Christ's service"):

The main key of the first brace given is B♭; the first two measures of the second brace of this excerpt are in its relative minor (G minor), with F♯ functioning as its leading tone. The latter two measures of this excerpt are again the tonic key of B♭, with the E♮ alteration resulting from a dominant chord.

The final cadence of nearly all hymn tunes is a progression to the tonic from either the dominant or dominant seventh chord. Internal (non-final) cadences of hymn tunes are more varied, including such progressions as V or V7 to I, I to V, V7 of V to V, VII₆ of V to V, and I to IV.

RHYTHM AND METER

Rhythm has already been mentioned in relation to melody as its time quality and its designation to the rate of chord structure change (harmonic rhythm). The rhythm of nearly all hymn tunes falls into the regular patterns of accented and unaccented beats governed by musical meter.[3]

Hymn tunes with two-beat measures having an accent on the first beat use such meters as $\frac{2}{2}$—DUKE STREET (B587, E544, L530, M157, P423, "Jesus shall reign where'er the sun"; B13, M101, "From all that dwell below the skies"; B70, "How great our God's majestic Name!"; L520, "Give to our God immortal praise"; L352, "I know that my Redeemer lives"; M438, "Forth in thy name, O Lord, I go"; P307, "Fight the good fight with all thy might"); $\frac{2}{4}$—ANTIOCH (B87, E100, L39, M246, P40, "Joy to the world! the Lord is come"); and $\frac{6}{8}$ (in fast tempo)—WORDS OF LIFE (B261, M600, "Wonderful Words of Life").

The three-beat pattern (-uu) in hymn tunes is found in such meters as $\frac{3}{2}$—ARLINGTON (B358, "This is the day the Lord has made"; B481, M511, "Am I a soldier of the cross"; B353, "Our God has built with living stones") and $\frac{3}{4}$—ST. CATHERINE (B352, E558, L500, M710, "Faith of our fathers"; B123, M183, P366, "Jesus, thy boundless love to me").

The six-beat pattern, with its main accent on beat one and a secondary accent on beat four, is utilized in such meters as $\frac{6}{8}$ (in slow tempo)—STILLE NACHT (B91, E111, L65, M239, P60, "Silent night, holy night") and $\frac{6}{4}$—THE CALL (E487, M164, "Come, my Way, my Truth, my Life"). The more extended compound meters—$\frac{9}{8}$ and $\frac{12}{8}$—are mainly found in gospel hymns. Examples are "Blessed assurance, Jesus is mine" in $\frac{9}{8}$ (B334, M369, P341) and "I will sing of my Redeemer" with its stanzas in $\frac{9}{8}$ and refrain in $\frac{12}{8}$ (B575).

The rhythms of hymn tunes are basically simple and straightforward in keeping with their role as music for the congregation. Part of this rhythmic

---

[3] Plainsong and Anglican chant are two bodies of congregational music that are comparatively non-metrical. Metered texts can be sung to plainsong, for example, "Of the Father's love begotten" See Chapter 5, "Early Church and Pre-Reformation Traditions," page 88.

simplicity is found in repetition. The four phrases of OLD 100TH (B253, E380, L564, 565; M95, P591, "Praise God, from whom all blessings flow"; B5, E377, 378; L245, M75, P220, "All people that on earth do dwell"; E380, L550, "From all that dwell below the skies"; L531, "Before Jehovah's awe-some throne"; M621, "Be present at our table, Lord"), for example, have the same rhythmic pattern. Other hymn tunes whose melodies repeat basically the same rhythmic pattern are ST. DENIO (B6, E423, L526, M103, P263, "Immortal, invisible, God only wise"), ST. THEODULPH or VALET WILL ICH DIR GEBEN (B126, E154, L108, M280, P88, "All glory, laud, and honor"; E74, "Blest be the King whose coming"), TOPLADY (B342, E685, L327, M361, "Rock of Ages, cleft for me"), and WEBB or MORNING LIGHT (B485, E561 L389, M514, "Stand up, stand up for Jesus").

Within each meter there are frequently recurring rhythmic patterns. For example, in $\frac{4}{4}$ there is often the use of shorter note values followed by a longer note at the cadences of the first and/or second phrases. This is illustrated by LEONI or YIGDAL (B34, E401, L544, M116, P488, "The God of Abraham praise"), HYMN TO JOY (B7, E376, L551, M89, "Joyful, joyful, we adore thee"; B47, "God, who stretched the spangled heavens"; B585, "Tell It Out with Gladness"; M702, "Sing with all the saints in glory"), and PROMISES (B335, M374, "Standing on the promises").

Poetic meter[4] determines the rhythmic patterns of hymns. Iambic hymn texts use tunes that begin on an unaccented upbeat. Examples are EIN' FESTE BURG, (B8, E687, 688; L228, 229; M110, P259, 260, "A mighty fortress is our God") and AZMON (B216, E493, L559, M57, P466, "O for a thousand tongues to sing"; B11, "My God, how wonderful You are"; B268, "The love of Christ who died for me"; M422, "Jesus, thine all-victorious love"; M608, "This is the Spirit's entry now"; P386, "O for a world where everyone"). Conversely, hymns with trochaic texts use tunes that begin on a downbeat, such as MENDELSSOHN (B88, E87, L60, M240, P31, "Hark! the herald angels sing") and HYFRYDOL (E460, L158, P144, "Alleluia! Sing to Jesus"; B77, M196, P2, "Come, thou long-expected Jesus"; E657, L315, P376, "Love divine, all loves excelling"; B36, "Praise the Lord! ye heav'ns adore him"; B535, "I will sing the wondrous story"; L288, "Hear us now, our God and Father").

TEXTURE

The texture of most hymn tunes is *homophonic* or *chordal*, with the lower voice parts moving more or less in the same rhythm as the soprano melody. In

[4]Poetic meter is discussed in more detail in Chapter 1 of this textbook, "The Hymn and Literature."

unison tunes, however, the texture is generally more *contrapuntal*, with a greater rhythmic independence of the accompanying voices. Examples of contrapuntal hymn tunes are Ralph Vaughan Williams' harmonizations of LASST UNS ERFREUEN (B27, L527, M62, E400, P455, "All creatures of our God and King") and SINE NOMINE (B229, M166, M711, "All praise to thee"; B355, E287, L174, M711, P526, "For all the saints"). Some popular tunes designed to be sung in harmony utilize counterpoint in the form of independent voice parts, such as the tenor and bass repetitions of "crown him" in DIADEM (B200, M155, "All hail the Power of Jesus' name"), and the alto-tenor-bass repetitions against the longer melody notes of PROMISES (B335, M374, "Standing on the promises").

FORM

Hymns are usually in *strophic* form, using the same music for each stanza. The number of phrases of the hymn tune correspond to its text, ranging generally from as few as four (as in OLD 100TH, B5, E377, 378; L564, M75, P220, "All people that on earth do dwell"; B253, E380, L564, 565; M95, P591, 592; "Praise God, from whom all blessings flow"; M621, "Be present at our table, Lord") to as many as eight (as in TERRA PATRIS or TERRA BEATA, B43, L554, M144, P293, "This is my Father's world"; B529, "Forever with the Lord"; M111, "How can we name a Love"). There will sometimes be a refrain of four or more additional phrases. Within its overall strophic form, examination of the phrases encountered in hymn tunes shows an interesting variety of patterns.

A pattern especially found in shorter hymn tunes consists of four different phrases (designated as ABCD). Short tunes with the ABCD pattern include OLD 100TH, ST. ANNE (B74, E680, L320, M117, P210, "O God, our help in ages past"; B51, "Creator God, creating still"; B73, "God moves in a mysterious way"; B626, "We bind ourselves in freedom's chains;" P255, "Now praise the Lord, all living saints"), ST. PETER (E644, L345, "How sweet the name of Jesus sounds"; B385, P439, "In Christ there is no east or west"; B580, "O God of love, enable me"; L477, "O God of Jacob, by whose hand"; M549, "Where charity and love prevail"), and MARYTON (B279, E660, L492, M430, P357, "O Master, let me walk with thee (you)"; B364, "Come, Holy Spirit, Dove divine"; M654, "How blest are those (they) who trust in Christ"). Longer tunes also following this through-composed structure include KRESMER (B636, E433, M131, P559, "We gather together"; B19, L241, "We praise thee (you), O God, our Redeemer"), EVENTIDE (B63, E662, L272, M700, P543, "Abide with me"), and SLANE (B60, E488, M451, P339, "Be thou my vision";

E482, L469, "Lord of all hopefulness").

Other patterns consist of one or more repetitions. One of the simplest of these phrase-repetition structures, involving only two different phrase pairs, may be diagrammed as AB AB CD AB, or more succinctly as AABA. This pattern is found in such hymn tunes as FOREST GREEN (B42, E398, M152, "I sing the almighty power of God"; E78, P43, "O little town of Bethlehem"; B79, Blessed be the God of Israel; B491, "Make room within my heart, O God"; B639, E705, P414, "As men (those) of old their first fruits brought"; M539, "O Spirit of the living God"; M709, "Come, let us join our friends above"; P292, "All beautiful the march of days"; P412, "Eternal God, whose power upholds"), and NETTLETON (B15, E686, L499, M400, P356, "Come, thou fount of every blessing"; B507, "Would You bless our homes and fam'lies"; P355, "Hear the good news of salvation").

Another pattern involves a repeated phrase or pair of phrases and contrasting phrases (AAB); it is known in German music as *bar form*. Many chorales are in bar form, including EIN' FESTE BURG (B8, E687, 688; L228, 229; M110, P259, 260, "A mighty fortress is our God") and LOBE DEN HERREN (B14, E390, L543, M139, P482, "Praise to the Lord, the almighty"). The number of phrases in the "B" portion of bar form varies. When diagrammed in more detail, the bar form of EIN' FESTE BURG is AB AB CDEFB; the bar form of LOBE DEN HERREN is A A BCD.

Some hymn tunes have repetitions of internal phrases such as the ABCD-DEF pattern of ITALIAN HYMN or MOSCOW (B247, E365, L522, M61, P139, "Come, thou Almighty King") and the ABABCCAB pattern of MADRID or SPANISH HYMN (B231, M158, P150, "Come, Christians, join to sing"). Phrases in hymn tunes are sometimes repeated with an ending variation to effect a final cadence, as in the $AB_1 AB_2$ pattern of HAMBURG (B144, M298, P101, "When I survey the wondrous cross"; B374, "Your supper, Lord, before us spread") and the $AB_1 AB_2 CD$ [5] pattern of RESCUE (B559, M591, "Rescue the perishing").

A study of hymn tune phrases will reveal a number of additional patterns. A study of phrase relationships within hymn tunes, including repeated phrases and the technique of sequential development discussed earlier in this chapter, is important to understand how hymn melodies are constructed.

TYPES OF HYMN TUNES

The hymnal contains a wide variety of hymn tunes representing a number

---

[5]The final cadential measure of B also appears in D.

of different musical traditions. Not every hymn tune will fit into one of the categories described here, but they constitute most of the music used for present-day congregational singing in America.

Plainsong

With roots in the Middle Ages, plainsong is also known as Gregorian chant (After Gregory I, who was Pope from 590 to 604). Plainsong is modal, based on the medieval church modes. It also has flexible rhythm articulated by means other than regular accentuation. Gregorian chant's modality and rhythmic flexibility are traits that account for its distinctive sound. Although traditionally sung without harmony and accompaniment, plainsong may also be sung congregationally in unison with a harmonized accompaniment. Well-known examples of plainsong hymn tunes are DIVINUM MYSTERIUM (B251, E82, L42, M184, P309, "Of the Father's love begotten") and VENI (VENI,) EMMANUEL (B76, E56, L34, M211, P9, "O come, O come, Emmanuel").

One type of plainsong, called the psalm tone, is used for chanting prose psalms from the Bible, as in the following setting of Psalm 8. [6]

[Musical Example, L290.] Reprinted from *Lutheran Book of Worship*, copyright © 1978, by permission of Augsburg Press.

The division of the psalm is marked by an asterisk (*). The first note (‖O‖) in each part of the tone is a reciting note, to which one or more syllables or words are sung. In this method the Psalm is pointed for singing, the point (´) above a syllable (or word) indicates the syllable (or word) where singers move from the reciting note to the following notes. The most important feature of this type of chant, as distinguished from the ordinary hymn tune, is that it seeks to accomodate natural speech.

Another type of chant which seeks to utilize the accentuations of natural speech is Anglican chant, which is written in four voice parts and accompanied. Anglican chant, which may be derived from plainsong, consists of two or four short phrases of simple harmonic progressions, as in William Boyce's setting of the VENITE EXULTEMUS (M91).

---

[6]Instructions for chanting psalm tones are given in *The United Methodist Hymnal* (1989), on page 737. Psalm tones are given on pages 290-91 of the *Lutheran Book of Worship*. Another setting of Psalm 95 (in a modern translation) is at L95.

Canticle of Praise to God
(Venite Exultemus)

1. O come, let us sing unto the Lord; let us heartily rejoice in the
3. For the Lord is a great God, and a great
5. The sea is His, and He made it; and His hands pre-
7. For He is the Lord our God; and we are the people of His pasture and the

10. Glory be to the Father and to the Son, and

(1) strength of our sal - vation. 2. Let us come before His presence with thanks - giving;
(3) King a - bove all gods. 4. In His hand are all the corners of the earth;
(5) pared the dry land. 6. O come let us wor- ship and fall down,
(7) sheep of His hand. 8. O worship the Lord in the beauty of holiness;
9. For He cometh, for He cometh to judge the earth;
(10) to the Ho - ly Ghost; As it was in the be- ginning, is now, and ev - er shall be,

(2) and show ourselves glad in Him with psalms.
(4) and the strength of the hills is His also.
(6) and kneel be fore the Lord our Maker.
(8) let the whole earth stand in awe of Him.
(9) and with righteousness to judge the world, and the peo - ples with His truth.
(D.S. to Vs 9)
(optional D.C. to 10)
(10) world without end. A men.

WORDS: Psalm 95:1-7; 96:9, 13
MUSIC: William Boyce

2. The Hymn and Music
39

Lutheran Chorale

In addition to Anglican chant, a large body of German and Scandinavian hymn tunes known as chorales developed from the impetus of the Protestant Reformation in those countries. The chorales reflect a variety of musical styles and melodies ranging from medieval plainsong and the song of the 16th-century Meistersinger, to the baroque continuo accompanied lied. Because of his masterful chorale harmonizations, many persons associate the chorale chiefly with J. S. Bach.

The phrase structure of chorales is often the German bar form (AAB), mentioned on page 37. In accord with the poetic structure of German chorale texts, few chorale tunes are in common, long, or short meter; instead, they use a wide variety of other hymn meters. There are two main styles of rhythmic movement in the chorale. One consists of the sturdy rhythms with regular patterns of mostly quarter notes and a few longer note values, especially for phrase endings. This style is sometimes called the "isometric" ("same meter") chorale; it was common in the 18th century and is now associated with the Bach chorale harmonizations. Most of the older chorales found in American hymnals are isometric. The other style, known as the "rhythmic chorale," consists of more irregular and often syncopated rhythms, such as those often found in the Reformation-era chorales, which were originally sung without accompaniment. This is illustrated by the original rhythm (E687, L228, P259) of Luther's EIN' FESTE BURG.[7]

Chorales can be harmonized in the Bach style using a number of nonharmonic tones (PASSION CHORALE, B137, E168, M286, P98),[8] or in a simpler style that uses nonharmonic tones sparingly, and then mostly at cadences (LOBE DEN HERREN, B14, E390, L543, M139, P482).[9]

Calvinian Psalm Tune

The practice of singing Psalms in meter (metrical psalms) to simpler tunes than chorales arose from the practice of the Reformation theologian John Calvin of Geneva. These psalm tunes may be divided into two categories: (1) those of the French language Genevan Psalter, characterized by a wide variety of hymn meters; (2) those of the English and Scottish psalters, largely falling into the patterns of common, long, and short meter. The French psalm tunes,

---

[7]For the well-known isometric version, see B8, E688, L229, M110, P260.
[8]The original and isometric settings of PASSION CHORALE at L116 and L117 are harmonized more simply than in Bach's style.
[9]For a detailed treatment of the musical style of the chorale, see Johannes Riedel, *The Lutheran Chorale—Its Basic Traditions* (Minneapolis: Augsburg Press, 1967).

EIN' FESTE BURG

like the Reformation-Era chorales, are more often characterized by irregular rhythms and/or syncopations, as in RENDEZ À DIEU (E301, 302, 413; M565, P218, 502):

Most of the English and Scottish psalm tunes in current American hymnals are isometric and in ¼ meter. This is illustrated by WINCHESTER OLD (E94, P58, "While shepherds watched their flocks"; L264, "When all your mercies, O my God"; M470, "My God, I love thee"; M603, "Come, Holy Ghost, our hearts inspire"; P162, "O Lord, our God, how excellent"; P191, "God is our refuge and our strength"; P239, "How happy is each child of God") and DUNDEE (E126, "The people who in darkness walked"; E526, "Let saints on earth in concert sing"; E709, P269, "O God of Bethel, by whose hand"; L464, "You are the way; through you alone"; P234, "I to the hills will lift my eyes").

Both of these major groupings of psalm tunes reflect the extreme application of the Calvinian principle of simplicity in church song with seldom more than one note per syllable. Furthermore, most of these tunes (except a few longer Genevan melodies like RENDEZ À DIEU) consist of four short unrepeated (ABCD) phrases, as in OLD 100TH (B5, 253; E377, L564, M75, 95, 621; P220, 591). The psalm tunes used today are harmonized in a simple style, rarely using the nonharmonic tones characteristic of the Bach chorales.

Victorian Part-Song Tune

In Victorian England, a large body of hymn tunes were composed that reflected the rich and often chromatic harmonies of the contemporary secular part-song. In addition to their harmonic emphasis, these tunes are often characterized by repeated note melodies, such as ST. AGNES (B225, L316, M175, P310 "Jesus, the very thought of thee (you)"; E510, P126, "Come, Holy Spirit, heavenly Dove"; B116, "Our Savior's infant cries were heard"; B498, "O God, we ask for strength to lead"; B505, M445, "Happy the home when God is there"; B506, "O God, to those who here profess"; E343, "Shepherd of souls, refresh and bless"; M561, "Jesus, united by thy grace"). They are also characterized by stagnant bass lines, as in LANCASHIRE (B621, E555, L495, M580, P447, "Lead on, O King Eternal"; B164, M303, P118, "The day of resurrection"; E563, "Go forward, Christian soldier"; M571, "Go, make of all disciples"). A third characteristic is mild repeated rhythms, as illustrated by ST. AGNES.

Other familiar Victorian part-song hymn tunes illustrating one or more of these musical traits are ST. GERTRUDE (B493, E562, L509, M575, "Onward, Christian soldiers"; M555, "Forward through the ages"), AURELIA (B350, E525, L369, M545, P442, "The church's one foundation"; B272, "I lay my sins on Jesus"; P443, "O Christ, the great foundation"), and LAUDES DOMINI (B221, E427, L546, M185, P487, "When morning gilds the skies"; P130, "Let every Christian pray").

Folk Tune

Although melodies of folk origin (existing first in oral tradition) have been used with hymns for centuries, folk melodies from a number of countries have achieved a prominent place in most recent American hymnals. An examination of the index of sources for most of our hymnals will reveal the majority of these tunes are from Great Britain and America. They fall largely into five categories: (1) the carol, (2) the English folk tune, (3) the Welsh folk tune, (4) the American folk hymn tune, and (5) the American spiritual.

1. Carol. The carol, a form of a hymn whose words and music are typically joyful and festive, is a "strophic song, often traditional and usually (but not always) connected with the celebration of Christmas."[10] The carol has been redefined in the light of 20th-century use "as a quasi-religious song of folk-like spirit with reference to the joyful observance of something new in

---

[10]"Carol," *The New Harvard Dictionary of Music*, 1986, 141.

the life of Christ."[11] Carols in their medieval origin were associated with dance; some carols still used are characterized by dance-like rhythms, such as IN DULCI JUBILO (B96, E107, L55, M224, P28, "Good Christian men (friends), rejoice"), THE FIRST NOWELL, (B85, E109, L56, M245, P56, "The first Nowell"), and GREENSLEEVES (B118, E115, L40, M219, P53, "What child is this"). If "folk-like spirit" is accepted as a main determinant of which hymns and tunes are carols, then Lowell Mason's arrangements from Handel's *Messiah*, ANTIOCH (B87, E100, L39, M246, P40, "Joy to the world! the Lord is come") and STILLE NACHT (B91, E111, M239, P60, "Silent night, holy night") might well be regarded as carols. On the other hand, more stately texts and tunes such as ADESTE FIDELES (B89, E83, L45, M234, P41, "O come, all ye faithful") and MENDELSSOHN (B88, E87, L60, M240, P31, "Hark! the herald angels sing"), would seem to fit more appropriately in the category of Christmas hymns.

2. English Folk Tune. Folk tunes other than carols were brought into English hymnals in the first decade of this century. In contrast to the harmonic interest of the Victorian hymn tunes, these melodies, adapted from secular folk songs and harmonized, are noted for their melodic interest. The English folk tunes often fall into four lines of paired phrases having one or more lines repeated, as in FOREST GREEN (B42, E398, M152, "I sing the almighty power of God"; E78, P43, "O little town of Bethlehem"; B79, "Blessed be the God of Israel"; B491, "Make room within my heart, O God"; B639, E705, P414, "As men (those) of old their first fruits brought"; M539, "O Spirit of the living God"; M709, "Come, let us join our friends above"; P292, "All beautiful the march of days"; P412, "Eternal God, whose power upholds") and KINGSFOLD (B120, M179, P308, "O sing a song of Bethlehem"; E292, "O Jesus, crowned with all renown"; E480, "When Jesus left his Father's throne"; L391, "And have the bright immensities"; M285, "To mock your reign, O dearest Lord"; M606, "Come, let us use the grace divine"; P434, "Today we all are called to be Disciples"; P601, "Blest be the God of Israel").

3. Welsh Tunes. Welsh folk or folklike tunes usually consist of a pattern of four lines with one or more of them repeated, as found in ST. DENIO (B6, E423, L526, M103, P263, "Immortal, invisible, God only wise"; B168, "We welcome glad Easter") and LLANGLOFFAN (E68, P15, "Rejoice! rejoice, believers"; E607, M435, P289, "O God of every nation"; M425, "O crucified Redeemer"; L430, "Where restless crowds are thronging"; P291, "O God of

---

[11]"Carol," *A Dictionary of Protestant Church Music*, 1975, 74. A book-length treatment of this subject is Erik Routley's *The English Carol* (London: Herbert Jenkins, 1958).

earth and altar"; P448, "Lead on, O King eternal"). The sturdy rhythms of these Welsh tunes contrast with the lilting dancelike English carol tune.

4. American Tunes. The American folk hymn tunes consist largely of folk melodies derived from secular folk songs set to sacred texts by rural singing-school teachers, and published in early 19th-century shape-note tunebooks. As first published, American folk hymns were set in three or four voice parts in open score with the melody in the staff immediately above the bass. They were harmonized in a style using "forbidden" harmonies and progressions. For example, NEW BRITAIN or AMAZING GRACE (B330, E671, L448, M378, P280) appeared in William Walker's *Southern Harmony* (1835) without thirds (first chord), and some parallel fifths (bracket 1, treble and tenor), and octaves (bracket 2, treble and bass).

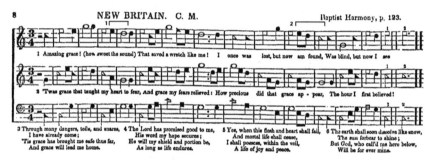

As they appear in current hymnals, however, American folk hymns are made more acceptable to people conditioned to Victorian harmonies, as in E. O. Excell's well-known 1900 reharmonization of NEW BRITAIN or AMAZING GRACE (see B330, M378, P280).

NEW BRITAIN or AMAZING GRACE also illustrates another important trait of American folk hymn tunes: the use of "gapped scales" employing less than the normal seven diatonic notes for their melodies. (They are generally harmonized using all seven notes.) The pentatonic scale is used for NEW BRITAIN or AMAZING GRACE and other folk hymns.[12]

American folk hymns make extensive use of repeated phrases, the most common pattern being AABA, as found in NETTLETON (B15, E686, L499, M400, P356, "Come, thou fount of every blessing"; B507, "Would you bless our homes and fam'lies"), and CLEANSING FOUNTAIN (B142, M622, "There is a fountain"). This repetition pattern is slightly varied in FOUNDATION (B338, E636, L507, M529, P361, "How firm a foundation"), whose

[12]See Chapter 8 in this textbook, "American Traditions," for discussion of additional folk hymns and spirituals.

form is $A_1A_2BA_2$, and NEW BRITAIN or AMAZING GRACE, whose phrases consist of an $A_1A_2BA_1$.

5. Spirituals. Spirituals are a distinct type of American folk hymn characterized by text repetitions of phrases and usually a chorus. Although the African-American spiritual is better known, spirituals have been a part of the oral hymn repertory of both Whites and Blacks since at least the early 19th century.

The spiritual, although in a similar musical style to the folk hymn, is often characterized by livelier rhythm, sometimes involving syncopation, as in JACOB'S LADDER (B474, E453, M418) and BREAK BREAD or LET US BREAK BREAD or BREAK BREAD TOGETHER (B366, E325, L212, M618, P513). The African-American spiritual was originally improvised, a practice facilitated by the use of a slow tempo and long-note values. Some of these longer notes which originally provided opportunity for improvisation are found in such spirituals as WERE YOU THERE (B156, E172, L92, M288, P102), BALM IN GILEAD (B269, E676, M375, P394), and BREAK BREAD or LET US BREAK BREAD. Spirituals associated with Whites stemmed from the frontier revivals of the early 19th century and were published with music in shape-note tunebooks along with other folk hymns. White spirituals, although not generally characterized by syncopation, do exhibit driving, marchlike rhythms, as in PROMISED LAND (B521, M724, "On Jordan's stormy banks I stand").

Gospel Hymn Tune

The gospel hymn was developed in latter 19th-century America and reflects much of the simple musical style of contemporary popular song. Gospel hymns use simple major-key melodies and corresponding simple harmonies consisting largely of the tonic, subdominant, and dominant chords in slow harmonic rhythm. They generally make fuller use of chromatic melodies (sometimes with chromatics added by the singers) than most other bodies of hymn tunes. Although gospel hymns are frequently in simple meters such as $\frac{2}{4}$ and $\frac{3}{4}$, they make greater use of compound meters than any other body of hymn tunes. Gospel hymns may use straightforward rhythms, but dotted rhythms are more characteristic, such as the dotted eights and sixteenth rhythms of (THE) OLD RUGGED CROSS (B141, M504) and the dotted quarter and repeated eighths of CONVERSE (B182, L439, M526, P403, "What a friend we have in Jesus"). Some gospel hymns also make use of syncopated rhythms, as in JESUS LOVES ME or CHINA (B344, M191, P304) and SWEET

SPIRIT or MANNA (B243, M334, P398, "There's a sweet, sweet Spirit in this place"). Gospel hymns are mainly homophonic, but variety of texture is sometimes found in the use of "echo" voices, as in the alto, tenor, and bass parts of (THE) OLD RUGGED CROSS (B141, M504).

Innovative Hymn Tunes

Some present-century hymn tunes fall into one of the categories described; other more current hymn tunes are innovative and do not fit a simple characterization. The following descriptive list of innovative hymn tunes will show how some composers have sought to create new interest in this simple form.

SINE NOMINE (B355, E287, L174, M711, P526, "For all the saints"; B229, M166, "All praise to thee, for thou, O King divine")—a "Baroque Trio" (bass, middle voice(s), and melody; some have one or more stanzas in harmony). Two devices found in this hymn tune common to a number of other innovative hymn tunes are its "walking" bass line and its downbeat in the accompaniment before the voices enter.

PURPOSE (E534, "God is working his purpose out")—a unison tune with a free accompaniment. The melody is given out a measure later in canon at a lower octave by a "walking" bass.

SHILLINGFORD (E130, M260, "Christ, upon the mountain peak")—a unison tune setting of a hymn depicting the mystery of Christ's transfiguration, is an angular melody of varied measure lengths supported by haunting dissonant harmonies. While opening and closing in A♭, this innovative tune has internal cadences on C and D.

AUTHORITY (M264, "Silence, frenzied, unclean spirit!")[13]—a unison setting of a hymn depicting Jesus casting out demons, expresses this tense scene with bold dissonance and insistent repeated quarter notes on the same pitch. The latter half of AUTHORITY is more relaxed with less pitch repetition and dissonance in keeping with the lessening of tension in the hymn text. In keeping with the prayer for healing, AUTHORITY concludes its final stanza with full cadence ending on a Picardy third.

SINGABILITY AND MEMORABILITY

John Wilson pointed out "singability" and "memorability" as two important factors which make for successful hymns tunes. "The need for 'singability' is obvious: there are many excellent melodies that are not congregationally singable. The reason for 'memorability' is that the greater part of congrega-

[13]This tune was also published in *The Hymn*, 36, 1 (Jan. 1985): 9.

tional singing is (musically) done from memory."[14] As Erik Routley pointed out,[15] hymn tunes are folk songs being passed along by word of mouth. A melody that is difficult to memorize will be hindered in its acceptance as a congregational song, even though it might be quite attractive. Wilson has described traits of the hymn tune's melodic outline, rhythm, harmony, and structure that contribute to its success. Having examined the traits of a hymn tune, it is instructive to evaluate its potential for congregational use by asking the questions, "Is it singable?" "Is it memorable?" "Why or why not?"

MATCHING TUNE AND TEXT

For a happy marriage of hymn text and tune, they must be compatible in meter, accent, mood, and association. If a hymn text consists of four lines of eight syllables each (long meter), its tune must also have four phrases with notes to fit eight syllables per phrase. Closely associated with meter is a consideration of accent. Although ANTIOCH (B87, E100, L39, M246, P40) and "Amazing Grace" (B330, E671, L448, M378, P280) are both in common meter, the trochaic (long-short) accents of ANTIOCH, suitable for "Joy to the world! the Lord is come" do not fit "Amazing Grace! how sweet the sound" The initial unaccented syllable of "Amazing Grace" would be accented if sung to ANTIOCH.[16]

Hymn tunes themselves cannot communicate nonmusical ideas, but they can express general moods, such as majesty, joy, solemnity, reflection or meditation, and march-like enthusiasm. Although "All hail the power of Jesus' name" and the tune AMAZING GRACE or NEW BRITAIN are both in common meter, the majestic character of this hymn text simply does not fit the more subdued mood of this tune.

Finally, a hymn tune must not be tied too strongly to previous associations to be compatible with a particular text. So strongly identified are such tunes as NICAEA (B2, L165, M64, 65, "Holy, holy, holy! Lord God Almighty") and EIN' FESTE BURG (B8, L228, L229, M110, "A mighty fortress is our God") with their texts that it would be difficult for them to function as tunes for other words without reminding us of their more familiar associations. Tunes with secular associations for a particular congregation usually cannot be used with hymns without difficulties. Stephen Foster's tune to "Beautiful Dreamer" can

---

[14]John Wilson, "Looking at Hymn-Tunes: The Objective Factors," in, *Duty and Delight: Routley Remembered*, ed. Robin A. Leaver, James H. Litton and Carlton R. Young (Carol Stream, IL: Hope Publishing Co.; Norwich, England: Canterbury Press, 1985), 123-4.

[15]Erik Routley, *Christian Hymns Observed* (Princeton, NJ: Prestige Publications, 1982), 1-3.

[16]Note similar considerations above in Chapter 1 of this textbook, "The Hymn and Literature."

be sung to "Blessed assurance, Jesus is mine," but the widespread knowledge of this tune by Americans as a love song renders it unsuitable for use as a hymn tune.

QUESTIONS FOR THOUGHT AND DISCUSSION

1. What are the forms (ABCD, ABB, and so forth) of the following hymn tunes: BEECHER (B208, B248, B470, M384), OLD 134TH, (B30, B388), HYMN TO JOY (B7, B47, L551, M89, M702), ST. THEODULPH (B126, L108, M280), SAVANNAH (M385, M562), and EBENEZER (L233, M108, 586)?

2. How well do the following hymn texts and hymn tunes fit each other in regard to hymn meter, accent, mood, and association?

"Holy, holy, holy! Lord God Almighty!" and NICAEA

"Just as I am, without one plea" and WOODWORTH

"O for a thousand tongues to sing" and HAMBURG

"Amazing grace! how sweet the sound" and ARLINGTON

"All hail the pow'r of Jesus' name!" and ST. AGNES

"Jesus shall reign" and MARYTON

3. The following questions are applicable in considering hymn tunes for congregational singing. Apply them to several familiar hymn tunes in your hymnal.

A. How singable is the hymn tune for congregational use? (Consider the range, *tessitura*, and difficulty.)

B. How suitable is the style of the hymn tune for its intended use? (How familiar? For which group? For what occasion?)

C. Is there another readily available hymn tune that fits the hymn text better than the one given? (Consult the metrical index.)

3

THE HYMN AND SCRIPTURE

Scripture is the basic raw material for most good hymns. A hymn cannot be useful unless and until it relates closely to the revealed truth about God and God's mighty acts as written in the Scriptures. The effectiveness, therefore, of any hymn is measurable in large part by the extent to which it functions as a vehicle for scriptural truth.

From one standpoint the entire history of the hymn could be delineated according to its varying relationship to the Scriptures.[1] Generally speaking, the line of evolution is from the actual singing of parts of the Bible (the psalms, for example) through the strict paraphrasing of extended passages and the dutiful use of biblical allusion, language, and figures of speech, to the free expression of scriptural thought and teaching in contemporary terms.

VARIATIONS IN HYMN/SCRIPTURE RELATIONSHIP

Using the familiar Shepherd Psalm (23) one can illustrate the evolutionary process of moving from scriptural psalm to original hymn. First, there is Psalm 23 in the original Hebrew or in a vernacular prose version such as those found in responsive reading sections of many hymnals (B1, L225, M754, 873). In this form the Psalm may be intoned or chanted to a form of plainsong[2] or to Anglican chant.[3] There are newer translations and more contemporary ways of singing the Psalms, such as those in *The Jerusalem Bible* set to a modern type of chant by the French Jesuit, Joseph Gelineau.[4]

[1] This has been done by Louis F. Benson. See *The Hymnody of the Christian Church* (New York: George H. Doran, 1927. Reprint, Richmond: John Knox Press, 1956), "The Relation of the Hymn to Holy Scripture," 57-95.
[2] See the *Lutheran Book of Worship*, 290-91.
[3] See Chapter 2, "The Hymn and Music," page 40, the VENITE EXULTEMUS.
[4] Joseph Gelineau, *The Grail/Gelineau Psalter* (Chicago: G. I. A. Publications, 1963).

Then there are the literal metrical versions of this Psalm that are little more than rearrangements of the biblical words into patterns of meter and rhyme that accommodate simple measured tunes. Possibly the most famous version (among the scores that exist) is from the *Scottish Psalter* of 1650: "The Lord's my Shepherd, I'll not want" (L451, M136, Pl70).

James Montgomery's version of Psalm 23 is a slightly freer and more poetic paraphrase than the Scottish Psalter version. It appeared in his *Songs of Zion, Being Imitations of Psalms* (1822):

> "The Lord is my Shepherd, no want shall I know,
>   I feed in green pastures, safe-folded I rest;
> He leadeth my soul where the still waters flow,
>   Restores me when wandering, redeems when oppressed."[5]

A step further away from the original biblical text is seen in the New Testament allusions incorporated in the free paraphrase which Henry W. Baker included in the appendix to his 1868 edition of *Hymns Ancient and Modern*, "The King of love my shepherd is" (E645, 646; L456, Ml38). In the third stanza Baker actually breaks away from the Psalm, personalizing it further by inserting a related idea from the parable of the good shepherd recorded in Luke 15:3-7:

> "Perverse and foolish oft I strayed,
>   But yet in love he sought me,
> And on his shoulder gently laid,
>   And home, rejoicing, brought me."

Then in stanza four the hymnist adds to the comforting rod and staff of the shepherd the symbol of the cross for guidance through the shadow of death:

> "In death's dark vale I fear no ill,
>   With thee, dear Lord, beside me,
> Thy rod and staff my comfort still;
>   Thy cross before to guide me."

---

[5]This four-stanza paraphrase may be found in many 19th and 20th-century hymnals. See, for example, *Baptist Hymnal* (Nashville: Convention Press, 1956), 57, and *The New Church Hymnal* (Waco, TX: Lexicon Music, Inc., 1976), 325.

Finally, there are hymns on the shepherd theme that are original compositions. For example, "Savior, like a shepherd lead us" (B61, E708, L481, M381, P387) starts with a thought that may be from Psalm 23 but could just as easily have been inspired by the "I am the good shepherd" passage in John 10. Essentially, however, this is an original work, bearing only the suggestion of a relation to a particular Scripture passage and carrying the unmistakable impress of its author, Dorothy A. Thrupp.[6]

In these five examples related to Psalm 23, the progression from the precisely biblical to the clearly invented and original can be traced. These representative examples epitomize the affinity of the Christian hymn with Scripture.

EXAMPLES OF HYMNS BASED ON SCRIPTURE

Though the book of Psalms is the natural and most used source of their inspiration, hymnists have also turned to other portions of the Old Testament and the New Testament as bases for their hymns. For example, passages from the Old Testament prophets have had unusual appeal. The following instances demonstrate that the prophet Isaiah has been a particularly fertile source for hymnic ideas.

The anonymous author of "How firm a foundation" (B338, E636, 637; L507, M529, P361) quotes, almost literally, verses from Isaiah in three stanzas:

Scripture	Hymn

"Fear thou not; For I am with thee: be not dismayed; for I am thy God: I will strengthen thee; yea, I will help thee; yea, I will uphold thee with the right hand of righteousness." (Isa. 41:10)	" 'Fear not, I am with thee;
	    O be not dismayed,
	For I am thy God,
	    and will still give thee aid;
	I'll strengthen thee, help thee,
	    and cause thee to stand,
	Upheld by My righteous,
	    omnipotent hand.' "

"When thou passest through the waters, I will be with thee; and through the rivers, they shall not overflow thee: (Isa. 43:2a)	" 'When thro' the deep waters
	    I call thee to go,
	The rivers of woe
	    shall not thee overflow;

---

[6]Another example: Joseph H. Gilmore's "He leadeth me! O blessed thought" (B52, L501, M128) was inspired by thoughts from a prayer meeting devotional talk on Psalm 23.

For I will be with thee
  thy troubles to bless,
And sanctify to thee
  thy deepest distress.' "

"when thou walkest through the fire, thou shalt not be burned; neither shall the flame kindle upon thee." (Isa. 43:2b)

" 'When thro' fiery trials
  thy pathway shall lie,
My grace, all sufficient,
  shall be thy supply;
The flame shall not hurt thee;
  I only design
Thy dross to consume,
  and thy gold to refine.' "

The 17th-century German hymn "Comfort, comfort ye (now) my people" (E67, L29, P3) is based on Isaiah 40:1-8—a passage made familiar to many from its use by Handel for the opening tenor recitative in *Messiah*. Isaiah 33:20-21 is alluded to in the first two stanzas of John Newton's "Glorious things of thee are spoken" (B398, E522, 523; L358, "Glories of your name are spoken," M731, P446).

There are numerous hymns that refer to parts of Isaiah's experience in the temple, partially because Isaiah 6:1-8 includes the famous thrice-holy hymn of the cherubim and Isaiah's poignant response of commitment "Here am I; send me." These include:

- "Day is dying in the west" (M687)
- "God himself is present" (L249)
- "Hark, the voice of Jesus calling" (B591)
- "Here am I, send me" (B597)
- "Holy, holy, holy" (B2, E362, L165, M64, P138)
- "Holy God, we praise thy (your) name" (E366, L535, M79, P460)
- "Isaiah in a vision did of old" (L528)
- "Let the whole creation cry" (L242)
- "O day of rest and gladness" (L251)
- "Take my life, lead me, Lord" (B287)
- "The voice of God is calling" (M436)

William Williams's "Guide me, O thou great Jehovah" (B56, E690, L343; "Guide me ever, great Redeemer," M127, P281) is predominantly based on the Old Testament. Its general setting is the pilgrimage of the children of Israel from Egypt to Canaan. Its verses, however, constitute a veritable mosaic of Scripture, drawing upon ideas from both Old Testament and New Testament:

"Guide me, O thou great Jehovah, (Deut. 8:14-20; Ps. 78:52)
    Pilgrim through this barren land; (Heb. 11:13; Ex. 17:1)
I am weak, but thou art mighty; (Ps. 6:2; Isa.1:24; Ps.24:8)
    Hold me with thy powerful hand; (Ps. 139:10; Deut. 9:29)
Bread of heaven, (Ex. 16:4, 12, 18)
    Feed me till I want no more." (John 6:48-51)

"Open now the crystal fountain, (Ex. 20:11; Ps. 78:15-16)
    Whence the healing stream doth flow; (2 Cor. 10:4; Rev. 22:1-2)
Let the fire and cloudy pillar (Ex. 13:21)
    Lead me all my journey through; (Deut. 8:2; Ps. 5:8)
Strong deliverer, (Ps. 18:2; 70:5)
    Be thou still my strength and shield." (Ps. 28:7, 144:2)

"When I tread the verge of Jordan (Josh. 3:8, 17)
    Bid my anxious fears subside; (1 Chron. 28:20; Isa. 35:4)
Death of death and hell's destruction, (2 Tim. 1:10; Heb. 2:14)
    Land me safe on Canaan's side; (Num 32:32)
Songs of praises, (Ps. 27:6)
    I will ever give to thee." (Ps. 34:1; 146:2)

A prime example of literal paraphrase of a New Testament narrative is Nahum Tate's "While shepherds watched their flocks"(E94, 95; M236, P58, 59), a metrical version of the nativity story recorded in Luke 2:8-14. Other writers often start their hymns with a description of an event in the Gospels, recalling some specific action of Jesus' ministry in order to remind the hymns' users of contemporary situations in which Christ's ministry may continue. Such is the case with Henry Twells's "At even, ere the sun was set" and Edward H. Plumptre's "Your hand, O Lord, in days of old" (L431), both based on the account of Jesus' healing the sick recorded in Mark 1:32-33. Both hymns go beyond description and recall a prayer for Christ's healing presence amid the needy circumstances of today's world.

A few passages from the letters of the apostle Paul have been choice themes for hymnic treatment. One of these is: "But may it never be that I should boast, except in the cross of our Lord Jesus Christ, through which the world has been crucified to me, and I to the world" (Gal. 6:14, NASB), reference to which is found in all the following hymns:

- "Ask ye what great thing I know" (B538, M163)
- "Beneath the cross of Jesus" (B291, E498, L107, M297, P92)
- "In the cross of Christ I glory" (B554, E441, 442; L104, M295, P84)
- "The head that once was crowned with thorns" (E483, L173, M326, P149)
- "When I survey the wondrous cross" (B144, E474, L482, M298, 299; P100, 101)

Another Pauline passage that has inspired hymnists is Philippians 2:4-11. "At the name of Jesus" (B198, E435, L179, M168, P148) is a 19th-century expression of its essential truths by the British woman, Caroline M. Noel. The American clergyman, F. Bland Tucker has given it a 20th-century interpretation in his "All praise to thee, for thou, O King divine" (B229, E477, M166).

The doxological hymns in the Book of Revelation have also inspired hymn writing. For example, "Worthy is the Lamb that was slain to receive power, and riches, and wisdom, and strength, and honour, and glory, and blessing" (Rev. 5:12) is echoed in these hymns:

- "Blessing and honor" (L525)
- "Come, let us join our cheerful songs" (E374, L254)
- "Glory be to God the Father" (L167)
- "O God of God, O Light of light" (L536)
- "Ye (You) servants of God" (B589, E535, L252, M181, P477)

BIBLICAL IMAGES AND EXPRESSIONS

Hymnists through the years have used biblical images to impress upon the singing congregation and evoke from it the truths of the faith. Many of these biblical images both illuminate and adorn the truths being expressed. Some of these images, though quite natural for the culture of biblical times, or even for the cultures of the hymnists using them in the 18th and 19th centuries, may need to be reexamined today because of the continuing cultural revolution of our time.

Shepherd

The image of shepherd used in the hymns discussed above may not have meaning for persons who have lived all their lives in urban settings, where shepherds and sheep are rarely encountered except on the television screen. If one idea of the concept "shepherd" is that of a reliable leader guiding one through hard and unfamiliar places when the going gets rough and confusing, then "The Lord is my guide" might be a more apt image for some urban folk.

Moreover, even when the word shepherd is a familiar concept, it connotes differing ideas to many people. "Shepherd" can either be conceived as the strong hero who relentlessly seeks the lost and wounded lambs and defends them from the wolves, or he can be the tender ethereal creature who gently carries the lamb "in his bosom." It was characteristic of the 19th century to ignore the idea of the "tough shepherd" and focus on that of the "tender shepherd." While the latter figure may be permissible in children's hymns, the idea of the tough shepherd would seem to come nearer the truth as portrayed in Scripture. The contrast is clear when comparing Clement of Alexandria's hymn in F. Bland Tucker's paraphrase: "Jesus, our mighty Lord" (E478) (The literal translation is "Bridle of colts untamed"!) with Mary L. Duncan's:

> "Jesus, tender Shepherd, hear me.
> Bless Thy little lamb tonight;
> Through the darkness be Thou near me,
> Watch my sleep til morning light."[7]

Rock of Ages

"Trust in the Lord for ever, for the Lord God is an everlasting rock" (Isa. 26:4, RSV).

There is a marginal reading in the *King James Version* of the above verse which has "Rock of Ages"—a familiar image in hymnody. This phrase can be thought of in two ways: in the Old Testament, Elijah hid himself in the cave of a rock to get out of a storm (1 Kings 19). In the New Testament, Christ tells the story of the house built on the rock that stands when the storms come, in contrast to the house built on the sand that falls (Matt. 7:24-27). Which image carries the greater truth? If the rock conjures up the image today of a sort of "bomb shelter" to which one can run and symbolically hide from life's dangers and demands, it could encourage a rather spineless religion. But if "Rock of Ages" calls to mind the firm foundation of faith on which one stands to face life's temptations and threats, then it can support a strong and adventurous faith.

The "Rock of Ages" idea as "foundation" is found in John Newton's "Glorious things of thee are spoken" (B398, E522, 523; "Glories of your name are

---

[7]This children's hymn can be found in many hymnals of the late 19th and early 20th centuries. See *The Hymnal* (Philadelphia: Presbyterian Board of Christian Education, 1933), 449.

spoken," L358, M731, P446), in Nicholai F. S. Grundtvig's "Built on the Rock the church doth stand" (tr. Carl Doving, B351, L365—"Built on a rock the Church shall stand") and the anonymous "How firm a foundation" (L507). The "Rock of Ages" as "protection and escape" seems to be the idea of Edward Hopper's "Jesus Savior, pilot me" (L334, M509); Augustus Toplady's "Rock of Ages, cleft for me" (B342, L327); and William O. Cushing's "O safe to the Rock that is higher than I" with its chorus:

> "Hiding in Thee, hiding in Thee,
>   Thou blest 'Rock of Ages,'
> I'm hiding in Thee."[8]

Ancient of Days

The expression "Ancient of days" (referring to God) found in several familiar hymns is often regarded as poetic nonsense since few worshipers know its scriptural base. The term is found in only one passage of the Bible: Daniel 7:9, 13, 22. In apocalyptic imagery the writer employs it to signify the eternal God, "one advanced in days," seated majestically on a throne of judgment. Hymnists seeking to express the worship and adoration due God alone have incorporated the phrase with its majestic associations into songs of objective praise, as in the first stanzas of these hymns:

- "Immortal, invisible, God only wise" (B6, E423, L526, M103, P263)
- "Come, Thou Almighty King" (B247, E365, L522, M6l, Pl39)
- "O worship the King" (B16, E388, L548, M73, P476)

Lord (of) Sabaoth

The word *Sabaoth* is Hebrew for "hosts" or "armies" and is used in the Old Testament to designate God's mighty power. It is retained untranslated in the older versions of the New Testament verses (Romans 9:29; James 5:4) which refer to "the Lord of Sabaoth." The phrase entered into hymnic expression early on and nowhere more memorably than in the 4th century *Te Deum laudamus* with its quotation of the seraphic song from Isaiah 6:

> "Holy, holy, holy, Lord God of Sabaoth;
> heaven and earth are full of the majesty
> of thy glory" (L3, M80)

---

[8]Found in many earlier hymnals. See *Baptist Hymnal* (Nashville: Convention Press, 1956), 271.

The most familiar use of the phrase "Lord Sabaoth, his name" (B8, E687, 688; M110, P260)[9] occurs in Frederic H. Hedge's translation of Luther's *"Ein' feste Burg."* It is also found in several other contemporary hymns.[10] Because of similarities in their appearance and spelling, many worshipers have mistaken "Sabaoth" for "sabbath," thereby missing altogether the true significance of the term.

Alpha and Omega

Better known than "Sabaoth," "Alpha and Omega," the first and last letters of the Greek alphabet, is found in Revelation (1:8, 11; 21:6; 22:13) as a title for Christ: the first and the last, the beginning and ending of all things.

The words are present in stanza one of Prudentius' Latin hymn of praise, translated by John Mason Neale, "Of the Father's love begotten" (B251, E82, L42, M184, P309), and Charles Wesley also used them in "Love divine, all loves excelling" (B208, E657, L315, M384, P376). In characteristic fashion, Wesley links the "Alpha and Omega" reference from Revelation with a similar idea in Hebrews 12:2, incorporating its prayer that Jesus will indeed be "the author and finisher of our faith."

While these and numerous other biblical expressions can easily be misunderstood by hymn singers, with proper explanation, hymns using these images can leap to new life and significance.

BIBLICAL NAMES AND PLACES

Traditionally, hymn writers have made reference to biblical names and places that, for people unfamiliar with the Bible, often need to be explained. An alphabetical listing of some of the names most commonly found would include:

Babel (Gen. 11:9)	Emmanuel (Immanuel, Matt. 1:23)
Bethlehem (Matt. 2:1-8)	Galilee (Matt. 3:13)
Calvary (Luke 23:33)	Gethsemane (Matt. 26:36)
Canaan (Num. 33:50-53)	Gilead (Jer. 8:22)
Ebenezer (1 Sam. 7:12)	Golgotha (Matt. 27:33)
Eden (Gen. 2:8)	Israel (Deut. 6:4)
Edom (Gen. 32:3; 36:21)	Jacob (Gen. 25:26)

---

[9]The *Lutheran Book of Worship* (228, 229) provides a new translation, which changes the phrase to "Lord of hosts is he!"

[10]See, for example "Praise the Lord, the King of Glory" by Delma B. Reno (B232): "Lord of Sabaoth His name."

Joseph (Gen. 30:24)	Moses (Ex. 2:10)
Jerusalem (Luke 2:22)	Mt. Pisgah (Deut. 34:1)
Jesse (1 Sam. 16:1-22)	Nazareth (Luke 2:51)
Jordan (Josh. 1:2)	Pharisee (Luke 18:10)
Lebanon (Ps. 29:5)	Sharon (Song of Sol. 2:1)
Madedonian (call, Acts 16:9)	Siloam (John 9:7-11)
Martha (Luke 10:41)	Stephen (Acts 6:5)
Mary (Matt. 2:11)	Zion (Sion, Ps. 48:11)
Messiah (John 4:25)	

The terms that refer in narrative fashion to persons and places, such as Mary, Joseph, Jesus, Bethlehem, Nazareth, Gethsemane, and Golgotha, are not so difficult for those with some knowledge of the gospel story. Names found in the Old Testament, however, often carry symbolic meanings that may require explanation.

Eden

This term may refer poetically to the garden where the first man and woman dwelt; thus, it may be associated with the creation, as in the following hymn:

> "Mine is the sunlight!
>> Mine is the morning
> Born of the one light
>> Eden saw play!"
> (B48, E8, M145, P469, "Morning has broken")

The references to Eden also include the bliss of the garden before the fall and are associated with the glories of heaven, especially in gospel songs. For instance, here is Fanny Crosby's "My Savior First of All" (B528):

> "Oh, the dear ones in glory, how they beckon me to come,
>> And our parting at the river I recall;
> To the sweet vales of Eden they will sing my welcome home,
>> But I long to meet my Savior first of all."

Jordan/Canaan

Similarly the use of *Jordan* and *Canaan* in hymnic expression often bears no literal reference to a particular river or to the land promised to the

Israelites in Old Testament times. These two proper names are often found together, particularly in 18th-century hymns:

> "When I tread the verge of Jordan,
>   Bid my anxious fears subside;
> Death of death and hell's destruction,
> [Bear me thro' the swelling current,]
>   Land me safe on Canaan's side."
> (B56, E690, M127, P281, "Guide me, O thou great Jehovah"; L343
>   "Guide me ever, great Redeemer").

> "On Jordan's stormy banks I stand
>   And cast a wishful eye
> To Canaan's fair and happy land
>   Where my possessions lie."
> (B521, M724, "On Jordan's stormy banks I stand")

The symbolism is that of passing over Jordan—the river of death, into the happy promised land of Canaan—the joys of heaven.[11]

Zion (Sion)

One of the most common proper names found in hymnody is Zion (or Sion). It is used to convey more than one idea. In the following instances, it transfers the earthly Mount Zion (Jerusalem, to which the Jews climbed for worship at the temple) into a heavenly idea:

> "The hill of Zion yields
>   A thousand sacred sweets,
> Before we reach the heavenly fields,
>   Or walk the golden streets."
> (B524, M732, 733, "Come, we that love the Lord")

> "The ladder is long, it is strong and well-made,
>   has stood hundreds of years and is not yet decayed;
> Many millions have climbed it and reached Sion's hill,
>   many millions by faith are climbing it still:"
> (E453 "As Jacob with travel")

---

[11]Many spirituals also make use of this imagery. For example, "Deep River" (African-American) and "Poor Wayfaring Stranger" (Anglo-American).

Other hymns using Zion in reference to heaven include: "Jerusalem, the golden" (B527, E624, L347), "Alleluia! Sing to Jesus" (E460, 461; L158, P144), and "Oh (O), what their joy" (E623, L337, M727).

In some hymns Zion refers to the church—the people of God on earth:

"Sure as thy (your) truth shall last,
 To Zion shall be giv'n
The brightest glories earth can yield,
 And brighter bliss of heaven."
(B354, E524, L368, M540, P441 "I love thy (your) kingdom, Lord")

"Christ is made the sure foundation,
 Christ the head and cornerstone;
Chosen of the Lord and precious,
 Binding all the church in one;
Holy Zion's help forever,
 And her confidence alone."
(B356, E518, L367, M559, P416, 417 "Christ is made the sure foundation")

Hymns using this word picture include "Glorious things of thee are spoken" (B398, E522, 523; M731, P446; "Glories of your name are spoken," L358), "O Zion, haste" (B583, E539, M537), "Praise God. Praise Him" (L529), and "Zion, praise thy Savior, singing" (E320).

GUIDES TO BIBLICAL SOURCES OF HYMNS

Alongside the information for authors or sources, many hymnals also indicate the scriptural references for terms such as those previously discussed. Some hymnals even place an appropriate verse of Scripture above each hymn printed.[12]

For teachers, pastors, ministers of music, and other church leaders, a convenient index now found in most hymnals is one variously called an Index of Scripture or Index of Scriptural Bases for Hymns.[13] These indices are a ready tool for correlating appropriate hymns with public Bible readings and/or sermon texts. Insofar as possible, correlation should be sought so that a service

[12]See, for example, *The Worshipping Church* (Carol Stream: Hope Publishing Co., 1990) and *The Baptist Hymnal* (Nashville: Convention Press, 1991).
[13]"Scripture Bases for Hymns Index" (B737-739); "Index of Scripture" (M924-926); "Index of Scriptural Allusions" (P687-90); "Index of Scriptural References," (E1031-1039). The *Lutheran Book of Worship* has a scriptural index entitled "Scripture References in Hymns" in its Minister's Desk Edition (468-69).

of worship or instruction may form one artistic and logical whole. It will also help worshipers and learners become more keenly aware of the scriptural foundations of many of the finest hymns.[14]

Churches that adhere closely to the Christian year can correlate their lectionaries with appropriate hymns by using suggested listings such as "Hymns for the Church Year" found in the *Lutheran Book of Worship* (929-31) and *A Liturgical Index to The Hymnal, 1982*.[15] Through available resources,[16] a meaningful hymn-Scripture correlation can be established. For example:

THE ASCENSION OF OUR LORD
(Observed the seventh week of Easter)

Epistle: Acts 1:1-11—Our Lord takes leave of His discples with the promise of His everlasting presence till He comes.

Gospel: Mark 16:14-20—The exalted Lord shows Himself to be the One to whom all power in heaven and earth is given.

Hymns:
"Look, ye saints (oh, look)! the sight is glorious:" (B169, L156)
"The head that once was crowned with thorns" (L173)
"Crown Him with many crowns," (B161, L170)
"A hymn of glory let us sing" (L157)
"Hail, thou once despised Jesus" (E495, M325)

Generally speaking, worthy hymns are biblical in the sense that they are either based directly upon, or express truths consonant with, holy Scripture. Therefore, drawing attention to their scriptural connections will not only enhance their meaningful use in worship and evangelism, but it will also lead in an appealing way to a more interested consideration and study of the Bible. Many churchgoers today would not have any notion of the meaning of "Ebenezer" or "Mt. Pisgah" (to mention only two Old Testament place names) if the former had not been encountered in "Come, thou fount of ev'ry blessing" (B15, L499, M400, P356) and the latter in

---

[14]A further resource for leaders, going much beyond the sometimes meager indication of biblical bases in some hymnals is Donald A. Spencer, *Hymn and Scripture Selection Guide*, Revised and Expanded Edition (Grand Rapids: Baker Book House, 1993).
[15]The detailed index was prepared by Marion C. Hatchett and published as No. 5 in the Episcopal Church's *Hymnal Studies* (New York: The Church Hymnal Corporation, 1986).
[16]See reference especially to Boushong in the "Selected Bibliography."

"Sweet hour of prayer" (B445). Careful attention to scriptural allusions in hymnody can lead to a renewed interest in Bible study as well as more intelligent hymn singing!

QUESTIONS FOR DISCUSSION/PROJECTS FOR ACTION

1. Compare and contrast the influence of the Psalms on hymn composition in the 18th, 19th, and 20th centuries.

2. What is the meaning of biblical images like "milk and honey," "throne of David," "Paschal Lamb," "Jesse's stem," "Edom," and "Star of the East" found in the following hymns?

"Jerusalem the golden" (E527, E624, L347)

"Lord, enthroned in heavenly splendor" (E307, L172, P154)

"Brightest and best of the stars of the morning" (E117, 118, L84, P67)

3. Using a hymnal concordance (see "Selected Bibliography"), locate hymns mentioning these biblical names: Emmanuel (Immanuel), Gilead, Sharon, Stephen, Bethel, Israel.

4. Look up the meaning of the following biblical words no longer in today's common language but still found in hymns: Manna, psaltery, seraph, timbrel. Find hymns where these words occur.

5. Using a source such as McDormand and Crossman's *Judson Concordance to Hymns* or a tool such as Spencer's *Hymn and Scripture Selection Guide*, find hymns for worship and/or evangelism appropriate for use with the following Scripture passages: Isaiah 40:1-11, Psalm 91, Colossians 3:15-17, Matthew 5:1-12.

6. For Sunday School lessons on the following Bible selections, choose appropriate related hymns: Genesis 1, Psalm 103, John 20:19-29, Philippians 2:5-11.

7. Using such aids as the "Biblical Characters" section of the topical index in Erik Routley's *Rejoice in the Lord* (Grand Rapids: William B. Eerdmans Publishing Co., 1958), 593-594, or Judy Hunnicutt's *Index of Biblical Characters in Hymns* (Ft. Worth: The Hymn Society), plan a hymn service around one of the following: David, Jacob, John the Baptist, Paul, Mary, the Prophets, the Apostles.

8. In what ways could a pastor, minister of education, or Sunday School teacher be convinced that a thorough study of Christian hymnody could enhance Bible study?

4
THE HYMN AND THEOLOGY

I t has been said that hymns are the poor person's poetry and the ordinary person's theology. Hymns are the most popular kind of verse in living use because they express what common folk have believed through the ages and what can be affirmed today as true and reliable.

THE HYMN—A BEARER OF "GRASS-ROOTS" THEOLOGY

The recitation of creeds and confessions of faith makes up an important part of the public worship of many Christians. In those worshiping groups where this is not the normal practice, however, the hymn stands as an alternate means of objectifying belief corporately. Replete with the lyric expression of universal doctrine distilled from the church's 20 centuries of experience, the hymnal is truly a book of "grass-roots theology." For the person in the pew, a hymn like "O God, our help in ages past" (B74, E680, L320, M117, P210) sets forth in strong, vivid, and adequate language the eternity and omnipotence of God. A song like "The Solid Rock" (B406, L293, M368, P379) voices the singer's simple confession of faith in Jesus Christ as all-sufficient Redeemer. The hymnal is not a formal volume of systematized dogma; however, by its general arrangement and its biblical content, it is clearly theological.

The hymnal is often overlooked as a ready means of presenting and teaching Christian doctrine. More Christians' basic beliefs are formulated by singing hymns than by preaching or Bible study. Certainly one's disposition toward, or away from, right belief is subtly, but indelibly, influenced by the hymns one repeatedly sings. When talking about their faith, average churchgoers can quote more stanzas of hymns than they can verses of Scripture. This fact, far from lessening the importance of preaching and Bible teaching, is simply a testimony to the importance of the hymnal as a practical textbook in doctrine. Moreover, it focuses attention on the critical requirement that the content of the hymns taught to young and old, insofar as possible, accurately reflect theological and biblical truth.

Besides nurturing the faith, hymns figure prominently in sharing it. Christians from New Testament times onward have proclaimed their beliefs through song, thereby spreading the tenets of the faith. Many of the early Christian hymns were forged in theological controversy and consequently are creedal in nature. [1] Furthermore, every great religious awakening of the past has gone forward on the wings of song. [2] And to the degree that hymns have been clearly theological, they have become the folk songs of the church militant. The evangelizing power of Christian song cannot be denied.

Because hymns were born out of the conscious human need of their authors to express their faith and devotion, they also minister to the spiritual needs of those who know and sing them. Thus, the hymnal is a theological guidebook for meeting the challenges of daily living and the spiritual problems encountered in ordinary human relationships.

When Charles Wesley sought longingly for a thousand tongues to sing the praises of the One whose name calms fears and bids sorrows cease, ("O for a thousand tongues to sing" B216, E493, L559, M57, P466), he wrote from his own experience of the reassuring and comforting love of God revealed in Christ. When Christians today sing the exuberant affirmations of this great hymn (written on the anniversary of Wesley's conversion experience), they, too, may be calmed and strengthened in their lives.

When John G. Whittier penned "Dear Lord and Father of mankind" [3] (B267, E652, 653; L506, M358, P345), he was stating his quiet Quaker confidence in the eternal goodness of God and his sense of the wholeness of life given to those who are faithful in God's service. The confident singing of this hymn, amid the pressures of today's world, can undergird faith and purpose for one's own Christian walk. Since there is a great reservoir of helpful spiritual truth within the covers of a good hymnal, it can function as a reliable handbook for believers, sustaining them in the daily round.

Thus, the hymn is a ready tool for the major functions of today's church: worship, education, evangelism, and ministry. In worship it can serve as a corporate affirmation of a congregation's faith. In education it can make the doctrines of the faith memorable for Christian growth. In evangelism it can dramatize the truths of the gospel for mission appeal. In daily ministry

[1] See the sections on Greek and Latin hymnody in Chapter 5 of this textbook, "Early Church and Pre-Reformation Traditions."

[2] For examples, see Chapter 10 of this textbook, "The Hymn in Proclamation."

[3] The stanzas of this hymn are an excerpt from a 17-stanza poem entitled "The Brewing of Soma," written in 1872.

its assuring lines can be constantly at hand to help in spiritual emergencies involving every kind of human need. The hymn effectively functions in all of these areas because it is a proved expression of Christian theology couched in appealing lyric and mediated through personal experience. [4]

THE HYMN IN THEOLOGICAL CONTROVERSY

The great hymns of the early centuries of the Christian church, such as the expanded *Gloria in excelsis Deo* and the *Te Deum laudamus*, were sung creeds. Moreover, the content of such hymns as Clement of Alexandria's "Jesus, our mighty Lord" (E478) and Prudentius's "Of the Father's love begotten" (B251, E82, L42, M184, P309) are best understood and appreciated when it is recognized that they originated in the midst of theological struggle between those considered to be of the Orthodox faith and those of the Gnostic and Arian persuasions. [5] Here, the Trinitarian doxology became an integral part of medieval hymnody and psalmody. Not only was the *Gloria Patri* (the Lesser Doxology) appended to the chanting of every psalm in the divine offices, but, in the 19th century, praise to the Trinity became part and parcel of practically every hymn translated by the Oxford Reformers. [6] Consider, for example, the following hymns, all of which include a Trinitarian doxology in their last stanzas:

- Prudentius, "Of the Father's love begotten" (B251, E82, L42, M184, P309)
- Gregory the Great, "Father, we praise thee" (E1, 2; M680, P459)
- Anonymous (7th century), "Christ is made the sure foundation" (M559, P416, 417)
- Rabanus Maurus, "Come, Holy Ghost (Spirit), our souls inspire" (E503, 504; M651, P125)
- Peter Abelard, "O what their joy and their glory must be" (E623, L337, M727)
- Bernard of Cluny, "Jerusalem, the golden" (B527, E624)
- Francis of Assisi, "All creatures of our God and King" (B27, E400, L527, M62, P455)

---

[4] Each of these hymnic areas, as they relate to the work of the churches, are treated in detail in "Part III: The Hymn in Practice" of this textbook.

[5] See Chapter 5 of this textbook, "The Early Church and Pre-Reformation Traditions."

[6] The members of the Oxford Movement even appended doxologies to existing hymns in their eagerness to imitate the medieval hymn. See Erik Routley, *Church Music and the Christian Faith* (Carol Stream, Il.: Agape, 1978), 98.

These hymns also demonstrate that though often "born of controversy, the hymns that survive are those which express the universal faith of Christendom."[7] "Hymns which are exaggerated or one-sided in their doctrinal emphasis do not come into general use, and sooner or later are discarded."[8] If hymns are not discarded altogether, those parts which are unsuitable for universal use are generally omitted. Therefore, most of the polemic elements in hymns have been largely excised for those who use them today. For example, Samuel J. Stone's "The church's one foundation" (B350, E525, L369, M545, P442) was in 1866 a rigid assertion of High Church dogma in disdainful opposition to those who were embracing the liberating accents of science and the higher criticism. However, certain hostile allusions in the hymn have more recently been omitted, such as:

"Though there be those that hate her [the Church]
    And false sons in her pale,
Against or foe or traitor
    She ever shall prevail."[9]

Consequently, the parts of the hymn which remain in use constitute a sound lyrical exposition of what most Christians believe about the church.[10]

Theological understandings that are quite meaningful in one generation may be rejected in later generations. Christian theologians are constantly struggling for better insight into the truth of God; this struggle is often reflected in the emendation or abridgement of hymns. For example, recent debate concerns the use of sexist language in hymns. Some theologians and worship leaders feel the pains of separation in the Christian community that result from noninclusive language in many (even classic) hymns. In their opinion, if such hymns are to continue to be effective in public worship, their sexist imagery—exclusively male images of God, exclusively female images of the church and nature, and the use of "generic" man (that is, mankind, and so forth)—must be modified and in most instances eliminated.

[7]Kenneth L. Parry, *Christian Hymns* (London: SCM Press, Ltd., 1956), 8.
[8]Robert Guy McCutchan, *Hymns in the Lives of Men* (New York, Abingdon-Cokesbury Press, 1945), 178, quoted from Howard Chandler Robbins, *Ecumenical Trends in Hymnody,* pamphlet issued by the Federal Council of Churches.
[9]Albert E. Bailey, *The Gospel in Hymns* (New York: Charles Scribner's Sons, 1950), 377.
[10]See an article critical of the doctrine of the church set forth in this hymn, Helen Bruch Pearson, "The Battered Bartered Bride," *The Hymn* 34, 4 (October, 1983): 216-220.

An example of the kinds of emendation advocated is seen in the following excerpts from Henry van Dyke's "Joyful, joyful, we adore thee" (B7, E376, L551, M89, P464):

Original	Emendation
"Thou our Father, Christ our Brother	"We on earth are all thy children;
All who live in love are Thine;	All who live in love are thine;
Father-love is reigning o'er us	All creation sings before us,
Brother-love binds man to man."	Raise we now the glad refrain."[11]

A classic example from another time is Reginald Heber's richly poetic "From Greenland's icy mountains" which accurately stated the ardent convictions of 19th-century Englishmen in the days when the Christian missionary thrust was conceived as parallel to and intermingled with the spreading of the British Empire. But now the spiritually patronizing attitude implied by the questions in stanza 3 has caused this hymn to fall into disuse:

"Can we, whose souls are lighted
With wisdom from on high,
Can we to men benighted
The lamp of life deny?"[12]

The few hymnals that still include this hymn usually omit the following stanza because of the words "heathen" and "vile" (in reference to those who are objects of Christian missions):

"What though the spicy breezes
Blow soft o'er Ceylon's isle,
Though every prospect pleases,
And only man is vile;
In vain with lavish kindness
The gifts of God are strown;
The heathen in his blindness
Bows down to wood and stone."

[11]Most hymnals either alter stanza 4 of this hymn or omit it altogether. Such changes in hymn texts seeking to avoid gender-specific references to God and humanity may be found in collections like *Because We Are One People: Songs for Worship* (Chicago: Ecumenical Women's Centers, 1975). See also Brian Wren, *What Language Shall I Borrow? God-talk in Worship* (New York: Crossroad, 1989) for a thorough treatment of this issue by one who is a leading champion of inclusivity in God language used in hymn writing.
[12]*Baptist Hymnal* (Nashville: Convention Press, 1956), 449.

Hymns that express outmoded attitudes concerning the nature and mission of the church are being replaced. Newer hymns such as Jeffery W. Rowthorn's fervent prayer, "Lord, you give the great commission" (E528, M584, P429), Georgia Harkness's exuberant "Tell it out with gladness" (B585), and Sylvia Dunstan's straightforward "Go to the world!" [13] are inspired, however, by the same basic Christian belief. This belief is that God's good news should be shared the world over with all persons so that their lives may be transformed into the abundant life Christ died to give them.

John Wesley had a keen sense of the importance of the hymn for encapsulating Christian dogma. He spoke of his collection of hymns as "a little body of experimental and practical divinity." [14] Furthermore, he was quite impatient with those who tried to mend his brother Charles' hymns to make what they thought to be better theological sense out of them. Yet, John himself engaged in a considerable bit of emendation in order to satisfy his own theological and poetic requirements.

For instance, the second stanza of Charles Wesley's great hymn on the indwelling spirit of love, "Love divine, all loves excelling" (B208, E657, L315, M384, P376) originally read: "Take away our *power* of sinning." The questions concerning this were on this wise: "Is not this expression too strong?" "Can God take away our power of sinning without taking away our power of free obedience?" This extreme view of Christian perfection, [15] though a cherished ideal of Charles Wesley, was so objectionable to John that he completely omitted this stanza in later hymnals. In American editions the stanza is retained but with "power of" changed to "bent to." Other wordings that have been changed are "second rest" becoming "promised rest" (in stanza 2) [16] and "sinless" becoming "spotless" (in stanza 4).

This doctrine of sinless perfection was a cause of much controversy in 18th-century England. One of its stoutest and most vituperative opponents was Augustus M. Toplady, the author of "Rock of Ages, cleft for me" (B342, E685,

---

[13]"Go to the world! Go into all the earth. Go preach the cross where Christ renews life's worth, Baptizing as the sign of our rebirth. Alleluia. Alleluia." Sylvia G. Dunstan, *In Search of Hope and Grace* (Chicago: G.I.A. Publications, 1991), 84-85. (© Copyright 1991. G.I.A. Publications. Used by Permission.*) Ms. Dunstan was a minister of the United Church of Canada (1955-1993) whose hymns (40 in the above collection) have appeared in recently published hymnals and supplements.

[14]John Wesley, preface to *A Collection of Hymns for the Use of the People Called Methodists* (London, 1780) quoted in numerous places, including Carlton R. Young's *Companion to the United Methodist Hymnal.* See Richard Watson and Kenneth Trickett, *Companion to Hymns and Psalms* (Peterborough: Methodist Publishing House, 1988), 22.

[15]Also evident in the original version of stanza 4: "Finish then thy new creation; Pure and sinless let us be."

[16]However, *The United Methodist Hymnal* returns to "second rest" (M384).

L327, M361).[17] Yet today, Toplady's "Rock of Ages" and Wesley's "Jesus, lover of my soul" (B180, E699, M479, P303), in spite of the strong theological differences between their authors, have stood side by side as two of the most loved hymns in the English language. This fact is dramatic proof of the truth stated above: though born of controversy, the great hymns express the one universal faith. They provide a powerful prod for Christians, regardless of denominational label, to continue to struggle toward the ultimate goal of unity expressed by Jesus in his high-priestly prayer: "That they may be one, even as we are one" (John 17:22).

THE HYMNAL'S TABLE OF CONTENTS–A THEOLOGICAL INDICATOR

A glance at the table of contents and topical index of a standard hymnal usually reveals the range and depth of its presentation of Christian doctrine. The manner and order of presentation may differ from hymnal to hymnal, yet most of the cardinal points of doctrine will find a place in a book claiming acceptance and respect by large bodies of believers. For example, the hymns may be arranged according to the seasons of the Christian year in a liturgically-oriented hymnal; a book reflecting the beliefs and practices of worshiping groups inclined toward the free church tradition might list many of the same hymns under a heading such as "Jesus Christ" and the various events in Christ's life and ministry.

By a similar token, hymns concerning the third person of the Trinity may be arranged systematically under "The Christian Year—Pentecost Season" in one hymnal; another may group these hymns under "God—The Holy Spirit."[18] Hymns concerned primarily with the subject of outreach may appear in one hymnal under the heading of "The Church—Evangelism and Missions"; in another hymnal many of the same hymns will be found under the heading of "The Christian Year—Epiphany Season." Thus, even the categorization of the hymns by subject headings reveals the theological stance of a hymnal's editors, publishers, and users.

Furthermore, the number and variety of hymns under particular headings can be a clue to the theological bent of the hymnal's compilers. For example, hymns and gospel songs dealing with confession, repentance, and salvation in one hymnal may number several times those on the same subjects in another hymnal. The latter hymnal, however, may have a much richer and

[17]Insight into this dreadful controversy is afforded by Albert E. Bailey's account in *The Gospel in Hymns* (New York: Scribner's Sons, 1960), 117-21.
[18]However, in some hymnals both categories may be found. For example, *The United Methodist Hymnal* has hymns listed concerning "The Holy Spirit" (M943) and "Pentecost" (M937).

larger quantity of hymns on social concern and the relevancy of the gospel to the problems people encounter in today's world.

HYMN PATTERNS

Christian ministers, whether musicians or nonmusicians, have the opportunity and obligation to understand their hymnbook theologically. They should apply certain learned expository techniques to the task of revealing the theological teachings and implications of individual hymns. One way this may be done is to consider the patterns of thought in specific hymns.

Objective-Subjective

One approach is to regard hymns in terms of their objectivity and/or subjectivity. In its address, a hymn can be either objective (God, a person, or a thing is the main object of attention and concern,) or it can be subjective (the focus of attention being on the poet or singer—the one who originally created the hymn or the one who recreates the hymn when singing it).

For example, a quick analysis of a hymnal's table of contents will show how the hymns under the heading "God" are either addressed to God or they are exhorting others or even one's own soul to make God the object of worship and thanksgiving. [19] Sometimes there may be emphasis on only one aspect of the Godhead (for example, on Christ [20] or the Holy Spirit). [21]

God is the chief object of prayer and praise in true hymnic expression. Inanimate objects such as sunlight ("Heavenly Sunlight") or a cross ("The Old Rugged Cross") may certainly be referred to in worshipful song, but when they become the principal objectives of attention, they tend to be exalted to a status equal to or above God. In singing such songs, one may unwittingly express a theological position that is foreign to one's actual beliefs.

Subjectivity is predominantly found in many popular hymns. While a healthy subjectivism is necessary to a wholehearted involvement of one's total person in a relationship with God, subjectivity must be disciplined lest it lead to self-centeredness. Consequently, the use of songs weighted heavily toward subjectivity, like "O That Will Be Glory" (B520) and "Pass me not, O gentle Savior" (B308, M351) should be balanced with God-centered hymns such as "All praise to Thee" (B229, E477, M166) and "All hail the power of Jesus' name" (B200, 201, 202; E450, 451; L328, 329; M154, 155; P142, 143).

[19]For example, of the 95 selections under "Praise of the Triune God" in M, some 30 are directly addressed to God. Similarly, look in B at hymns number 1-40, in which those not directly addressed to God bring God to mind as the object of praise.
[20]For example, see hymns B75-236, E439-499, L22-159, M153-327, P299-312.
[21]For example, see hymns B237-245, E500-516, L486-513, 160-164, 376-403; M328-336, P313-326.

Some hymns and gospel songs combine the objective with the subjective by changing the object of address between or within successive stanzas. For example, Isaac Watts' hymn on the atonement, "Alas, and did my Savior bleed" (B139, 145; L98; M294, 359) is written with Christ, the Savior, as the supreme object of attention, yet Christ is referred to in the third person. With stanza 3 or 4 (beginning "Thus might I hide my blushing face"), the hymn takes a more subjective turn; in the final stanza, Christ is addressed directly, with the climaxing words of commitment: "Here, Lord, I give myself away,'Tis all that I can do."

Similarly, in Cecil Frances Alexander's "Jesus calls us o'er the tumult" (B293, E549, 550; L494, M398), Jesus is spoken of in the third person—the singer addressing other worshipers. The final stanza is an intimate prayer to Jesus: "…by thy mercies (in your mercy), Savior, may we (make us) hear thy (your) call." A similar kind of shift to and from direct address to God can be observed in gospel hymns such as "He leadeth me! O blessed thought" (B52, L501, M128) and "Jesus, keep me near the cross" (B280, M301).

Paradox and Contrast

Some hymns make creative use of the poetic devices of paradox and contrast. This should be expected when the many paradoxes implicit in the Christian faith are recalled: the burden of the teaching of Jesus was that whosoever would save his life shall lose it, and whoever would lose his life for Christ's sake would find it (Matt. 16:25); whoever would be chief must be servant of all (Matt. 20:27).

Charles Wesley's "Thou hidden source of calm repose" (M153) is rich in paradox, especially in its final two stanzas:

> "Jesus, my all in all thou art,
>   My rest in toil, my ease in pain,
> The healing of my broken heart,
>   In war my peace, in loss my gain,
> My smile beneath the tyrant's frown,
>   In shame my glory and my crown."

> "In want my plentiful supply,
>   In weakness my almighty power,
> In bonds my perfect liberty,
>   My light in Satan's darkest hour,

In grief my joy unspeakable,
　　My life in death, my heaven in hell." [22]

The "I know not" hymns express some of the great contrasts implicit in the faith. Using the theme of 2 Timothy 1:12, Daniel Whittle movingly contrasts the "I know not's" of the author or singer with the Pauline assurance: " 'I know whom I have believed' " (B337, M714). The hymn of Evelyn Atwater Cummins, "I know not where the road will lead" (E647) also effectively illustrates this pattern of contrast.

The Hebrew Pattern

A frequently overlooked thought design in many hymns is known as the Hebrew pattern, identified thus because of its prevalent use in Hebrew poetry, particularly the Psalms.[23] It consists of the conventional threefold plan: thesis, antithesis, and synthesis. The thesis in the hymn contemplates God in all God's perfection as holy, eternal, omnipotent, and loving. The antithesis presents the contrasting human situation with its sinfulness, ephemerality, weakness, and rebellion against God. In the synthesis, our sinfulness is caught up in God's holiness, our mortality into divine immortality, our weakness into God's power, and our rebellion into joyful reconciliation with the All-Merciful.

This pattern is most clearly discernible in the hymns of Isaac Watts, possibly because the poet followed closely the psalmodic model even when he was not paraphrasing a psalm. "O (our) God, our help in ages past" (B74, E680, L320, M117, P210), based on Psalm 90, can be analyzed as follows:

THESIS
　　Stanza 1: "O God, our help…"
　　　　　　2: "Under the shadow…"
　　　　　　3: "Before the hills…"
　　　　　　4: "A thousand ages…"

ANTITHESIS
　　　　　　5: "Time, like an…"
　　　　　　6: "The busy tribes of flesh and blood,
　　　　　　　　With all their cares and fears,
　　　　　　　　Are carried downward by the flood,

---

[22]See also the reference to George Matheson's use of paradox in "Make me a captive, Lord" in Chapter 1, "The Hymn and Literature," page 21.
[23]See Carl F. Price's "Hymn Patterns" in *Religion in Life*, Summer 1947.

And lost in following years." [24]

SYNTHESIS
> 7: "O God, our help…"

Watts' hymn on the Holy Spirit, "Come, Holy Spirit, heavenly Dove" (E510, P126) also follows the Hebrew model:

THESIS
> Stanza 1: "Come, Holy Spirit…"

ANTITHESIS
> 2: "Look how we grovel…"
> 3: "In vain we tune…"
> 4: "And shall we then…"

SYNTHESIS
> 5: "Come, Holy Spirit…"

An example of this pattern in a more recent hymn may be seen in Frank Mason North's "Where cross the crowded ways of life" (E609, L429, M427, P408):

THESIS
> Stanza 1: "Where cross the crowded…"

ANTHITHESIS CONTRASTING WITH THESIS
> 2: "In haunts of wretchedness..."
> 3: "From tender childhood's..."
> 4: "The cup of water..."

SYNTHESIS
> 5: "O Master, from..."
> 6: "Till sons of men…"

There are other hymns cast in this mold. [25]

[24] If we had more of Watts' original paraphrase in our hymnals, the antithesis would include the quoted stanza.
[25] See, for example, "Praise, my soul, the King of heaven" (B32, E410, M66, P478), "O for a closer walk with God" (E683, 684; P396, 397), and "O thou, in whose presence" (M518).

THEOLOGICAL INTERPRETATIONS

In addition to the analysis of patterns, theological meanings in hymns can also be highlighted through an exegesis of their content on a stanza-by-stanza basis. This can be done by verbal exposition either in a broad summary statement or by a detailed analysis. Some clergymen and other church workers have prepared short devotional commentaries on specific hymns; others have developed entire sermons using one or more hymns as sermon texts. A list of sources containing sermons and devotional thoughts may be found in the "Selected Bibliography" under "Sermons/Devotional Talks Based on Hymns."

Doctrinal content can also be brought into focus by paraphrasing a hymn's poetry in succinct prose. For example, John Greenleaf Whittier's hymn "Immortal love, forever full" (B480) could be paraphrased in the following manner:

Hymn	Paraphrase
"Immortal love, forever full, Forever flowing free, Forever shared, forever whole, A never—ebbing sea!"	The eternal love of God, though constantly offered, is inexhaustible.
"We may not climb the heav'nly steeps, To bring the Lord Christ down; In vain we search the lowest deeps, For him no depths can drown."	Christ's presence is not found only in the highest reaches of the stratosphere; it is also found in the deepest ocean valleys.
"The healing of his seamless dress Is by our beds of pain; We touch him in life's throng and press, And we are whole again."	His healing presence can touch our busy, harried lives and restore wholeness.
"O Lord and Master of us all, Whate'er our name or sign, We own thy sway, we hear thy call, We test our lives by thine."	Regardless of our label, we all claim You, Lord, as Supreme Master and Model of our lives.

In summary, Whittier's theology in this hymn postulates the boundless love of God that is freely given to those who acknowledge Christ as sovereign Lord in their present circumstance and need. Such basic doctrine becomes recognizable and clear when the stanzas are paraphrased.

CONCLUSION

The early 19th-century German poet Goethe once said that noble architecture is frozen music. A 20th-century hymnologist has rightly asked in response: "May we not say that a noble hymn is frozen theology that melts in the fervor of devotional song?"[26] Indeed we may. Yet, regardless of the richness and correctness of a hymn's theological content, the hymn itself becomes a genuine expression of Christian belief only when the singer utters it from the heart.

Here is the crux of the matter of the hymn as theology. Regardless of the precision and correctness of the theological teaching of a hymn, its doctrine remains frozen in moribund wording and lifeless musical notation until its meaning is devoutly embraced by the one who sings it. George Herbert aptly states this in his poem "A True Hymn":

"The fineness which a hymn or psalm affords
Is when the soul unto the lines accords."[27]

QUESTIONS FOR DISCUSSION/PROJECTS FOR ACTION

1. In what ways have specific hymns influenced your own beliefs?

2. Compare the table of contents of your hymnal with the contents of another church's or denomination's hymnal to determine their main theological emphases.

3. Some people have objected to the theology in the following songs:

"Pass me not, O gentle Savior" (B308, M351)

"I come to the garden alone" (B187, M314)

"O That Will Be Glory" (B520)

Can you find reasons for such objections? Do you agree or disagree with these objections?

4. Do you know of other hymns whose theology is objectionable?

5. Choose 10 hymns from your hymnal that are totally objective in address and direction. Then choose 10 more that are subjective.

6. Make a list of your 25 favorite hymns and analyze them for subjectivity/objectivity.

Continued on next page

---

[26]Frank B. Merryweather, *The Evolution of the Hymn* (London: William Clowes and Sons, Ltd., 1966), 17.

[27]Herbert, "A True Hymn" in *The Temple: Sacred Poems and Private Ejaculations.* ed. John N. Wall, Jr., *The Classics of Western Spirituality* (New York: Paulist Press, 1981), 294.

7. Can you find and block out on paper the Hebrew pattern in these hymns?

"A mighty fortress is our God" (B8, E687, 688; L228, 229; M110, P259, 260)

"Praise, my soul, the king of heaven" (B32, E410, L549, M66, P478)

8. Choose one of the following three hymns. Write out in simple prose the thought contained in each of its stanzas. Then summarize the hymn's theological teaching in one or two sentences.

"Look, ye saints (oh, look)! the sight is glorious" (B169, L156)

"Lord, speak to me, (us), that I (we) may speak" (B568, L403, M463, P426)

"Abide with me: fast falls the eventide" (B63, E662, L272, M700, P543)

9. What are some ways you might lead others to consider more carefully the theology of the hymns they sing?

PART II:
THE HYMN IN HISTORY
AND CULTURE

5

EARLY CHURCH AND PRE-REFORMATION TRADITIONS

W hen considering the worship song of the first-century Christians, one is inevitably drawn to the Old Testament Psalter, which constituted the first Christian book of praise. For Christians who were converted Jews, the well-known psalms may have been their primary means of singing worship. Although the embryonic Christian community was soon to add new songs that expressed its newfound hope and joy in Christ, even these songs were to be based on psalmodic models.

OLD TESTAMENT BACKGROUNDS

The nativity canticles in the Gospel of Luke are much like the Psalms both in form and content. It is significant that at the conclusion of the Last Supper, Jesus and His disciples sang a hymn that was most likely a portion of the traditional psalms used for Passover—The Great Hallel (Ps. 113-118.) [1]

The Psalms, the most quoted Hebrew Scripture in the New Testament, are the base upon which all subsequent church song has been built. Whether intended for corporate or private worship, they voice universal sentiments which have constituted the themes of musical devotion throughout the centuries. Since they appear and reappear in varied forms and styles throughout the history of congregational song,[2] their supreme importance for worship prior to the formation of the Christian church needs only to be recognized here.

NEW TESTAMENT SONG
Nativity Canticles

Having come into a new and unprecedented knowledge of a loving fellowship through faith in the risen Christ, the first Christians felt the need to give

[1]Other references to singing in the New Testament speak of songs which cannot with certainty be linked to the canonical Psalter.
[2]See elsewhere in this chapter, for example, the third part of the famous *Te Deum laudamus*.

fresh expression to their feelings in new songs of Christian experience. This is evidenced in the exuberant lyrics connected with the nativity of Jesus: the song of Mary (Luke 1:46-55), the song of Zacharias (Luke 1:68-79), the song of the angels (Luke 2:14), and the song of Simeon (Luke 2:29-32).

In later times these songs came to be known by their first words (incipits) in the Latin: the *Magnificat* (usually sung at Vespers or Evensong in liturgical churches) (E-S185-189; L6, M199, P600); the *Benedictus* (sung at the morning hours) (E-S190-195; L2, M208, P601, 602);[3] the *Gloria in excelsis Deo* (the "Greater Doxology," expanded from the angelic message into a much longer song of prayer and praise) (E-S201-204; L-pages 58-59, 79-80, 100-102; M82, 83; P566, 575); and the *Nunc dimittis* (sung at Compline, Vespers, or Communion) (E-S196-200; L-pages 73, 93-94, 116, 159-60; M225; P603, 604, 605). The central note struck by these first truly Christian songs is one of exulting joy occasioned by the fulfillment of ancient prophecy in the miraculous coming of Jesus Christ.

Pauline Hymn Fragments

In various other places in the New Testament, particularly in the letters of the apostle Paul, hymn-like fragments, possibly quoted from early worship usages in the churches, can be found. For example, there appear to be snatches from doctrinal hymns which sound very much like the material from which the early creeds came:

> "He was revealed in flesh,
>   vindicated in spirit,
>   seen by angels,
> proclaimed among Gentiles,
>   believed in throughout the world,
>   taken into glory."
> (1 Tim. 3:16b, NRSV)

Some of these fragments may have come from hymns used liturgically. For example, here is a fragment from a baptismal hymn:

> "Sleeper, awake!
>   Rise from the dead,
>   and Christ will shine in you." [4]

[3]Two 20th-century hymnists who have made paraphrases of the Benedictus are James Quinn SJ (B79) and Michael Perry (M209). The other canticles are also the basis for some contemporary hymns, most notably Timothy Dudley-Smith's paraphrase of the Magnificat, "Tell out, my soul" (B81, E437, M200).
[4]One 20th-century hymn based on this fragment is F. Bland Tucker's "Awake, O sleeper, rise from death" (E547).

There is a reference to the spontaneous use of hymns and prayers in the Jerusalem church recorded in Acts 4:24-31. This marvelous incident affords just one glimpse of how the first Christians broke into singing compositions which were part of a great reservoir of poetry and prose regularly used in their common worship. Even in unlikely circumstances, as when Paul and Silas were beaten and locked in stocks at Philippi (Acts 16:25), they gave voice to well-known songs in praise to God.

The use of Christian song as an instrument of instruction is evident in parallel exhortations from Paul's writings: "Do not get drunk with wine, for that is debauchery; but be filled with the Spirit, as you sing psalms and hymns and spiritual songs among yourselves, singing and making melody to the Lord in your hearts" (Eph. 5:18-19, NRSV); "Let the word of Christ dwell in you richly; teach and admonish one another in all wisdom; and with gratitude in your hearts sing psalms, hymns and spiritual songs to God" (Col. 3:16, NRSV).

Doxological Hymns

Certain doxological (praise) hymns describing a visionary heavenly worship in the Book of Revelation provided another rich store of praise literature for the New Testament Christians. Among the many examples[5] is "The song of Moses, the servant of God, and the song of the Lamb":

> "Great and amazing are your deeds,
>> Lord God the Almighty!
> Just and true are your ways,
>> King of the nations!
> Lord, who will not fear and glorify your name?
>> For you alone are holy.
> All nations will come and worship before you,
>> for your judgments have been revealed."
> (Revelation 15:3-4, NRSV)

The fact that the early churches actually engaged in singing praise is clear from the record of Pliny the Younger, governor of Bithynia, who in A.D. 112 reported to the Emperor Trajan that the Christians in his province held their worship assemblies on Sunday mornings before dawn and sang antiphonal hymns of praise to Christ as God.[6]

---

[5]See Revelation 1:4-8; 5:9-10; 11:17-18; and 19:1-3, among others.
[6]See Henry Bettenson, *Documents of the Christian Church* (London: Oxford University Press, 1946. Second ed., 1963), 3-5.

GREEK HYMNODY

Greek was the language of culture in the Eastern Mediterranean areas where the Christian movement got its start. Consequently, the Hebrew Scriptures, originally translated into Greek (the *Septuagint*) in the 3rd and 2nd centuries B.C. to meet the needs of Jews in Egypt, were also appropriated by the first Greek-speaking Christians. Since the New Testament was originally written, for the most part, in Greek, it was natural that the worship materials used by the early churches existed in this language as well.

Early Prose Hymns

Our Greek hymnic legacy stems from three distinct types. The relatively few earliest hymns were prose-like, coming from New Testament times and the era immediately thereafter. Besides the biblical hymns already mentioned, two hymns from these early centuries have continued to maintain an important place in the worship of the Greek church; through translation, they also hold a place in other churches to this day.

One is *Phos Hilaron*—the famous "Lamplighting Hymn" of the 3rd century A.D. which was sung at the approach of night both in the family circle of Christian homes and at the gathering of the church for corporate devotion. Addressed to the heavenly Father and using the metaphor of light, this hymn is one of pure praise. In an older translation by John Keble, it is known as "Hail! Gladdening Light, of His pure glory poured." Later translations or paraphrases are those of Robert Bridges, "O Gladsome light, O grace of God the Father's face" (E36, M686)[7] and F. Bland Tucker, "O gracious Light, Lord Jesus Christ" (E25, 26).

The other hymn is a morning song—an expanded Greek form of the angels' message at Christ's birth, upon which the fully developed *Gloria in excelsis Deo* of the Western church was based. This previously mentioned "Greater Doxology" is chanted as a canticle in liturgical churches with the familiar first line, "Glory to God in the highest" or "Glory be to God on high" (E-S201-204; L-pages 58-59, 79-80, 100-102; M82, 83; P566, 575).

Classical Meters

The second type of Greek hymn was written in classical meter. One of the earliest of these is "Shepherd of eager youth" by Clement of Alexandria (c. 160-c. 215). Clement was a leading Christian Gnostic scholar and head of

---

[7]At L279 the translation beginning "Oh, gladsome light of the Father immortal" is by the American poet, Henry W. Longfellow.

the catechetical school at Alexandria. The original poem on which this hymn is based was appended to his guidebook in Christian morals and manners, variously called *The Pedagogue*, *The Tutor*, or *The Instructor*. Not a hymn for children as some translations might indicate, it was written for the guidance and inspiration of Christian converts who were nurtured under the rule of the Word of Christ (*Logos*). "Shepherd of eager youth" is a 19th-century paraphrase by the American Congregational minister, Henry M. Dexter, which has fallen from use. F. Bland Tucker (1895-1984) made a more contemporary paraphrase beginning:

> "Jesus, our mighty Lord, our strength in sadness,
> > The Father's conquering Word, true source of gladness" (E478).

Synesius of Cyrene (c. 375-c. 430), a philosopher-statesman and bishop in North Africa, wrote 10 hymns which set forth the great themes of Christian doctrine in terms of Neoplatonic philosophy. The hymn "Lord Jesus, think on me" (E641, L309, P301) is a translation of the final hymn of the group. It is a prayer to Jesus for forgiveness and inner purity (st. 1), for inward peace and rest (st. 2), for a guiding controlling hand (st. 3), and for a future life of peace and joy (st. 4). These are universal needs.

Other early Greek hymns were originally in the form of prayers. Most notable are the eucharistic prayers in the *Didache* (Teaching of the 12 Apostles)—a 2nd-century manual of church order. From these prayers for the church, F. Bland Tucker paraphrased the hymn "Father, we thank thee who has planted" (E302, 303; "Father, we thank you, for you planted," M563, 565).

The original of "Let all mortal flesh keep silence" (B80, E324, L198, M626, P5) is a prayer associated by tradition with the liturgy of St. James (according to tradition the half-brother to our Lord) at the Jerusalem church. It was first intended for use at the Communion, but can also be used as a call to worship, a Christmas hymn, or for general use. Its plainsong-like tune, PICARDY, comes from 17th-century France.

Prose Canons

The third and most important type of Greek hymn came into existence after the decline of the classical meters. Though in prose format, these hymns have rhythmical affinities with Hebrew poetry. Reaching their culmination with the great *canons* of the 8th and 9th centuries, they are still included in the service books of the Orthodox church. It is to this type of source that John

Mason Neale (1818-1866) dedicated his unusual gifts to produce treasured English translations.

Andrew of Crete, also known as Andrew of Jerusalem (660-732), is the earliest writer in this category who still claims attention. He was actually born in Damascus, but embraced the monastic life while under the influence of the Patriarch of Jerusalem (hence his second name). However, after living both at the monastery of Mar Saba in the Judean desert and at Constantinople for a time, he was appointed Bishop of Crete (hence the name by which he is usually known).

Andrew is considered the originator of that characteristic worship form referred to above as the *canon* (*kanon*). The most exalted form of Greek hymnody, the canon is an extended poem; it consists of eight (sometimes nine) odes, each of which is made up of several stanzas. These odes are based on scriptural songs such as the song of Moses (Exodus 15) and the nativity canticles of Luke's Gospel. In the Greek liturgy they are sung at the office of Lauds (early morning).

Andrew's most celebrated work was the "Great Canon," which consisted of some 250 penitential stanzas; it was chanted during the Lenten season prior to Holy Week. These exceedingly long and tiresome works are more metered than rhymed. Thus, they would be somewhat comparable to modern free verse. Neale was the first to make translations of selections from these immense works for use in English worship. Without benefit of guidance as to form (neither from the original Greek nor from the example of any other translators), he made hymns which often bear more the stamp of his own genius than his originals. The only hymn attributed to Andrew, that has, until recently, been found in standard hymnals, is "Christian, dost thou see them." [8] Set by Neale in question-answer format, it challenges the Christian to spiritual combat with evil foes.

John of Damascus (d. c. 780) is generally considered the greatest of all the Greek hymnists. Like Andrew of Crete, he was educated at the cloister of Mar Saba. This desolate monastery hanging on a bare cliff located between Jerusalem and the Dead Sea was an important center for hymn writing in the 8th century. After a political career as chief councillor for the caliph of Damascus—the leading civil ruler of the Muhammadan faith—John and his foster brother, Cosmas (the Younger), gave up their earthly possessions and retired to Mar Saba. There they were under the

---

[8] American Methodists extended its use the longest in *The Methodist Hymnal* (1935), 275 (ST. ANDREW OF CRETE) and *The Methodist Hymnal* (1966), 238 (WALDA).

tutelage of a learned Sicilian monk named Cosmas (the Elder).

John devoted himself to a life of writing, compiling huge works in the areas of science, philosophy, and theology. His main contribution, however, was in the realms of hymnody and music. Indeed, what Gregory the Great (540-604) achieved in the collection and codification of Christian chant in the West, John achieved in the East, thereby giving great impetus to the development of music and hymnody in the Greek church. John's fame as a hymn writer rests mainly on his composition of both words and music for the *canon*—the form originating with Andrew—which he perfected. The subject matter of his six canons was the incarnation conceived as the entire Christ-event: birth, earthly ministry, death, resurrection, and ascension.

The most famous of these canons is the one for Easter, variously known as the "Golden Canon," "King of Canons," and "Queen of Canons." It is generally recognized as the grandest piece of Greek sacred poetry in existence. From the first ode of this canon comes the hymn "The day of resurrection" (B164, E210, L141, M303, P118) in the free translation of Neale. This is a glorious hymn of victory, making allegorical use of the Jewish Passover theme to apply to the triumph of Christ in the resurrection.

Another Easter hymn, also by John in the original, is "Come, ye (you) faithful, raise the strain" (E199, 200; L132, M315, P114, 115). It is translated by Neale from the first ode of the Canon for St. Thomas Sunday (the first Sunday after Easter Sunday). Based on the song of Moses (Ex. 15:1-18), this hymn employs the imagery of Israel's crossing of the Red Sea, applying it to Christ's deliverance from the waters of death to the joys of the resurrected life.

Anatolius (9th century) was a hymnist active in Constantinople—the great center of culture, politics, and learning, as well as another focal point of hymn writing for the Greek church. There in a secluded monastery known as the Studium of St. John, a group of holy men gave themselves to constant prayer and study. Under the inspiring example of their abbot, Theodore of the Studium (c. 759 - c. 825), many of the monks also were devoted to hymn writing. Most likely a pupil of Theodore, Anatolius wrote over a hundred hymns, including the original of "The day is past and over" (M683). This appealing prayer, intended for use upon retiring, has been freely translated by Neale. In its altered form it has found a place in evening worship and in Christian homes as a lullaby for children at bed time.

Traits of Greek Hymnody

The majority of Greek hymns in current use are characterized by objectivity (for example, "Glory be to God on high"). This is true in part because they sprang up at the time the great doctrines concerning the mysteries of the Trinity and incarnation were being hammered out in the creeds. For the most part, they were conceived liturgically (that is, with the intention of glorifying the great scriptural lessons which were part and parcel of the daily and weekly orders of public worship). Consequently, little opportunity is given for personal response to these doctrinal statements and scriptural expositions. The mind of the Greek hymn writer gloried in revealed truth, losing itself in sustained praise and ecstatic contemplation.[9]

In contrast to this prevailing objectivity, there are a few compositions among the shorter hymns (for example, Synesius's "Lord Jesus, think on me") which reflect a tender introspection; in their affecting simplicity, they continue to appeal. The words of a British scholar may aptly describe our hymnic legacy from Greek Christians: "the fountain of Christian hymnody is pure at its source."[10]

LATIN HYMNODY: 4TH AND 5TH CENTURIES

Christian song in the Latin West developed at a time parallel to the later stages of Greek hymnic activity. Hymnody was slower winning its way in the West because non-scriptural hymns were often forbidden—an intended safeguard against heresy. In fact, the introduction of hymn singing in the Western church came by way of theological controversy.

The church was torn by doctrinal factions in the 4th and 5th centuries. Arius (c. 250-336), an influential leader in Alexandria, had led the battle against orthodoxy over the issue of the nature of Jesus Christ. To him, Jesus was a derived creature and therefore not fully divine. Though Arius was banished by his superiors, his teachings continued to be spread by means of appealing hymns, often sung in nightly processions. With the blessing of Emperor Theodosius (378-396), Bishop John Chrysostom of Constantinople organized processions of orthodox hymn singers as a counterforce. Although confusion and even bloodshed sometimes resulted, the Christian custom of singing at evening was thereby greatly strengthened.[11]

---

[9]Neale and the other translators left their unmistakable imprint on the Greek hymns by carefully excising references which ascribe great honor and power to the virgin Mary and concluding with Trinitarian formulas, in keeping with 19th-century Anglo-Catholic worship practices.
[10]Frederick John Gillman, *The Evolution of the English Hymn* (London: George Allen and Unwin, Ltd., 1927), 51.
[11]Erik Routley, *Hymns and Human Life* (New York: Philosophical Library, 1953), 20-21.

Hilary of Poitiers

It was this custom of nightly polemical singing which greatly impressed the energetic Hilary (c. 310-366). He fought so strenuously against the Arian heresy in the West that he came to be called "The Hammer of the Arians." Though none of his rugged hymns survived, he is important historically as the pioneer of hymn singing in the West, thereby exerting a powerful influence on the true popularizer of Western hymnody, Ambrose.

Ambrose of Milan

Ambrose (c. 340-397) led the battle against Arianism in Milan where he had been made bishop by popular demand. When besieged in his basilica by the heretical soldiers of the Arian Emperor Valentinian and his mother Justina, he composed simple, singable hymns for his followers to relieve their weariness during the long night watches. Ambrose's hymns were shorter and more disciplined than those of Hilary. Moreover, adopting the meter of the marching rhythm of soldiers, he standardized the form known in modern English hymnody as "Long Meter"—four lines of iambic tetrameter.[12]

Of the near 100 hymns attributed to Ambrose, only four can be proved as his. But his pioneering work was so significant for metrical hymnody in the West that the term "Ambrosian" is applied to all hymns produced at this

time in the meter that he established, even though they may have been composed by some of his numerous imitators and disciples. Many of these hymns (especially those that came into being after the Arian struggle had calmed down and the church was again more serene) represent the earliest "office hymns" for use in the prescribed hours of prayer in the monasteries. These hymns are austere in their simplicity and largely objective in content.

Three of Ambrose's hymns in English translation which continue to be used are:

© 1980 Charles Massey, Jr.

Ambrose of Milan

---

[12]Information about Ambrose's hymns comes mainly through the references of his disciple and devoted friend, Augustine of Hippo. For an explanation of meter, see Chapter 1, "The Hymn in Literature," pages 17-18.

"O Splendor of God's glory bright" (E5, M679, P474) or
"O Splendor of the Father's light" (L271)

"O Trinity, O blessed Light" (L275) or
"O Trinity of blessed light" (E30)

"Savior of the nations, come" (E54, L28, M214, P14)

The first and second titles are translations of Ambrose's morning hymn, *Splendor paternae gloriae*. Addressed especially to Christ as the Light of the world, it asks for divine guidance throughout the day. The third and fourth titles are translations of *O lux beata, Trinitas*, an evening hymn in praise of the triune God. In both these hymns the imagery of light is prominent. Light is a symbol found in Scripture and in earlier hymnody before Ambrose (for example, the famous "Lamplighting Hymn" previously mentioned). The final hymn, translated from *Veni, redemptor gentium*, is popularly used at Advent and comes to us principally through the German of Martin Luther in various composite English translations. Intended for congregational singing in the monastic communities, these songs set the standard for a great body of systematic hymnody that was to develop throughout the Middle Ages.

Niceta of Remesiana

Contemporary with Ambrose was Niceta (c. 335 - c. 414), missionary bishop of Remesiana in Dacia (Serbia), who also utilized hymns to wage battle for the Orthodox faith. He is the probable author of at least part of the *Te Deum laudamus*—the most famous extrabiblical hymn of the Western church. This extended composition has enjoyed wide use for 15 centuries, not so much for its intrinsic poetic qualities as for its clear testimony to the Christian faith.

In the English version included in the 1549 and 1552 *Book of Common Prayer*, it falls into three parts. The first two parts found in earlier Greek versions were (1) a paean of praise to God the Father and incorporated the "trice holy" of Isaiah (6:3) and (2) a confession of faith in Christ concluding with prayer that the redeemed may share in God's everlasting glory. The third part was a later addition consisting of petitions culled from the Psalms.

In this composite hymn, the essentials of the Christian faith are set forth in expressions of majesty and beauty, broadly outlining New Testament doctrine. Though given varying kinds of musical settings for congregational singing, the *Te Deum* presently remains principally in choral settings used throughout the Christian world for days of special thanksgiving and commemoration.[13]

Aurelius Clemens Prudentius

Prudentius (348-413) was a Spaniard who gave up a career in law to devote his life to Christian study and writing. Historians honor him as the first poet of the West to bring scholarly study and religion together, enlivening classic prosody with the vigor of a living faith. Excerpts from the original poems of Prudentius were used throughout the Middle Ages. The most popular one to survive is "Of the Father's love begotten," J. M. Neale's translation of *Corde natus ex Parentis* (B251, E82, L42, M184, P309).

Written in the early 5th century, this hymn is another intended to promote orthodox doctrine concerning the nature of Christ in opposition to Arian teachings. Based on Revelation 1:8, it affirms Christ to be "Alpha"—the source of all things—and "Omega"—the end of all things—and therefore coeternal with God the Father. Although the hymn is particularly appropriate for worship at Christmas, its praise of the Trinity makes it suitable also for general use. The plainsong tune, DIVINUM MYSTERIUM, can be sung antiphonally between two bodies of singers who then come together on the refrain in the last line of each stanza: "Evermore and evermore."

Another excellent Prudentius hymn used at Epiphany is *O sola magnarum urbium* found in translation variously as "Earth has many a noble city" (E127) and "O chief of cities, Bethlehem" (L81).

St. Patrick

Patrick (c. 372-466), apostle and patron saint of Ireland, is remembered for his authorship of the famous *Lorica* or "Breastplate Hymn." It came into being originally as an incantation, but survives today as a lengthy credal hymn in the translation of Mrs. Cecil F. Alexander's "I bind unto myself today" (E370, L188). While somewhat rough in its grammar and loose in its poetic construction, it possesses the devotional fire of a courageous heart.

The characteristics of these early 4th and 5th-century hymns may be summarized: some of the originals may have had little or no rhyme and accent,

---

[13]Many world-famous composers, including Palestrina, Cherubini, Graun, Purcell, Handel, Tallis, Berlioz, Verdi, Vaughan Williams, and Walton have created music for the *Te Deum*. Other church composers have treated it in choral "Service" settings for Morning Prayer in the Episcopal and Lutheran churches. In some hymnals it is set out either to be sung by the congregation in free paraphrase to a hymn tune (E366), to some contemporary form of plainsong (L, pp. 139-141), or to be read in unison with a response sung after each of the three parts. (M80)

most of them utilized the "Ambrosian" metrical form of iambic tetrameter, and in content they were primarily creedal, forwarding the orthodox doctrines in the struggle against heresies.

THE DARK AGES

The five centuries following the collapse of the Roman empire (A.D. 476) are often referred to as "the Dark Ages." During these centuries, however, intellectual and cultural work of the highest order was accomplished, especially by the scholars and missionaries of the Benedictine order. This period forms a prelude, as it were, to medieval history and can be considered dark only by comparison to what followed. In this era (A.D. 500-1000), the foundations of medieval civilization were laid in every area of human endeavor. It is not surprising then, that several important hymnists pursued their creative work during this relatively obscure time.

Gregory the Great

Pope Gregory I (590-604)—called Great because of his accomplishments in the realms of administering, missions, theological writing, and preaching—is remembered primarily for his contributions in the fields of liturgy and music, which he collected and codified for the Western church. The few hymns attributed to Gregory may not be actually his. The most popular of those connected with his name, *Nocte surgentes vigilemus omnes*, translated by Percy Dearmer as "Father, we praise you (thee)" (E1, 2; L267, M680, P459), has been determined by recent scholarship to have been written in the 10th century. A simple morning hymn of objective praise, it is set in the unusual Sapphic meter,[14] in contrast to the more popular Ambrosian meter. The tune traditionally assigned to it, CHRISTE SANCTORUM, is a French "church melody" from the 17th century.

Venantius Honorius Clementainus Fortunatus

Fortunatus (c. 530-609)—considered the last link between the classical and the medieval world—was born and educated in northern Italy. After traveling extensively in troubadour fashion as poet and secretary to the Frankish King Sigbert, he left court and settled at Poitiers, where, toward the end of his life, he became bishop. It was at Poitiers, for the reception into the

[14]Sapphic meter refers to the verse form used by the Greek lyric poetess, Sappho (600 B.C.), a stanza of which falls in the rare pattern for hymnody: 11.11.11.5. Later, in the time of the Thirty Years War, however, Sapphic meter was used in German chorales, as described in Chapter 6, "Reformation Traditions," page 102.

convent of St. Croix of a relic of the true cross, that Fortunatus wrote his greatest hymn, *Vexilla regis proderunt*. Translated by Neale as "The royal banners forward go" (E161,[15] 162; L124, 125), it is sung at Evensong on Passion Sunday and daily until Wednesday in Holy Week. VEXILLA REGIS is the traditional plainsong melody for the text.

For use at Easter is his well-known *Salve, festa dies*, in John Ellerton's paraphrase, "Welcome, happy morning!" (E179, L153). Becoming more popular recently is the translation "Hail thee, festival day!" (L142, M324, P120). Particularly when sung to the Vaughan Williams tune, SALVE FESTA DIES, this hymn gives exuberant expression to the Christian joy resulting from the Easter proclamation of Christ's triumph in the resurrection.[16]

One of the most venerable hymns from this period is *Urbs beata Jerusalem*, the second part of which (beginning *Angularis fundamentum*) is translated "Christ is made the sure foundation" (B356, E518, L367, M559). This 7th-century anonymous lyric, based on 1 Peter 2:5, Ephesians 2:20, and Revelation 21:2, is widely used for the dedication of church buildings.

Theodulph of Orleans

Theodulph (c. 760-821) was born a barbarian but became a great Christian pastor and poet. So great was his poetic genius that he was called to the court of Carolus Magnus (Charlemagne), king of the Franks, to establish schools for the instruction of monks and other churchmen. He is remembered for his one hymn *Gloria, laus et honor*, familiar today in Neale's translation, "All glory, laud, and honor" (B126, E154, 155; L108, M280, P88) that was composed about 820 while Theodulph was imprisoned in Angers by order of King Louis I. Based on the Gospel account of the triumphal entry into Jerusalem (Mark 11:1-10 and John 12:12-19), it is one of the best Palm Sunday processional hymns, picturing the only occasion when public homage was paid to Jesus.[17]

---

[15]E161 is a different translation, "The flaming banners of our King," made by the Canadian theologian, John Webster Grant (1919-1994).

[16]Another Fortunatus hymn extensively used at passiontide is his *Pange lingua gloriosi proelium certaminus* in Neale's translation "Sing, my tongue, the glorious battle" (E165, 166; L118, M296). This is considered by many his finest. M296 has a translation by Percy Dearmer.

[17]Among several hymn interpretations to various of these hymns available is a clever dramatization of "All glory, laud, and honor" for children's choir with accompaniment of handbells, flutes, Orff bar instruments, and percussion by Hal H. Hopson, entitled *The Singing Bishop* (Dallas: The Chorister's Guild, 1978).

Rabanus Maurus

Although the authorship of *Veni, Creator Spiritus* has been variously attributed to Charlemagne, Ambrose, and Gregory the Great, it may be the work of Rabanus Maurus (776-856), Bishop of Fulda and Archbishop of Mainz. This fervent prayer for the coming of the Holy Spirit exists in several English translations, evidencing its prominent use in connection with ordinations of clergy, consecrations of bishops, the laying of foundation stones, and the consecration of churches. It was the only metrical hymn admitted to the English *Book of Common Prayer* (1549) at the time of the English Reformation. "Creator Spirit, by whose aid" (E500, L164) is the paraphrase by John Dryden (1631-1700), the chief literary figure of the Restoration Era. "Come, Holy Ghost, our souls inspire" (E503, 504; L472, 473; M651, P125) is the earlier, more literal translation of John Cosin (1594-1672), Bishop of Durham. A more contemporary translation is "O Holy Spirit, by whose breath" (E502) by John Webster Grant. Consecrated by the worship of centuries, this hymn continues to find use at occasions where the gifts of the Holy Spirit are celebrated.

Not until the 19th century was any of this hymnody of the early Christian centuries translated into English. This finally happened as a result of the work of the Oxford Movement—a powerful force within 19th-century Anglicanism to revitalize the church by reasserting its ancient spirit and reclaiming its original power. This movement prompted a reexamination of the church's oldest documents and a reemphasis on its worship ritual and literature.

THE MIDDLE AGES

"The Middle Ages" is a convenient designation for the period extending from the waning of the Dark Ages to those times when the spirit of the Renaissance became dominant in political, social, and artistic life. For the student of Christian hymnody, it has special interest as the age which approached most nearly the realization of Western Christendom as a cultural unity. This was made possible by the absolute supremacy of the papacy in all temporal matters and by the missionary and conserving zeal of the special orders of monks—the Benedictine, Cluniac, and Cistercian, and the new mendicant orders—the Franciscan and Dominican. Most of the hymnists of this period came from the ranks of these orders.

Little hymnody has survived from the 11th century. But with the perfection of new forms of Latin verse using rhyme and accent, and the development of a contemplative life style in the cloisters, some of the finest songs relating to all that was true and holy in people's lives were produced in the

12th century. These songs were written in veneration of the virgin Mary, the apostles, and the saints, and were often refined into mystical meditations on the joys of heaven, the vanity of life, and the suffering of Christ.

Abelard

Peter Abelard (1079-1142), brilliant theologian, philosopher, and teacher, wrote an entire hymnal (*Hymnarius Paraclitensis*) for the use of the convent of the Paraclete (near Nogent-sur-Seine in France) which was under the charge of his beloved Heloise. From this Latin hymnal Neale has given us the English "O what their joy and their glory" from the original, (E623, L337, M727) *O quanta qualia*, a hymn celebrating the joy and peace of heaven. It is traditionally sung to O QUANTA QUALIA, a French "church melody" from the Paris Antiphoner of 1681.

The American Episcopal clergyman F. Bland Tucker translated a useful lyric for Good Friday from this Abelard hymn cycle: "Alone thou goest forth, O Lord" (E164).

Benard of Clairvaux

Many hymns have been ascribed to the greatest of the medieval men of the church, Bernard of Clairvaux (1091-1153). Bernard may not be the author of *Jesu, dulcis memoria*,[18] but the hymn profoundly bears the stamp of his mind, and may be taken as representative of his spirit.

Bernard was the most influential monk of his day, brilliantly debating with philosophers and theologians, passionately preaching to great throngs of people, and skillfully arbitrating among statesmen and popes. He was the founder and abbot of the model monastery at Clairvaux (near Troyes in northeastern France) and the preacher of the Second Crusade. *Jesu dulcis memoria* was inspired by passages from the Song of Solomon and repeats the name of Jesus in a manner that must have been enchanting to singers and hearers alike. It has supplied English and American hymnbooks several translations of sterling worth, including these two most familiar.

- "O Jesus, joy of loving hearts" (E649, 650; L356)
- "Jesus, the very thought of thee (you)" (B225, E642, L316, M175, P310)

---

[18]Twentieth-century scholarship makes it difficult to resist the conclusion that the hymn is the work of an Englishman at the end of the 12th century. See E. J. E. Raby, "The poem DULCIS IESU MEMORIA" in *Bulletin of the Hymn Society of Great Britain and Ireland* 33 (October 1945): 1-6.

The first is the altered translation of the American Congregationalist poet and preacher, Ray Palmer (1808-1887), who is best known for his "My faith looks up to Thee" (B416, E691, M452, P383). The second translation is the work of the British Roman Catholic scholar, Edward Caswall (1814-1878), to whom we are also indebted for other fine translations from both Latin and German sources.[19]

Bernard of Cluny

The other great Bernard (12th century, of the Cluny monastery) is known as the poet of *De contemptu mundi* ("Of Scorning the World")—a bitter satire that laments the moral corruption of his time. In contrast to the evil and darkness of that age, the hymn depicts the golden glories of the celestial city. From Bernard's poem of 3,000 lines, Neale translated 218, which have been arranged at various times into several different hymns. Of these, only "Jerusalem, the golden" (B527, E624, L347) has survived. Its durability could be due as much to its tune, EWING (named for the 19th-century Englishman who composed it), as to its lofty recital of the joys of heaven.

Sequence Hymns

A most significant hymnic development of the Middle Ages was the invention of *tropes* and *sequences*. *Tropes* were both musical and textual accretions to the prescribed liturgy. Their purpose was to amplify, augment, or elucidate the Mass. The particular type of trope associated with the Alleluia chant of the Mass became known as a *sequence*, and lengthy melismas were developed on the final syllable of the Alleluia. Then, as an aid to the musical memory of those singing them, special hymn-like texts were set to these extended vocalized passages. Yet another development came in the proliferation of thousands of these texts as independent entities to be sung for the various seasons and festivals of the Christian year.

During the Counter-Reformation, the Council of Trent (1545-1563) reduced the number of sequences to four: (1) the *Victimae paschali* for Easter;[20] (2) the *Veni, Sancte Spiritus* ("the Golden Sequence") for Pentecost (from which we have "Come, thou Holy Spirit bright"—E226, and "Come, Holy Ghost, God and Lord"—L163); (3) the *Lauda Sion* by Thomas Aquinas for the Feast of Corpus Christi (on which "Zion, praise thy Savior"—E320—is based); and (4) the *Dies irae* by Thomas of Celano (13th century) for the Requiem Mass.

[19]See, for example, "When morning gilds the skies" (B221, E427, M185, P487) and "Glory be to Jesus" (E479, L95).
[20]See Chapter 6, "Reformation Traditions," page 99.

5. Early Church and Pre-Reformation Traditions

In 1727 a fifth sequence was added—the *Stabat mater dolorosa*—attributed to Jacopone da Todi (1230-1306), for use on Good Friday. From this the hymn "At the cross, her station (vigil) keeping" (E159, L110) was translated. This hymn survives from a great body of medieval literature gathered about the cult of the virgin Mary.[21] Its roots are probably traceable to the 14th-century *laudi spirituali* (praise songs) which glorify the sufferings of Mary and Christ, and were sung by wandering bands of "flagellants." These heretical groups traveled about in macabre processions scourging themselves for the sins of the world and pathologically brooding on sorrow.

Francis of Assisi

St. Francis of Assisi (1182-1226), the most remarkable personality of the early 13th century (who founded the mendicant order bearing his name), is intimately connected with the origins of the *laudi* which resulted from the combination of Provencal (southern French) song style with the Italian vernacular. Known as "God's Troubadour," Francis attracted numerous followers, including two of the above-mentioned authors: Jacopone da Todi and Thomas of Celano, the saint's biographer.

Francis's famous "Canticle to the Sun," *Altissimu, onnipotente, bon Signore*, is said to be the first genuine religious lyric in the Italian language. It reflects the saint's child-like identification with all creation in the joyous praise of the Eternal. One translation is by the British clergyman, William H. Draper (1855-1933), "All creatures of our God and King" (B27, E400, L527, M62, P455). A second translation is by Howard Chandler Robbins, American pastor and teacher (1876-1952), "Most high, omnipotent, good Lord" (E406, 407). The exciting traditional tune, LASST UNS ERFREUEN can be sung antiphonally with good effect.

© 1980 Charles Massey, Jr.

Francis of Assisi

[21]Numerous composers, including the following, have set the *Stabat Mater* polyphonically: Josquin, Palestrina, Lassus, A. Scarlatti, D. Scarlatti, Pergolesi, Schubert, Dvořák, Gounod, Liszt, Verdi, Poulenc, Penderecki, Kodaly, Persichetti, and Virgil Thomson.

Thomas Aquinas

The most learned representative of the Domincan order in the 13th century was Thomas Aquinas (c. 1227-1274), the master schoolman who consumated the medieval scholastic method (founded by Abelard) in his monumental *Summa Theologica*. In addition to the sequence hymn *Lauda sion*, Thomas was the author of several other hymns which were primarily expositions of the mysteries of the Eucharist. Of these communion hymns, the best known is *Adoro te devote*, translated by J. R. Woodford (1820-1885) as "Thee we adore, O hidden Savior" (L199). It is also found in a composite translation as "Humbly I adore thee" (E314).

Carols

In the 13th, 14th, and 15th centuries, the humanizing influence of Francis of Assisi helped produce a great flowering of religious folk song, generally known as *carols*. Representative of this free, folksy kind of devotional expression are three carols found in most hymnals from German and French sources.

Surrexit Christus hodie, in the anonymous translation "Jesus Christ is risen today" (E207, L151), is an Easter carol which appeared originally in German and Bohemian manuscripts of the 14th century.

In dulci jubilo, in Neale's translation "Good Christian men (friends), rejoice" (B96, E107, L55, M224, P28), is a macaronic carol (mixture of two languages) from 14th-century Germany. Songs like these, which combined the Latin of the church with the vernacular of the people, were common in Germany and elsewhere towards the close of the Middle Ages. The happy and joyous vein of the text is suitably matched with its swinging melody IN DULCI JUBILO, making it one of the most popular Christmas songs.

O filii et filiae is probably the work of a French Franciscan, Jean Tisserand (d. 1494). As translated by Neale, it is a lovely narrative Easter carol, "O sons and daughters, let us sing" (E203, L139, M317, P116, 117). The tune O FILII ET FILIAE is a lilting folk melody of the same period. The gradual unfolding of the Easter story stanza by stanza, together with its repetitive Alleluia, makes it particularly useful for teaching to children. It demonstrates the close connection that may have once existed between the trope and the carol. *O filii et filiae* was originally a trope on the *Benedicamus Domino* chant, which usually closes the singing of the offices.

Later Contributions (14th to 18th Centuries)

Latin hymnic production declined from the late 14th century onward, paralleling the decline in the dominant influence of the church. However, the following hymns are representative of several excellent ones which have survived this era of decadence.

"O come, O come, Emmanuel" (B76, E56, L34, M211, P9), an anonymous hymn first appearing in print in 1710 but doubtless existing in oral tradition from earlier times, is useful in Advent in preparation for the celebration of Christmas. We have it in various composite translations, including the work of John Mason Neale, Henry Sloan Coffin, and Lawrence Hull Stookey. "The strife is o'er" (B172, E208, L135, M306, P119), an anonymous 17th-century hymn translated by Francis Pott (1832-1909), is a staple for worship at Eastertide. "Jerusalem, my happy home" (B517, E620, L331) is an anonymous 16th-century English hymn on heaven. It is based upon translations from a 15th-century source[22] and is appealingly set to the American folk tune, LAND OF REST.

"I love thee, Lord, but not because" (E682) and "My (O) God, I love thee" (L491, M470) are alterations of Edward Caswall's translation of a 17th-century Latin poem based on a Spanish sonnet which examines one's motives for loving God. They are often attributed to Francis Xavier (1506-1552), the Jesuit missionary and preacher. "On Jordan's bank(s) the Baptist's cry" (E76, L36, P10) is a translation by John Chandler (1806-1876) of an Advent hymn by the distinguished French ecclesiastic and educator, Charles Coffin (1676-1749), who wrote over a hundred such hymns for *The Paris Breviary* (1736). "O come, all ye faithful" (B89, E83, L45, M234, P41, 42) is a translation by Frederick Oakeley (1802-1880) of *Adeste fidelis laeti triumphantes*, written by the English layman, John Francis Wade (c. 1710-1786), who also composed its tune. Wade's popular hymn exists in over a hundred English translations. The tune ADESTE FIDELES exhibits the fuging characteristics of many tunes of its time in both England and America.

The Latin Legacy

Hymns from the Latin are widely varied in their characteristics because they were produced over such a lengthy period of church history. Because many were born in theological controversy, they are creedal in content, and give militant expression to what was considered the orthodox faith of the time. Because many were generated within the monastic life, they are otherworldly and reflective in nature, giving expression to personal devotion, particularly to

[22]Attributions of authorship have been made for this hymn to Joseph Bromehead (1747-1826) and F. B. P. (16th century), but evidence for neither is conclusive.

the crucified Jesus. Because many were written for use in the canonical hours, they are seasonal in their liturgical intent. Because several are the products of the common folk, they are carol-like in nature, giving vent to simple religious joys. Because most were the result of an irrepressible universal urge to glorify God, they possess a dominant element of praise and thanksgiving.

Our rich Latin hymnic legacy is unfortunately neglected and forgotten. To reclaim the best of it for contemporary use is the responsibility and privilege of today's worshiping communities.

6
REFORMATION TRADITIONS

THE CHORALE-REFORMATION TO 1618

The Protestant Reformation brought about a renewal of congregational song in much of Europe. Hymns known as chorales developed in Germany and Scandinavia. In other areas metrical psalmody developed, and psalters were published in French, Dutch, and English.

© 1980 Charles Massey, Jr.
Martin Luther

The German and Scandinavian chorales received their impetus from the thought and work of the German reformer Martin Luther (1483-1546). Luther was not only a theologian but also a musician, and he believed music to be of utmost importance in worship.[1] As a part of Luther's emphasis on the priesthood of all believers, he advocated full involvement of the people and restored congregational singing to a prominent place as part of their liturgy. For example, the Gradual in Luther's *Deutsche Messe* (German Mass) became a Gradual hymn, a "Hymn of the day" functioning as a "musical and poetic commentary of all of the [Scripture] lessons and chiefly on the meaning or theme to be communicated by the service."[2] In 1524, seven years after Luther's 95 Theses were first posted, the first Lutheran hymn collection

[1]For a concise treatment of Luther's views on music, see Carl F. Schalk, *Luther on Music: Paradigms of Praise* (St. Louis: Concordia Publishing House, 1988).
[2]Philip H. Pfatteicher and Carlos Messerli, *Manual on the Liturgy: Lutheran Book of Worship* (Minneapolis: Augsburg Publishing House, 1979), 80. Quoted in Carl Schalk, *The Hymn of the Day and its Use in Lutheran Worship* (St. Louis: Concordia Publishing House, 1983), 5-6.

appeared—the *Achtliederbuch* (*Book of Eight Songs*, eight hymns and four melodies)—which included four hymn texts by Luther.[3]

Of the 37 hymns attributed to Luther, five appear in many current hymnals:

- *Ein' feste Burg ist unser Gott* ("A mighty fortress is our God," B8, E687, 688; L228, 229; M110, P259, 260)—based on Psalm 46
- *Aus tiefer Not schrei ich zu dir* ("Out of the depths I cry to thee," E666, L295, M515, P240)—based on Psalm 130
- *Von Himmel hoch da komm ich her* ("From heaven above to earth I come," E80, L51, P54)—a Christmas hymn for children based on a secular song, *Aus fremden Landen komm ich her* ("Good news from far abroad I bring")
- *Christ lag in Todesbanden* ("Christ Jesus lay in death's strong bands," E185, 186; L134; M319; P110)—an Easter hymn based on earlier hymns, including the Latin Easter sequence, *Victimae paschali laudes* (E183)
- *Nun komm der heiden Heiland* ("Savior of the nations, come," E54, L28, M214, P14)—an Advent hymn modeled on Ambrose's *Veni redemptor genitum* (E54, L28, M214).

Although Luther led the revolt against the abuses of the Roman Catholic church, he continued to make use of its texts and tunes: "He modified Roman Catholic tunes and texts to fit his new theology. As a result, people recognized familiar hymns and chants and felt at home in the new church. He used music which was already familiar to the majority of the people in Germany."[4]

Luther may well have composed the melodies to "A mighty fortress" and to some of his other texts, but this is uncertain. Most surely he used melodies that reflected the German Meistersinger tradition, including EIN' FESTE BURG.[5] Several recent American hymnals (E687, 688; L228, 229; P259, 260) give both the original rhythmic and the altered isometric versions of EIN' FESTE BURG. (See also page 41.) Luther's "A mighty fortress" (B8, E687, 688; L228,

---

[3]The actual title is *Etlich Cristlich Lider* (Some Christian Songs). A facsimile edition was published as an insert in the 1956 *Jahrbuch für Liturgik und Hymnologie* (Yearbook for Liturgy and Hymnology), which contains an introduction by Konrad Ameln.

[4]Johannes Riedel, *The Lutheran Chorale, Its Basic Traditions* (Minneapolis: Augsburg Publishing House, 1967), 38. For further information on the varied sources upon which Luther drew for the chorale, see Carl F. Schalk, "German Hymnody," *Hymnal Companion to the Lutheran Book of Worship*, ed. Marilyn Kay Stulken (Philadelphia: Fortress Press, 1981), 19-22.

[5]This melody has been compared to Hans Sachs' famous "Silberweise" (Silver Tone). See ibid., 39, and *Troubadours, Trouveres, Minne- and Meistersinger* ed. F. Gennrich, v. 2 of *Anthology of Music*, ed. K.G. Fellerer (Cologne, Germany: Arno Volk Verlag, 1960), 64-65.

229; M20, P259, 260), which became the "Battle hymn of the Reformation," mirrors his strong personality. This chorale depicts Luther's struggle with Satan (st. 1), including his belief in the presence and power of devils (st. 3), and the triumph of Christ and God's kingdom over the forces of evil (st. 4).

The last hymnal in which Luther was involved was the *Geystliche Lieder* (Leipzig, 1545, known as the Babst hymnal after its printer). It contained a preface by Luther followed by 129 hymns, and is considered the most representative German hymnal of its period.[6]

Other 16th-century chorales in current use include Nikolaus Herman's (c. 1480-1561) Christmas text and tune LOBT GOTT IHR CHRISTEN ("Let all together praise our God," L47), and an early chorale text by Johann Lindemann (1549-1631), *In dir ist Freude* ("In thee is gladness," L552, M169), published at Erfurt in 1598 to be sung to a triple meter balletto melody of the Italian Giovanni G. Gastoldi (1556-1622). It is known by its German tune name, IN DIR IST FREUDE. One year later, 1599, the "King and Queen of Chorales" appeared. These were Lutheran pastor Philipp Nicolai's (1556-1608) texts and tunes: *Wachet auf, ruf uns die Stimme* ("Wake, awake, for night is flying," L31, M720; " 'Sleepers, wake!' A voice astounds us," E61, 62; P17) and *Wie schön leuchtet der Mogenstern* ("O Morning Star, how fair and bright," L76, M247, P69; "How bright appears the Morning Star," E496, 497). These two bar-form (AAB) chorale melodies reflect the Meistersinger tradition, and the texts of both are rich in biblical imagery.

In the first two decades of the 17th century, three chorale melodies were composed which still maintain a place in most hymnals. Hans Leo Hassler's PASSION CHORALE (1601), originally set to a love song, became the setting of Paul Gerhardt's O *Haupt voll Blut und wunden*, based on a Medieval Latin poem—"O sacred Head, now (sore) wounded," B137; E168, 169; L116, 117; M286). Melchior Vulpius' tune GELOBT SEI GOTT (1609) is associated in English with the 20th-century Easter hymn, "Good Christians all (Christian friends), rejoice and sing" (E205, L144, P111; see also P530). A third familiar chorale melody from this era is Melchior Teschner's ST. THEODULPH (1615) named after Theodulph of Orleans. Theodulph of Orleans was author of the Latin Palm Sunday hymn *Gloria, laus et honor* ("All glory, laud and honor," B126; E154, 155; M280; P88; VALET WILL ICH DIR GEBEN, L108), a text still associated with this tune.

The Lutheran movement spread especially to Denmark, Norway, Sweden, and Finland where it became the state church. The early Scandinavian

---

[6]A facsimile of this hymnal has been published with an introduction by Konrad Ameln (Kassel: Bärenreiter-Verlag, 1966).

Lutheran contributions found in most current hymnals stem from *Piae Cantiones (Sacred Songs)*,[7] a compilation of Theodoric Petri of Nyland (the largely Swedish-speaking province of southern Finland now referred to as Uusimaa), published in 1582. From this collection of old Scandinavian hymns and carols four melodies are now in use: DIVINUM MYSTERIUM ("Of the Father's love begotten," B251, E82, L42, M184, P309) is an adaptation of an 11th-century Sanctus trope. Of the five hymnals cited in this volume, only *The Hymnal 1982* (E82) has DIVINUM MYSTERIUM in the triple meter to be found in *Piae Cantiones*. The other hymnals print this tune in equal note values. PERSONET HODIE (E92, M248, P46) is associated with an English translation of the Christmas carol from *Piae Cantiones*, "On this day earth shall ring." PUER NOBIS NASCITUR, originally in a Trier manuscript (15th century), appeared in a $\frac{4}{4}$ meter in *Piae Cantiones* with the Latin trope known in English as "Unto us a boy is born." (E98).[8] The fourth melody, TEMPUS ADEST FLORIDUM, widely associated with John Mason Neale's "Good King Wenceslaus," is also the setting for a 20th-century Christmas hymn, "Gentle Mary laid her child," (B101, P27).

17TH CENTURY:
THE THIRTY YEARS' WAR AND A RENEWAL OF THE HYMN

An estimated 20,000 hymns had been written in Germany by the end of the 16th century; by 1618 (the beginning of the Thirty Years' War) this total had only increased to perhaps 25,000. The tragic political-religious conflict known as the Thirty Years' War (1618-48) exerted a profound positive influence on German hymnody. As described by Moore, "It was in this period of desolation and darkness of the night that there came about a real revival in the writing of hymns." [9]

Among the writers to participate in this renewal was the Lutheran pastor Johann Heermann (1585-1647), author of the hymn *Herzliebster Jesu, was hast du verbrochen* (1630). This hymn has been translated and supplemented by Robert Bridges as "Ah, holy Jesus, how hast thou offended" (E158, L123, M289, P93). The tune HERZLIEBSTER JESU is Johann Crüger's reworking

---

[7]*Piae Cantiones* is described in Erik Routley's *The Music of Christian Hymns* (Chicago: C.I.A., 1981), 18B-19B. A facsimile edition of *Piae Cantiones* with an introduction by Timo Mäkinen was published in 1967 in the series *Documenta Musicae Fennicae* by Edition Frzer, Helsinki, Finland. See page 158, footnote 52.
[8]A triple meter version of this tune as altered by Michael Praetorius, known under the shorter name, PUER NOBIS, appears in several American hymnals ("What star is this, with beams so bright," E124, P68; "That Easter day with joy was bright," E193, P121; "On Jordan's banks the Baptist's cry," L36).
[9]Sydney H. Moore, *Sursum Corda, Being Studies of Some German Hymn Writers* (London: Independent Press, Ltd., 1956), 21. For a detailed discussion of this conflict, see "Thirty-Years' War" in *Encyclopedia Britannica*, 15th ed., Vol. 18, 333-44.

of the Genevan Psalter setting of Psalm 23.

The best known hymn to appear during the Thirty Years' War is *Nun danket alle Gott* ("Now thank we all our God," B638; E396, 397; L533, 534; M102; P555), written around 1636 by the Lutheran pastor Martin Rinkart and later set to music by Johann Crüger. This hymn of thanksgiving, originally intended as a table blessing, is based on the Apocryphal book of Ecclesiasticus 50:22-24 and includes only a brief allusion at the close of stanza 2 to the suffering experienced during this disastrous political conflict:

> "And keep us in His grace,
>   And guide us when perplexed,
> And free us from all ills
>   In this world and the next."

These lines are followed by the triumphant praise of Rinkart's closing stanza, his paraphrase of the *Gloria Patri* (B252, M70, 71; P577, 578, 579). "Now thank we all our God," known as the *Te Deum* of Germany, has become not only the German national hymn of praise and thanksgiving, but also a popular expression of gratitude among English-speaking peoples.

The tragic Thirty Years' War is more fully reflected in a hymn by the German nobleman, Matthäus von Löwenstern (1594-1648)—*Christ, du Beistand deiner Kreutzgemeine*, 1644. This hymn was translated and paraphrased by Philip Pusey as "Lord of our life and God of our salvation" (L366). While Bailey states that Pusey's version of 1834 reflects the situation in England at the time of the Oxford Movement,[10] nevertheless, it retains the atmosphere of the original (as well as its use of the classical Sapphic meter—11.11.11.5). Germans sing this hymn to a 17th-century tune; in English, "Lord of our life" is commonly sung to ISTE CONFESSOR (ROUEN), a French Roman Catholic tune published in 1746. It is ironic that one of the finest Protestant hymns of this bloody war is sung to a Roman Catholic tune!

The Sapphic meter of Löwenstern's hymn is one sign of the early 17th-century literary flowering and refining of German language and poetry. The effect of the Thirty Years' War was to make hymnody more personal and subjective. Hymns from this time written for family devotions typically emphasize trust in God and a yearning for eternal life, and those dealing with Christ's passion gained a prominent place.[11]

---

[10]Albert Edward Bailey, *The Gospel in Hymns* (New York: Charles Scribner's Sons, 1950), 324.
[11]For a detailed treatment in English of the development of the German chorale, see Carl Schalk, "German Hymnody" in *Hymnal Companion to the Lutheran Book of Worship* by Marilyn Kay Stulken (Philadelphia: Fortress Press, 1981), 19-33.

The introspective qualities of the 17th-century German hymn are most fully exemplified in the work of the Lutheran minister Paul Gerhardt (1607-76), regarded, next to Luther, as the greatest German hymnist. Gerhardt is the most beloved and the most frequently represented writer in German hymnals today.[12] Four of his hymns are often included in American hymnals:

- *Frölich soll mein Herze springen* ("All my heart this night (today) rejoices," P21; "Once again my heart rejoices," L46)—a Christmas hymn originally containing 15 stanzas;
- *O Haupt voll Blut und wunden* ("O sacred Head, now (sore) wounded" B137; E168 169; L116; M286; P98)—Gerhardt's translation of part of a medieval poem on the suffering of Christ on the cross;
- *Befiehl du deine Wege* ("Give to the winds thy (your) fears," M129, P286)—a personal hymn of trust in God; and
- *O Jesu Christ, mein schönstes Licht* ("Jesus, thy boundless love to me," B123, L336, M183, P366)—a personal hymn giving the believer's response to the love of Jesus.

The subjective character of Gerhardt's hymns is illustrated in "Jesus, thy boundless love to me" (1653) (translated in Georgia by John Wesley and published in 1739), in which the personal pronouns "I," "me" and "my" abound.

Hymn tunes of the 17th century, in contrast to the earlier Meistersinger practice, were generally no longer composed by the author of the hymn text, but rather by specialist musicians. Congregational singing was further popularized in this time by the adoption of the *Kantional* style, in which the melody appeared in the highest voice and the lower parts were harmonized in

Paul Gerhardt

note-against-note treatment.[13] In addition, the Italian *basso continuo* style exerted harmonic influence upon the chorale melodies in that they were most

---

[12]Forty of Gerhardt's hymns are found in the German Lutheran hymnal, *Evangelischen Kirchensangbuch*, edition for the Lutheran Church in Bavaria (Munich: Evang. Presserverband für Bayern e. V., 1957). Further references to this hymnal indicate this Bavarian edition.
[13]Riedel, *The Lutheran Chorale*, 56-57.

often fitted for accompaniment by a keyboard instrument such as the organ.[14]

Gerhardt's friend and colleague at St. Nicholas Church in Berlin, organist-composer Johann Crüger (1598-1662), was his musical counterpart in the development of the chorale. Crüger's chorale tune collection of 1644, *Praxis pietatis melica (Practice of Piety in Song)*, was, in its numerous editions, the most important Lutheran hymnal of its century. Crüger tunes in American hymnals include:

- HERZLIEBSTER JESU—"Ah, holy Jesus" (E158, L123, M289, P93)
- JESU, MEINE FREUDE—"Jesus, priceless treasure" (L457, M532, P365; "Jesus, all my gladness," E701)
- JESUS, MEINE ZUVERSICHT—"Let thy blood in mercy poured" (E313), "Jesus Christ, my sure defense" (L340), and "Jesus lives! The victory's won" (L133)
- NUN DANKET—"Now thank we all our God" (B638, E396, 397; L533, 534; M102, P555)
- NUN DANKET ALL UND BRINGET EHR or GRÄFENBERG—to texts of English origin—(E374, 509, 627; M193, 266; P230, 325)
- SCHMÜCKE DICH—"Deck thyself (yourself), my soul, with gladness" (E339, M612, P506); "Soul, adorn yourself with gladness," (L224)

Crüger's tunes such as HERZLIEBSTER JESU are harmonically conceived. His melodies also reflect influences of the Genevan Psalter tunes, such as the repeated opening notes in his HERZLIEBSTER JESU and NUN DANKET.[15] Crüger's friend and successor as organist of St. Nicholas Church in Berlin was Johann George Ebeling (1637-76) who also composed chorale settings including: DIE GÜLDNE SONNE, the tune to Gerhardt's *Die güldne Sonne voll Freud und Wonne* ("Evening and morning," L465) and WARUM SOLLT' ICH, a tune to Gerhardt's *Fröhlich soll mein Herze springen* ("All my heart this night (today) rejoices," P21).[16]

The increasingly personal and intimate character of German hymns of the mid-17th century is exemplified by those of Johann Franck (1618-77), lawyer and friend of Crüger. His hymns include *Schücke dich, o liebe Seele* ("Deck thyself (yourself), my soul, with gladness," E339, M612, P506; "Soul, adorn yourself with gladness," L224); and *Jesu meine Freude* ("Jesus, all my gladness,"

---

[14]*Evangelisches Kirchensangbuch*, "The Period of the 30 Years' War," 742.
[15]For a detailed discussion of Crüger's style, see Riedel, *The Lutheran Chorale*, 64-69.
[16]Eight of Ebeling's melodies are in the 1957 German Lutheran hymnal.

E701; "Jesus, priceless treasure" (L457, 458; M532; P365). Another personal hymn (both text and tune) written in 1641 by Georg Neumark (1621-81), a young student who later became court poet at Weimar, is *Wer nur den lieben Gott lässt walten*,"If you will only let God guide you" (B57); "If you but trust in God to guide you" (L453); "If thou but suffer (trust in) God to guide thee" (E635, M210). In contrast to the hymns of Franck and Neumark there is a later hymn of 1671, *Tröstet, tröstet, meine Lieben*, "Comfort, comfort ye (you) (now) my people" (E67, L29, P3), a paraphrase of Isaiah 40:1-8 written by the hymnal compiler Johannes Olearius (1611-84).[17] This text is traditionally sung to PSALM 42 (or FREU DICH SEHR) from the Genevan Psalter.

LATE 17TH AND 18TH CENTURY PIETISM

Pietism, that began with Philipp Jakob Spener at Frankfurt in 1670, was a reaction to the ever-increasing formality and rigidity within the established church. It sought to give new life to the church and to underline the importance of a personal Christian experience. Pietistic hymns emphasized the tension between the transcendence of God and the personal relationship in repentance, conversion, and assurance of salvation. The personal emphasis of Pietism was foreshadowed in earlier chorale texts, such as those of Gerhardt, Franck, and Neumark. Note the personal Pietistic emphasis in one of the earliest hymns, *Sei Lob und Ehr dem höchsten Gut* ("Sing praise to God who reigns above (the highest good)," B20, E408, L542, M126, P483) by Spener's lawyer and friend, Johann Jakob Schütz (1640-90):

> "Sing praise to God who reigns above,
> 　　The God of all creation,
> The God of power, the God of love,
> 　　The God of our salvation;
> With healing balm my soul he fills,
> 　　And ev'ry faithless murmur stills:
> To God all praise and glory!" [18]

Another Pietist, of the Reformed (Calvinistic) church in Germany, was Joachim Neander (1650-80). Though he lived only to the age of 30, he bequeathed us one of the most popular chorales, *Lobe den Herren, dem mächti-*

---

[17]Olearius' *Geistliche Singe-Kunst* (*Sacred Song-Art*, Leipzig, 1671), one of the most important Lutheran hymnals of the 17th century, included 302 of his hymns in its first edition. Five of his hymns remain in the 1957 German Lutheran hymnal.
[18]Different translations of the hymn are found at L524 and E375.

gen König der Ehren ("Praise to (ye) the Lord, the Almighty," B14, E390, L543, M139, P482), a hymn of adoration and personal testimony. Also a gifted musician, Neander composed the tunes WUNDERBARER KÖNIG ("God himself is present," L249) and UNSER HERRSCHER, ("God of love and God of power," M578; "He is risen, he is risen," E180; "Open now thy gates of beauty," L250; and "See the morning sun ascending," M674).

The leading hymnist of the Pietist movement, Johann A. Freylinghausen (1610-1739), was son-in-law and successor to the great Pietist leader at the Halle university and orphanage, August H. Franke. Freylinghausen's *Geistreiches Gesangbuch* (first part, 1704; second part, 1714) appeared in numerous editions and supplied hundreds of hymns and tunes for the Pietist movement including the tune GOTT SEI DANK (or GOTT SEI DANK DURCH ALLE WELT) "Lord, our Lord, Thy glorious name," P163; "On this day, the first of days," E47; "Spread, (O) Oh, spread, almighty (thou mighty) Word," E530, L379.[19]

The most mystical of the Pietists whose hymns survive was Gerhard Tersteegen (1697-1769), a Reformed minister who later became an independent religious teacher and leader. In addition to *Gott ist gegenwärtig* ("God himself is with us (present)," E475, L249), Tersteegen's mysticism is expressed in the following stanza of *Verborgne Gottesliebe du* ("Thou hidden Love of God, whose height," M414, stanza 5), as translated by his contemporary John Wesley:

> "Each moment draw from earth away
> My heart that lowly waits thy call;
> Speak to my inmost soul and say,
> 'I am thy love, thy God, thy all!'
> To feel thy power, to hear thy voice,
> To taste thy love, be all my choice."

THE MORAVIANS

The Moravians (also known as the Hussites, Bohemian Brethren, and the *Unitas Fratrum*—Unity of Brethren) were the much-persecuted followers of John Hus of Bohemia (both Bohemia and Moravia are provinces in present-day Czech Republic), who was martyred in 1415. Hus's followers gave new emphasis to congregational singing. Their hymns were first published in a Czech hymnal in 1501, more than two decades before the first Lutheran hymnal. The earliest Moravian hymnic contribution commonly found in current

---

[19]A dozen tunes from Freylinghausen's *Gesangbuch* appear in the current German Lutheran hymnal. For a description of this musical style, see "The Freylinghausen Tradition" in Riedel, *The Lutheran Chorale*, 70 ff.

American hymnals is the tune MIT FREUDEN ZART ("Sing praise to God who reigns above;" B20, E408, M126, P483; "With high delight let us unite," L140; "Lord Christ, when first thou cam'st (you came) to earth," E598, L421, P7). The most significant early Moravian hymnal in the German language was Michael Weisse's *Ein New Gesengbuchlen*[20] of 1531 that included 155 hymns written or translated by Weisse. Over three-fourths of the hymns in Weisse's collection entered into German Lutheran hymnic use in the 16th and 17th centuries.[21] In addition to several Weisse texts and tunes in *Hymnal of the Moravian Church* (1969), his tunes FREUEN WIR UNS ALL IN EIN ("Hark! A thrilling voice is sounding," L37) and GOTTES SOHN IST KOMMEN ("Once he came in blessing," E53) are in major American hymnals.

After three centuries of persecution, a turning point came for the Moravians in 1722 when they were given refuge on the estate of the German nobleman, Count Nicolaus Ludwig von Zinzendorf (1700-60). Under his leadership at Herrnhut (the Lord's Shelter), the Moravians were mobilized into a great missionary force. Zinzendorf was a prolific hymn writer, and hymn singing played an important part in Moravian life. There was "No visitor to Herrnhut but was struck by the amazing 'hymn-meetings,' *Singstunden*, which he [Zinzendorf] conducted there. He seems to have felt a continual necessity to create. He would give forth one line, which the congregation would then sing; by that time the second line would be ready, perfect in rhythm, rhyme and sense. Many of his hymns indeed, improvised in this fashion, have been lost, since no one, in the earlier years at any rate, was deputed to copy them down."[22]

Because of their improvisatory nature, some of Zinzendorf's best hymns should be credited to the editing of Christian Gregor (1723-1801), Moravian bishop, organist, hymnist, and leader. From his critical and careful revision we have such hymns as *Herz und Herz vereint zusammen* (Christian hearts, in love united, B378) and *Jesu, 'geh voran* (Jesus, still lead on, L341).[23] One other Zinzendorf hymn found in American hymnals, *Christi Blut und Gerechttigkeit*, was translated by John Wesley as "Jesus, thy (your) blood and righteousness"

[20]A facsimile of Weisse's hymnal with an introduction by Konrad Ameln was published by Bärenreiter in 1957.
[21]Marilyn Kay Stulken, *Hymnal Companion to the Lutheran Book of Worship*, No. 37.
[22]Moore, *Sursum Corda*, 84.
[23]Although Gregor, who compiled the first standard Moravian hymnal in 1778 and their first printed tunebook in 1784, has no hymns generally included in American hymnals, he is represented by one hymn text and one hymn tune in the current German Lutheran hymnal and by 15 hymns, 7 tunes, and numerous harmonizations in *Hymnal of the Moravian Church* (Bethlehem, PA, and Winston Salem, NC: The Moravian Church in America, 1969). See *Choral-Buch* by Christian Gregor. A Facsimile of the First Edition of 1784; introduction by Martha Asti; translation of the Author's Preface by Karl Kroeger; edited by James Boeringer. Published for the Moravian Music Foundation Press, Winston Salem, NC, and Bethlehem, PA; (London and Toronto: Associated University Presses, 1984).

(L302). These hymns express the Pietist-Moravian emphasis on personal Christian experience.

OTHER 18TH CENTURY DEVELOPMENTS

In addition to later Pietist hymnists and the Moravians, there were other writers of the 18th century whose chorale texts are found in current American hymnals. Three representative hymnists are Erdmann Neumeister (1671-1756), Benjamin Schmolck (1672-1737), and Matthias Claudius (1740-1815).

Neumeister, a Hamburg Lutheran pastor and conservative who opposed the Pietists and Moravians, wrote many cantata texts for the Christian year which were set to music by J. S. Bach and others. Although a half dozen of Neumeister's hymns are found in current German hymnals, only one has achieved wide use in English: *Jesus nimmt die Sünder an* ("Sinners Jesus (Jesus sinners) will receive," B563, L291). This hymn has the distinction of being known in English as a gospel hymn, its musical setting being in a popular American style. (At L291, however, it is set to the chorale melody, MEINEN JESUS LASS ICH NICHT.) James McGranahan (1840-1907) used four of its six lines in each stanza and the final couplet of the sixth stanza as the following refrain:

> "Sing it o'er and o'er again;
>> Christ receiveth sinful men;
> Make the message clear and plain:
>> Christ receiveth sinful men."

The leading hymnist of the non-Pietist Lutherans in the first half of the 18th century was Benjamin Schmolck, a pastor in Silesia (between the present-day Czeck Republic and Poland) who served under difficult circumstances in a predominantly Roman Catholic region. The hardships of his ministry rendered him bedridden and blind in his later years. Of his nearly 1,200 hymns, 11 appear in the German Lutheran hymnal and two are often found in American hymnals: *Tut mire auf die schöne Pforte* ("Open now thy gates of beauty," L250), a personal hymn for the beginning of worship; and *Liebster Jesu, wir sind hier* ("Dearest Jesus, we are here," L187, P493), a baptismal hymn.

Matthias Claudius, the son of a Lutheran pastor, was one of the few German lay writers of hymns. Although he was a freethinker in early adulthood, he was brought to a deepened faith through a serious illness. His one hymn in

American hymnals is *Wir pflügen und wir streuen* ("We plow the fields, and scatter," E291, L362, P560); a harvest hymn, which was an especially appropriate expression for the author who was a one-time agricultural commissioner. The tune WIR PLÜGEN is by Claudius' contemporary Johann A. P. Schulz (1747-1800), a well-known composer of German art songs and an opponent of the Enlightenment (German: *Aufklärung*), which sought to reconstruct hymnody in rationalistic terms and provide hymns with a new vocabulary to accord with the spirit of the age. For example, conversion became self-improvement; sanctification, betterment; God, the Supreme Being; and piety, virtue.[24] Hymns by Luther and Gerhardt were either remodeled or replaced by the rationalists.

By the close of the second decade of the 19th century, the winds of the Enlightenment had run their course, and the movement to restore the older hymnody was well on its way. One influence of the rationalistic mindset, that every measure should have an equal number of beats, remains in the chorale melodies of many current American hymnals. This practice resulted in the development of the isometric ("same meter") chorale. Many of the older chorales (for example, Luther's EIN' FESTE BURG)[25] in American hymnals are cast in this isometric form.

By the time of Freylinghausen's famous Pietist hymnal in the early 18th century, the newly composed chorales clearly reflected the baroque solo song style; they were mostly arias for single voice with *basso continuo* (frequently harpsichord and cello) accompaniment. These chorale arias were published with only melody and figured bass parts. The keyboard instrumentalist would improvise the missing parts.[26] Although chorale arias were adapted in simpler arrangements for use in congregational singing, hymns for the soloist took precedence over hymns for the congregation. These solo chorales reflected the aesthetic principles of the late baroque, with melodies constructed to allow the singer and accompanist ample opportunity for embellishment.

Many of the later chorale melodies were built on the intervals of the triad (such as WIR PLÜGEN, L362, and UNSER HERRSCHER, E180, L250, M578); some of them used dance rhythms (such as NEUMARK, B57, E635, L453, M142). These are only two of many stylistic traits which show the influence of general musical developments upon the chorale.[27]

The composer most commonly associated with the chorale in the 18th

[24]Moore, 103.
[25]See Chapter 2, "The Hymn and Music," pages 39 and 41.
[26]An illustration of the practice of ornamenting a chorale aria is found in Riedel, 73 ff.
[27]See "The Freylinghausen Tradition (ca. 1644-1756)" in Riedel, 70-89.

century is Johann Sebastian Bach. Bach's genius lay not in composing new hymn tunes, but in harmonizing and embellishing the rich body of church song that already existed. He made extensive use of the chorale in his cantatas and passions, harmonizing most of the melodies in four parts for singing by trained choirs. Some of his ingenious harmonizations are found in hymnals today, either intact or simplified for congregational use. Bach's best known chorale harmonizations are those for the PASSION CHORALE ("O sacred Head, now (sore) wounded," B137; E168, 169; M286; P98), which he used in both his *Christmas Oratorio* and *St. Matthew Passion*. Other Bach chorale harmonizations in current American hymns include:

- WAS FRAG' ICH NACH DER WELT ("Now yield we thanks and praise," E108; "Our God, to whom we turn," P278)
- DU FRIEDENSFÜRST, HERR JESU CHRIST ("The day is past and over," M683)
- ERMUNTRE DICH ("Break forth, O beauteous heavenly light," B114, E91, M223, P26)
- ICH HALTE TREULICH STILL ("God, bless your church with strength, P41)
- JESU, JOY OF MAN'S DESIRING ("Come with us, O blessed Jesus," E336, L219; "Jesus, joy of our desiring," M644)
- JESU, MEINE FREUDE ("Jesus, priceless treasure," M532, P365)
- NUN KOMM, DER HEIDEN HEILAND ("Savior of the nations, come," E54, L28, M214)
- O WELT, ICH MUSS DICH LASSEN ("The duteous day now closeth," E46; "O food to pilgrims given," E309, M631)
- ERHALT UNS HERR ("O Christ, the healer," M265)
- CHRIST LAG IN TODESBANDEN ("Christ Jesus lay in death's strong bonds," E186, L134, M319, P110)
- VATER UNSER ("Thou hidden love of God, whose height," M414; "Our Father, Lord of heaven and earth," P590)
- SALZBURG ("Let the whole creation cry," P256; "Songs of thankfulness and praise," E135; "At the Lamb's high feast we sing," E174; "Why are nations raging," P159; "Holy Spirit, Lord of love," P524)
- WACHET AUF ("'Sleepers, wake!' A voice astounds us," E61, P17; "Wake, awake, for night is flying," L31, M720; "Praise the Lord through every nation," E484)
- WIE SCHÖN LEUCHTET DER MORGENSTERN ("O Morning Star,

how fair and bright," L76, M247, P69; "How bright appears the Morning Star," E497; "Rejoice, rejoice this happy morn," L43; "All hail to you, O blessed morn" L73; "He is arisen! Glorious Word" L138; "O Holy spirit, enter in," L459).

Alongside the Protestant development of the chorale came the growth of hymn singing among Roman Catholics in German-speaking countries. Several German Catholic hymn tunes now appear in American hymnals, including LASST UNS ERFREUEN ("All creatures of our God and King," B27, E400, L527, M62, P455; "Ye watchers and ye holy ones," E618, M90, P451; "Praise God, from whom all blessings flow," M94), published in 1623 at Cologne; and GROSSER GOTT ("Holy God, we praise thy (your) name," E366, L535, M79, P460), published at Vienna about 1774.

19TH CENTURY

The 19th century was primarily a time of rediscovery for German Protestant church song, its rich heritage having been both ignored and weakened by the Rationalists. Original versions of the old chorales were restored to German Lutheran hymnals, such as Friedrich Layriz's *Kern des deutschen Kirchengesangs* (*Core of German Church Song*, 4 vols., Nördlingen, 1844-55). Scholars produced monumental scholarly studies concerned with the history of the chorale form.[28] This was also the time when a large number of German hymns were translated into English by such translators as Catherine Winkworth in England and Robert Massie in Scotland.

Although the 19th-century focus was on past heritage, some new German hymns were written. Karl Johann Philipp Spitta (1801-59), pastor from Hanover, was the leading Lutheran hymnist of his century. He was a hymnal compiler and author of *Wir sind des Herrn, wir leben oder sterben* ("We are the Lord's," L399). Another 19th-century German hymn now in American hymnals is *Walte, walten nah und fern* ("Spread, O (Oh) spread, thou mighty (almighty) word," E530, L379), a missionary hymn by Jonathan Friedrich Bahnmaier (1774-1841), outstanding Lutheran preacher and university professor at Tübingen.

The largest number of 19th-century German musical contributions to the development of the chorale are those of Felix Mendelssohn (1809-47). His large choral works contain harmonizations for the chorales NUN DANKET

---

[28]Two monumental works treating the melodies of German church song are Johannes Zahn's *Die Melodien der deutsche Kirchenlieder* (6 vols., 1889-93), which includes some 8,806 melodies to German Evangelical hymns, and Wilhelm Bäumker's *Das katholische deutsche Kirchenlied* (4 vols, 1883-1911), a basic study of German Roman Catholic Church song from 1470 to 1800 containing 451 melodies.

("Now thank we all our God," B638, E397, M102, P555); MUNICH ("O Word of God (O Christ, the Word) Incarnate," E632, M598, P327; "I lay my sins on Jesus," L305; "O Jesus, I have promised," L503); "We sing the glorious conquest," E255; "On Pentecost they gathered," P128; and BRESLAV ("He sat to watch o'er customs paid," E281; "We sing the praise of him who died," E471). His most famous tune MENDELSSOHN ("Hark! the herald angels sing," B88, E87, L60, M240, P31, 32) was adapted from his cantata *Festgesang*, 1844. Although represented in American hymnals, tunes by Mendelssohn and other great composers (such as Mozart, Haydn, Beethoven) have not found general acceptance in German hymnals.

Several 19th-century contributions have come from Lutheran churches of Scandinavia. *Kirken den er et gammelt Hus* ("Built on the Rock (a rock) the church doth stand," B351, L365) was written by Nikolaus Frederik Severin Grundtvig (1783-1872). He and Sören Kierkegaard were the most influential religious personalities of 19th-century Denmark. The tune KIRKEN for Grundtvig's hymn was composed by Ludvig Matthias Lindeman (1812-87), an outstanding Norwegian organist of his time and the compiler of a Norwegian Lutheran hymnal.[29]

The largest number of Scandinavian[30] hymns in American hymnals are from Sweden.[31] This nation's greatest hymnist was Johan Olof Wallin (1779-1839), Archbishop of Sweden in 1837, whose hymnal of 1819 served the Church of Sweden without revision for over a century. His hymns still occupy the leading place in Swedish hymnals. His best known hymn in English translation is the Christmas text, *Var hälsad, sköna morgonstund* ("All hail to you, O blessed morn," WIE SCHÖN LEUCHTET, L73). Other hymns of Wallin are *Vi lova dig, o store Gud* ("We worship you, O God of might," L432) and *Du som fromma hjartan vaarder* ("Christians, while on earth abiding," WERDE MUNTER, L440).

---

[29]Additional contributions of these Scandinavians are found in the *Lutheran Book of Worship* (1978). Hymns of Grundtvig are: *Det dimer nu til Julefest* ("The bells of Christmas," L62), *Dejlig er den Himmel blaa* ("Bright and glorious is the sky," L75), *Den signede Dag* ("O day full of grace," L161), *Herren strækker ud sin Arm* ("Cradling children in his arm," L193), *Guds Ord det er vort Arvegods* ("God's Word is our great heritage," L239), *Du, som gaar ud* ("Spirit of God, sent from heaven abroad," L285), and *Fred til Bod for bittert Savn* ("Peace, to soothe our bitter woes," L338). Hymn tunes of Lindeman are: FRED TIL BOD ("Hallelujah! Jesus lives," L147; "Peace to soothe our bitter woes," L338), DU SOM GAAR UD ("Spirit of God, sent from heaven abroad," L285), NAAR MIT ÖIE ("Come to Calv'ry's holy mountain," L301), GUD SKAL ALTING MAGE ("Jesus, priceless treasure," L458), and HER VIL TIES ("Saviour, like a shepherd lead us," L481).
[30]Articles on the hymnody of Denmark (Edward A. Hansen), Norway (Mandus A. Egge), Iceland (Shirley McCreedy), Sweden (Joel W. Lundeen), and Finland (Toivo K. Harjunpaa) are among the historical essays in Marilyn Kay Stulken, *Hymnal Companion to the Lutheran Book of Worship* (Philadelphia: Fortress Press, 1981).
[31]Information on many Swedish hymns now in English translation and a summary of Swedish hymnody are found in J. Irving Erikson, *Twice-Born Hymns* (Chicago: Covenant Press, 1976).

Another Scandinavian hymnist was the Swede, Caroline Vilhelmina Sandell-Berg (1832-1903), whose hymns reflect the spiritual awakening which swept Northern Europe in the latter part of the 19th century. Two of her hymns found in American hymnals are *Tryggare kan ingen vara* ("Children of the heavenly Father"—to a Swedish melody of unknown origin: TRYGGARE KAN INGEN VARA, B55, L474, M141) and *Blott en dag ett ögonblick i sänder* ("Day by day and with each passing moment" (BLOTT EN DAG, B66). The latter hymn is set to a tune by Oscar Ahnfelt (1813-82), a popular singer associated with Sweden's greatest lay preacher and religious leader, Carl Olof Rosenius. The most popular Scandanavian hymn in America is *O store Gud* ("How Great Thou Art," O STORE GUD, B10, L532, M77, P467), written in 1886 by the Swedish preacher, religious editor, and parliament member, Carl Boberg (1850-1940). Set to a Swedish melody of unknown origin, this hymn was made popular in America through the Billy Graham meetings beginning in 1955.[32]

The most popular 19th-century German text in American hymnals is the Austrian *Stille Nacht, heilige Nacht* ("Silent night, holy night," B91, L65, M239, E111, P60). This beloved Christmas song was written in the village of Oberndorf (near Salzburg) for Christmas in 1818 by the Catholic priest Joseph Mohr (1792-1848) and set to music by his church's acting organist, Franz Gruber (1787-1863). This Christmas hymn, first sung by two voices to guitar accompaniment because the church organ was out of order, has achieved international popularity.

20TH CENTURY

Although the practice of hymn writing is alive in 20th-century Germany, few of the more recent hymns have been translated and published in American hymnals. The multilingual hymnal, *Cantate Domino* (3rd ed., 1974),[33] contains a representative number of recent German hymns in English translation. The two hymnists with the largest number of contributions to *Cantate Domino* (CD) are Dieter Trautwein (five texts and one tune) and Rolf Schweizer (one text and four tunes). Trautwein (b. 1928), a Lutheran minister at Frankfurt (Main), has written such provocative hymns as *Kommt Gott als Mensch in Dorf und Stadt* (CD60, 1964, "God will, when he comes to earth," tr. by Fred Kaan, 1972). It depicts his view of how God would react upon return-

[32]The popular version in English under the title "How Great Thou Art" is Stuart W. K. Hine's translation of a Russian version, which in turn was based on a German translation of the Swedish original. Much of Hine's version represents an addition to the original including the fourth stanza, added in 1948. For a translation of nine stanzas of Boberg's Swedish original, see "O mighty God, when I behold the wonder" in *The Covenant Hymnal* (Chicago: Covenant Press, 1973), 19. See also Carlton R. Young, *Companion to The United Methodist Hymnal* (Nashville: Abingdon Press, 1993), 409-411.
[33]See Chapter 9, "Cultural Perspectives," pages 233-234.

ing in human form. Trautwein is also the author of *Wir sind nicht irgendwer und nicht nur ungefähr* (CD73, 1965, "We're not just anyone; we're not just nobodies," tr. by F. Pratt Green, 1972), an innovative hymn based on 1 Peter 1:4-19. In this hymn, the refrain is sung and the stanzas are spoken above a background of improvised music. Schweizer (b. 1936), a church music director in Pforzheim, has composed pop-style hymn tunes with syncopations and off-beat entrances. These characteristics are evident in his 1963 setting of Paul Stein's *Singet dem Herrn ein neues Lied* (CD47, 1963, "Sing to the Lord a new song," tr. by F. Pratt Green, 1972).[34]

In addition to recent hymnists represented in *Cantate Domino*, another German hymnist who has contributed to current American hymnals is Heinz Werner Zimmerman (b. 1930), a well-known Lutheran church music composer who has composed CARPENTER, 1970, ("Praise the Lord," P225), LITTLE FLOCK, 1971 ("Have no fear, little flock," L476).[35] The German theologian Dietrich Bonhoeffer (1906-45) wrote *Von guten Mächten wunderbar geborgen* ("By gracious powers so wonderfully sheltered," INTERCESSOR, E695, M517, P342; LE CÉNACLE, E696) while in a Nazi prison. The German composer Hugo Distler (1908-42) composed the tune TRUMPETS (adapted by Jan Bender for Martin Franzmann's "Weary of all trumpeting," E572, M442). Bender (1909-1994), born in Holland of a German mother and Dutch father, lived primarily in Germany and in the United States. Bender's tune WITTENBERG NEW was composed for Franzmann's 1967 hymn commemorating the 450th anniversary of the Reformation, "O God, O Lord of heav'n and earth" (L396).

The leading recent Scandinavian hymn writer whose hymns are available in English[36] is Anders Frostenson (b. 1906), a minister of the Church of Sweden who is represented by six hymns in *Cantate Domino*. Frostenson's hymns are remarkable fresh expressions of biblical events, as in " 'It's Jesus we want,' requested the Greeks" (*Vi ville dig se, så grekerna bad*, 1971, tr. by Fred Kaan, 1972, CD33) and *De såg ej dif blott timmermannens* ("They saw you as the local builder's son," 1962, tr. by Fred Kaan, 1973, CD81). Also noteworthy are Frostenson's contemporary portrayals of faith and love in *Ton sig sträcker efter frukten* ("Faith, while trees are still in blossom," 1960, tr. by Fred Kaan, 1972, CD44, M508) and *Guds kärlek är som stranden och som gräset* ("The love of God is broad like beach and meadow," 1968, tr. by Fred Kaan, 1972, CD49, M120). Another Scandinavian whose hymns have been published in English translation is the Norwegian

[34]Another Schweizer tune is his setting of Psalm 92, "How good to give thanks" (CD16).
[35]See Chapter 2, "The Hymn and Music."
[36]*Songs and Hymns from Sweden* ed. by Anders Frostenson and tr. by Fred Kaan (London: Stainer & Bell, Ltd., 1976). See the review of this collection in *The Hymn* 29, 1 (January 1978): 47-48.

Svein Ellingsen (b.1929), an artist as well as hymn writer and regarded as the most outstanding Norwegian hymnist of his time. Twenty-four of his original texts and 14 of his translations were published in the 1985 *Norsk Salmebok,* the hymnal of The [Lutheran] Church of Norway. Fourteen of his hymns have been translated into English by Hedwig T. Durnbaugh and published with music by Norwegian composers in *Praises Resound!* (1991).[37] One of these hymns, "In the stillness of the evening" with a tune by Harald Herresthal (I DE SENE TIMERS STILLHET), was published in *Hymnal: A Worship Book* (1992).[38]

The centuries-old chorale tradition given its principal impetus by Martin Luther thus remains alive in Germany and in Scandinavia. As this tradition's 20th-century contributions become increasingly available in English, some of them will likely find a place in the repertory of America's congregations.

THE METRICAL PSALM
French and Continental

Just as Luther gave the chorale its impetus, his contemporary—the French-Swiss Reformation theologian John Calvin (1509-64)—was the guiding hand behind the metrical psalm. A more radical reformer than Luther, Calvin rejected the musical heritage of the Roman Catholic Church, including organs, choirs, and humanly composed hymns. He advocated singing only Scripture in worship, primarily the Psalms versified like hymns so that each could be sung to a particular tune. Furthermore, in Calvin's view the metrical

© 1980 Charles Massey, Jr.
John Calvin

psalms were to be sung only in unison and without instrumental accompaniment. The result of this philosophy of church song was the production of a series of gradually enlarged psalters in French, beginning with Calvin's Strassburg Psalter of 1539, continuing with other psalters published in Geneva, and culminating with the Genevan Psalter of 1562, which included all 150 psalms plus the Ten Commandments and the *Nunc dimittis.* The complete Genevan Psalter contained 125 tunes in 110 different meters.

Calvin, unlike Luther, was neither composer nor poet, but he was fortunate to

[37](Oslo: Norsk Musikforlag A/S).
[38](Elgin, IL: Brethren Press; Newton, KS: Faith and Life Press; Scottdale, PA: Mennonite Publishing House).

have the assistance of others who did have these talents. Calvin's *Psalter* was versified in the French language by Clement Marot (*ca.* 1497-1544), who was succeeded several years after his death by Theodore de Béze (1519-1608). The chief musical contributor to the Genevan Psalter was Louis Bourgeois (*ca.* 1510-*ca.* 1561), who came from Paris to be director of music at St. Peter's Cathedral in Geneva, where Calvin preached for a number of years. In keeping with a common practice of the time, Bourgeois used many first phrases of secular chansons in his Genevan Psalter melodies. It is uncertain just how many were derived from other sources. Bourgeois' great influence upon this work has been attested by Pratt: "To him is plainly due the individual style that sets the French Psalter apart from all others of its age." [39] Among the Genevan Psalter tunes in present-day American hymnals are:

- DONNE SECOURS[40] ("Hope of the world," L493, P360, E472)— a Dorian melody attributed to Bourgeois and set to Marot's version of Psalm 12.
- O SEIGNEUR ("When morning gilds the skies," L545)
- LE CANTIQUE DE SIMÉON or NUNC DIMITTIS ("O gladsome light," M686; "Now may your servant, Lord," P605)
- OLD 100TH ("All people that on earth do dwell," B5, E377, 378; M75; "Be present at our table, Lord" M621; "Praise God, from whom all blessings flow," B253, M95)—Originally to Psalm 134; attributed to Bourgeois but with a first line from a secular chanson.
- OLD 107TH ("The Lord will come and not be slow," L318,)— original 7.6.7.6.6.7.6.7 meter changed to C.M.D. in British-American use.
- OLD 113TH ("I'll praise my Maker while I've breath," B35, E429, M60, P253)
- OLD 124TH ("Your kingdom come! O Father, hear our prayer," L376; "Now Israel may say," P236; or GENEVA 124, "Go forth

[39]Waldo Selden Pratt, *The Music of the French Psalter of 1562* (New York: Columbia University Press,1939. Reprinted. New York: AMS Press,1966), 62. This study, the most comprehensive treatment of the Genevan Psalter in English, contains all 125 tunes of the 1562 edition in modern notation.
[40]The Genevan tune titles are often supplied with either French names or with the word "Old" before a number. The French titles are the incipits of the original French psalm texts. For example, DONNE SECOURS are the opening words of Psalm 12. All the tune titles beginning with the word "Old" refer to the English use of the Genevan tunes. A famous example is OLD HUNDREDTH, which refers to the use of that Genevan tune for Psalm 100 in English. Another system of designation is simply to name the tunes GENEVAN, with the number of the original psalm following, as in GENEVAN 47 (P194).

for God," M670; or TOULON, "Lord of all good," P375; "I greet Thee, who my sure Redeemer art," P457)

- OLD 134TH (or ST. MICHAEL, "Stand up and bless the Lord," B30, M662; "How can we sinners know," M372; "O come and dwell in me," M388; "O day of God, draw nigh," B623, M730)—originally to Psalm 101 and in the metrical pattern 11.11.10.4, this tune has been considerably altered in English use.

- RENDEZ À DIEU ("Bread of the world in mercy broken," M624, P502; "Father, we thank you," M565; "New songs of celebration render," P218)—attributed to Bourgeois.

- PSALM 42 ("Comfort, comfort you my people," P3; or FREU DICH SEHR, L29; "Praise and thanks and adoration," L470)— this melody, eventually taken over into German use, was later used by Bach in seven of his cantatas.

The melodies of the Genevan Psalter gained extensive use in the 16th and 17th centuries. They were spread not only in French-speaking areas but also through numerous translations in Germany, Holland, England, and Scotland, and from these lands to the American colonies. The acceptance of these French Psalter tunes was so great in Holland that their circulation there, even in our own century, is probably wider than that within their original French Protestant domain.[41]

Early English Psalms

Just as the first psalm versions of Marot had been written while he served in the court of Francis I of France, the beginnings of the first significant English psalter also took place amid royalty. Before 1549, Thomas Sternhold (1500-1549), a servant in the courts of Henry VIII and Edward VI, published 19 psalm versions (which he sang to ballad tunes for his own private devotions) and dedicated them to young King Edward. A second edition containing 37 psalms appeared in 1549 after Sternhold's death. In 1551, his friend John Hopkins (d.1570), a clergyman and schoolteacher from Suffolk, added seven new versions to the previous 37. By the time this English Psalter was completed in 1562 (the same year of completion as the Genevan Psalter) Hopkins had contributed more than 60 psalm versions, thus giving it its popular designation—the Sternhold and Hopkins Psalter.

[41]Pratt, 69.

Before the completion of the English Psalter, however, political-religious developments in England caused English-language psalters to be both published and used on other than English soil. After the death of Edward VI in 1553, Roman Catholic Queen Mary (known as "Bloody Mary") succeeded to the throne. Under Mary's reign, many Protestants fled from persecution to the Continent, and especially to Geneva. Editions of the Anglo-Genevan Psalter appeared in 1556, 1558, and 1561, the first being the initial English-language psalter to include tunes. (Each of its 51 psalms had its proper tune, including some tunes reflecting Genevan influences.) The most lasting legacy from the Anglo-Genevan Psalter was that of William Kethe (d.c. 1593). Among his 25 versions in the 1561 edition was his rendition of Psalm 100, "All people that on earth do dwell" (B5; E377, 378; L245; M75; P220, 221). It was set to the tune previously used with Psalm 134 in the Genevan Psalter, known to English-speaking churches as OLD 100TH.

The complete English Psalter of 1562, which included many psalms from the Anglo-Genevan Psalter, was actually the work of at least 12 persons, but chiefly Sternhold and Hopkins. This Sternhold and Hopkins Psalter, later known as the Old Version (to distinguish it from the 1696 *New Version* of Tate and Brady), was the official psalter of the Anglican Church until the second decade of the 19th century. Its metrical versions have passed out of common use today.

The influence of Sternhold and Hopkins upon current hymnody is musical rather than textual. Several of its tunes remain in common use. This complete psalter (the official title is *The Whole Book of Psalms, collected into English metre*), was published in melody-only edition (most melodies in double common meter) in 1562 in London by John Day. It was published in a harmonized version in part-books (the melody in the tenor) in 1563. From Day's edition of 1562, the first four lines of the C.M.D. tune for Psalm 132 have become the presently used tune ST. FLAVIAN ("Lord, who throughout these forty days," E142, P81; " 'Thy kingdom come!' on bended knee," E615; "Be known to us in breaking bread," P505; "When in the night I meditate," P165). Other musical editions of Sternhold and Hopkins which have bequeathed tunes to present-day hymnals are:

- William Daman's *Psalmes* (1579), containing the S.M. tune to Psalm 14, later named by Ravenscroft SOUTHWELL ("Lord Jesus, think on me," E641, L309, P301).

- William Daman's *Booke of Musicke* (1591, his psalms printed by Este) containing the C.M. tune WINDSOR ("Jesus, the very thought of thee," E642; "My God, how wonderful thou art," E643; "There is a green hill far away," L114).
- Thomas Este's *Psalmes* (1592), containing the C.M. tune to Psalm 84, WINCHESTER OLD ("While shepherds watched their flocks by night," E94, P58; "My God, I love thee," M470; "Come, Holy Ghost, our hearts inspire," M603; "O Lord, our God, how excellent," P162; "God is our refuge and our strength," P191; "How happy is each child of God," P239).
- Thomas Ravenscroft's *Psalmes* (1621), which included the common meter tunes BRISTOL ("Hark! the glad sound! the Savior comes," E71 and DURHAM ("When all thy mercies, O my God," E415).

In addition to these musical editions of Sternhold and Hopkins, another early English psalter is important for its music; Archbishop (of Canterbury) Matthew Parker's Psalter of about 1567 contained nine tunes of the pioneer Anglican composer Thomas Tallis (c. 1505-1585), including:

- TALLIS' CANON or THE EIGHTH TUNE ("All praise to (thee) you, my God, this night," B449, E43, L278, M682, P542; "O gracious Light, Lord Jesus Christ," E25; "Go with us, Lord, and guide the way," P535),
- TALLIS' ORDINAL ("We stand united in the truth," B625; "Come now, and praise the humble saint," E260; "The great Creator of the worlds," E489; "Thy mercy and Thy truth, O Lord," P186), and
- THIRD MODE MELODY ("I heard the voice of Jesus say," E692, L497; "To mock your reign, O dearest Lord," E170).

Scottish Psalms

Beginning about 1550, Sternhold's English psalter was used in Scotland. A few years later the Scots, along with the English who fled from persecution to Geneva, used the Anglo-Genevan Psalter. The great Scottish reformer John Knox was pastor to the Genevan congregation of refugees for two years. After Knox's return to his homeland in 1559, the Scots began to revise the Anglo-Genevan Psalter. This process resulted in their own psalter in 1564 as a part of

The Forme of Prayers and Ministration of the Sacraments. Only about a third of this book's metrical psalms were of Scottish authorship. The Scottish Psalter contained 105 tunes (melodies only) and is regarded as musically superior to the Sternhold and Hopkins Psalter because of its greater use of French psalm tunes.

Two early editions of the Scottish Psalter are of musical interest. The 1615 edition added 12 "common tunes" (tunes which could be used with a number of psalms cast in the same meter) to the "proper tunes" (tunes to be sung to only one metrical psalm). One of his psalter's "Common tunes" (also in common meter) is used today with several hymns:

- DUNDEE ("You are the way; through you alone," L464; "My God, how wonderful thou art," L524; "The people who in darkness walked," E126; "Let saints on earth in concert sing," E526; "O God of Bethel, by whose hand," E709, P269; "I to the hills will lift my eyes," P234). First called "French Tune," DUNDEE was introduced to England by Ravenscroft in 1621 under the name "Dundy Tune."

The 1635 edition of the Scottish Psalter, edited by skilled musician Edward Miller, had 31 common tunes harmonized (their melodies being in the tenor), including:

- CAITHNESS ("O Lord, throughout these forty days," L99; "Christ, when for us you were baptized," E121, P70; "O God, to those who here profess," E352; "O for a closer walk with God," E684, P396; "The heavens above declare God's praise," P166; "The earth and all that dwell therein," P176) and
- LONDON NEW ("This is the day the Lord hath made," E50; "O God, whom neither time nor space," E251; "God moves in a mysterious way," E677)—originally named NEWTOUN. This melody with its frequent leaps is in marked contrast to the more usual stepwise psalm tunes of its time.

LONDON NEW was introduced into English use by John Playford in his *Psalms & Hymns in Solemn Musick* (1671) and *The Whole Book of Psalms* (1677), the latter remaining in circulation for a hundred years. Through Playford's and other English psalters, several Scottish psalm tunes gained a place in the repertory of English psalmody.

Although editions of the Scottish Psalter after 1564 included music, the new Scottish Psalter adopted in 1650 contained no music. The 1650 *Scottish Psalter* is the source of several metrical psalms in American use, including:

- "The Lord's my Shepherd; I'll not want"—Psalm 23 (L451, M136, P170)
- "How lovely is thy dwelling place"—Psalm 84 (B523, E517)[42]

Although hymnals began to appear in Scotland by the late 19th century,[43] the Scottish Psalter continued to be used well into the present century, its latest edition printed in 1929.[44] The 1929 Scottish Psalter was used until 1973 along with the 1927 edition of the Church of Scotland's *Church Hymnary*, when the third edition of the *Church Hymnary* was published. In this edition, the metrical psalms and other scriptural paraphrases lost their time-honored special place and were mingled with the hymns. The small Free Kirk of Scotland, however, still sings only the psalms. When entering a Free Kirk, one is handed a Bible with metrical psalms bound in the book. The Church of Scotland and the Free Church are both working on new metrical versions of the psalms, thus preserving, but also developing, the tradition.[45]

Later English Psalmody

Although the Sternhold and Hopkins Psalter remained England's most widely used collection until the mid-19th century, its leading rival, *A New Version of the Psalms of David, fitted to the tunes used in Churches*, made its initial appearance in 1696. The *New Version* was authored by two Irishmen, Nahum Tate (1652-1715), who had been made poet laureate by William III, and Nicholas Brady (1659-1726), a royal chaplain at that time. The *New Version* was dedicated to the King, who with his council designated it as "allowed and permitted to be used in all Churches, Chappels, and Congregations, as shall think fit to receive the same."

In contrast to strict metrical renderings of the Old Version of Sternhold and Hopkins, the *New Version* made a freer and more polished literary paraphrase of the psalms. This aroused such objections as the following: "David

---

[42]In addition to stanzas 1 and 2 from the 1650 Scottish Psalter, two more stanzas of Psalm 84 have been paraphrased by the American hymnist Carl P. Daw, Jr. (b. 1944) and appear in these two recent hymnals.

[43]These are listed in Millar Patrick, *Four Centuries of Scottish Psalmody* (London: Oxford University Press, 1949), 219. This book is a definitive work on Scottish psalmody.

[44]*The Scottish Psalter* (London: Oxford University Press, 1929).

[45]We are indebted to Alan Luff and Alisdair Fraser of the Hymn Society of Great Britain and Ireland for this information.

speaks so plain," said one old man, "that we cannot mistake his meaning, but as for Mr. Tate and Brady, they have taken away my Lord, and I know not where they have laid him."[46] The *New Version* was never fully accepted by the Anglican Church, and it was used primarily by those who were most ready to sing hymns along with the psalms, particularly in the churches of London.[47] Indeed, the polished metrical psalms of Tate and Brady seemed much more like hymns than those of the older psalters. One Psalm from the *New Version* remaining in American use is Psalm 42, "As pants the hart (longs the deer) for cooling streams" (E658, L452).

No music was included in the 1696 edition of the *New Version*, but a *Supplement* in 1708 provided tunes, with several attributed to William Croft (1678-1727):

- ST. ANNE (to Watts' version of Psalm 90, "O (Our) God, our help in ages past," B74, E680, L320, M117, P210)
- HANOVER ("Ye servants of God, your master proclaim," M181, P477; "O (Oh) worship the King," E388, L548)
- ST. MATTHEW ("Thine arm, O Lord, in days of old," E567)

This *Supplement* also included a familiar scriptural paraphrase of the announcement of the birth of Christ from Luke 2, "While shepherds watched their flocks by night" (E94, 95, M236, P58, 59). Thus while the *New Version* did not achieve as widespread acceptance as the Old Version, the *New Version* did gain a lasting place for some of its psalm versions, as well as its Christmas Gospel paraphrase.

American

The Anglican and Reformed metrical psalmody was brought across the Atlantic by a number of groups who settled in colonial America, notably the Pilgrims and the Puritans. The Pilgrims settled at Plymouth, Massachusetts, in 1620, bringing with them the Ainsworth Psalter (1612),[48] which they used until the close of the century. Nearly a decade later the Puritans established the Massachusetts Bay Colony (1628), bringing with them the Sternhold

---

[46]Quoted in Millar Patrick, *The Story of the Church's Song*. Revision of original 1927 ed. for American use by James Rawlings Sydnor (Richmond: John Knox Press, 1962), 98.
[47]Louis F. Benson, *The English Hymn*. Reprint of the original 1915 ed. (Richmond: John Knox Press, 1962), 50.
[48]This was a psalter complied by Henry Ainsworth, an English separatist minister and Hebrew scholar at that time in Amsterdam. Its 39 tunes drew from both English and Genevan sources. A detailed study of this psalter is Waldo S. Pratt, *The Music of the Pilgrims* (Boston: Oliver Ditson Co., 1921. Reprinted. New York: AMS Press, 1966). A more recent study is Lorraine Inserra and H. Wiley Hitchcock, *The Music of Henry Ainsworth's Psalter*. I.S.A.M. Monograph No. 15 (New York: Institute for Studies in American Music, 1981).

and Hopkins Psalter (1562). In other American colonies settled by French and Dutch Protestants, psalters from their respective homelands were used.

In 1640 at Cambridge, Massachusetts, the Puritans published the Bay Psalm Book, the first book of any kind to be printed in British North America. (For its actual title, see the accompanying photo of the title page on page 124.) The Puritan ministers sought to provide in the Bay Psalm Book a rendering of the psalms that was smoother and closer to the original Hebrew than those of Sternhold and Hopkins. The early editions of the Bay Psalm Book contained no music but was referenced to the Ravenscroft Psalter for tunes. Beginning with the ninth edition of 1698, music was provided, drawing from psalm tunes well known in England.[49] Although no psalm versions from the Bay Psalm Book remain in use in today's congregational repertory, this psalter was widely used for over a century in New England, England, and Scotland.[50]

18th-Century Psalmody

In the 18th century, the Bay Psalm Book was gradually replaced by other psalters. Watts' *The Psalms of David Imitated* was first reprinted in America by Benjamin Franklin's press at Philadelphia in 1729. The revival fervor of the Great Awakening shortly thereafter caused many congregations to adopt Watts' *Psalms and Hymns*. A number of Watts' metrical psalms were also found in John Wesley's "Charlestown Collection" of 1737.[51] Some denominations changed with little difficulty from the older psalters to updated versions or to hymns, while others, notably Presbyterians, experienced major controversies.[52]

19th-Century Psalmody

After the colonies gained political independence, various psalter editions sought to accommodate Watts' *Psalms* to America by removing references to Britain: Barlow (1785), Dwight (1801), Worcester (1815), and Winchell (1818). The second of these, edited by Timothy Dwight (1752-1817), an army chaplain under George Washington and later president of Yale, included the

---

[49]The tunes and musical instructions in this edition were taken from Playford's *Brief Introduction to the Skill of Musick* (London, 8th ed., 1679).

[50]Two significant studies of the Bay Psalm Book are Zoltan Haraszti, *The Enigma of the Bay Psalm Book*, published with a facsimile of the first edition of this psalter (Chicago: University of Chicago Press, 1956) and Irving Lowens, "The Bay Psalm Book in 17th-Century New England," in *Music and Musicians in Early America* (New York: W.W. Norton, 1964). Tunes from the ninth edition are given in Richard G. Appel, *The Music of The Bay Psalm Book 9th Edition* (1698) I.S.A.M. Monographs No. 5 (New York: Institute for Studies in American Music, 1975).

[51]See Chapter 7, "British Traditions."

[52]See Benson, *The English Hymn*, 161-218, for a detailed treatment of "The Era of Watts in America."

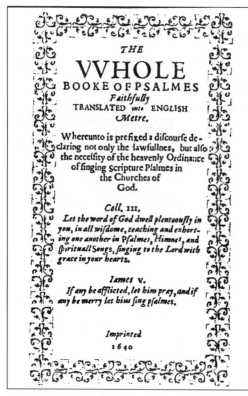

Title page–Bay Psalm Book, 1640

editor's version of Psalm 137, "I love thy (your) kingdom, Lord" (B354, E524, L368, M540, P441), the earliest American congregational song remaining in common use. In the 18th and early 19th centuries, most American denominations changed from singing only metrical psalms to singing freer psalm versions and the hymns of Isaac Watts and other English authors.

In the latter 19th century, a second psalm paraphrase gained a place in the broad stream of American hymnody. "O my soul, bless God the Father (your Redeemer)" (B21, P223), a version of Psalm 103, was first published in 1871 in the United Presbyterian *Book of Psalms*.

20th-Century Psalmody

Although metrical psalms in America were superseded by hymns in most of its churches by the early 19th century, several denominations of the Calvinist tradition continue to use them. In 1893 the United Presbyterian Church invited all Presbyterian and Reformed denominations to work on a new psalter, a project involving nine denominations and resulting eventually in the 1912 *Psalter*. This psalter is still in print and is used by two small Dutch-American denominations, the Protestant Reformed and the Netherlands Reformed Churches.[53] When the United Presbyterian Church began hymn singing, they added hymns to this same psalter when

---

[53]Much of this section is based on the article of Emily R. Brink, "Metrical Psalmody in North America: A Story of Survival and Revival," *The Hymn* 44, 4 (October 1993): 20-24. An earlier version appeared in the *I.A.H. Bulletin* 20 (June 1992, International Fellowship for Research in Hymnology): 122-123. The 1912 *Psalter* is available in a 1927 edition (which includes a chorale section in the back) from Eerdmans, 225 Jefferson, Grand Rapids, MI 49503.

they produced their 1927 *Psalter Hymnal*. A major Dutch-American denomination—the Christian Reformed Church— took the same path in their 1934 *Psalter Hymnal*. Another important musical step was taken in the 1934 *Psalter Hymnal* when they reached back to the Reformation and restored the Genevan Psalter tunes, a tradition that continues in the 1987 *Psalter Hymnal*. The Genevan tradition is especially preserved by the Canadian Reformed Churches, whose *Book of Praise* (1972, 2nd ed., 1974) is the only current complete Genevan Psalter with English texts.[54]

© 1980 Charles Massey, Jr.
Timothy Dwight

A surge of new metrical psalmody has been experienced in North American churches from the 1980s. This development was encouraged by a combination of language changes, new Bible translations, and the growing use of the lectionary. For example, Episcopalians were provided all the shorter psalm portions for their Eucharistic Lectionary in Christopher Webber's *A New Metrical Psalter* (1985). In the same year, the Reformed Church in America published its hymnal, *Rejoice in the Lord,* which included more than 60 metrical psalms in a section entitled "Psalms Praise Him."[55] In 1986 the Presbyterian Church (U.S.A.) released two psalm collections: *Singing Psalms of Joy and Praise,* a collection of texts by Fred Anderson, and *A Psalm Sampler* by the Psalter Task Force, which prepared both metrical and responsorial psalms for *The Presbyterian Hymnal* (1990).[56]

Even though most English-speaking churches no longer use metrical psalters, the tradition begun by John Calvin at Geneva has left its imprint on today's congregational song, since practically every major hymnal includes

---

[54]*Book of Praise: Anglo-Genevan Psalter* (Winnipeg: Premier Printing, Ltd., 1984). Available from Premier Printing, Ltd., 1249 Plessis Road, Winnipeg, Manitoba, Canada R2C 3L9.
[55]*Rejoice in the Lord: A Hymn Companion to the Scriptures,* ed. Erik Routley (Grand Rapids, MI: Wm. B. Eerdmans Publishing Co., 1985).
[56]Among other psalters in use in North America is the Associate Reformed Presbyterian Church's psalter, entitled *Bible Songs* (Due West, SC: Executive Board, Associated Reformed Presbyterian Church, 1930, 7th ed., 1975). Although restricted to the metrical psalms, the music of *Bible Songs* is largely American, making use of many gospel-hymn tunes. Along with the psalter, most A.R.P. congregations use hymnals as well. Also using a metrical psalter is the Reformed Presbyterian Church of North America. Their psalter is *The Book of Psalms for Singing* (Pittsburgh: Board of Education and Publication, Reformed Presbyterian Church of North America, 1973; 2nd ed. 1975). This psalter, although incorporating American musical settings, makes fuller use of the European heritage than does the *Bible Songs* volume. For example, it includes such familiar psalm tunes as DUNDEE, CRIMOND, ST. ANNE, and TALLIS' ORDINAL.

tunes from the Genevan and later psalters, as well as English language metrical psalms drawn from the psalters of England, Scotland, and America. Furthermore, a revival of metrical psalmody in the closing decades of the 20th century has been felt in a number of North American churches.

7
BRITISH TRADITIONS

THE GATHERING STREAMS
Sixteenth-century English reformers chose to follow John Calvin of Geneva rather than Martin Luther of Wittenberg. This had decisive consequences for the song of the Christian church in England. Because the Lutheran chorale was rejected by the British reformers,[1] the development of true hymnody, instead of metrical psalmody, was long delayed. Consequently, British worship song from the Reformation until the 18th century is largely the story of the metrical psalm. (See the preceding chapter.)

George Wither
While psalmody continued to be dominant in the established church and among Nonconformists, there were rumblings of discontent. Several early attempts were made to widen the sphere of church song. Most notable was the publication by George Wither (1588-1667) of *Hymns and Songs of the Church* (1623), probably the very earliest English-language hymnal. In addition to the conventional paraphrases of Scripture, it contained some true hymns for festivals and special occasions. While it won a royal patent, its concession to hymns was jealously opposed by the Company of Stationers; the patent had to be withdrawn, and Wither's bold experiment eventually came to naught. Nonetheless, the book was popular with the young people for a time, and its attraction was doubtless enhanced by the inclusion of 16 tunes by the most eminent composer of the day, Orlando Gibbons (1583-1625). None of Wither's delightful

---

[1]There was a brief period in the days of Henry VIII (1491-1547) that Lutheranism seemed likely to have some influence in English reform. Miles Coverdale's *Goostly Psalmes and Spirituall Songes* (1537-43) represented an attempt to import Lutheran hymnody into England but this book was soon suppressed (burned). After some hesitation, Archbishop Cranmer (1489-1556) came down on the side of Calvin, thus turning church song in the direction of metrical psalmody. See Robin A. Leaver, *Goostly Psalmes and Spirituall Songes* (Oxford: Clarendon Press, 1992).

lyrics have survived, but the Gibbons's tunes remain a noble legacy.[2]

George Herbert

The century that produced Wither also marked the emergence of a remarkable group known as the metaphysical poets, including: John Donne (1573-1631), Dean of St. Paul's in London; Richard Crashaw (d. 1649); Nicholas Ferrar (1592-1637); and George Herbert (1593-1633). Most were members of a distinguished circle that gathered about Izaak Walton (1593-1683), author of *The Compleat Angler* (1683),a monument of English literature. All wrote devotional poetry intended mainly for private reading and contemplation, and various lines from many of their poems were later extracted as hymns.

The best known poet is George Herbert, the masterful orator of the University of Cambridge and self-effacing rector of the village church at Bemerton near Salisbury, who is generally considered one of the saintliest characters in the history of literature. Herbert's hymns have been taken from a little book entitled *The Temple* (1633). This collection, published posthumously, contains some of the quaintest and most profound poems in the English language.

Herbert's hymns have been included in numerous hymn collections, and today he is mainly remembered for the one he entitled "Antiphon," known by its first line "Let all the world in every corner sing" (B28, M93, P468). It has been set by Robert G. McCutchan (ALL THE WORLD) and Erik Routley (AUGUSTINE). Herbert's "Come, my Way, my Truth, my Life" to Ralph Vaughan Williams's appealing tune, THE CALL (M164), is also included in several collections.

John Milton

The verse of Herbert's younger contemporary, John Milton (1608-74), represents a different development in the early history of the English hymn. While Herbert and his group produced religious verse that subsequently was adapted for congregational singing, Milton's "hymns" are actually free paraphrases of portions of the Psalms. Relaxing the adherence to the exact content and language of the Psalms by gifted men like Milton was a necessary step toward the eventual breaking altogether of metrical psalmody's stranglehold on congregational song. Two excellent hymns based on Psalms are Milton's legacy to present-day singing: "The Lord will come and not be

---

[2]These tunes are still named according to the numbering given them in Wither's hymnbook. See, for example, SONG 1 (E315, 499, 617; L206; P385, 604); SONG 13 (M355, 465, 550, 699, altered and named CANTERBURY; P321; E670); SONG 34 (E21, 264; L505); SONG 67 (E697, L438).

slow" (E462, L318), based on portions of Psalms 85, 82, and 86, and "Let us, with a gladsome mind" (E389, P244), based on Psalm 136.

Richard Baxter

Often called the greatest of the Protestant schoolmen, Richard Baxter (1615-91) was also one of the pioneers of hymn making and hymn singing. At a time when most of his fellow Puritan clergymen were disapproving music in church, he was its champion. At a time when most of his contemporaries were paraphrasing the Psalms, he boldly wrote original lyrics. Few of Baxter's hymns are now found in use. His "Lord, it belongs not to my care," poignantly expressing Christian trust, has dropped out of hymnals after three centuries of service. However, in the revision by John Hampden Gurney (1802-62), his hymn exalting God's praises in heaven and on earth—"Ye holy angels bright" (E625)—anticipates the style and content of the hymns that soon were to come from the pioneering pen of Isaac Watts. Though generally unrecognized, Baxter is nevertheless a real herald of the modern English hymn.

Samuel Crossman

Samuel Crossman (1624-83) wrote about the intimacies of the faith. Dean of Bristol Cathedral, he is remembered for one poignant hymn on the Passion of our Lord, "My song is love unknown" (E458, L94, P76), suitably set to John Ireland's LOVE UNKNOWN. The naive directness and charm of this hymn strikes an old-world note that undoubtedly contributes to the high regard in which it is still held today.

John Bunyan

John Bunyan (1628-88), the great allegorist who spent much of his adult life in jail as punishment for preaching in a Baptist church, is represented in most hymnals by "He (All) who would valiant be" (E564, E565; L498). Originally "Who would true valour see," this hymn was written as the epilogue to a chapter in Part II of *Pilgrim's Progress* (1684) that follows the conversation between Great Heart and Valiant-for-Truth, and is a summary of all that Bunyan was attempting to say in his epic story. Most likely Bunyan would have been pleased for this poem to be sung, since he cast it in metrical form and was known to have encouraged the singing of hymns in worship. The hymn sounds a needed note of urgency and bold venture which is admirably captured in the bracing vigor and direct rhythms of both ST. DUNSTAN'S by Winfred Douglas (1867-1944) and Vaughan Williams's arrangement of the Sussex folk melody, MONK'S GATE.

Thomas Ken

This period of the development of congregational hymnody is perhaps best represented by Thomas Ken (1637-1711). Ken occupied many positions during a varied career—rector of Little Easton, curate of Brightstone on the Isle of Wight, chaplain to Princess Mary at The Hague, chaplain of the English fleet at Tangiers, Bishop of Bath and Wells. His contributions to hymnody, however, came in connection with his positions at Winchester Cathedral, where he was a member of the cathedral staff as chaplain to the bishop and fellow at Winchester College where he had been a scholar. He prepared for the boys of the college his *Manual of Prayers for the Use of the Scholars of Winchester College* (1674), to which his famous morning and evening hymns were later appended. Ken was well-known in his lifetime for strength of conviction and fidelity to conscience—qualities that ring out in his hymns: "Awake, my soul, and with the sun" (E11, L269, P456), and "All praise to (You) thee, my God, this night" (B449, E43, L278, M682, P542).

Ken also wrote a midnight hymn that has not survived. As the final stanza of all three of these hymns he wrote his well-known doxology beginning "Praise God, from whom all blessings flow" (B253; M94, 95; P592, 593). This doxology has most likely been sung more than any other four lines in the English language to a wide variety of tunes.

Benjamin Keach

An adventurous pioneer in writing hymns with the express purpose of having them sung in public worship was Benjamin Keach (1640-1704), pastor of a Particular Baptist church in the vicinity of London. As early as 1673 he introduced to his congregation the singing of his own hymns at the observance of the Lord's Supper. In view of the fact that Baptists at this time were generally opposed to such a practice, Keach's pioneering effort is all the more remarkable. He defended his church's singing of hymns in *The Breach Repaired in God's Worship, or Singing of Psalms, Hymns and Spiritual Songs Proved to be an Holy Ordinance of Jesus Christ* (1691). He reinforced it with the publication of *Spiritual Melody* (1691), a collection of 300 hymns. Practically all of these hymns were of poor quality. None has survived into current use, but the name of Benjamin Keach remains in the history of congregational hymn singing as a valiant pioneer.

An Anonymous Folk Ballad

Among these early writers of hymns was the anonymous author of

"Jerusalem, my happy home" (B517, E620, L331). This famous 26-stanza hymn on the subject of eternal life was probably written in the early 17th century. It exists in manuscript in the British Library, where it is headed "A Song Mad [sic] by F.B.P. to the tune Diana." Little is known of this tune and its author, but the hymn's fervid images of heaven constitute a delightful mixture of biblical and English garden allusions that Routley calls both its defense and its splendor.[3]

Nahum Tate

The name of Nahum Tate (1652-1715) is to be associated principally with metrical psalmody;[4] however, a supplement to the *New Version of the Psalms by Dr. Brady and Mr. Tate* (1700) included also some paraphrases of passages of Scripture other than the Psalms. Among these was "While shepherds watched their flocks by night" (E94, 95; M236; P58)—Tate's paraphrase of Luke 2:8-14. This is the only "hymn" to survive from the man who in his day wrote considerably for the stage and who later became both poet laureate and royal historiographer. Today he needs no greater monument than "While shepherds watched their flocks by night," one of the finest hymnic descriptions of the appearance of the angels to the shepherds at the birth of Jesus.

THE CONFLUENCE OF THE CALVINIST AND LUTHERAN STREAMS

Lutheran hymnody and Calvinian psalmody—the two major streams of church song stemming from the Reformation—for generations had developed along parallel lines in England, Scotland, and Wales. Finally, in the early 18th century they converged and blended in the person and work of Isaac Watts.

Isaac Watts

As we have seen, Isaac Watts (1674-1748) had his forerunners: Milton and Tate who struggled toward a lyrical freedom within the tradition of scriptural paraphrase; Herbert and Crossman who composed superb devotional verse which on occasion found use in public praise; and Wither and Keach who actually championed the singing of hymns in public worship. Therefore, Watts cannot properly be thought of as the inventor of the English hymn.

[3]Erik Routley, *Hymns and Human Life* (London: John Murray, 1952), 305. The hymn could have existed in Latin originally. A version of it has been attributed to Joseph Bromehead; see Chapter 5, "Early Church and Pre-Reformation Traditions," page 96.
[4]See Chapter 6, "Reformation Traditions," pages 121-122.

© 1980 Charles Massey, Jr.

Issac Watts

Watts possessed both the vision for and the ability to join two main streams—paraphrases of Scripture and devotional lyric poetry—and to produce the two types of true English hymn for which he is justly famous. These two types resulted from his twofold theory of congregational praise:

1. Truly authentic praise for Christian folk had to go beyond the mere words of Scripture to include original expressions of devotion and thanksgiving.

2. If the Psalms were to be used in Christian worship, they must be renovated by giving them Christian content.

Watts put the first part of his theory into practice by the publication of his *Horae Lyricae* (1705) and *Hymns and Spiritual Songs* (1707). From the latter volume came his finest hymns, among which are some of the greatest in the English language:

- "Alas, and did my Savior bleed" (B139, 145; M294, 359; L98, P78)
- "Am I a soldier of the cross" (B481, M511)
- "Come, let us join our cheerful songs" (E374, L254)
- "Come, we that love the Lord" (B524, 525; M732, 733)
- "Come, Holy Spirit, heavenly dove" (E510, P126)
- "I sing the almighty power of God" (B42, E398, M152, P288)[5]
- "Nature with open volume stands" (E434, L119)
- "When I survey the wondrous cross" (B144, E474, L482, M298, 299; P100, 101)

[5]This hymn appeared in *Divine Songs Attempted in Easy Language for the Use of Children* (1715).

Demonstrating the second of his principles, Watts brought the Psalter up to date. He made its use meaningful for the Christian worshipers of 18th-century England and America by carrying this idea of New Testament praise back into the Psalter in his *Psalms of David Imitated in the Language of the New Testament* (1719). This volume contained such great paraphrases as:

- Psalm 23—"My shepherd will supply my need" (B68, E664, P172)
- Psalm 72—"Jesus shall reign" (B587, E544, L530, M157, P423)
- Psalm 90—"O (Our) God, our help in ages past" (B74, E680, L320, M117, P210)
- Psalm 98—"Joy to the world" (B87, E100, L39, M246, P40)
- Psalm 100—"Before Jehovah's (the Lord's) awesome (eternal) throne" (E391, L531)
- Psalm 117—"From all that dwell below the skies" (B13, E380, L550, M101, P229)
- Psalm 118—"This is the day the Lord has made" (B358, E50, M658, P230)
- Psalm 146—"I'll praise my Maker while I've breath" (B35, E429, M60, P253)

With hymns like these, Watts set the model for the English hymn where others had tried and only partially succeeded. He was able to create a position for hymns whereby all hymn writers after him are indebted to him.

While it may be an oversimplification to say that before Watts English churches sang psalms, and after him they sang hymns, it can be affirmed that until Watts the use of true humanly composed hymns was the exception rather than the rule. "To Watts more than to any other man is due the triumph of the hymn in English worship."[6]

The School of Watts

By both teaching and example, Watts gave great impetus to hymn writing in England. His successors in the "school of Watts" include:

Joseph Addison (1672-1719)
"The spacious firmament on high" (E409)
"When all thy (your) mercies, O my God" (E415, L264)

---

[6]Bernard Manning, *The Hymns of Wesley and Watts* (London: The Epworth Press, 1942), 81.

Philip Doddridge (1702-51) [7]
"Awake, my soul, stretch every nerve" (E546)
"Great God, we sing that mighty hand" (P265)
"Hark, the glad sound" (E71, 72; L35)
"O God of Bethel" (E709, P269)
"O happy day that fixed my choice" (B439, M391)

Joseph Hart (1712-68)
"Come, ye sinners, poor and needy" (B323, M340)

Anne Steele [8] *(1716-78)*
"Father of mercies, in thy (your) word" (L240)

Traits of the Watts Hymn

Watts's hymns bear characteristics that left their mark on the form and content of the English hymn for decades.

Form:

1. It is simple: (a) in meter—only common, long, and short meter was used; (b) in vocabulary—predominantly Anglo-Saxon words, with preference for monosyllables.

2. It is striking in its opening line, tersely proclaiming the theme of the entire hymn like a headline.

3. It is frequent in its use of repetition and parallelism, following the structural principle of the Psalms.

4. It is often half-rhymed with liberal use of imperfect rhymes or mere assonances.

5. It is dramatic in its climax, usually expressed in a final stanza.

Content:

1. It is comprehensive in scope and cosmic background. [9]

2. It is Calvinistic in theology: emphasis on doctrines dealing with

[7]See Erik Routley, "The Hymns of Philip Doddridge" in G. F. Nuttall, ed. *Philip Doddridge 1702-51* (London: Independent Press, Ltd., 1951), 46-78, for a thorough analysis of Doddridge's hymns from scriptural, theological, literary, and societal perspectives.

[8]Miss Steele was the foremost of a group of Baptist hymnists, including Benjamin Beddome (1717-93), Samuel Stennett (1727-95) (B219, 521; M724), Robert Robinson (1735-90) (B15, 18; E686, M400, P356), and Samuel Medley (1738-99), who, because their hymns possess a quality unsurpassed before or since, constitute a "Golden Age of Baptist Hymnody."

[9]Watts was the "master of the enormous conception" (a Routley phrase) who in wondering awe sang of the omnipotence of God, the spaciousness of nature, the vastness of time, and the dreadfulness of eternity.

the glory and sovereignty of God, the depravity of human nature, the security of the elect, and the all-sufficient atonement of Jesus Christ on the cross for the sins of humankind.

3. It is Christian in focus: Christ exalted and adored above all else as the very center of worship.

4. It is liturgical in purpose: inspired by the setting of public worship and conceived for the use of the people of the congregation in public praise.

5. It is scriptural in flavor: faithfully paraphrasing Scripture and masterfully incorporating biblical language, allusion, and thought.

With these characteristics the prototype of English hymn was set. Thus was brought into being a class of "religious song which his (Watts's) own ardent faith made devotional, which his manly and lucid mind made simple and strong, which his poetic feeling and craftsmanship made rhythmical and often lyrical, and which his sympathy with people made hymnic."[10]

Isaac Watts is the one man who most changed the course of English-speaking congregational praise. Though his own hymns made rather slow headway in many congregations in the latter part of the 18th century, they "rode to the dominating position they ultimately held on the wings of Revival."[11] And that revival came with the inspired and indefatigable work of the Wesleys. There was, however, an element of reciprocity here, for Watt's hymns were, in turn, a potent factor in promoting that Evangelical Revival.

The Wesleys

The first hymnbook to be published on North American soil for use in Anglican worship was John Wesley's *Collection of Psalms and Hymns* (Savannah, GA, printed in Charleston, SC, 1737).[12] Of its 70 hymns, exactly one half were from Watts, the others were hymns of inner experience and evangelical concern. This early collection showed John's tempering of the Calvinistic stream of hymnody (psalmody) with the warmer current of Lutheran pietistic devotion that had been picked up from the Moravians.

---

[10]Louis F. Benson, *The English Hymn* (London: George H. Doran Co., 1915), 206. This book is still the classic on the subject.

[11]Arthur P. Davis, *Isaac Watts* (London: Independent Press, 1943), 207.

[12]Facsimile reprints: *John Wesley's First Hymnbook: A Collection of Psalms and Hymns* (Charleston: The Dalcho Historical Society, 1964) and (Nashville: The United Methodist Publishing House, 1988).

Moravian Influences

The Moravians exerted powerful influence on the Wesleys. During their voyage to Georgia (1735), John Wesley (1703-91) and his brother Charles (1707-88) were impressed with the devout singing of the Moravians on board. John maintained contact with these Moravians while in Georgia, learning and translating several of their hymns for inclusion in *Psalms and Hymns*, 1737, and later collections. After the Wesleys returned to England, it was perhaps under Moravian influence that they underwent their "heartwarming" and life-changing conversion experiences. Thereafter, they set out on their mission to evangelize England, Wales, and Ireland.

© 1980 Charles Massey, Jr.
John Wesley

Wanting to learn more of Moravian life-style and worship, John Wesley soon journeyed to Herrnhut, the Moravian settlement on the border of Bohemia, where he spent several weeks in fellowship and prayer and again came under the spell of fervent Moravian hymn singing. As a result, John Wesley became an ardent lover of their hymnody while rejecting their pietistic excesses. He was the first important translator of Moravian and other German hymns into English.

Contemporary hymnals are in great debt to John Wesley for these translations of German hymns:

- "Jesus, thy (your) blood and righteousness" (L302)
- "Give to the winds thy fears" (M129, P286)
- "Jesus, thy boundless love to me" (B123, L336, M183, P366)
- "Thee will I love, my strength" (L502)
- "Thou hidden love of God" (M414)

Charles Wesley

Not to overlook his work as translator, tune-book editor, and music critic,[13] John Wesley probably made his main contribution to English hymnody in the collecting, editing, publishing, and promoting of his brother Charles's hymns.

[13]See Carlton R. Young, *Music of the Heart: John and Charles Wesley on Music and Musicians* (Carol Stream: Hope Publishing Company, 1995).

The picture of England during the opening decades of the 18th century was a sorry one—morals had decayed, education was practically nonexistent, sanitation was neglected, literature and the theater were debauched, intemperance was rampant, crime was widespread, politics were corrupt, and the clergy for the most part were idle and uncaring. Into such a despicable scene came the Wesleys like a cleansing fire. The astute organizer and promoter of the movement was John Wesley. Much of the success of this remarkable religious awakening, however, must be attributed to the singing of Charles Wesley's hymns.

These hymns resulted from a genuine conversion experience in Charles's life (actually coming prior to John's). Before this crucial turning point he, like John, was an ordained Anglican clergyman and, together with John, a missionary of sorts for a brief period to the Georgia colony. He was a gifted poet. But it was not until he claimed a deeply personal relationship with Jesus Christ as Redeemer and Lord (Whitsunday, 1738) that the gift of sacred song was released in him. Immediately he wrote what many consider his first hymn, "Where shall my wondering soul begin?" (M342).

"Thereafter hardly a day or an experience passed without its crystallization in verse. The result, 6500 hymns on hundreds of Scripture texts and on every conceivable phase of Christian experience and Methodist theology."[14]

To list the Wesleyan hymns in current use would require too much space. Methodist collections would be expected to contain the most Wesley hymns,[15] but no hymnal could be considered complete without most of these:

- "And can it be that I should gain" (B147, M363)
- "Come, O thou traveler unknown" (E638, 639; M387)
- "Come, thou long-expected Jesus" (B77, E66, L30, M196, P1, 2)
- "Christ the Lord is risen today" (B159, E188, 189; L130, M302, P113)
- "Christ, whose glory fills the skies" (E6, 7; L265, M173, P462, 463)
- "Depth of mercy" (B306, M355)
- "Hail the day that sees him rise" (B165, E214, M312)
- "Hark! the herald angels sing" (B88, E87, L60, M240, P31)
- "Jesus, lover of my soul" (B180, E699, M479, P303)
- "Lo, he (Jesus) comes with clouds descending" (B199, E57, 58; L27, M718, P6)

[14]Edward Albert Bailey, *The Gospel in Hymns* (New York: Charles Scribner's Sons, 1950), 84.
[15]*The United Methodist Hymnal* (M) contains over 50 hymns by the Wesleys.

- "Love divine, all loves excelling" (B208, E657, L315, M384, P376)
- "O for a thousand tongues to sing" (B216, E493, L559, M57, P466)
- "Praise the Lord who reigns above" (B33, M96)
- "Rejoice, the Lord is king" (B197, E481, L171, M715, 716; P155)
- "Soldiers of Christ, arise" (E548, M513)
- "Ye servants of God" (B589, E535, M181, P477)

Wesleyan Hymn Traits
The following characteristics are evident:

Form:
1. The Wesleyan hymn is rich in the variety of poetic meters. Not content to remain with the old psalm meters, Wesley had superb mastery of at least 20 meters.
2. It is so constructed that sound and sense coincide. Wesley rarely fails to make the ends of his lines correspond with natural pauses in thought, thus making them very suitable for singing.[16]
3. It is bold and free in scriptural paraphrase. Rather than keeping strictly to a restatement of the original, Wesley makes imaginative comment on his scriptural passages.
4. It is skillful in the mixture of Anglo-Saxon and Latin vocabulary.
5. It is masterful in the use of the conventional 18th-century literary devices—careful rhyme, repetition, anaphora, chiasmus, and so forth.[17]

Content:
1. The Wesleyan hymn is replete with Christian dogma. Reflecting Moravian influence, Wesley is Arminian in theology. His hymns taken together constitute a body of expertly condensed doctrine, or, in the words of John Wesley, "a body of experimental and practical divinity."[18]
2. It is full of scriptural allusion. Wesley's hymns are always disciplined by biblical truth, and many of them are finely wrought

[16]Manning, *The Hymns of Wesley and Watts*, 59.
[17]See Chapter 1, "The Hymn and Literature," pages 20-24. Two sources for further study in this connection are Henry Bett, *The Hymns of Methodism in Their Literary Relations* (London: Epworth Press, 1945); Bernard L. Manning, *The Hymns of Wesley and Watts* (London: Epworth Press, 1942). See also Austin Lovelace, *The Anatomy of Hymnody* (Nashville: Abingdon Press, 1965; repr. G. I. A. Publications, 1982).
[18]From the famous Preface to *A Collection of Hymns for Use of the People Called Methodists* (London: 1780).

biblical mosaics.[19]

3. It is expressive of passionate Christian experience. Every mood of the Christian soul is reflected with a fervor which is free of vulgarity and mawkish excess. The predominant note is one of joy and confidence.

4. It is simple and smooth, speaking directly of important matters dealing with God and the souls of human beings. With disarming simplicity and directness, Wesley confronted plain men and women with the central concerns of the faith. The hymns are democratic in design and evangelistic in purpose.

5. It is mystical, glowing with a luminous quality transfiguring history and experience.[20] This comes in the audacity of intimacy with which Wesley talks to God as friend—a quality that makes his hymns timeless and universal in their appeal.

Methodist Tunes

Because his restless genius expressed itself in meters never before utilized by hymnists, Charles Wesley posed a challenge to writers of hymn tunes. John Wesley, who, along with Martin Luther before him and General Booth (Salvation Army) after him, seemed to believe that the devil should not have all the good tunes, constantly looked for music wherever he could find it. Therefore, by challenging and encouraging composers, both amateur and professional, the Wesleyan Revival unleashed a flood of new hymn tunes, some of which have proved to be of permanent value.

Many of these "old Methodist tunes" were highly florid and repetitive; others, however, being intended for "all sorts and conditions of men," were simple and folk-like in style.[21]

---

[19]See Bailey, *The Gospel in Hymns*, 95-97, where the scriptural tapestry of "Love divine, all loves excelling" is unraveled.

[20]Manning, *The Hymns of Wesley and Watts*, 29-30.

[21]The tunes that Wesley and his followers used are those:
1. of straightforward psalm type: DUKE STREET (B587, E544, L352, M101, P307); ST. THOMAS (B354, E411, L368, M540, P441),
2. of suave, flowing type: RICHMOND (E72, M417, P233); SAGINA (B147, M363),
3. in architectonic structure: DARWALL (B197, E625, L261, M715, P155); GOPSAL (E481, M716),
4. of florid nature: DIADEM (B200, M155, P143); EASTER HYMN (B159, E207, L151, M302, P123),
5. in the folk style of the Moravians: AMSTERDAM (B33, M96); SAVANNAH (E188, M385). These two tunes, together with some 40 others, were published in a small tunebook, *A Collection of Tunes Set to Music as they are commonly sung at the Foundery*. See a facsimile reprint of this "Foundery Collection," bound with a reprint of Wesley's *Collection of Psalms and Hymns* (Charles-town, 1737), with a preface by Rev. G. Osborn (London: T. Woolner, n.d.). A reprint (no publisher or place) was made by Bryan F. Spinney in 1981. See also Carlton R. Young, *Music of the Heart* (Carol Stream: Hope Publishing, 1995).

But whether they are of the sophisticated tradition of Purcell and Handel (Handel set three Wesley hymns.[22]) or of the popular tradition (sung by the folk in the fields and even in the jails!), many of the tunes are unforgettable. To hum or whistle them brought to mind the memorable texts to which they were matched; and one could again be confirmed in the faith. This was a distinctly Wesleyan use of hymns.[23]

> "These hymns were composed in order that the men and women whom Hogarth depicted in his terrible pictures might sing their way not only into experience but also into knowledge; that the cultured might have their culture baptized and the ignorant might be led into truth by the gentle hand of melody and rhyme. This disciplined fervor was what made it possible for English hymnody to have a classical age before it fell into corruption and decay."[24]

It was this fervor that helped re-Christianize Britain, providing sufficient personal faith and moral backbone to save it from the agonies that overtook France during the French Revolution.

To summarize: the Calvinist stream (aside from the metrical psalm) produced the liturgical hymn of Watts; the pietistic Lutheran stream nourished the evangelical hymn of the Wesleys. Together, these two types of classic hymnody "reformed the Reformation."[25]

FULL COURSE: THE EVANGELICAL REVIVAL

While the Wesleys dominated their age, and most of their contemporaries and followers are dwarfed by comparison, the evangelical hymn stream was also fed by other swift-flowing tributaries of revival inspiration.

George Whitefield and the Calvinistic Methodists

The first of these sources was the powerful preacher, George Whitefield (1714-70). After the Wesley brothers, Whitefield was the third most important herald of the revival movement. A member with the Wesleys of the famous Oxford Holy Club (dubbed "Methodist" by its detractors), he was

---

[22]See John Wilson, "Handel's tunes for Charles Wesley's hymns" *The Hymn Society of Great Britain and Ireland Bulletin* 163 (May, 1985): 32-37.
[23]See Carlton R. Young "John Wesley and the Music of Hymns" in *Companion to the United Methodist Hymnal* (Nashville: Abingdon Press, 1993), 11-14.
[24]Erik Routley, *Hymns and Human Life* (London: John Murray, 1952), 71-72.
[25]Martha Winburn England and John Sparrow, *Hymns Unbidden* (New York Public Library, 1966), 40.

spiritually reborn before the Wesleys' conversions. It was also he (possibly because of his Welsh connections) who led the way in England into preaching in the open air after the established churches shut their doors to him.

Although not a hymn writer himself, Whitefield did edit an influential hymnbook.[26] He also gave great impetus to the Welsh revival, which thrived on fervent hymn singing. Whitefield's principal contributions to hymnody came after he broke with the Wesleys for theological reasons to become a leader among the Calvinistic Methodists in the west of England and in Wales.

William Williams

The chief of the Welsh revival hymnists was William Williams (1717-91), who produced 800 hymns in Welsh and over a hundred in English. His greatest hymn is "Guide me, O Thou great Jehovah" (B56, E690, L343, M127, P281). It is a hymn supremely representative of Welsh religious verse of his time. Its spirit, character, nature imagery, and emotional style is very much like that of Hebrew poetry. Known as "the Welsh Watts" and "the sweet singer of Wales," Williams is little sung today except for this masterpiece.

The greatest legacy of the Welsh to hymnody is the appealing folk-like character of their tunes, supported by strong fundamental harmonies to give them an admirable congregational quality and provide solid, deep-rooted and vigorous singing. The 20th century has discovered the enduring qualities of such tunes as: HYFRYDOL (B77, E460, L158, M196, P2), CWM RHONDDA (B56, E690, L343, M428, P420), ST. DENIO (B6, E423, L526, M103, P263), EBENEZER (TON-Y-BOTEL) (E381, L233, M108, P129), and LLANGLOFFAN (E68, M425, P15).[27] Welsh tunes possess a singable quality that renders them durable under hard use. They continue to be identified with the hearty kind of congregational singing that is characteristic of spiritual revival.

John Cennick

In Whitefield's circle was John Cennick (1718-55). He was typical of many in that age whose denominational loyalty swung indecisively from one religious group to another. In his brief life he first followed the Wesleys, then Whitefield, but ended as minister among the Moravians. He is the author of the so-called "Wesley Graces"—"Be present at our table, Lord (M621) and

---

[26]*Hymns for Social Worship...* (London: William Strahan, 1753) contained Whitefield's familiar alteration of Wesley's original "Hark, how all the welkin rings."
[27]Tunes now used from Wales, however, are primarily products of the 19th century (CWM RHONDDA excepted). See Chapter 9, "Cultural Perspectives," pages 225-227. The most authoritative source on Welsh hymn texts and tunes in English is Alan Luff, *Welsh Hymns and Their Tunes* (Carol Stream: Hope Publishing Company, 1990).

"We thank thee, Lord, for this our food." His most-used hymns are "Children of the heavenly King" and the original form of Charles Wesley's "Lo, he comes with clouds descending."[28]

Thomas Olivers

Converted by Whitefield's preaching, Thomas Olivers (1725-99), a Welsh shoemaker, became one of Whitefield's itinerant preachers, later switching his allegiance to the Wesleys. In hymnody he is remembered for his Christianization of the 13 articles of the Jewish Yigdal (a sort of creedal doxology) which he heard chanted to its traditional melody one Friday evening in the Great Synagogue, Duke's Place, London. "The God of Abraham praise" (B34, E401, L544, M116, P488), the opening line of Olivers' version, continues to be sung in England and the United States.[29]

Lady Huntingdon

A second rallying point for the Evangelical Revival centered in the person and work of Selina (1707-91), Countess of Huntingdon. She was a brilliant noblewoman who used her wealth and influence to sponsor itinerant preachers and patronize hymnists and musicians. She edited hymnals and commissioned the outstanding musician, Felice de Giardini, to compose tunes for the numerous chapels she either purchased or paid to have erected.[30]

Edward Perronet

One of Selina's protégés was Edward Perronet (1726-92), a man of French Huguenot ancestry. Though brought up in the Church of England, Perronet worked energetically with the Wesleys for eight years. A volatile and strong-willed young man, he broke with them and served for a while as a chaplain for Lady Huntingdon, eventually becoming an independent pastor in Canterbury.

Perronet's hymnic fame rests on his masterful "All hail the power of Jesus' name" (B202, E450, L328, M154, P142), often considered the grandest of all church songs on the lordship of Jesus Christ. This popular hymn is sung to

[28]Cennick is treated insightfully as a minor master of simple, tasteful verse in Erik Routley, I'll Praise My Maker (London: Independent Press, 1951), 248-258.
[29]In the late 19th century, a complete recasting of the Yigdal in a metrical version more faithful to the Hebrew was done through the collaboration of three American clergymen: Rabbi Max Landsberg and two Unitarian ministers, Newton Mann and William C. Gannett, all of Rochester, New York. The Mann-Gannett version is most often found now in hymnals, but with Olivers's original opening line. However, L544 retains the greater part of Olivers's work.
[30]See the informative article by S. E. Boyd Smith, "The Effective Countess: Lady Huntingdon and the 1780 edition of A Select Collection of Hymns", The Hymn 44, 3 (July, 1993): 26-32.

three well-known tunes: MILES LANE—its first tune—by the young Canterbury organist, William Shrubsole (1760-1806) (B201, E451, L329); CORONATION—the oldest American hymn tune in continuous use—by Yankee tunesmith, Oliver Holden (1765-1844) (B202, E450, L328, M154, P142); and DIADEM—a florid "Methodist tune"—by the 19th-century lay musician, James Ellor (1819-99) (B200, M155, P143). Perronet's hymn was considerably altered by the prominent Baptist preacher, historian, and editor, John Rippon (1751-1836), who is credited with adding the lines which now almost always constitute the final stanza:

> "O that with yonder sacred throng
> We at his feet may fall!
> We'll join the everlasting song,
> And crown him Lord of all."[31]

Thomas Haweis

A second follower of Lady Huntingdon was Thomas Haweis (1734-1820), who served as a manager of her chapels, in addition to holding various posts in the established church. Haweis was an important promoter of hymn singing and the author of a collection of hymns, *Carmina Christo*, or *Hymns to the Saviour* (1792). He was also assistant for a time to Martin Madan, chaplain of Lock Hospital chapel, and one of the founders of the London Missionary Society. The most musical of Lady Huntingdon's chaplains and the composer of several tunes, Haweis is remembered mainly for the suave "Methodist tune" RICHMOND (E72, M417, P233).

Olney Hymns

A third source of Evangelical Revival hymns emerged within the established church under the robust leadership of the Olney curate, John Newton (1725-1807). The story of Newton's early profligate career as a slave trader, his miraculous conversion, and his late flowering in the Anglican ministry is one of the great romances of Christian hymnic history.[32]

Newton is remembered for his hymns written for the epoch-making little

---

[31]Rippon figures prominently in British hymnic circles because of his *A Selection of Hymns from the Best Authors* (London, 1787) and its sequel, *A Selection of Psalm and Hymn Tunes from the Best Authors* (London, 1791), both of which were widely used in America, as well as England.
[32]See a dramatic portrayal of the life and work of Newton based on his private journals by John Pollock, *Amazing Grace: John Newton's Story* (San Francisco: Harper and Row Publishers, 1981). For a shorter account with copious annotations and illustrative material, see Bernard Braley, *Hymnwriters 2* (London: Stainer and Bell, 1989), 1-57.

collection *Olney Hymns* (1779), in which he collaborated with his poet friend, William Cowper. *Olney Hymns* was compiled (according to the custom of local hymnbooks prevailing at that time) for the parish church at Olney, that is, "for the use of plain people," who gathered weekly in the parish house for informal prayer and praise.

Newton's hymns express a virile confidence in God and a passionate zeal for souls. They were written to be sung in corporate worship. Those hymns for which he is remembered include:

- "Amazing grace! how sweet the sound" (B330, E671, L448, M378, P280)
- "Glorious things of thee are spoken" (B398, E522, 523; M731, P446); (Glories of your name are spoken" L358)
- "How sweet the name of Jesus sounds" (B453, E644, L345)
- "May the grace of Christ our Savior" (E351); (third stanza of "God, the Father of Your People" B382)
- "On what has now been sown" (L261)

William Cowper (1731-1800), who excelled in lyrics of personal devotion, although suffering periodic lapses into depression and insanity, contributed 67 hymns to the book. With characteristic industry, Newton wrote 281 hymns for the collection. Like Watts, Newton was a Calvinist. He wrote his best hymns from a churchly intent. On the other hand, personal experience and evangelical concern are clearly expressed in his hymns still sung today.

Cowper's hymns are illustrative of the hesitating faith of the solitary Christian.[33] Those in common use include:

- "God moves (O God,) in a mysterious way" (B73, E677, L483, P270)
- "Heal us, Emmanuel, hear our prayer" (M266)
- "O for a closer walk with God" (E683, 684; P396, 397)
- "Sometimes a light surprises" (E667)
- "There is a fountain filled with blood" (B142, M622)

---

[33]In *I'll Praise My Maker: Studies in English Classical Hymnody* (London: Independent Press Ltd., 1951), 61-144, Erik Routley gives a fuller treatment to Cowper and his hymns than to any of the 10 other hymnwriters with whom he deals. A more general human interest approach to Cowper is made by Bernard Braley in *Hymnwriters 1* (London: Stainer and Bell, 1987), 29-53.

Augustus Toplady

One hymnist influenced at many points by the Evangelical Revival, but somewhat apart from both the Wesleyans and the Anglicans, was Augustus Toplady (1740-78). Nourished in the established church, he was converted to Methodism but later turned Calvinist and entered the Anglican ministry as one of the earliest members of the Evangelical (Low Church) Party that included John Newton, Thomas Haweis, and others. Toplady's vituperative theological battles with the Wesleys is one of the most interesting episodes in British hymnic history.[34] Most of that controversy is now forgotten and the memorable residue is Toplady's world-famous penitential hymn "Rock of Ages, cleft for me" (B342, E685, L327, M361). Despite some confusing images and a musical setting that has taken a toll on the hymn's once great popularity, it continues to have great power in voicing a universal human need for confessing sin and receiving God's forgiveness.

John Fawcett

A Baptist contemporary of Toplady was John Fawcett (1740-1817), whose fidelity to his struggling congregation at Wainsgate, in spite of opportunities to leave for more secure positions in London and Bristol, is of special romantic interest. Although greatly impressed by Whitefield's preaching, Fawcett was connected for a while with the Methodists. Later, he was ordained a Baptist minister and spent his life as a clergyman and educator. Fawcett is remembered for two hymns of parting: "Blest be the tie that binds" (B387, L370, M557, P438) and "Lord, dismiss us with thy blessing" (E344, L259, M671, P538). The latter hymn is more precisely a dismissal hymn, but the former is also frequently used at the end of worship. Together, they bring lasting recognition to a dissenting minister who, during his lifetime, sought little of it.

Anonymous Hymns

Several of the hymnic masterpieces of this revival period were produced anonymously, including:

- "Come, thou almighty King" (B247, E365, L522, M61, P139)
- "How firm a foundation" (B338, E636, L507, M529, P361)
- "Praise the Lord! ye (O) heavens adore him" (B36, E373, L540)

[34]See Chapter 4, "The Hymn and Theology."

The tunes to which these hymns are usually set furnish a cross section of the typical musical resources for evangelical hymnody. "Come, thou almighty King" is usually found with ITALIAN HYMN (MOSCOW) by Felice de Giardini (1716-96), Italian composer and violinist. Befriended by Lady Huntingdon, Giardini wrote several tunes for the famous Lock Hospital Collection compiled by Martin Madan (1726-90).[35] This is the only tune from that collection which has survived. FOUNDATION, sung to "How firm a foundation," is an anonymous American tune representative of a rich shape-note tradition that matched folk melodies to scores of hymns from the Evangelical Revival.[36] HYFRYDOL, often found with "Praise the Lord, ye heavens adore him," is a tune composed about 1830 by Roland (or Rowland) Hugh Pritchard (1811-87), a prominent Welsh amateur musician.

THE ROMANTIC FLOOD

Charles Wesley pioneered in bringing the hymn into the domain of true poetry. While much of what he wrote was rhymed dogma for teaching new converts, his muse often took wings because he was blessed with the natural gifts of a poet and was trained in the disciplines of 18th-century literary expression. Outside of Methodism, William Cowper was the poet of the Evangelical Revival. His sensitive gifts often expressed the deep personal aspects of the Christian faith.

But the full acceptance of poetic emotion into hymnic expression had to await the flowing of that great stream in English literature known as the Romantic Movement. It broke over England at the turn into the 19th-century with such inspired works as the *Lyrical Ballads* (1798) of William Wordsworth, *Childe Harold* (1812) of Lord Byron, and similar masterpieces by the "Romantics"—Scott, Coleridge, Southey, Shelley, and Keats.

The principal characteristics of the works of the "romantic" hymn writers were the lyric expression of emotion, the imaginative description of natural beauty, and a careful regard for elegance of form. These were incorporated in English hymnody through the work of Bishop Reginald Heber of the established church, and James Montgomery, a layman connected with the Moravians, the Methodists, and the Anglicans.

---

[35]Madan is probably the alterer of the hymn "Hail, thou once despised Jesus" (E495, M325), also attributed to his contemporary, John Bakewell (1721-1819).
[36]Concerning American shape-note hymnody, see Chapter 8, "American Traditions," pages 181-185.

Reginald Heber

The movement toward the "literary hymn" was led by Bishop Heber (1783-1826) in his attempt to compile a national church hymnal made up of the contributions of people like Robert Southey (1724-1843), Sir Walter Scott (1771-1832), and other romantic poets. Until his untimely death in India, Heber had gathered over a hundred hymns, more than half being his own, that were published posthumously in 1827. The three distinguishing characteristics of this collection were: (1) its hymns were arranged in the order of the Christian year; (2) they

© 1980 Charles Massey, Jr.

Reginald Heber

were emotionally sensitive, albeit restrained ; and (3) they were couched in romantic images and elegant forms, thus joining the mainstream of Romantic Literature. These mark a significant development in the evolution of the English hymn and are aptly demonstrated by Heber's own hymns.

His "Brightest and best of the stars (sons) of the morning" (E117, 118, L84, P67)—(for Epiphany); "The Son of God goes forth to war" (L84)—(for St. Stephen's Day, December 26); and "Bread of the world in mercy broken" (E361, M624, P502)—(for communion), show his concern to make hymns fit the various emphases of the Prayer Book and the ecclesiastical year. Second, as evidence of his concern for sober restraint, his "Holy, holy, holy" (B2, E362, L165, M64, P138) praises not the intimate God of the mystics, nor the fearful God of the Calvinists, but the transcendent Lord "perfect in power, in love and purity." Third, his "God, that madest (who made the) earth and heaven" (L281, M688) and "From Greenland's icy mountains" (the first real missionary hymn after Watts's "Jesus shall reign") beautifully exhibit his romantic use of the imagery of nature as background for hymnic thought.[37]

James Montgomery

While considered no greater poet than many of his contemporaries, James Montgomery (1771-1854), journalist of Scottish Moravian background, hymnal

[37]An informal attractive study of Heber, his hymns, and their contexts is Bernard Braley, *Hymnwriters 1* (London: Stainer and Bell, 1987), 55-100.

editor, and social prophet, nevertheless had the poetic gift which expresses the inner life in forms of beauty suitable for the corporate worship of ordinary Christians. Montgomery's hymns possess something of the enthusiasm and subjectivity of the Wesleys combined with the churchliness and objectivity of Watts. Not only have such qualities contributed to the continuous use of Montgomery's hymns, but one scholar thinks they entitle him to be called "the typical English hymnwriter" of the 19th century.[38] Consequently, Montgomery's hymns continue to wear well. Their number and current usefulness demonstrate the claim made for him as "the greatest of Christian lay hymnwriters."[39] His hymns sung today include:

- "Angels, from the realms of glory" (B94, E93, L50, M220, P22)
- "Be known to us in breaking bread" (P505)
- "Go to dark Gethsemane" (B150, E171, L109, M290, P97)
- "Hail to the Lord's (All hail to God's) Anointed" (E616, L87, M203, P205)
- "In the hour of trail" (L106)
- "Prayer is the soul's sincere desire" (M492)
- "Stand up and bless the Lord" (B30, M662, P491)

Heber and Montgomery represent the two principal streams that moved 19th-century British hymnody on its triumphant way. Following Watts, Heber was a continuing fountainhead of the churchly stream of hymnody. Montgomery, following more closely the model of the Wesleys, fed the evangelical stream with his hymns of personal renewal and devotion.

THE EVANGELICAL STREAM

The pioneering work of Heber, though seminal for the onrush of liturgical hymnody soon to come within Anglicanism, came while evangelical hymnody was in full stream. Appearing first among the independents, the evangelical hymn that emphasized individual experience also won its way gradually into the established church use. In the early decades of the 19th century, no strong line of demarcation developed between Anglicans and Dissenters insofar as a great many of the hymns they produced are concerned.

It has already been noted that the Wesleys lived and died as ministers of the

[38]Ibid., 125. Routley also furnishes an insightful critical appreciation of some 35 of Montgomery's hymns in *I'll Praise My Maker*, 179-217. For an extensive recent study with pictures and in scrapbook format, see Bernard Braley, *Hymnwriters 2* (London: Stainer and Bell, 1989), 59-119.
[39]Routley, *Hymns and Human Life*, 124.

Church of England and that Newton, Cowper, and Toplady wrote their hymns of individual piety in connection with that church. It was not long before scores of clergymen (Anglican and Dissenting) and many lay persons were also writing hymns of personal devotion. Although many of the Oxford Movement (some even reverting to the Roman Catholic Church) produced a high churchly hymnody (*see listing to follow*), many gave expression to deeply felt personal emotion, thus making their hymns hardly distinguishable from those of the Evangelicals. From a long list of hymnists representing widely differing theological backgrounds, the following gave voice to expressions of personal experience and evangelical feeling:

Clergy

John Ernest Bode (1816-74), Anglican
- "O Jesus, I have promised" (B276, E655, L503, M396, P388, 389)

Horatius Bonar (1808-89), Scottish Free Church (Presbyterian)
- "Blessing and honor and glory and power" (L525, P147)
- "I heard the voice of Jesus say" (B551, E692, L497)
- "I lay my sins on Jesus" (B272, L305)
- "Here, O my (our) Lord, I (we) see thee (you) (E318, L211, M623, P520)

George Croly (1780-1860), Anglican
- "Spirit of God, descend upon my heart" (B245, L486, M500, P326)

Frederick William Faber (1814-63), Anglican, Roman Catholic
- "Faith of our fathers, living still" (B352, E558, L500, M710)
- "My God, how wonderful thou (You) art (are)" (B11, E643, L524)
- "There's a wideness in God's mercy" (B25, E469, 470; L290, M121, P298)

Edwin Hatch (1835-89), Anglican
- "Breathe on me, Breath of God" (B241, E508, L488, M420, P316)

Thomas Kelly (1769-1855), Anglican, Independent
- "Look, ye saints (oh, look)! the sight is glorious" (B169, L156)
- "The head that once was crowned with thorns" (E483, L173, M326, P149)
- "We sing the praise of him who died" (E471, L344)

Henry Francis Lyte (1793-1847), Anglican
- "Abide with me" (B63, E662, L272, M700, P543)
- "God of mercy, God of grace" (E538, P203)
- "Jesus, I my cross have taken" (B471)
- "Praise, my soul, the king of heaven" (B32, E410, L549, M66, P478, 479)

George Matheson (1842-1906), Scottish Free Church
- "Make me a captive, Lord" (B278, M421, P378)
- "O love that wilt not let me go" (B292, L324, M480, P384)

Lay Persons
Sarah Flower Adams (1805-48), Unitarian
- "Nearer, my God, to thee" (B458, M528)

Cecil Frances Alexander (1818-95), Anglican
- "All things bright and beautiful" (B46, E405, M147, P267)
- "Jesus calls us o'er the tumult" (B293, E549, 550; L494, M398)
- "Once in royal David's city" (E102, M250, P49)
- "There is a green hill far away" (E167, L114)

John Bowring (1792-1872), Unitarian
- "In the cross of Christ I glory" (B554, E441, 442; L104, M295, P84)
- "Watchman, tell us of the night" (E640, P20)

Elizabeth Cecilia Clephane (1830-69), Scottish Free Church
- "Beneath the cross of Jesus" (B291, E498, L107, M297, P92)

Charlotte Elliott (1789-1871), Anglican
- "Just as I am, without one plea" (B303, 307; E693, L296, M357, P370)

Arabella Katherine Hankey (1834-1911), Anglican
- "I love to tell the story" (B572, L390, M156)

Frances Ridley Havergal (1836-79), Anglican
- "I am trusting you, Lord Jesus" (L460)
- "I gave my life for thee" (B606)
- "Like a river glorious" (B58)
- "Lord, speak to me (us), that I (we) may speak" (B568, L403, M463, P426)
- "Take my life and let it (that I may) be consecrated" (B277, 283; E707, L406, M399, P391)

Thomas Moore (1779-1852), Roman Catholic
- "Come, ye disconsolate" (B67, M510)

Dorothy Thrupp (1779-1847), Anglican
- "Savior, like a shepherd lead us" (B61, E708, L481, M381, P387)

Anna Laetitia Waring (1823-1910), Anglican
- "In heavenly love abiding" (B348)

It should be noted that many in the previous listing were women, who with some exceptions, were evangelicals connected in some way to the families of clergy. Those in the established church, together with their men folk, constituted a Low Church party throughout the 19th century which gave great impetus to personal Bible study and prayer. This explains the themes of personal piety that permeate their hymnody.

THE CHURCHLY STREAM

Until the early years of the 19th century, hymn singing had not been an integral part of the official Service Orders for

© 1995 Charles Massey, Jr.

Frances Ridley Havergal

the worship of the Church of England. At the time of the English Reformation in the 16th century, Archbishop Cranmer dispensed with hymns altogether.[40] His rubrics for the *Book of Common Prayer,* insofar as music was concerned, provided only for the singing of canticles, psalms, and anthems.

Actually, however, the singing of hymns was allowed in public worship as a result of the work of the hymnic giants, Watts and Wesley. Through a liberal interpretation of psalmody, Watts's Christianized Psalms were admitted. It was then only a step from the use of his free psalm paraphrases to his true hymns, especially since they were liberally laced with Scripture. Moreover, the Methodist hymnic cause brought infiltration from within. The Wesleys remained clergymen of the established church to the end of their lives, and their revival enthusiasm was shared by other ministers of that communion. As indicated before, these clergymen constituted a lively Evangelical wing (including George Whitefield, Martin Madan, John Newton, Augustus Toplady, Roland Hill, and others), in which hymn singing was welcome.

Though hymns were officially proscribed in the public worship of their church, Anglicans were encouraged to use hymns in other ways. For instance, paraliturgical services in which hymn singing was fostered sprang up within the established church. The *Olney Hymns* were intended by Newton and Cowper for prayer meetings during the week in the Olney manor house rather than for Morning and Evening Prayer on Sunday in the parish church. The chapels of charity hospitals were also centers of hymnic activity.[41] And the early Methodist meetings, regardless of where they were held, were considered extraliturgical services of the church.

Many Anglicans, therefore, were gradually won over to this great interest in hymns and their singing. In the first decades of the 19th century, numerous individuals made and published collections of hymns for use in the parish churches.

The Oxford Movement

The popularity of the evangelical type hymn caused considerable alarm among the leaders of the Establishment. Some wanted to counteract it with hymns expressing the ideals of the Oxford Movement, including lyrics that expressed the various emphases of the Christian year in the *Book of Common Prayer.*

[40]The one exception was the *Veni, Creator Spiritus.*
[41]The Lock Hospital and the Foundling Hospital were two of the most prominent charity institutions in whose chapels hymn singing was not only allowed, but for which now well-known collections of hymns were published. See, for example, the source of "Praise the Lord! ye (O) heavens adore him" (B36, E373, L540).

The Oxford Movement[42] was a High Church school of thought which sought to restore the Anglican church to the glory of former times when it reigned supreme in all matters temporal and spiritual. John Keble and John Henry Newman, two of the prominent leaders of the movement, felt that the drastic severing with the past which the Reformation had appeared to effect, had cut the English church off from the Holy Catholic Church. Thus, in an attempt to restore liturgical and apostolic continuity, they sought to recover some of the lost treasures of the Breviaries and Service Books of the early Greek and Latin churches. It was under the impetus of this Oxford Movement,[43] with its Romantic reverence for history, that Greek, Latin, and German hymns in translation entered the mainstream of English hymnody.[44] In many ways they served as models for the original hymns the Oxford Reformers were beginning to write. The High Churchmen and members of their families soon were producing a steady stream of liturgical hymnody.

Listed below are those hymnists whose verses are still sung, with an indication of the liturgical purpose for which their hymns were written.

Clergy
Henry Alford (1810-71)
- "Come, ye (you) thankful people, come" (B637, E290, L407, M694, P551)—(Harvest Thanksgiving)
- "We walk by faith, and not by sight" (E209, P399)—(Feast of St. Thomas)

Henry Williams Baker (1821-77)[45]
- "O God of love, O King of peace" (B619, E578, L414, P295)—(For Times of Trouble)
- "The King of love my shepherd is" (E645, 646; L456, M138, P171)—(For General Use or Funerals)

[42]Erik Routley suggests the movement should be called the London Movement because it was there that much of the early action centered. See his *A Short History of English Church Music* (London: Mowbray's, 1977), 55.

[43]Also called the Tractarian Movement since its promoters urged their views in a series of *Tracts for the Times*, the logic of which drove many into the Roman Catholic Church. John Keble has been called the spark plug of the movement as a result of the famous Assize Sermon he preached at Oxford in 1833. See Albert E. Bailey, *The Gospel in Hymns* (New York: Charles Scribner's Sons, 1950), 161-4, 186-90.

[44]See the sections dealing with these traditions in Chapters 5 and 6. John Wesley should be remembered for pioneering the translation of German hymns in the 18th century. However, the main flow of translation from this language did not come until the 19th century with the work of Catherine Winkworth and others.

[45]For an interesting study of Baker with particular focus on his work with *Hymns Ancient and Modern*, see Bernard Braley, *Hymnwriters 2*, 121-145.

Sabine Baring-Gould (1834-1924)
- "Now the day is over" (E42, L280, P541) (Evening)
- "Onward, Christian soldiers" (B493, E562, L509, M575)—
  (Processional)
- "The angel Gabriel from heaven came" (E265, P16)—
  (Annunciation)

John Ellerton (1826-93)[46]
- "Savior, again to thy (your) dear name we raise" (E345, L262,
  M663, P539)—(Choir Festival)
- "The day Thou gavest (you gave us), Lord, is (has) ended"
  (E24, L274, M690, P546)—(Evening Vespers)

William Walsham How (1823-97)[46]
- "For all the saints who from their labors rest" (B355, E287,
  L174, M711, P526)—(All Saints' Day)
- "O Word of God incarnate" (L231, M598, P327); "O Christ,
  the Word Incarnate" (E632)—(The Scriptures)
- "We give thee but thine own" (B609, L410, P428)—(Offertory)

John Keble (1792-1866)
- "Blest are the pure in heart" (E656)—(Presentation of Christ
  in the Temple)
- "God, our Lord, a king remaining" (P213)—(Christ the King)
- "New every morning is the love" (E10)—(Morning)

Henry Hart Milman (1791-1868)
- "Ride on! ride on in majesty" (E156, L121, P90, 91)—
  (Palm Sunday)

John Samuel Bewley Monsell (1811-75)
- "Fight the good fight" (E552, 553; L461, P307)—
  (19th Sunday after Trinity)
- "Sing to the Lord of harvest" (B641, L412)—
  (Harvest Thanksgiving)

---

[46]For delightful human interest treatments of both Ellerton and How and their hymns see Bernard Braley, *Hymnwriters 1*, 101-193.

Edward Hayes Plumptre (1821-91)[47]
- "Rejoice, ye pure in heart" (B39, E556, 557; L553, M160, 161; P145, 146)—(Choir Festival)

Walter Chalmers Smith (1824-1908) (Divine service)
- "Immortal, invisible, God only wise" (B6, E423, L526, M103, P263)

Samuel John Stone (1839-1900)
- "The church's one foundation" (B350, E525, L369, M545, P442)—(The Creed)

Christopher Wordsworth (1807-1885)
- "Alleluia, alleluia! Hearts and voices heavenward rise" (E191)—(Easter)
- "Gracious Spirit, Holy Ghost" (E612, P318)—(Pentecost)
- "O day of rest and (of radiant) gladness" (E48, L251, P470)—(Sunday)
- "Songs of thankfulness and praise" (E135, L90)—(Epiphany)

Lay Persons
Matthew Bridges (1800-94)
- "Crown Him with many crowns" (B161, E494, L170, M327, P151)—(Coronation)

William Chatterton Dix (1837-98)
- "As with gladness men of old" (B117, E119, L82, P63)—(Epiphany)
- "What child is this" (B118, E115, L40, M219, P53)—(Christmas)

Robert Grant (1779-1838)
- "O (Oh) worship the King" (B16, E388, L548, M73, P476)—(Divine service)

Dorothy Frances Bloomfield Gurney (1858-1932)
- "O perfect love, all human thought transcending" (B512, L287, M645, P533)—(Wedding)

[47]An account of the life and varied scholarly interests of Plumptre is given in Bernard Braley, Hymn-writers 3 (London: Stainer and Bell, 1991), 37-69.

Folliott Sandford Pierpoint (1835-1917)
- "For the beauty of the earth" (B44, E416, L561, M92, P473)—
  (Communion)

William Whiting (1825-78)
- "Eternal Father, strong to save" (B69, E608, L467, P562)—
  (Mariners)

Hymns Ancient and Modern

Aside from these individual achievements, the greatest hymnic legacy of the Oxford Movement was *Hymns Ancient and Modern* (1859-61), a collection that reflected four decades' activity in the production of individual hymnals for parochial use.[48] The sheer number of these collections prevented most of them from being successful. Recognizing the need for unanimity in the church's hymnic usage, certain leaders—chief among them being Henry W. Baker (1821-77)—united to compile one book which would command general confidence. An appeal was made to the clergy and their publishers to withdraw their individual collections and to support this new combined venture. The result was *Hymns Ancient and Modern*, which experienced immediate and overwhelming success, becoming possibly the most popular English hymnal ever published.

This collection, which has gone through many subsequent editions[49] in its blending of the old and the new, set a standard to which most later responsible hymnals have adhered. Many of the previously-listed hymns first appeared in *Hymns Ancient and Modern*. It contained also the finest work of those leaders who were translators from the Latin, Greek, and German languages.[50]

The musical character of this pivotal collection also contributed to its popularity. Under the musical editorship of William H. Monk, composers contributed a type of hymn tune which (whatever may be its artistic merits) satisfied the musical tastes of the churchgoers of the last four decades of the 19th century and beyond. Consequently, this book (including its later editions) is the original source for such now well-known Victorian tunes by the following composers:

[48]See John Julian, *Dictionary of Hymnology* (London: John Murray, 1907), 334-38 for the listings of over one hundred hymnals compiled in this period.
[49]The history of the editions of this influential book up until its publication can be read in W. K. Lowther-Clarke, *A Hundred Years of Hymns Ancient and Modern* (London: Clowes, 1960). See also: *Historical Companion to Hymns Ancient and Modern*, (London: Clowes, 1962).
[50]See above in Chapters 5, 6 and 7 under Greek, Latin, and German hymnody concerning the contributions of outstanding translators such as Edward Caswall, John M. Neale, Jane Borthwick, Catherine Winkworth, among others.

John Bacchus Dykes (1823-76)
- DOMINUS REGIT ME (E646, P174)
- MELITA (B69, E608, L294, P562)
- NICAEA (B2, E362, L165, M64, P138)
- VOX DILECTI (B551)

William H. Monk (1823-89)
- DIX (adapted) (B44, E119, L82, M92, P63)
- EVENTIDE (B63, E662, L272, M700, M543)

Joseph Barnby (1838-96)[51]
- LAUDES DOMINI (B221, E427, L546, M185, P130, 487)

These tunes influenced and were imitated by many other late 19th-century writers including:

John Goss (1800-80)
- LAUDA ANIMA (E410, L549, M66, P478)

Henry Smart (1813-79)
- REGENT SQUARE (B94, E93, L50, M220, P22)

John Stainer (1840-1901)
- CROSS OF JESUS (E160, P509)

Arthur Sullivan (1842-1900)
- FORTUNATUS (E179, L153)
- ST. GERTRUDE (B493, E562, L509, M555)
- ST. KEVIN (E199, M315, P115)

Alexander Ewing (1830-95)
- EWING (B527, E624)

Hymns Ancient and Modern also dipped back into the past to include the hymns of those associated with the "dissent" of the Nonconformists and the "enthusiasm" of the Methodists. It therefore brought together into one large

---

[51]For a collected edition of Barnby's tunes, see *Hymn-Tunes by Joseph Barnby* (London: Novello, 1897). Around 1900 Novello also published the collected tunes of Dykes, Stainer, and Sullivan.

collection the two mainstreams of hymnody—the evangelical and the churchly. These two mainstreams had been running parallel in English religious life since the beginning of the century. With its initial publication in 1861, hymns reached the accepted and respected position they still hold today in the public worship of most groups. Later hymnals, even though admitting newer hymns, continued to reflect the character, aims, and ideals of *Hymns Ancient and Modern*. The contents of this hymnal therefore represent the mainstream of English hymnody throughout the remainder of the 19th century, as well as into the 20th century.

Carols

Another important development in the latter part of the 19th century was the revival of carols and their introduction into the congregation's repertoire. As a significant by-product of the Oxford Movement and a result of the general thrust toward historical research fostered under the influence of the Romantic Movement, carols from both medieval written sources and oral traditions were revived, edited, and made more generally known.

John Mason Neale and Thomas Helmore (1811-90) were not only leaders in the revival of medieval hymnody and plainsong, but also pioneers in adapting carols from certain ancient sources, notably *Piae Cantiones*.[52] Other researchers, among them William Sandys, H. R. Bramley, John Stainer, and R. R. Chope, published legendary songs from the oral tradition of the West Country of England. The unearthing of these old carols led also to the composition of new ones. Carols (chiefly but not exclusively of the Christmas variety) thus began to be incorporated into the regular worship of the churches.[53]

Hymnology

The 19th century also marks the burgeoning of hymnological research and commentary. This was but a part of broader scholarly activity asociated with the dawning of the study known as musicology. Aided and abetted by the Romantic passion for the past, the century produced several students of hymns who may be represented by four whose work spans the century: James Montgomery (1771-1854), John Mason Neale (1818-66),

[52]Published originally in Finland, *Piae Cantiones* (1582) yielded its riches to Helmore and Neale when a rare copy was brought to England in 1853. See Chapter 6, "Reformation Traditions," for a listing of the melodies from this source that are in current use. A 400th-anniversary reprint is Theodoricus Petri, *Piae Cantiones* (Helsinki: Edition Frazer, 1982).
[53]The fascinating story of the carol is told by Erik Routley in *The English Carol* (London: Oxford University Press, 1959).

Daniel Sedgwick (1814-79), and John Julian (1839-1913).

In a now famous essay prefixed to his *Christian Psalmist* (1825), Montgomery took stock of the Wattsian, Wesleyan, and other Evangelical hymns of his day and made value judgments mainly of a literary nature. Being no mean hymn-poet himself and fired by the ideals of the Romantic Movement, he produced a perceptive critical review that ranks as the first English work in hymnology.

A generation later, championing a scholarly and High Anglican theological standard, was John Mason Neale. Although known and renowned as a translator from the Greek and Latin and a writer of original hymns inspired by the ancient sources, Neale must also be reckoned a hymnologist. In an article entitled "English Hymnology: Its History and Prospects,"[54] he set forth, like Montgomery, his opinion concerning the merits of his predecessors in hymn writing. Although somewhat captious in its criticisms of Watts, Wesley, and the Evangelicals (mostly on doctrinal grounds), this lengthy article remains an important one for English hymnology.

Contemporary with (but in great contrast to) Neale was Sedgwick, a self-taught student and publisher of hymns who, by dint of industry and perseverance, became possibly the most prominent hymnologist of his time. He amassed an impressive library in the course of his work as a bookseller and became a valued consultant to the compilers of *Hymns Ancient and Modern* (1861), to Sir Roundell Palmer for his *Book of Praise* (1862), to Charles Haddon Spurgeon in *Our Own Hymnbook* (1866), and to Josiah Miller in his hymnological work, *Singers and Songs of the Church* (1869). Although he was limited in education and theological perspective, Sedgwick, through careful collection, comparison, and annotation of hymns and hymnological literature, may well qualify as the real father of English hymnology.[55]

John Julian, the prince of all hymnologists came a generation later. In his monumental *Dictionary of Hymnology* (1891),[56] he and others examined over 400,000 hymns. Although it is now in need of radical revision and updating, Julian is still the definitive reference book for the origins and history of Christian hymnody of all periods and nations.

[54]Published in *The Christian Remembrancer*, XVIII (October 1849), 303ff.
[55]Montgomery and Neale, though perceptive critics, did not give themselves, as did Sedgwick, to hymnology as a profession. See J. Vincent Higginson, "Daniel Sedgwick: Pioneer of English Hymnology" in *The Hymn* 4/3 (July 1953), 77-80.
[56]John Julian, *Dictionary of Hymnology* (London: John Murray, 1891). A revised edition with new supplement was published in 1907. More recent reprints in two volumes have been issued by Dover Publications, Inc. (New York, 1957) and by Kregel Publications (Grand Rapids, MI, 1987).

SUMMARY OF 19TH-CENTURY HYMNODY

Taking into account all these major developments, 19th-century British hymnody can be characterized in the following ways:

A. Under the impact of the Evangelical Revival, it was:
1. intense in its expression of personal devotion.
2. enthusiastic in proclaiming the evangelical faith.
3. produced mainly by Nonconformists.
4. fostered with vigor by the evangelical wing of the established church.

B. Under the impact of the Oxford Movement, British hymnody was:
1. produced to accompany the festivals of the liturgical year and the various emphases of the prayer book and the catechism.
2. enriched by a recovery of the treasures in the liturgical books of the early Greek and Latin churches.
3. influential on the work of tune writers who composed music for specific hymn texts.
4. written by many who espoused the Roman Catholic faith.

C. Under the impact of Romanticism, it was:
1. written in colorful, elegant language, appealing vividly to the imagination.
2. concerned with natural beauty as a backdrop for hymnic truth.
3. receptive of hymnic contributions from noted poets.
4. enriched by a reverence for the past, encouraging translations from ancient sources and oral traditions (carols), as well as fostering scholarly research (hymnology).

20TH-CENTURY CURRENTS

Dissatisfaction with Victorian hymnody had gathered momentum toward the end of the 19th century. Although more recent views have encouraged a more favorable reappraisal of that period, there is ample evidence that Victorian congregational song was in need of rejuvenation.

1900-1955—Protest and Change

Insofar as music is concerned, a small start toward hymnic revival was made by a group of composers in the latter decades of the 19th century. From Hubert Parry (1848-1918), professor, author, organist, and composer, came such broadly sweeping tunes as INTERCESSOR (E695, L283, M517, P342) and RUSTINGTON (E278, L408, P224). Because Charles V. Stanford (1852-1924), prominent conductor and composer, thought in expansive festival terms rather than congregational terms, his hymn tune contributions were minimal. He is remembered, however, for ENGELBERG, set now mostly to a baptismal hymn by John B. Geyer (b. 1932), "We know that Christ is raised" (E296, L189, M610, P495), or to Fred Pratt Green's popular hymn on music, "When in our music God is glorified" (B435, E420, M68, P264). Like Stanford, Basil Harwood (1859-1949), a cathedral and collegiate organist, wrote little for the churches; however, his THORNBURY (E444, L77) has enjoyed some success. These tunes signaled a new trend during a period of general musical complacency. However, the 1904 edition of *Hymns Ancient and Modern*, incorporating these and other tunes in this newer musical vocabulary, failed to win popular acceptance.

At this juncture several energetic men began to challenge the conventionalities of prevailing usage: Robert Bridges (1844-1930), poet laureate who had retired from an earlier career in medicine to give himself to literature and hymnody; George R. Woodward (1848-1934), a learned Tractarian priest of Oxford; Percy Dearmer (1867-1936), an Anglican vicar who became professor of ecclesiastical art in King's College, London; and Ralph Vaughan Williams (1872-1958), greatest British composer of his generation.

In 1899, Bridges prepared the *Yattendon Hymnal*[57] which championed the restoration of old metrical psalm, chorale, and plainsong tunes. To supply suitable words in English for many of these, Bridges found he had to make new translations or create completely new texts. This resulted in an excellent group of hymns, including "Ah, holy Jesus" (E158, L123, M289, P93), "O splendor of God's glory bright" (E5, M679, P474), and "All my hope on God is founded" (E665) ("All my hope is firmly grounded," M132). Woodward edited *Songs of Syon*[58] (1904, 1910), a much larger collection following the same general plan of Bridges (that is, reviving for British use

[57]*Yattendon Hymnal* (Oxford: Clarendon Press, 1899). The collection was issued earlier in two parts: Part I–hymns 1-25 (1895); Part II–hymns 26-50 (1897).
[58]*Songs of Syon* (London: Schott and Co., 1904, 1910).

the finest tunes from the Latin, Genevan, and German traditions and writing texts that could fit their unusual meters).[59]

The English Hymnal, 1906

Neither the *Yattendon Hymnal* nor *Songs of Syon* found wide use, but they made it easier for Percy Dearmer and his musical collaborator, Ralph Vaughan Williams, to achieve the successful publication of *The English Hymnal* (1906).[60] This hymnal was an important landmark for several reasons:[61]

1. It contained an often-quoted preface which declared the book to contain "the best hymns in the English language" and ventured the epic statement that "good taste is a moral rather than a musical issue."[62]

2. It included, for the first time in an Anglican book, a group of hymns embracing liberal theology and the social gospel, such as these hymns of American origin: Whittier's "Immortal love, forever full" (B480), Sears's "It came upon the midnight clear" (B93, E89, 90; L54, M218, P38), and Hosmer's " 'Thy kingdom come,' on bended knee."

3. It contained newly written hymns, including Gilbert Chesterton's "O God of earth and altar" (E591, L428, P291), Scott Holland's "Judge eternal, throned in splendor" (E596, L418), and Charles Kingsley's "From thee all skill and science flow" (E566).

4. Most memorably, it represented the first hymnic use of a large number of traditional English folk songs. Thanks to the sure editing of Vaughan Williams, many folk melodies were rescued from England's past: KINGSFOLD (B120, E292, L391, M179, P308), KING'S LYNN (E231, L178), and FOREST GREEN (B42, E78, M152, P43). Moreover, his craftsmanship was applied to composing original tunes, including RANDOLPH (M673, P540), DOWN

[59]Although he had as his musical editor Charles Wood (1866-1926), Cambridge music professor, Woodward harmonized many of the tunes himself. See, for example, PUER NOBIS NASCITUR (L36, P68). Insofar as texts are concerned, he is best remembered for his earlier work with carols ("This joyful Eastertide," E192, L149).

[60]*The English Hymnal* (London: Oxford University Press, 1906).

[61]For evaluations of *The English Hymnal* and its influence, see the following articles in *The Bulletin of the Hymn Society of Great Britain and Ireland* (henceforth BHSGBI): Erik Routley, *"The English Hymnal* 1906-56," No. 75 (Spring 1956): 17-26; A. J. B. Hutchings, "The Literary Aspects of *The English Hymnal*," (No. 76 (Summer 1956): 33-49; Cyril Taylor, *"The English Hymnal Service Book,"* No. 96 (Summer 1962): 111-18; Erik Routley, "Percy Dearmer, Hymnologist," No.111 (Winter 1967): 169-86.

[62]*The English Hymnal*, ix.

AMPNEY (E516, L508, M475, P313), and SINE NOMINE (B229, E287, L174, M711, P526). The latter two are generally considered among the great tunes of the 20th century.

The pioneering work of Vaughan Williams was followed by the labors of a group of prominent music teachers, including Walford Davies (1869-1941) and the Shaw brothers, Martin (1875-1958) and Geoffrey (1879-1943). Davies' hymn-tune style (more conventional than Vaughan Williams's but less so than most of the Victorians) has not worn well in the late 20th century. Martin Shaw, like Vaughan Williams, was versatile and uncompromising in his hymn-tune style. Along with the older composer, he was musical editor of both *Songs of Praise* (1926; enlarged ed., 1931)[63]—the direct successor of *The English Hymnal* and *The Oxford Book of Carols* (1928)[64]—the carol equivalent of *The English Hymnal*.

These books contained further adaptations of folk tunes, such as BESANÇON (M202, P12), COVENTRY CAROL (E247), NOËL NOUVELET (E204, L148), NOS ALLONS (L541), and ROYAL OAK (E405, M147, P267). Martin Shaw also wrote original tunes intended for unison singing in the chapel services of public schools. His PURPOSE (E534), first included in *Songs of Praise* (1931) and subsequently in many public school hymnals, is a good example of his broad melodic style.[65] His younger brother, Geoffrey Shaw, a public school musician, wrote tunes like LANGHAM. This tune has a forcible melody rising to a climax on the refrain of Laurence Housman's "Father eternal, ruler of creation" (E573, L413), for which it was written.

Songs of Praise was no less fresh and zestful in its selection of texts. Percy Dearmer, its editor, continued the liberal theological policy he had established in *The English Hymnal*, choosing, editing, translating, and writing hymns that boldly confronted the new mood of doubt and experimentation prevalent at the time. An example of his translation from the Latin is "Father, we praise thee (you) (E1, 2; L267, M680, P459). "He (All) who would valiant be" (E564, 565; L498), based on John Bunyan, is a good example of his adaptation of earlier English devotional poetry. "Draw us in the Spirit's tether" (M632, P504) reveals his talent as a hymnist in his own right.

[63]*Songs of Praise* (London: Oxford University Press, 1926; rev. and enlarged, 1931; renewed in the USA, 1959).
[64]*The Oxford Book of Carols* (London: Oxford University Press, 1928). Recently published is *The New Oxford Book of Carols*, ed. Hugh Keyte and Andrew Parrott (Oxford and New York: Oxford University Press, 1992).
[65]Martin Shaw's LITTLE CORNARD (P279) also has found some usefulness. "Public School" in Britain is the designation for what would be private schools in the USA.

Among other important hymn writers of the early 20th century, George Wallace Briggs (1875-1959), Anglican clergyman and educator, is outstanding.[66] His "Christ is the world's true Light" (E542) and "Come, risen Lord" (E305, 306; L209, P503) are typical of his contributions to *Songs of Praise*. His "God hath (has) spoken by his (the) prophets" (L238, M108) was one of "Ten New Hymns on the Bible" solicited by the Hymn Society (of America, now in the United States and Canada) and originally published in American hymnals. Cyril A. Alington (1872-1955), Anglican priest and Dean of Durham, also contributed "Good Christians all (Christian friends), rejoice and sing" (E205, L144, P111) to *Songs of Praise*.

Other writers of this period whose hymns achieved wide use are John Oxenham (1852-1941) (pseudonym for William A. Dunkerly), Congregationalist churchman and novelist, with his "In Christ there is no east or west" (B385, E529, L359, M548, P439, 440); Geoffrey A. Studdert-Kennedy (1883-1929), preacher and chaplain to the king, with his "Awake, awake to love and work" (E9); Jan Struther (pen name for Joyce Anstruther, 1901-53), poet and novelist, with her "Lord of all hopefulness" (E482, L469) and "When Stephen, full of power and grace" (E243); and Timothy Rees (1874-1939), World War II chaplain and Bishop of Llandaff, who wrote "Holy Spirit, ever living as the church's very life" (E511), "God is love, let heaven adore him" (E379), and "O crucified Redeemer" (M425).

In the area of tunes, David Evans (1874-1948), Welsh Presbyterian editor of the revised *Church Hymnary* (1927),[67] brought enrichment through his harmonizations of traditional tunes including CHRISTE SANCTORUM (M604, 680; P459, 529), GARTAN (B109, M242), LLANFAIR (M312, P113, 481), LLANGLOFFAN (L430, M425, 435), MADRID (B231, P150), NYLAND (E232, P389, 560), KUORTANE (L339), and SLANE (B60, E488, P339). Eric H. Thiman (1900-1975), Congregationalist organist and professor, served in nonconformist circles the role that Martin Shaw played in the established church.[68] Kenneth G. Finlay (1882-1974), Scottish shipbuilder and teacher, composed pleasing folklike melodies such as GARELOCHSIDE (L78). The latter two men were major contributors to *Congregational Praise* (1951),[69] which was the first collection from British noncon-

---

[66]For an appraisal of Brigg's contribution as hymn-poet, tune writer, and hymnologist, see an obituary by Erik Routley in BHSGBI, No. 88 (Winter 1960): 245-249.
[67]*The Church Hymnary Revised* (London: Oxford University Press, 1927) was authorized for use in the Church of Scotland and in Presbyterian churches there and elsewhere.
[68]Thiman's hymn tunes, though still found in British hymnals (and sung chorally in his numerous hymn-anthems), are little known in the United States.
[69]*Congregational Praise* (London: Independent Press, 1951).

formity to rise above the conventionality characterizing most of the denominational hymnals in the first half of the 20th century. *Congregational Praise* was published in the same year as *The BBC Hymn Book*,[70] and one year after the release of the third complete revision of *Hymns Ancient and Modern*.[71] These collections, in their breadth of vision and balanced regard for all the main traditions, typify the state of British hymnody at mid-20th century.

Other outstanding names connected with these hymnals include Walter K. Stanton (1891-1978), editor-in-chief of *The BBC Hymn Book* and composer of CANNOCK (L201); Cyril V. Taylor (1907-1991), who worked in several important posts including Canon at Bristol Cathedral, Warden of the Royal School of Church Music, and the composer of SHELDONIAN (L160, M537), MOWSLEY (E129, 195; P74), and ABBOT'S LEIGH, his finest tune (E379, 511, 523; L405, M584, 660; P132, 425, 429, 461);[72] and Sydney H. Nicholson (1875-1947), the leading contributor of new tunes to *Hymns Ancient and Modern Revised* (1950). That collection's content in both text and tune can be fairly represented by Nicholson's CRUCIFER, set to "Lift high the cross" by G. W. Kitchin (1827-1912) and M. R. Newbolt (1874-1956) (B594, E473, L377, M159, P371).

The British hymnic stream flowed deep and wide in the period 1900-1955. Periodically fed by fresh and sometimes turbulent springs (*English Hymnal*, 1906; *Songs of Praise*, 1926; *Hymns Ancient and Modern Revised*, 1950; and *The BBC Hymn Book*, 1951), it ran in full force near mid-century. Reinforced by subtle cross currents springing from the ecumenical movement, the Anglican main course exerted a favorable pressure on nonconformist hymnody which resulted in a general change of taste.

1955-1970—Innovation and Crisis

After 1955, British hymnody ran into troubled waters, stirred in part by the emergence of The Twentieth Century Church Light Music Group. Founded by Geoffrey Beaumont (1905-71), who in 1956 published the *Twentieth-Century Folk Mass* (sometimes called the "Jazz Mass"), this group of lay musicians produced tunes in various secular styles in the hope of

---

[70]*The BBC Hymn Book* (London: Oxford University Press, 1951). An excellent critical review of this book by Leonard Blake may be found in BHSGBI No. 58 (December 1951), 2-11.
[71]*Hymns Ancient and Modern Revised* (London: William Clowes & Sons, Ltd., 1950). See Erik Routley's appraisal of this book in BHSGBI No. 51 (April 1950):145-59.
[72]See an informative interview conducted by Harry Eskew, editor, with Canon Taylor in *The Hymn* 36, 1 (January 1984): 6-11.

popularizing the singing of familiar hymns for the evangelizing of youth.[73] Causing a shock wave in some church music circles, Beaumont deliberately wrote in the "big tune" style of the Broadway musical and succeeded in having two of his best tunes published in a standard Hymnal—*The Baptist Hymn Book* (1962),[74] a comprehensive and eclectic collection after the manner of *Congregational Praise*. Its chief claim to distinction may be its inclusion of Beaumont's CHESTERTON to H. W. Baker's "Lord, thy word abideth," and his GRACIAS to "Now thank we all our God" (Rinkart-Winkworth).

Other tune writers of this movement continued to compose music reminiscent of the popular stage songs of the 1920s and 1930s, but their creative output did not include innovative texts commensurate with their unconventional tunes. Many church leaders have regarded the style of this group as "old hat," patronizing, lacking in subtlety, and too compromising to have accomplished its goal of reaching the unchurched.

Another disturbance in the hymnic stream of the 1960s was caused by Sydney Carter (b. 1915), journalist and songwriter. Carter, a master in the use of modern satire, has written informal texts which are sung to folk melodies or to folk-like melodies newly composed.[75] One of his most widely known songs, "Lord of the dance" (M261, set to the early American Shaker tune, SIMPLE GIFTS), is written in the style of a carol, reminiscent of the medieval carol, "Tomorrow shall be my dancing day."[76]

Carter became the patron saint of a modern school of conversational style hymnody which included, among others, Malcolm Stewart (b. 1926). Stewart's songs, lacking Carter's irony and satire, are based mainly on narratives and incidents from the Bible sensitively arranged in an easy folk style.[77] The work of the "Church Light Music Group" and the "folk" hymnody of Carter and his follow-

---

[73]The work of this group may be seen in three representative collections, all published in London by Josef Weinberger, Ltd.: *Eleven Hymn Tunes by the Rev. Geoffrey Beaumont* (1957), *Thirty 20th Century Hymn Tunes* (1960), and *More 20th Century Hymn Tunes* (1962).

[74]*The Baptist Hymn Book* (London: Psalms and Hymns Trust, 1962). See review by Caryl Micklem, BHS-GBI No. 95 (Spring 1962): 118-20.

[75]Carter's "Folk" hymns were found in standard hymnals published after 1970. Roman Catholics were particularly hospitable to him; see *New Catholic Hymnal* (London: Faber Music Ltd., 1971), 99, and *Praise the Lord!* (Geoffrey Chapman, 1972), 92. He was also well represented in the hymnal supplements of the late 1960s and the 1970s.

[76]*The New Oxford Book of Carols*, 464-66. His most controversial song is "Friday Morning," the words of which are imaginatively put in the mouth of one of the thieves crucified with Jesus. See *Songs of Sydney Carter in the Present Tense* 2 (London: Galliard, Ltd., and New York: Galaxy Music Corporation, 1969), 6-7. The inclusion of this song in the *Book of Worship for United States Forces* (Washington: U. S. Government Printing Office, 1974), 286, caused a considerable furor. See *The Hymn* 27, 4 (October 1976): 134-35.

[77]See *Gospel Song Book* introduced by Sydney Carter (London: Geoffrey Chapman, 1970); also published as *Now Songs* (Nashville: Abingdon Press, n.d.).

ers represent significant deviations from the mainstream of British hymnody.

Simultaneously with these diverging currents, and in many respects in response to them, was the work of the Dunblane Consultations on church music and hymnody that took place among a group of clergy and musicians in the Scottish village of Dunblane from 1962 to 1969.[78] The purpose of the group's work was to produce an experimental hymnody with both musical and poetic integrity which could be friendly to a broad cross-section of contemporary worshipers. These church leaders were interested in achieving relevancy without succumbing to the pop culture. Their creative activity resulted in the release of two booklets, *Dunblane Praises I* (1964) and *Dunblane Praises II* (1967), some of the contents of which were more formally published in *New Songs for the Church I and II*.[79] This project inspired the early work of such hymnists as Brian Wren[80] and Erik Routley,[81] who later achieved major importance in contemporary hymnic history.

Despite the side currents of "light" and "pop" songs, the mainstream of British hymnody, reinforced by some of the creative efforts of the Dunblane Group, was soon to flow more deeply and widely again. The coming tide was not yet evident in *The Anglican Hymnbook* (1965).[82] This hymnal represented a conservative reaction, ignoring much in the mainline contemporary styles and omitting altogether the new "pop" styles in favor of the older schools of the 18th-century Evangelicals and the 19th-century Victorians. Though not presenting any development text-wise beyond *Hymns Ancient and Modern Revised*, this hymnal was slightly more adventurous in its tunes.

Textually, mainstream hymnody had for some time been reduced to a trickle, but thanks to hymnists like the Congregational minister, Albert F. Bayly (1901-84), it did not run completely dry. Bayly wrote his first hymns at the close of World War II and subsequently saw over a hundred of them published.[83] Bayly's work, while imaginatively relating the church's worship to

---

[78]Interesting descriptions of this group's workshops and their results may be found in Erik Routley, *A Panorama of Christian Hymnody* (Collegeville: The Liturgical Press, 1979), 188-9, and in Ian Fraser, "Beginnings at Dunblane" in *Duty and Delight*, ed. Robin A. Leaver, James H. Litton, Carlton R. Young (Carol Stream: Hope Publishing Co., 1985), 171-90.

[79]*New Songs for the Church*, Book 1–Psalms, Children's Songs, Ballads, Hymns, and *New Songs for the Church*, Book 2–Canticles (London: Galliard & Scottish Churches Council, 1969).

[80]Wren's first hymn written for public singing, "Lord Christ, the Father's almighty son" was included in *Dunblane Praises I* (1964).

[81]Routley's best-known hymn text, "All who love and serve your city" was originally published in *Dunblane Praises II* (1967).

[82]*Anglican Hymn Book* (London: Church Book Room Ltd., 1965). The title is somewhat misleading in that it represents only the evangelical side of the Anglican communion.

[83]Bayly published four booklets of hymns privately. They were titled *Rejoice, O People* (1950), *Again I Say Rejoice* (1967), *Rejoice Always* (1971), and *Rejoice in God* (1977), and are now out of print.

the issues of contemporary life, was thoroughly theological and basically conservative in language. After years of local use, his hymns achieved major representation in hymnals throughout the world.

Bayly's best-known hymn in the United States is "Lord, whose love in (through) humble service" (E610, L423, M581, P427).[84] Other hymns dealing with Christian responsibility in social and ecological concerns are "Lord of all good, our gifts we bring" (L411, P375), "Lord, save your world" (L420) and "What does the Lord require for praise and offering" (E605, M441, P405). Hymnal supplements released in the 1970s in England contained many of Bayly's hymns—a testimony to their usefulness as contemporary utterances yet tempered by a true classic poise.

Among other promising post-1950 hymnists was Donald W. Hughes (1911-67), headmaster of a boy's school, whose creative endeavors were cut short by an untimely death. His craft is evident in "Creator of the earth and skies" (E148, M450).

Post-1970—Revival and Opportunity

"New English Renaissance" [85] is the term applied to a group of writers and composers whose work appeared in several supplemental hymnals during the six-year period—1969-75. These hymnal supplements are vivid evidence of the rapidity of style change in more recent British hymnody. They also indicated a concern on the part of publishers to keep parent books in use while exploring for new treasures during an era that was characterized by trial and experimentation. By 1980 each major denomination had published at least one hymnal supplement.[86]

Hymns and Songs is important as the earliest of these supplemental books to include a sizable selection of the hymns of Fred Pratt Green (b. 1903), a Methodist clergyman and playwright who turned to hymn writing in retire-

[84]The words were originally published in "Seven New Social Welfare Hymns," 1961, by the Hymn Society of America.
[85]See Erik Routley, "Hymn Writers of the New English Renaissance" in *The Hymn* 28, 1 (January 1977): 6-10.
[86]*100 Hymns for Today* (London: William Clowes and Sons, Ltd., 1969) and *More Hymns for Today* (1980) are supplements to *Hymns Ancient and Modern Revised* (1950). *English Praise* (London: Oxford University Press, 1975) is a supplement to *The English Hymnal* (Revised edition, 1933). *Hymns and Songs* (London: Methodist Publishing House, 1969) is a supplement to *The Methodist Hymn Book* (1933). *Praise for Today* (London: Psalms and Hymns Trust, 1974) is a supplement to *Baptist Hymn Book* (1962). *Broadcast Praise* (London: Oxford University Press, 1981) is a supplement to the B.B.C. *Hymn Book* (1951).
The United Reform Church is a merger of the Presbyterians and Congregationalists in England. Therefore, *New Church Praise* (Edinburgh: The Saint Andrew Press, 1975) is a supplement both to *The Church Hymnary Revised* (1973) and *Congregational Praise* (1951). In most instances, the usable material in all the above-mentioned supplements has been incorporated into new editions of parent hymnals. See the "Selected Bibliography."

ment. He is generally considered the finest hymn writer that Methodism has produced since Charles Wesley.[87] With the exception of *English Praise*, all the supplements include some of his hymns, as do most of the standard hymnals produced after 1970. No less than 30 different hymns by Fred Pratt Green are found in the five hymnals to which this textbook is keyed. There are few Christian themes to which he has not contributed at least one hymn. In his direct and unaffected way, he has supplied hymns for:

Sunday—"The first day of the week" (B357, L246)

Opening of Worship—"God is here" (M660, P461)

The Lord's Supper—"Lord, we have come at your own invitation" (E348, P516)

Christ's Passion and Death—"To mock your reign, O dearest Lord" (E170, M285)

Life in Christ—"O Christ, the healer" (L360, M265, P380)

Thanksgiving—"For the fruit(s) of all (this) creation" (B643, E424, L563, M97, P553)

The Mission of the Church—"When the church of Jesus" (B396, M592); "The church of Christ, in every age" (B402, L433, M589, P421)

Musical Worship—"When in our music God is glorified" (B435, E420, L555, M68, P264)

Among a score of other hymns in current use, Green has contributed some useful translations such as "By gracious powers" (E695, 696; P342) from the German of Dietrich Bonhoeffer. This gifted hymnist also has the distinction of having written "A Hymn for the Nation," which was authorized for use in the churches at the 1977 observance of the jubilee of Queen Elizabeth II's accession to the British throne.[88]

Fred Kaan (b. 1929) is another hymnist on the contemporary scene. He is Dutch by birth, but has spent most of his career as a United Reform min-

---

[87]In June 1982, Emory University, Atlanta, Georgia, conferred upon Fred Pratt Green the degree, Doctor of Humane Letters (h.c.) in a specially called university convocation which coincided with the 50th anniversary meeting of the Hymn Society of America. Green's near 300 hymns are published in two volumes: *The Hymns and Ballads of Fred Pratt Green* (Carol Stream: Hope Publishing Company, 1982) and *Later Hymns and Ballads and Fifty Poems* (Carol Stream: The Hope Publishing Company, 1989) with commentary by Bernard Braley. The latter hymn enthusiast has written an extended essay on Green and his writings in *Hymnwriters 3* (London: Stainer and Bell, 1991), 122-77.

[88]See Erik Routley, "The Two Jubilee Hymns" in *The Hymn* 28, 3 (July 1977): 151-2.

ister in England and has written most of his hymns in English.[89] Kaan is a world Christian, a caring citizen of the modern city, and a passionate advocate of social action. These ideas permeate his hymns.[90] Combining inspiration with audacity, he often reveals a deft use of metaphor and double meaning. Often-published Kaan hymns include:

> **On the Life in Christ**—"We meet you, O Christ" (M257, P311);
> "Help us accept each other" (M560, P358)
> **On World Peace**—"We utter our cry" (B631, M439)
> **For Easter**—"Christ is risen" (B167, M313, P109)—a translation
> from the Spanish "Cristo vive" of Nicolas Martinez

The major contributor of new texts to *New Church Praise*[91] was Brian Wren (b. 1936), another minister of the United Reform Church. After serving as a pastor for a time, he worked with several ecumenical organizations in Great Britain before moving in the 1990s to the United States, where he works as a free-lance writer and lecturer on worship and hymn writing. The author of over a hundred hymns,[92] he is among the most prolific hymnists in the mainline tradition. In his hymn writing he has been judged to be "as theological as Pratt Green, and often as abrasive as Kaan."[93] He is the leading hymnic champion of inclusivity in God language and continues to write in a contemporary idiom that is frankly experimental and often controversial. His command of a straightforward, exhilarating style is evident in hymns such as:

> **For Easter**—"Christ is alive" (B173, E182, L363, M318, P108);
> "Christ is risen" (M307, P104)
> **For the Lord's Supper**—"I come with joy" (B371, E304, M617,
> P507); "This is a day of new beginnings" (B370, M383)

[89]For 10 years Kaan worked as an executive secretary with the World Alliance of Reformed Churches, with headquarters in the ecumenical center at Geneva, Switzerland. In 1978 he returned to England as a provincial moderator in the United Reform Church and later as team minister at Swindon Central Church and minister of Penhill United Reform Church.

[90]Though many of Kaan's works appeared in earlier volumes and in numerous hymnbooks, all his hymns written up to 1989 may be found in two collections: *The Hymn Texts of Fred Kaan* (London: Stainer and Bell; Carol Stream: Hope Publishing Company, 1985) and *Planting Trees and Sowing Seeds* (London: Oxford University Press; Carol Stream: Hope Publishing Company, 1989).

[91]There are reviews of this supplement by Norman P. Goldhawk in BHSGBI 134 (November 1975), 125-30 and by Carlton Young in *The Hymn* 28, 1 (January 1977): 28-30.

[92]See Wren's hymn collections listed in the Epilogue, footnote 27.

[93]Erik Routley, see note 84. Wren has written helpful articles giving encouragement to would-be hymn writers. See "Making Your Own Hymn" in BHSGBI 142 (May 1978): 21-24. See suggestions for those wanting to write hymns in *Faith Looking Forward* (last four unnumbered pages).

For the Transfiguration—"Christ, upon (Jesus on) the mountain peak" (E129, 130; M260, P74)

The Life in Christ—"Lord (Great) God, your love has called us here" (M579, P353)

The Mission of the Church—"There's a spirit in the air" (B393, M192, P433)

Christian Responsibility—"When Christ was lifted from the earth" (B562, E603, 604)

Among other hymn writers who have been active during the last quarter century, Timothy Dudley-Smith (b. 1926) is one of the most prominent. Ordained to the Anglican priesthood in 1950, he is allied with the evangelical wing of that communion and his earliest hymnic work was closely associated with Michael Baughen and others of the Jubilate Group in the production of *Youth Praise 1* and *2* (1966, 1969), *Psalm Praise* (1973), and *Hymns for Today's Church* (1982, 1987). Serving as the Bishop of Thetford from 1981 until his retirement in 1992, Dudley-Smith continues to write hymns rich in biblical imagery and spiritual insight.[94] His most popular hymn is his paraphrase of the Magnificat, "Tell out, my soul, the greatness of the Lord" (B81; E437, 438; M200). Other hymns in current use based directly on Scripture include:

Psalm 8—"How great our God's majestic name" (B70)
Isaiah 2:1-4; Micah 4:1-4—"Behold a broken world" (M426)
Isaiah 9:67—"See, to us a child is born" (B104)
1 Corinthians 13—"Not for tongues of heaven's angels" (P531)
Revelation 4 and 5—"Heavenly hosts in ceaseless worship" (B40)

The Jubilate Group (mentioned above) was founded in the early 1960s by Michael Baughen (b. 1930, now Bishop of Chester) and included text and tune writers intimately connected with young people's work. The group "wished to extend their singing beyond the foursquare ways of metrical hymnody, and the unpredictability of Anglican chant!"[95] as they sought to meet the challenges of a new generation.

[94]His hymns written up until 1992 are published in three volumes: *Lift Every Heart: Collected Hymns 1961-1983 and some early poems* (London: Collins Liturgical Publications; Carol Stream: Hope Publishing Company, 1984); *Songs of Deliverance: 36 New Hymns written between 1984 and 1987* (London: Hodder and Stoughton; Carol Stream: Hope Publishing Company, 1988); and *A Voice of Singing: Thirty-six New Hymns 1988-1992* (London: Hodder and Stoughton; Carol Stream: Hope Publishing Company, 1993).
[95]*Come Rejoice!* (London: Marshall Pickering; Carol Stream: Hope Publishing Company, 1989), Preface.

Among some 40 authors and musicians in the group, the outstanding text writers (besides Timothy Dudley-Smith) are Christopher Idle (b. 1938), Michael Perry (b. 1942), Michael Saward (b. 1932), and James E. Seddon (1915-1983). The major figures in music are (besides Michael Baughen) Paul C. Edwards (b. 1955), David Peacock (b. 1949), and Norman Warren (b. 1934), all composers. Music arrangers include John Barnard (b. 1948), David Iliff (b. 1939) ,and Noel Tredinnick (b. 1949). Their work is reflected in a variety of Jubilate publications[96] and is finding its way into standard hymnals. Representative selections include:

> Baughen/Tredinnick—"Name of all majesty"-MAJESTAS (B207)
> Seddon—"Go forth and tell! O church of God" (B596)
> Saward—"Baptized in water" (B362, P492)
> Saward/Warren—"When God delivered Israel"-SHEAVES (P237)
> Idle—"Eternal light, shine in my heart" (P340) (paraphrase of Alcuin)
> Idle/Warren—"In the day of need"-SAMSON (P169)
> Perry/Warren—"Heal me, hands of Jesus"-SUTTON COMMON (M262)
> Perry/Warren—"The God of heaven"-GLORY (P180)

It is clear that the revival in writing hymn texts was a powerful stimulus for the composition of new tunes during this period. Outside the Jubilate Group, those who were most active in this field were John W. Wilson (1905-92), who composed LAUDS for Brian Wren's "There's a spirit in the air" (B393, M192, P433) and TRINITAS for Pratt Green's "Rejoice with us in God the Trinity";[97] Peter Cutts (b. 1937), who composed SHILLINGFORD for Wren's "Christ, upon the mountain peak" (E130, M260), BIRABUS for Routley's "All who love and serve your city" (E570, L436), and whose best known tune, BRIDEGROOM, is set to Carl Daw's "Like the murmur of the dove's song" (E513, M544, P314) and Dudley-Smith's "Not for tongues of heaven's angels" (P531); and Erik Routley (1917-82), who composed

[96]Their collections include *Hymns for Today's Church* (London: Hodder and Stoughton; Carol Stream: Hope Publishing Company, 1982, 1987), *Carols for Today* (London: Hodder and Stoughton; Carol Stream: Hope Publishing Company, 1986, 1987), *Carol Praise* (London: Marshall Pickering, 1987), *Come Rejoice* (London: Marshall Pickering; Carol Stream: Hope Publishing Company, 1989), *Psalms for Today* (London: Hodder and Stoughton; Carol Stream: Hope Publishing Company, 1990), and *Hymns for the People* (London: Harper Collins, 1993).
[97]Sixteen *Hymns of Today for use as Simple Anthems* (Croydon: The Royal School of Church Music, 1978), 35-37. In addition to this collection, Wilson selected and edited the tunes in its sequel, *Twenty-one Hymns Old and New for use as Simple Anthems* (Croydon: The Royal School of Church Music, 1985).

AUGUSTINE for George Herbert's "Let all the world in every corner sing" (E402, M93, P468) and SHARPTHORNE for Albert Bayly's "What does the Lord require" (E605, M441, P405).[98]

General characteristics found in the work of these tune writers are:

1. Melodies that are well crafted for unison singing, basically diatonic, sometimes folk-like, often lean and spare in style.
2. Rhythm that is free, flexible, and written often without meter signature.
3. Harmony which is uncomplicated and strong, sometimes modal, often minor in mode.

Australian Malcolm Williamson (b.1931), Master of the Queen's Music, is an accomplished composer who also writes hymn tunes. At home in a variety of musical styles, he composes his hymn tunes in a simplistic "pop" idiom that comes close to that of the Twentieth-Century Church Light Music Group. Unlike his contemporaries, he has no particular interest in setting new texts, but chooses those of the 18th-century evangelicals (Watts, Wesley, Kelly), the 19th-century Victorians (Ellerton, Wordsworth, Keble), and others from the various strands of traditional hymnody.[99] Two tunes in his offhand style in current use are CHRIST WHOSE GLORY (E6, P463) and MERCER STREET (E651).

Hymnological Activity

The flood of activity in 20th-century hymnody was accompanied by a commensurate growth in the work of hymnologists. Nowhere is this more evident than in the scholarly service rendered by the compilers of the numerous hymnal companions which appeared. Two important names connected with *Hymns Ancient and Modern* were W. H. Frere (1863-1938), who wrote an extended historical introduction for the "Historical Edition" of that collection in 1909; and Maurice Frost (1888-1961), who enlarged upon Frere's work to prepare the monumental *Historical Companion to Hymns Ancient and Modern* in 1962.[100] Frost was the most eminent of British hymnologists in the first half of the 20th century. His massive *Eng-*

[98]The more than 100 tunes of Routley, as well as his hymn texts, have been collected and published in *Our Lives Be Praise*, ed. Carlton R. Young (Carol Stream: Hope Publishing Company, 1990).
[99]Many of Williamson's tunes were published in *12 New Hymn Tunes* (London: Josef Weinberger, Ltd., 1962) and *16 Hymns and Processionals* (Carol Stream: Agape, 1975)
[100]Maurice Frost, editor, *Historical Companion to Hymns Ancient and Modern* (London: William Clowes & Sons, Ltd., 1962).

lish & Scottish Psalm & Hymn Tunes, c. 1543-1677,[101] is still an authoritative source.

In the field of Scottish hymnology, the outstanding scholars were James Moffatt and Millar Patrick, with their *Handbook to the Church Hymnary Revised* (1927, enlarged 1935).[102] Millar Patrick was the founder and first editor of the *Bulletin of the Hymn Society of Great Britain and Ireland* and the author of both *The Story of the Church's Song* and *Four Centuries of Scottish Psalmody*.[103]

Widely recognized as a scholar-apostle of the musical aspects of hymnody in England was John W. Wilson (1905-92), who served on the editorial committees of numerous hymn collections.[104] Wilson was a frequent contributor of essays to periodicals dealing with the technical and historical features of hymn tunes, many of which he was often the arranger and editor. For many years he served as an officer of the Hymn Society in Great Britain and Ireland, and as the organizer, promoter, and director of the annual hymn-singing event in Westminster Abbey known as *Come and Sing*.

Among several other hymnic scholars,[105] Alan Luff (b. 1928) and Robin A. Leaver (b. 1939) have been outstanding. Luff is an Anglican clergyman who speaks Welsh fluently. From 1979 to 1992 he was the Precentor at Westminster Abbey. His career has been intimately connected with the British Hymn Society for which he has served as secretary (1973-86), and more recently as its chairman. Though knowledgeable in many aspects of hymnody, especially psalmody (as well as being a singer, composer, and conductor), he is recognized as an authority on Welsh hymnody.[106]

Robin Leaver is an Anglican clergyman who was Lecturer in Worship, Wycliffe Hall, Oxford, and is a leading member of both the British and the American hymn societies, as well as former president of The International Fellowship for Research in Hymnology. After working part-time for a while

---

[101]Maurice Frost, *English & Scottish Psalm & Hymn Tunes*, c. 1543-1677 (London: Oxford University Press, 1953).

[102]James Moffatt and Millar Patrick, editors, *Handbook to the Church Hymnary with Supplement* (London: Oxford University Press, 1935).

[103]Millar Patrick, *The Story of the Church's Song* (Edinburgh: The Scottish Churches Joint Committee on Youth, 1927; reprinted and revised, James R. Sydnor, editor, Richmond: John Knox Press, 1962). Millar Patrick, *Four Centuries of Scottish Psalmody* (New York: Oxford University Press, 1949).

[104]Among others, Wilson served the following collections editorially: *Hymns for Church and School* (1964), *Hymns and Songs* (1969), *Broadcast Praise* (1981), and *Hymns and Psalms, A Methodist and Ecumenical Hymn Book* (1983).

[105]Included among others would be: Bernard Braley, Alan Dunstan, Norman Goldhawk, Bernard Massey, and Eric Sharpe.

[106]His most important work in this area is *Welsh Hymns and Their Tunes* (London: Stainer and Bell; Carol Stream: Hope Publishing Company, 1990).

in the United States, he accepted permanent employment in the United States in 1985. He has been professor of church music and director of the chapel at Westminster Choir College, Princeton, New Jersey as well as a member of the Graduate Faculty in Liturgical Studies at Drew University, Madison, New Jersey. The writer of many books and articles[107] in the realms of church music, theology, and liturgy, he is the author of two significant hymnological works: *Catherine Winkworth: The Influence of Her Translations on English Hymnody*[108] and *Goostly Psalmes and Spirituall Songes.*[109]

By far the most versatile of all 20th-century British hymnologists was Congregational clergyman, scholar, and musician, Erik Reginald Routley (1917-1982). Routley was a rare individual, equally competent in the theological and musical disciplines. For over three decades he exercised his unique gifts in the fields of biblical studies, hymnology, and worship.

A partial listing of his hymnological works includes:

I'll Praise My Maker (London: Independent Press, 1951)—A study of the hymns of certain authors who stand in or near the tradition of English Calvinism, 1799-1850.

Hymns and Human Life (London: John Murray, 1952)—A serious yet entertaining account of the human background of Christian hymnody.

Hymns of the Faith (Greenwich, CN: Seabury Press, 1956)—A devotional and theological study of 49 hymns considered to be among the most popular in English Protestantism.

The Music of Christian Hymnody (London: Independent Press, 1957)—The first extensive survey of hymn tunes in English, superseded by and expanded in *The Music of Christian Hymns* (Chicago: G.I.A. Publications, 1981.)

Hymns Today and Tomorrow (Nashville: Abingdon Press, 1968)—A series of essays loosely gathered about the theme of worship as drama in a changing society and the relation of music (including hymns) in its ordering.

---

[107]Leaver was the first editor (1982-85) of the quarterly, *News of Hymnody* (Bramcote: Grove Books).
[108]*Catherine Winkworth* (St. Louis: Concordia Publishing House, 1978).
[109]*Goostly Psalmes and Spirituall Songes* (Oxford: Clarendon Press, 1992).

A Panorama of Christian Hymnody (Collegeville, MN: The Liturgical Press, 1979), a series of topical and historical articles on various aspects of hymnody, illustrated by nearly 600 hymn texts.

An English-Speaking Hymnal Guide (Collegeville, MN: The Liturgical Press, 1979)—A sort of companion to the content of 26 "control hymnals," supplying concise information on each hymn and its author and/or translator.

Christian Hymns Observed (Princeton: Prestige Publications, Inc., 1982)—The author's final statement on Christian hymnody in the form of a succinct survey written in a uniquely engaging and popular style.

From 1947 to 1974, Routley served as editor of the *Bulletin of the Hymn Society of Great Britain and Ireland*, often furnishing the greater part of each quarterly issue with his own scholarly articles and reviews of hymnals. He served on the editorial board of many hymnals published during the last quarter of the 20th century and was the author of numerous periodical articles and other works pertaining to many aspects of hymnody.[110] Since he was a creator as well as a student of hymn texts and tunes, Routley has been representative of the whole of late 20th-century hymnic activity.[111]

Erik Routley

Owing much to the imaginative work of such scholars as these in England, the United States of America, and elsewhere, English hymnody continues in a vigorous state of revival. Its study is a matter of lively

[110]His crowning editorial achievement was the posthumously released official hymnal of the Reformed Church of America, *Rejoice in the Lord: A Hymn Companion to the Scriptures* (Grand Rapids: William B. Eerdman's Publishing Company, 1985).
[111]A memorial volume of essays, *Duty and Delight: Routley Remembered* (Norwich: Canterbury Press; Carol Stream: Hope Publishing Company, 1985) contains, in addition to its excellent essays, an almost complete bibliography of Routley's phenomenal output, both literary and musical.

interest, and its increasingly effective use is a cause for excitement and gratitude. Despite its detractors in some circles, the future of hymns and hymn singing continues to be bright!

8

AMERICAN TRADITIONS

THE EUROPEAN HERITAGE

Beginning in the 17th century, colonists from Europe arriving in the New World brought with them, along with other traditions, their Old World heritage of song. Two main types of congregational song were transplanted by these "Euramericans":

1. metrical psalmody[1]—from the English-, French-, and Dutch-speaking settlers, and

2. the chorale[2]—from the German and Scandinavian settlers. The transplanting was so effective that both traditions were maintained almost exclusively for nearly 100 years until the American singing school movement developed in the 18th century.

The Singing School

The singing school arose as a reform movement in early 18th-century New England. Harvard-educated ministers sought to improve what they regarded as poor congregational singing[3] by teaching their people to read music instead of singing by ear. In 1721, the Massachusetts pastor John Tufts compiled the first singing-school manual: *An Introduction to the Singing of Psalm Tunes* (11 eds. to 1744).[4] This modest volume was the first of hundreds

---

[1]See Chapter 6, section on "The Metrical Psalm," pages 115-122.
[2]See Chapter 6, section n "The Choral—Reformation to 1618," pages 98-101.
[3]One Massachusetts minister (Thomas Walter) described congregational singing as "an horrid Medley of confused and disorderly Noises." Gilbert Chase has made a strong case for viewing this singing as folk style. See Chase's *America's Music*. Rev. ed. (New York: McGraw-Hill, 1966), Chapter 2. See also Nicholas Temperly, "The Old Way of Singing," *Journal of the American Musicological Society* 34 (Fall 1981): 511-544.
[4]A facsimile reprint of the fifth edition contains an introduction by Irving Lowens (Philadelphia: Printed for *Musical Americana* by Albert Saifer, Publisher, 1954). Lowens treats the early history of Tuft's *Introduction* in his *Music and Musicians in Early America* (New York: The W. W. Norton Co., 1964), 39-57.

produced for singing school or church use. Each had two basic features: an introduction to the rudiments of music, and an anthology of music (usually with sacred texts) for singing.

By the latter 18th century the singing-school textbooks had become standardized in an oblong shape and were known as tunebooks because most of their tunes had only one stanza of text. In contrast to tunebooks, hymnals and psalters of this time generally contained texts only. Singing-school tunebooks included tunes for metrical psalms and hymns in addition to more elaborate noncongregational music (this category consisting of fuging tunes[5] and anthems).[6] The singing-school movement is important for American hymnody and American music history because in the latter 18th century, it brought forth our first native composers of hymn tunes. (The period of development for indigenous hymn texts was not to come until several decades later, in the 19th century.)

The earliest American hymn tune in common use today is CORONATION ("All hail the power of Jesus' name," B202, E450, L328, M154, P142), composed in 1793 by Oliver Holden (1765-1844),[7] a Massachusetts pastor, state legislator, music teacher, and tunebook compiler. Following the practice of the singing-school tradition, the melody was originally in the tenor voice. The latter portion of this tune was repeated with rests in the inner voice parts; these are features related to the fuging tune.

An example of a fuging tune now used in American hymnals is LENOX ("Blow ye the trumpet, blow," M379), composed by Lewis Edson (1748-1820) of Massachusetts, New York, and Connecticut, a blacksmith and singing-school teacher. LENOX (published in 1782 or 1783) begins with a homophonic section followed by an imitative section which is repeated, thus forming an ABB structure typical of the fuging tune. (See example on page 180.) In *The Methodist Hymnal*, LENOX appears in a "defuged" version with the imitative entrances filled in to bring it into conformity with present-day practice.

Both of these early American tunes—CORONATION and LENOX—have remained in continual use through their publication in *The Sacred Harp*[8] and other southern shape-note tunebooks. These tunes of the singing

---

[5]A good introduction to the fuging tune may be seen in Lowens, "The Origins of the American Fuging Tune" in *Music and Musicians in Early America*, 237-48.
[6]The anthem in early America is treated in Elwyn Wienandt and Robert H. Young, "The Beginnings of the American Anthem" in *The Anthem in England and America* (New York: Free Press, 1970), 169-205.
[7]See David W. McCormick, "Oliver Holden, 1764-1844," *The Hymn*, (July 1963): 69-77, 79.
[8]The most recent edition of *The Sacred Harp*, compiled by B. F. White and E. J. King, is *The Sacred Harp 1991 Edition* (Bremen, GA: Sacred Harp Publishing Co., 1991). Available from 1010 Waddell St., Bremen, GA 30110.

Lenox, from B. F. White and E. J. King, *The Sacred Harp.* 3rd ed. (Philadelphia: S. C. Collins, 1860), 40.

school thus represent the earliest of America's musical contributions to current hymnic practice.

FOLK HYMNODY

Introduction

Folk music is distinguished from cultivated music by the manner in which it is transmitted. Rather than conforming to one authentic version published in musical score, the folk song is transmitted by oral tradition, thus resulting in numerous variants. Since people hear and perform folk music from memory, a folk song may be sung in highly distinctive ways by different persons, especially if the singers come from contrasting cultures. American folk hymnody has both an unwritten and written history.

The melodies of American folk hymns are mostly related to the secular folk-song tradition brought by early settlers, primarily those from Great Britain. Some folk hymns have been traced by scholars, especially George Pullen Jackson (1874-1953),[9] to specific secular folk-song melodies. Others are related to "families" of folk melodies or are in a musical style very similar to the Anglo-American folk-song idiom. The most common style trait of

[9]Beginning with *White Spirituals in the Southern Uplands* (Chapel Hill: University of North Carolina Press, 1933; reprint, New York: Dover, 1964), Jackson's books are essential reading for a detailed knowledge of American folk hymnody. See his books listed in the bibliography of this text. See also *The Hymn* (October 1979): 240-42.

this tradition is the five-note (pentatonic) and other gapped scales. Another characteristic of these folk hymns is modal melody (for example, Dorian, Mixolydian, and so forth).

In its early history, the folk hymn existed solely in oral tradition. The written or printed history of the American folk hymn began when singing-school teachers either notated them from oral tradition (both words and music), took a printed hymn text (usually of English origin) and adapted a folksong melody to it, or composed a melody themselves in a style practically identical to that of other folk hymns. The earliest singing-school tunebook to contain a significant number of folk hymns surviving to the present was John Wyeth's *Repository of Sacred Music, Part Second*, published at Harrisburg, Pennsylvania in 1813.[10]

Shape-Note Hymnody

The printed folk hymn and the singing-school movement came together with the invention of shape notes, a device to simplify music reading first appearing in William Little and William Smith's tunebook, *The Easy Instructor* (Albany, NY, 1802).[11] Little and Smith's system (which corresponded to the Elizabethan sol-fa solmization brought by American colonists from England) used four shapes, three of which were repeated to form a diatonic scale:

fa sol la fa sol la mi fa

William Walker

Through shape-note tunebooks, folk hymns (along with New England psalm tunes, fuging tunes, and anthems) were widely circulated in the pre-Civil War period, especially in the rural South and Midwest.[12] Four leading shape-note tune books of this period, each containing a number of folk hymns, are Ananias Davisson's *Kentucky Harmony* (the first Southern shape-note tunebook, Harrisonburg, VA, 1816),[13] Allen Carden's *Missouri Harmony* (St. Louis, but printed in Cincinnati, 1820; later eds. to 1857), William Walker's *Southern Harmony* (Spartanburg, SC, but printed first in New Haven, CT, and later in Philadelphia, 1835; later eds. to 1854),[14] and B. F. White and E. J. King's *The Sacred Harp* (Hamilton, GA, but printed in

---

[10]See *Wyeth's Repository of Sacred Music, Part Second*, with a new introduction by Irving Lowens. Reprint of 2nd ed. of 1820 (New York: Da Capo Press, 1964).
[11]For a detailed study of this tunebook, see Lowens, *Music and Musicians*, 115-37.
[12]These tunebooks are listed in Richard J. Stanislaw, *A Checklist of Four-Shape Shape-Note Tunebooks* (New York: Institute for Studies in American Music, Brooklyn College, 1978).
[13]See *Kentucky Harmony*, Facsimile Edition with introduction by Irving Lowens. Reprint of 1st ed. of 1816 (Minneapolis: Augsburg Publishing House, 1976).
[14]See *Southern Harmony*, Facsimile of 1854 ed. (Lexington: The University Press of Kentucky, 1987).

William Walker

Philadelphia, 1844; later eds. to the present time).[15]

After about 1850, most shape-note tunebooks were printed in various seven-shape systems corresponding to the do-re-mi solmization advocated by Lowell Mason and other leading northern musicians. They united in the 1870s to use Jesse B. Aikin's seven-shape notation,[16] first published at Philadelphia in 1846 in his *The Christian Minstrel:*

do re mi fa sol la ti do

Folk hymns from oral tradition thus became part of the rural singing school through their publication in numerous shape-note tunebooks, some of which survive in present-day singings.[17] An increasing number of early American folk hymns (texts and tunes or hymn tunes for more recent texts) have appeared in most American hymnals of recent decades. Twelve of the most frequently found are:

- BEACH SPRING (L423, M581, "Lord, whose love in [through] humble service"; also B377, 604, 613, M605, P422) is a pentatonic melody in AABA' form originally published in duple meter in B. F. White and E. J. King's *The Sacred Harp* (Hamilton, GA; printed in Philadelphia, 1844).

[15]See *The Sacred Harp*, Facsimile of the 3rd ed., 1859, including as a historical introduction *The Story of the Sacred Harp* by George Pullen Jackson, with a postscript by William J. Reynolds (Nashville: Broadman Press, 1968). Description of these four tunebooks and biographical sketches of their compilers are found in Jackson, *White Spirituals*.

[16]A variety of seven-shape systems was developed because Aikin's shapes were thought to be patented (hence the term "patent notes" was used to refer to shape notes). A comparison of several of these seven-shape systems is given in Jackson, *White Spirituals*, 337.

[17]A singing is an informal gathering organized for fellowship and singing. Many singings take place annually on weekends, beginning by mid-morning and followed by a noonday break for "dinner on the grounds" and a concluding afternoon session. Though nondenominational, singings mostly take place in church buildings. Singings are generally organized into conventions, often on the county and state level. *The Sacred Harp* is by far the most widely used of the shape-note tunebooks. A list of "Traditional Sacred Harp Singings: Dates and Locations" is given in Buell E. Cobb, Jr., *The Sacred Harp, A Tradition and Its Music* (Athens: University of Georgia Press, 1978, 1989), 163-85. An annual *Directory and Minutes of Sacred Harp Singing* is available from the Sacred Harp Publishing Company, 1010 Waddell St., Bremem, GA 30110.

- **BOURBON** (E675, P393, "Take up your cross, the Savior said"; also E147, L127, P238) is a pentatonic modal melody first published in William Moore's *Columbian Harmony* (Wilson County, TN; printed in Cincinnati, 1825). This melody is related to KEDRON and to MORNING SONG.

- **CONSOLATION** or **MORNING SONG** (E583, M726, "O holy city, seen of John"; also E9, L33, M198, 226, P600) is an Aeolian melody, slightly florid like KEDRON, which appeared in Wyeth's *Repository of Sacred Music, Part Second* (Harrisburg, PA, 1813) to an earlier text.

- **DETROIT** (E674, L307, M390, P347, " 'Forgive our sins as we forgive' "; also L240) is a pentatonic modal melody first published in Ananias Davisson's *Supplement to the Kentucky Harmony* (Harrisonburg, VA, 1820).

- **FOUNDATION** (B338, E636, L507, M529, P361, "How firm a foundation, ye saints of the Lord") is a pentatonic melody originally entitled PROTECTION, but associated with this same text. It was first printed in another Shenandoah Valley tunebook, Joseph Funk's *Genuine Church Music* (Winchester, VA, 1832, later eds. to the present day; now entitled *New Harmonia Sacra*).

- **HOLY MANNA** (B379, "Brethren, we have met to worship"; L463, P268 "God, who stretched the spangled heavens,") is a pentatonic melody credited to William Moore of Wilson County, Tennessee, in his *The Columbian Harmony* (Cincinnati: Printed for the compiler by Moran, Lodge, and Fisher, 1825). At the annual Southern Harmony Singing at Benton, Kentucky, it is a long-standing tradition to begin with the singing of HOLY MANNA. "Brethren, we have met to worship," the hymn traditionally associated with HOLY MANNA, appeared as early as 1819 in George Kolb's *Spiritual Songster Containing a Variety of Camp Meeting and Other Hymns* (Frederick-town, MD), where it is attributed to George Atkins (identity unknown).

• **KEDRON** (set to six different texts; see E10, 163, L420, M109, P124, 283) is an Aeolian, hexatonic melody. It is one of the earliest folk hymns to be printed, appearing in 1799 at Boston in Amos Pilsbury's *United States Harmony.*

• **NETTLETON** (B15, E686, L499, M400, P355, "Come, Thou Fount of every blessing") was also published in Wyeth's tunebook under the tune name HALLELUJAH in duple meter with this same text.

• **NEW BRITAIN** or **AMAZING GRACE** (B330, E671, L448, M378, P280) is a pentatonic melody, probably the most popular American folk hymn. It first appeared in print in *Columbian Harmony, or Pilgrim's Musical Companion* (Cincinnati, 1829), compiled by Benjamin Shaw and Charles H. Spilman, where it is set to other texts. William Walker first published this tune to "Amazing grace, how sweet the sound" in his *Southern Harmony* (Spartanburg, SC; printed in New Haven, CT: Nathan Whiting, 1835). This folk hymn is equally popular among Black and White congregations and had the distinction of becoming an international hit in 1972 through the bagpipe recording of the Royal Scotch Dragoon Guards.[18]

• **RESTORATION** (B323, M340, "Come, ye sinners, poor and needy") is a pentatonic Aeolian melody which also seems to have been first published in 1835 in Walker's *Southern Harmony.*

• **TWENTY-FOURTH** or **DUNLAP'S CREEK** (set to four different texts; see E276, L122, 126, M658) is a hexatonic melody related to that of "Amazing Grace"; it was first published in two tunebooks of 1813: Wyeth's *Repository of Sacred Music, Part Second* and Robert Patterson's *Church Music* (Cincinnati).

• **WONDROUS LOVE**[19] (B143, E439, L385, M292, P85, "What wondrous love is this, O my soul, O my soul") is a Dorian,

[18]This folk hymn is the subject of an 87 minute video documentary, *Amazing Grace with Bill Moyers* (PBS Home Video 123; Beverly Hills, CA: Pacific Arts, 1990).
[19]For a comparative study involving this tune, see Ellen Jane Porter, *Two Early American Tunes: Fraternal Twins?* Papers of the Hymn Society of America, XXX (1975).

hexatonic melody first printed in the 1840 edition of Walker's *Southern Harmony*, where it bears the name "Christopher" as composer. In his later *Christian Harmony* (Spartanburg, SC, but printed at Philadelphia, 1867), Walker indicated this tune to be "Arranged by James Christopher, of Spartanburg, S. C. A very popular old Southern tune." The anonymous text Of WONDROUS LOVE, probably by an American, appeared in print as early as 1811 in two hymnals: the second edition of Stith Mead's *A General Selection of the Newest and Most Admired Hymns and Spiritual Songs Now in Use* (Lynchburg, VA) and Starke Dupuy's *A Selection of Hymns and Spiritual Songs* (Frankfort, KY).

Camp-Meeting Hymnody

In addition to its connection with the singing school, American folk hymnody was influenced by the growth of revivalism, particularly that of the frontier camp meeting. Beginning in the Carolinas and Kentucky in the first decade of the 19th century, the camp meeting revivals became a significant means of communicating the gospel in sparsely populated frontier areas. Singing was an important means of expressing the emotional fervor of these revival meetings. The need for simple and contagious songs, enough to appeal to unlettered frontier folk, brought into being a simplified folk hymn, a spiritual song, now commonly referred to as a spiritual. The basic technique of simplification in the spiritual is repetition, as in:

"Give me that old time religion,
Give me that old time religion,
Give me that old time religion,
It's good enough for me."[20]

Another way to construct a folk hymn was to add a chorus to a standard hymn such as the following, appended to Robinson's "Come, Thou Fount of every blessing" (B18):

"I am bound for the kingdom,
Will you go to glory with me?
Hallelujah, praise the Lord."

[20]Both White and Black versions of this spiritual are given in George Pullen Jackson, *White and Negro Spirituals*. Reprint of 1st ed. of 1943 (New York: Da Capo Press, 1975), 184-85.

A third way hymn texts were simplified in the camp-meeting tradition was to insert tag lines into a standard hymn text. An example is "glory hallelujah" in Cennick's "Jesus, my all to heaven is gone," as given in *The Sacred Harp*, 1991 Revision (324):

> "Jesus, my all, to heav'n has gone,
>   Glory Hallelujah;
> He whom I fix my hopes upon!
>   Glory Hallelujah!"

> *Chorus:*
> "I want a seat in Paradise,
>   Glory Hallelujah!
> I love that union never dies [*sic*],
>   Glory! Hallelujah!"

Numerous collections of camp-meeting hymn texts appeared in the early decades of the 19th century. Later their tunes were published (but in harmonized form) in such tunebooks as *The Sacred Harp* (1844) and John G. McCurry's *The Social Harp* (Hart County, GA, but printed at Philadelphia, PA, 1855). This latter collection has the largest single tunebook concentration of spirituals in this period.[21]

Two white spirituals to be found in present-day hymnals are WARRENTON ("Come, Thou Fount of every blessing"; refrain: "I am bound for the kingdom," B18) and PROMISED LAND ("On Jordan's stormy banks I stand"; refrain: "I am bound for the promised land," B521, M724). Both of these tunes[22] have British hymn texts, with refrains added during their association with early 19th-century American revivalism. Although PROMISED LAND now appears in a major key, its early version in shape-note tunebooks is in minor, as in this appearance in Walker's *Southern Harmony* (1835). (See page 187.)

Black Spirituals

African-American slaves developed an amazing repertory of spirituals (generally called plantation melodies)[23] over a period of two and a half cen-

---

[21]John Gordon McCurry, *The Social Harp* (Philadelphia: T. K. Collins, 1855; reprint ed. by Daniel W. Patterson and John F. Garst with an introduction by Daniel W. Patterson, Athens: University of Georgia Press, 1973).

[22]In addition to these two, the well-known tune BATTLE HYMN ("Mine eyes have seen the glory of the coming of the Lord," B633, M717) is regarded as a variant of a camp-meeting melody.

[23]For treatment of the musical traits of the spiritual, see Chapter 2, "The Hymn and Music," and Chapter 9, "Cultural Perspectives."

On Jordan's stormy banks I stand, And cast a wish - ful eye, To Canaan's fair and happy land, Where my possessions lie. I am

bound for the pro - mised land, I'm bound for the pro - mised land, O, who will come and go with me ? I am bound for the promised land

PROMISED LAND, from William Walker's *Southern Harmony* (Spartanburg, SC, but printed at New Haven, CT, 1835). The text, taken from a Methodist hymnbook, is by the English Baptist Samuel Stennett (1727-95). The identity of "Miss M. Durham," Walker's tune source, is unknown.

turies. The first collection of their spirituals is *Slave Songs of the United States*, 1867.[24] After the Civil War, Black spirituals branched into two streams. One stream—the grass roots spiritual—continued among the common folk. The other stream—the concert arrangements of spirituals harmonized in "correct" European style—was spread through popular performances of groups such as the Fisk Jubilee Singers (Fisk University in Nashville) beginning in 1871. While the grass roots spiritual continued to be sung by Blacks in their traditional ways, with less polished harmonies and free improvisations, the concert versions became known to the public at large.

African-American spirituals were not published in collections designed for congregational singing until the early to mid-20th century. Only in recent decades have they been included in most major American hymnals. As they appear in current hymnals, their harmonies are more akin to Victorian tunes and concert versions than to folk practices. The following Black spirituals[25] are among the more often included in American hymnals today:

[24]William Francis Allen, Charles P. Ware, and Lucy McKim Garrison (eds.), *Slave Songs of the United States* (New York: A. Simpson and Co., 1867; reprint, New York: Peter Smith, 1951; Rev. ed., New York: Oak Publications, 1965).
[25]The earliest of these spirituals to be published in a hymn collection seems to be "Were you there," in 1911, in *Songs of Evangelism* by Harvey R. Christie (Cincinnati: Standard Publishing Co.) and "We are climbing Jacob's ladder," 1905, in *Joy Bells of Canaan, Burning Bush Songs No. 2*, ed. by Arthur F. Ingler (Chicago: The Burning Bush). It is interesting that these earlier printings of Black spirituals were in revivalistic songbooks and that only in recent decades has it become acceptable to include these in denominational hymnals.

8. American Traditions

- "Every time I feel the Spirit" (M404, P315)
- "Go, tell it on the mountain" (B95, E99, L70, M251, P29)
- "He Never Said a Mumbalin' Word" (M291, P95)
- "I want Jesus to walk with me" (B465, M521, P363)
- "I will trust in the Lord" (B420, M464)
- "I've got peace like a river" (B418, P368)
- "Kum ba yah" (M494, P338)
- "Let us break bread together on our knees" (B366, E325, L212, M618, P513)
- "Lord, I want to be a Christian" (B489, M402, P372)
- "My Lord, what a morning" (M719, P449)
- "There is a balm in Gilead" (B269, E676, M375, P394)
- "We are climbing Jacob's ladder" (B474, M418)
- "Were you there when they crucified my Lord?" (B156, E172, L92, M288, P102)
- "When Israel was in Egypt's land" (E648, M448, P334)

White spirituals were published in shape-note tunebooks two decades before Negro spirituals began to appear in print. Both bodies of congregational folk song developed side by side in the pre-Civil War period, particularly in revivals and camp meetings. It is clear that these bodies of song intermingled and influenced each other, but the evidence is insufficient for either tradition to claim priority.[26] Regardless of their label, spirituals have become a deeply meaningful expression of a common faith for many American congregations.

In summary, American folk hymnody developed in the nineteenth century with a variety of associations: Anglo-American secular folk song, the singing school with its shape notation, revivalism (including the frontier camp meetings), and the African-American tradition (later influenced by the European tradition). All of these associations continue to influence congregational song.

19TH-CENTURY NORTHERN DEVELOPMENTS
Musical Reformers and Revivalists

In addition to folk hymnody and the singing school that flourished in the 19th-century South and the frontier areas of the Midwest, a second reform movement in American church music was developing in the urban

[26]The most extensive collection of sources documenting the early spiritual is Dena J. Epstein, *Sinful Tunes and Spirituals* (Urbana: University of Illinois Press, 1977).

North led by Lowell Mason (1792-1872) and others. This movement considered the music of the earlier American composers (such as Billings, Read, and Jeremiah Ingalls) generally inferior, preferring European music, which they regarded "scientifically" conceived (or correct). These reformers based their hymn tunes on European models, or they used melodies arranged from famous composers for congregational singing. Music education, including the introduction of music instruction in public schools, gradually replaced the singing school in the larger cities.

The dominant figure in this reform movement and the leading composer of hymn tunes of his time was Lowell Mason, whose main activities centered in Boston and in New York City.[27] Mason is particularly renowned for having pioneered in introducing music instruction on a regular basis into the Boston public schools in 1827. He composed or arranged some 1,600 hymn tunes and compiled some 80 music collections. Among the best known of his surviving hymn tunes are:

- ANTIOCH[28] (B87, E100, L39, M246, P40, "Joy to the world"), an arrangement (1839) of themes from Handel's *Messiah*.

- AZMON (B216, E493, L559, M57, P466,"O for a thousand tongues to sing," also B11, 268, M59,422, 608, P386), an arrangement (1839) from the music of Carl G. Gläser.

- BETHANY (B458, M528, "Nearer, my God, to thee"), a tune composed for this text in 1856.

- HAMBURG (B144, M298, P101, "When I survey the wondrous cross," also B374), arranged from a Gregorian chant in 1824.

- OLIVET (B416, E691, L479, M452, P383," My faith looks up to Thee"), a tune composed for this text in 1832.

Mason's leading contemporary in musical reform was Thomas Hastings (1784-1872),[29] who from 1832 onward was active in New York City. Hast-

[27]See J. Vincent Higginson, "Notes on Lowell Mason's Hymn Tunes," *The Hymn* 18 (April 1967): 37-42; George Brandon, "Some Classic Tunes in Lowell Mason's Collections," *The Hymn* 18 (July 1967): 78-79; and Carol A. Pemberton, "Praising God through Congregational Song: Lowell's Mason's Contributions to Church Music," *The Hymn* 44, 2 (April 1992): 22-30.
[28]John Wilson has shown ANTIOCH to have been arranged by British compilers set to other texts prior to Mason's. See "The Evolution of the Tune, 'Antioch,'" *The Hymn Society of Great Britain and Ireland Bulletin* 166, 11, 5 (January 1986): 107-114.
[29]See Lee Hastings Bristol, Jr., *The Hymn* 10 (October 1959): 105-10.

ings wrote some 600 hymn texts, 1,000 hymn tunes, and compiled more than 50 music collections. Two of Hastings's hymn tunes which survive are:

- ORTONVILLE (B219, "Majestic sweetness sits enthroned," B453, "How sweet the name of Jesus sounds"), composed for the first named hymn in 1837.

- TOPLADY (B342, E685, L327, M361, "Rock of Ages, cleft for me"), composed for this hymn in 1830.

While Mason and Hastings advocated hymn tunes in a devotional style characterized by simplicity and dignity, Congregationalist minister and journalist Joshua Leavitt (1794-1873) brought out (in his *The Christian Lyre*, New York, 1831) hymns set to secular melodies which Mason and Hastings regarded as unfit for religious use. Leavitt's collection sought to supply hymns (including some songs with choruses) suitable for the new urban revivalism of evangelist Charles G. Finney (1792-1875).[30] Among the anonymous hymn tunes bequeathed to current hymnals by *The Christian Lyre* are:

- ELLESDIE (B471, "Jesus, I my cross have taken"; B591, "Hark, the voice of Jesus calling").

- HIDING PLACE (L537, "O Jesus, king most wonderful").

- LIGHT (E667, "Sometimes a light surprises").

- PLEADING SAVIOR (E586, P305, "Jesus, thou (our) divine Companion"; L243, "Lord, with glowing heart I'd praise thee").

Although revivalistic in its orientation, *The Christian Lyre* also included the first publication of Presbyterian minister James W. Alexander's translation of Gerhardt's "O sacred Head, now wounded" (B137, E168 [st. 4], L116 and 117 [a composite tr.], M286, P98).

Mason and Hastings, alarmed by the secular orientation of *The Christian Lyre*, sought to supply the revival movement with more dignified church music in their *Spiritual Songs for Social Worship* (Utica, NY, and Philadelphia,

[30]See Paul Hammond, "The Hymnody of the Second Great Awakening," *The Hymn* 29 (January 1978): 19-28.

1833). This collection provided an introduction to the public for Ray Palmer's "My faith looks up to thee" (to Mason's OLIVET) and other widely used hymns of Hastings and others. Mason's associate during his later Boston years was George J. Webb (1803-87), a native of England. While on a ship bound for America, Webb composed music for a secular text, " 'Tis dawn, the lark is singing." This tune later came to be used with hymns and is now known as WEBB or MORNING LIGHT (B485, E561, L389, M514), the hymn tune for "Stand up, stand up for Jesus."

Denominational Hymnody

During the 19th century, most American denominations underwent a gradual transition from the use of metrical psalmody and Watts's and other hymns of English origin to the development of their own hymn writers. They also began to publish their own hymnals.[31] In this period a number of hymns emerged which are still found in American hymnals. Although some hymn texts of this period reflect the particular doctrines of individual denominations, those which have survived tend to embody beliefs held by most of America's Christians. These hymns, however, may best be treated according to their denominational origin.

Baptists. Massachusetts Baptist minister Samuel F. Smith (1808-95) produced one of America's enduring patriotic hymns, "My country, 'tis of thee" (AMERICA, B634, E717, L566, M697, P561), written in 1831 and first sung by a choir of Boston Sunday School children directed by Lowell Mason. This hymn's New England origin is reflected in such phrases as: "I love thy rocks and rills, Thy woods and templed hills." Smith was also one of the editors of *The Psalmist* (Boston, 1843), the leading Baptist hymnal of the first half of the century.

Three other Baptist ministers, whose hymns were written in the latter half of the century, are Joseph H. Gilmore (1834-1918), author of "He leadeth me! O blessed thought" (1862; B52, L501, M128); Sylvanus D. Phelps (1816-95), author of "Savior, Thy dying love" (1864; B607); and Adoniram J. Gordon (1836-95), composer of the hymn tune GORDON (1876; B210, M172, "My Jesus, I love thee"). Each of these hymns reflects the strong Baptist emphasis on a personal relationship to the Savior.

[31]The best survey of American denominational hymnals in the 19th century is in Louis F. Benson, *The English Hymn* (New York: George H. Doran, 1915; reprint, Richmond: John Knox Press, 1962). See Chapter 8 and portions of Chapters 9 and 10.

Congregationalists.[32] Congregationalists contributed a number of hymns. Their greatest contributions in the pre-Civil War period came from Ray Palmer (1808-87), author of "My faith looks up to Thee" (1830, B416, E691, L479, M452, P383), and translator of "Jesus, thou (O Jesus) joy of loving hearts" (1858, E649, 650, L356, P510, 511). Other Congregationalist contributors, all writing in the latter half of the century, are: Daniel March (1816-1909), the minister who wrote "Hark, the voice of Jesus calling" (1868, pub. 1878, B591, L381); Samuel Wolcott (1813-86), a missionary to Syria and later a pastor in this country who wrote the missionary hymn, "Christ for the world we sing" (1869, M568); John Zundel (1815-82), a native of Germany who gained fame as organist of Henry Ward Beecher's Plymouth Congregational Church, Brooklyn, composer of the hymn tune BEECHER (1870, B208, M384, "Love divine, all loves excelling"; also B248, 470, E470, P343); Washington Gladden (1836-1918), minister and early advocate of the social application of the gospel who wrote "O Master, let me walk with Thee (you)" (1879, B279, E659, 660, L492, M430, P357); and Ernest W. Shurtleff (1862-1917), minister who wrote "Lead on, O King Eternal" (1887, B621, E555, L495, M580, P447, 448).

Episcopalians. The earliest 19th-century Episcopalian hymn found in today's hymnals is "'Take up thy (your) cross,' the Savior said" (B494, E675, L398, M415, P393), written in 1833 by Connecticut minister Charles W. Everest (1814-77). A second Episcopal contribution is the hymn tune CAROL ("It came upon the midnight clear," B93, E89, L54, M218, P38), composed in 1850 by the music critic Richard S. Willis (1819-1900). The popular Christmas hymn "O little town of Bethlehem" (1868, B86, E78, 79, L41, M230, P43, 44) was written for Sunday School children by the famed preacher Phillips Brooks (1835-93) following a visit to Bethlehem.[33] The organist of his Holy Trinity Church in Philadelphia, Lewis Redner (1831-1908), composed its tune, interestingly named ST. LOUIS.

The missionary hymn "O Zion, haste, thy mission high fulfilling" (B583, E539, L397, M573) was written in 1868 by the English-born Philadelphian Mary Ann Thomson (1834-1923). Another of this century's patriotic hymns, but one not restricted to a single nation, is "God of our fathers (the ages), whose almighty hand" (B629, E718, L567, M698, P262). This hymn

[32]Congregationalists have merged with the Evangelical and Reformed Church to form the United Church of Christ.
[33]See J. Vincent Higginson, "Phillips Brooks and Sunday School Music," *The Hymn* 19, 2 (April 1968): 37-43.

was written in 1876 for America's centennial by Daniel C. Roberts (1841-1907). The unusual hymn tune (NATIONAL HYMN) with fanfares was composed in 1892 for the centennial of the United States Constitution by the New York organist, George W. Warren (1828-1902).

Methodists. Only one Methodist American hymn writer of the 19th century (apart from a number of gospel hymnists) is commonly represented in today's hymnals. The artist and editor Mary A. Lathbury (1841-1913)[34] wrote the hymn "Break thou the bread of life" (B263,[35] M599, P329) in 1877 for the summer assemblies at Lake Chautauqua, New York. Miss Lathbury's beautiful evening hymn, "Day is dying in the west" (St. 1 and 2, 1877; st. 3 and 4, 1890; M687) has declined in use along with the gradual passing of vesper services.

Presbyterians. Three Presbyterians whose hymns are commonly found in current hymnals are Elizabeth P. Prentiss (1818-78),[36] George Duffield, Jr. (1818-88), and Edward Hopper (1816-88). Mrs. Prentiss, an invalid who authored the religious best seller *Stepping Heavenward* (1869), wrote "More love to thee, O Christ" (1856, B473, M453, P359). Duffield, one of a family of Presbyterian ministers, wrote "Stand up, stand up for Jesus" (WEBB, B485, 487, L389, M514) during the 1858 revival in Philadelphia. Hopper, pastor of the Presbyterian Church in Sag Harbor, Long Island, New York, wrote "Jesus, Savior, pilot me" (1871, L334, M509).

Quakers. The one Quaker hymnist of the past century whose hymns are still being sung is one of the giants of American poetry, John Greenleaf Whittier

© 1980 Charles Massey, Jr.
John Greenleaf Whittier

[34]See Gladys E. Gray, "Mary Artemisia Lathbury," *The Hymn* 14 (April 1963): 37-46.
[35]The additional two stanzas given in this hymnal were written by Englishman Alexander Groves and were published in 1913.
[36]Mrs. Prentiss and her minister husband were first Congregationalists and later became Presbyterians.

(1807-92).[37] Although he did not write hymns as such, hymns have been extracted from his poems. Two of his hymns that survive are: "Dear Lord and Father of mankind" (1872, B267, E652, 653, L506, M358, 499, P345) and "Immortal Love, forever full" (1866, B480).

Unitarians. One hymn by an American Unitarian from the first half of the 19th century has found a firm place in current hymnals. "It came upon the midnight clear" (B93, E89, 90, L54, M218, P38) was written in 1849 by Edmund H. Sears (1810-76), a Massachusetts minister. With no mention of Jesus, this hymn focuses upon the portion of the angels' message dealing with peace and forecasts its eventual achievement on earth. The Unitarian hymnist of the last century with the largest number of hymns in use today is Samuel Longfellow (1819-92), brother of the poet Henry Wadsworth Longfellow. Samuel Longfellow wrote:

- "Bless thou the gifts our hands have brought" (ca. 1886, M587).

- "Holy Spirit, Truth divine" (1864, L257, M465, P321).

- "Now, on land and sea descending" (1859, M685, P545).

Samuel Longfellow and his fellow hymnist Samuel Johnson (1822-82) edited the Unitarian hymnals of 1845 and 1864.[38] Unitarians have also contributed the patriotic hymn "Mine eyes have seen the glory of the coming of the Lord" (1861, B633, M717) by Julia Ward Howe (1819-1910), an influential speaker and advocate of abolition and pacifism. A Unitarian hymn which anticipated the space age, "Eternal Ruler of the ceaseless round" (E617, L373), was written in 1864 by John W. Chadwick (1840-1904) for his graduation from Harvard Divinity School.

Nondenominational. One 19th-century American poet, essayist, and critic who never affiliated with any church is James Russell Lowell (1819-91). He is the author of "The Present Crisis" (1845), an antiwar poem from which we have the hymn "Once to every man and nation" (B470). Katharine Lee Bates (1859-1929), an English professor at Wellesley College and daughter of a Congregationalist minister, also did not affiliate with any denomination. She

[37]See David H. Kidder, "John Greenleaf Whittier's Contribution to American Hymnody," *The Hymn* 8 (October 1957): 105-11.
[38]Two of Johnson's hymns in *The Hymnal 1940* (Episcopal) are "Life of ages, richly poured" and "City of God, how broad and far."

wrote "O beautiful for spacious skies" (B630, E719, M696, P564). This patriotic hymn, written after the author visited the Rocky Mountains in 1893, is reflective of America's experience of geographical expansion to the West in that century.

Mention should also be made of the anonymous American Christmas hymn for children, "Away in a manger, no crib for a bed" (B103, E101, L67, M217, P24, 25). This hymn appeared in 1885 in Philadelphia.

Most of America's major denominations during the 19th century made some contribution to current hymnody. However, two principal church groups, the Roman Catholics and Lutherans, had not yet developed a considerable original hymnody because of their strong ties to their European heritages. Roman Catholics were singing very little in the vernacular, and Lutherans were using either German chorales (increasingly in English translation) or the hymns of their English-speaking neighbors.

Although the hymnody of America's churches in the 19th century is characterized by much diversity, the hymns that have continued in current use reflect certain emphases:

1. Americans have been well supplied with national hymns, including "My country, 'tis of thee," "Mine eyes have seen the glory," "God of our fathers," and "O beautiful for spacious skies." All of these were perhaps an outgrowth of the sense of patriotism necessary to weld the United States into a cohesive nation.

2. America's involvement in the modern worldwide missionary movement is illustrated by such hymns as "Hark, the voice of Jesus calling," "Christ for the world we sing," and "O Zion, haste."

3. The few hymns written for seasons of the church year focus mostly on Christmas, including "O little town of Bethlehem," "It came upon the midnight clear," and "Away in a manger."

4. There is an emphasis on hymns of devotion to Jesus, such as "More love to Thee, O Christ" and "Savior, Thy dying love"; there are also hymns of a personal relationship to Christ, such as "He leadeth me" and "Jesus, Savior, pilot me."

5. Much 19th-century American hymnody is concerned with the afterlife. This is especially true of folk and gospel hymnody. Among the hymns mentioned in this section, note the reference to heaven in the final stanzas of "He leadeth me," "More love to

Thee, O Christ," "Away in a manger," and "Jesus, Savior, pilot me." The emphasis on heaven gave hope to most Americans who worked long and hard but with little realization of riches in this life.

6. There are a few hymns reflecting a growing social concern, such as "It came upon the midnight clear," and "Once to every man and nation."

7. Finally, with the exception of women hymn writers, the hymn text writers from the 19th-century churchly stream of American congregational song were nearly all clergymen rather than laypersons.

GOSPEL HYMNODY

Just as the rural camp meeting in the early decades of the 19th century produced its popular hymnody, the urban revivals in the latter decades brought forth a body of popular church song—a type known as the gospel song or the gospel hymn. The use of these terms to refer to this body of revival hymnody can be traced to two popular collections: Philip P. Bliss' *Gospel Songs* (1874) and Bliss and Ira D. Sankey's *Gospel Hymns and Sacred Songs* (1875). Gospel hymn texts utilized the same devices of simplification found in the camp-meeting hymn. The musical style of the gospel hymn has been described in Chapter 2, "The Hymn and Music."

William Batchelder Bradbury

Sunday School Era

Although the term "gospel hymnody" emerged in the mid-1870s, this hymnody actually appeared more than a decade earlier, especially in collections designed for America's rapidly growing Sunday Schools. Some of the common features of the gospel hymn were anticipated in hymn tunes of Lowell Mason and Thomas Hastings. But Mason's student, William B. Bradbury (1816-68), a leading composer of Sunday School music, is the first composer in this idiom whose works survive to any extent in current American hymnals. The compiler and publisher of numerous collections with titles designed to appeal to Sunday School children (for example, *Fresh Laurels*, New York, 1867; *Golden Chain*, New York, 1861), Bradbury composed the musical settings for:

- "Jesus loves me" (1862, CHINA or JESUS LOVES ME, B344, M191, P304),

- "He leadeth me" (1864, B52, L501, M128),

- "Sweet hour of prayer" (ca. 1861, B445, M496),

- "Just as I am, without one plea" (1849, WOODWORTH, B307, E693, L296, M357, P370),

- "My hope is built on nothing less" (1863, SOLID ROCK, B406, L293, M368, P379), and

- "Savior, like a shepherd lead us" (BRADBURY, B61, M381, P387).

Two successors to Bradbury in providing music for the Sunday School were Baptists Robert Lowry (1826-99)[39] and William H. Doane (1832-1915). Lowry, a pastor who succeeded Bradbury as editor of Sunday School songbooks for the New York firm of Biglow and Main, wrote both words and music. He wrote both text and tune of "Shall we gather at the river"[40] (1864, B518, M723), the tune NEED for "I need Thee every hour" (1892, text by Baptist Annie S. Hawks, B450, M397), and the tune SOMETHING FOR JESUS (1871) for "Savior, Thy dying love" (1864, text by Baptist Sylvanus D. Phelps, B607). Doane, president of a Cincinnati firm manufacturing woodworking machinery, found time to compose more than 2,200 hymn tunes and compile more than 40 collections. He is particularly known for his musical settings of hymns by Fanny Crosby (1820-1915), such as:

---

[39]See John F. Zellner, III, "Robert Lowry: Early American Hymn Writer," *The Hymn* 26 (October 1975): 117-24, and 27 (January 1976): 15-21. See also Roger William Walworth, *The Life and Hymnological Contributions of Robert Lowry (1826-1899)*, (D.M.A. diss., The Southern Baptist Theological Seminary, 1994).

[40]This hymn has been arranged for solo voice by Aaron Copland in his collection, *Old American Songs Newly Arranged* (New York: Boosey & Hawkes, 1950).

- "I am Thine, O Lord," (1875, B290, M419),

- "Jesus, keep me near the cross" (1869, B280, M301),

- "Pass me not, O gentle Savior" (1868, B308, M351),

- "Rescue the perishing" (1869, B559, M591), and

- "To God be the glory" (1875, B4, M98, P485).

Doane also composed the tune to Elizabeth P. Prentiss' previously mentioned hymn, "More love to thee."

Fanny Crosby, the remarkable leading poet of the gospel hymn movement,[41] was a blind Methodist teacher from New York who wrote about 8,000 hymn texts. A recognized popular secular poet before she turned to writing hymns, she incorporated in her hymns such words of sentiment found in the popular song of her day as "gentle," "precious," and "tenderly." In addition to her hymns set by Doane, other texts of Crosby still in use include: "All the way my Savior leads me" (1875, tune by Lowry, B62), "Blessed assurance, Jesus is mine" (1873, tune by Methodist Phoebe P. Knapp, B334, M369, P341), and "Jesus is tenderly calling thee home" (1883, tune by George C. Stebbins, B316).

One of the most popular gospel hymns of the Sunday School era is "What a friend we have in Jesus" (B182, L439, M526, P403), written in 1855 by Joseph M. Scriven (1819-86), a native of Ireland who lived in Canada from 1844, and set to music in 1868 by the distinguished American composer Charles C. Converse (1832-1918). Another popular gospel hymn of this era was "I love to tell the story" (B572, L390, M156), written in 1866 by Londoner Katherine Hankey (1834-1911) and set to music in 1869 by William G. Fischer (1835-1912), a college music professor who from 1868 was associated with J. E. Gould (composer of PILOT) in a Philadelphia piano business.

Moody-Sankey Era

The 1870s gospel hymnody was a major force in urban revivalism, especially through the meetings of evangelist Dwight L. Moody (1837-99) and his musical associate Ira D. Sankey (1840-1908). During the Moody-Sankey

---

[41]An authoritative biography of Fanny Crosby is *Fanny Crosby* by Bernard Ruffin (Philadelphia: United Church Press, 1976).

era, the hymns previously associated with the Sunday School came to be known as gospel hymns. In their mass meetings, Sankey introduced many gospel hymns as he accompanied himself at his portable reed organ. Much of Moody and Sankey's work was related to the Young Men's Christian Association (founded in London, 1844; in Boston and Montreal, 1851), an organization which utilized the popular hymns of Bradbury, Lowry, Fischer, and others. Moody and Sankey first met at a YMCA convention at Indianapolis in 1870. Sankey was selected to direct music at Moody's church in Chicago. In 1872, when Moody was invited to hold evangelistic meetings in England, he first sought the services of the more experienced musicians Philip Phillips (1834-95)[42] and then Philip P. Bliss (1838-76); both declined. Moody then invited the less-experienced Sankey, who during their British tour gained international fame. Such was the demand for the hymns used by Sankey that a series of popular gospel hymn collections emerged. Although he was more important as a compiler and a popularizer of gospel hymnody than as a composer, Sankey composed two tunes in the hymnals of this study (SANKEY, B413; TRUSTING JESUS, B417).

Sankey did much to spread gospel hymnody through the collection he began in London in 1873 entitled *Sacred Songs and Solos*. This was a small 16-page pamphlet that by 1903 became a mammoth volume of 1,200 selections. Its American counterpart, the "Gospel Hymns Series," began with Bliss and Sankey's *Gospel Hymns and Sacred Songs* (1875), followed by numbers 2 (Bliss and Sankey), 3, 4, 5, and 6 (Sankey, McGranahan, and Stebbins), and culminating in *Gospel Hymns Nos. 1-6 Complete* (1894).[43]

Sankey's co-compilers, all associated with Moody at various times, were more successful than he in writing gospel hymns. Bliss, a Pennsylvanian like Sankey, was an evangelistic singer who worked with Moody and with the evangelist Daniel W. Whittle (1840-1901). Bliss wrote words and music to such popular gospel hymns as "Wonderful Words of Life"[44] (1874, first line: "Sing them over again to me," B261, M600), "'Man of sorrows!' what

---

[42]Phillips' *Hallowed Songs* (Cincinnati, 1865) was at first used by Sankey in London before compiling his own collection. Phillips, known internationally for his services of song, did much to popularize gospel hymnody and prepare the way for Sankey.

[43]This collected edition has been reprinted with a new introduction by H. Wiley Hitchcock (New York: Da Capo Press, 1973). See Esther Heidi Rothenbusch, "The Role of *Gospel Hymns Nos. 1 to 6* (1875-1894) in American Revivalism" (Ph.D. diss., The University of Michigan, 1991).

[44]Since gospel hymn tunes are not normally sung to more than one text and often are given tune names in hymnals that are a shortening of their hymn titles, tune names for most of the gospel hymns treated here are not listed.

a name" (B175, M165), and the music to "I gave My life for thee" (1873, text by Frances R. Havergal, 1858, B606), and "It Is Well with My Soul" (1876, first line: "When peace, like a river, attendeth my way," Horatio G. Spafford, 1873: B410, M377; hymn without refrain, L346).[45]

James McGranahan (1840-1907), who after Bliss's death became Whittle's song leader, composed music for such gospel hymns by Whittle as "I Know Whom I Have Believed" (1883, first line: "I know not why God's wondrous grace," B337, M714) and "There shall be showers of blessing" (1883, B467). McGranahan also composed the music to Bliss's "I will sing of my Redeemer" (1876, tune 1877, B575) and a German hymn of 1718 by Neumeister, "Christ Receiveth Sinful Men" (1883, first line: "Sinners Jesus will receive," B563).

George C. Stebbins (1846-1945), an evangelistic singer with Moody and others for some 25 years, composed the music to such popular gospel hymns as "Jesus is tenderly calling thee home" (1883, text by Crosby, B316), "Take time to be holy," (text by William D. Longstaff, B446, M395), and "Have Thine own way, Lord" (1907, text by Adelaide A. Pollard, B294, M382).[46] Daniel B. Towner (1850-1919), the youngest of Moody's associates whose hymns survive, is especially important as an educator of evangelistic musicians, for he was head of the Music Department of Moody Bible Institute in Chicago from 1893 until his death. Of the more than 2,000 compositions credited to him, two which remain in use are settings of "Trust and Obey" (1887, first line: "When we walk with the Lord," text by John H. Sammis, B447, M467) and "Grace Greater than Our Sin" (1910, MOODY, first line: "Marvelous grace of our loving Lord," text by Julia H. Johnston, B329, M365).

Three gospel hymnists of this period not associated with Moody whose surviving hymns were produced in the late 19th century are John R. Sweney (1837-99), William J. Kirkpatrick (1838-1921), and Will L. Thompson (1847-1909). Sweney, a Presbyterian and a popular song leader for summer assemblies, composed more than 1,000 gospel tunes and compiled more than 60 collections. He wrote tunes for four gospel hymns from the 1880s to 1891 which remain in use: "Tell me the story of Jesus" (1880, text by Crosby, B122), "More about Jesus would I know" (1887, text by Pennsylvania Presbyterian Eliza E. Hewitt, B600), "There is sunshine in my soul today" (1887, text by

[45]Although VILLE DU HAVRE has a refrain, its straightforward rhythm and harmonic variety are more typical of "churchly" hymnody than of gospel hymnody. Other Bliss tunes in this more churchly idiom are those to "'Man of Sorrows,' what a name" (1875, B175) and "More holiness give me" (1873, Baptist Hymnal, 1956, No. 338).

[46]Like Bliss, Stebbins also composed hymn tunes in other idioms. His tune EVENING PRAYER ("Savior, breathe an evening blessing," Baptist Hymnal 1956, No. 34), for example, is in a typical Victorian hymn-tune style.

Hewitt, B430),[47] and "My Savior First of All" (1891, first line: "When my life-work is ended, and I cross the swelling tide" by Crosby, B528).

Kirkpatrick, a Methodist active in Philadelphia, was associated with the publication of about 100 gospel hymn collections of various publishers. He wrote words and music for the invitation hymn, "Lord, I'm Coming Home" (1892, first line: "I've wandered far away from God," B309) and the music for "Jesus Saves" (1882, first line: "We have heard the joyful sound," text ca. 1882 by Priscilla Owens, B581), and "'Tis so sweet to trust in Jesus," text by Louisa M. R. Stead, B411, M462). In addition to his music to gospel hymns, Kirpatrick composed CRADLE SONG, a well-known setting to "Away in a manger" (E101, P24). Thompson, a music publisher from Ohio, composed both words and music for two well-known gospel hymns: "Softly and tenderly Jesus is calling" (1880, B312, M348) and "Jesus is all the world to me" (B184, M469).

© 1980 Charles Massey, Jr.

Ira David Sankey

The Early 20th Century

Following the era of Moody and Sankey, the pattern of each evangelist's having their own professional musicians became the norm. Among the musicians associated with evangelists, particularly important contributions to gospel hymnody were made by Charles M. Alexander (1867-1920) and Homer A. Rodeheaver (1880-1955). Alexander, who was briefly associated with Moody in 1893, became famous through his meetings with evangelists Reuben A. Torrey (1856-1928) and later J. Wilbur Chapman (1859-1918) in America, England, and Australia. Alexander, the opposite in personality from Sankey, eliminated all vestiges of dignity and formality in his revival services, leading the singing with wide sweeping motions of his hands and preferring improvised trills and cadenzas on the piano to simple organ accompaniment. In keeping with the lighthearted mood of his song services, Alexander popularized "The Glory Song" (1900, first line: "When all my

---

[47]It is of interest that both Sweeney and Kirkpatrick were associated with Civil War military bands, a factor that may have influenced their gospel hymn melodies. Note, for example, the trumpet-call like melody to Kirkpatrick's setting of JESUS SAVES (B581).

labors and trials are o'er," text and tune by Charles H. Gabriel, B520), a gospel hymn which lent itself to interpretive effects. Although not a composer, Alexander compiled widely used collections of gospel hymns; some of his copyrights are solos and congregational hymns still in use, the latter category including "One day when heaven was filled with His praises" (ca. 1909, CHAPMAN, by Charles H. Marsh, text by J. Wilbur Chapman, B193).

Rodeheaver became famous as the song leader for William (Billy) Sunday (1862-1935). His approach to music in evangelism (similar to Alexander's) was enhanced by his vocal and trombone solos. To those who criticized his use of a secular-sounding gospel hymn, Rodeheaver replied: "It was never intended for a Sunday morning service, not for a devotional meeting—its purpose was to bridge the gap between the popular song of the day and the great hymns and gospel songs, and to give men a simple, easy lilting melody which they could learn the first time they heard it, and which they could whistle and sing wherever they might be."[48]

Rodeheaver established his own music publishing firm in 1910, later locating it at Winona Lake, Indiana (now a part of Word Music, Incorporated). Rodeheaver composed little but published many gospel hymns; two of his most popular copyrights were "In the Garden" (1912, first line: "I come to the garden alone," text and tune by C. Austin Miles, B187, M314) and "The Old Rugged Cross" (1913, first line: "On a hill far away stood an old rugged cross," text and tune by George Bennard, B141, M504).

The music editor for Rodeheaver from 1912 until his death in 1932 was the prolific Charles H. Gabriel (b. 1856), who produced numerous gospel hymn collections. Like Bliss and Lowry before him, Gabriel wrote both words and music of gospel hymns. Hymns of Gabriel still in use include "Send the Light" (1890, first line: "There's a call comes ringing o'er the restless wave," B595), "I stand amazed in the presence" (1905, B547, M371), and the music to "Higher Ground" (text 1892, "I'm pressing on the upward way," Johnson Oatman, Jr., B484) and "Since Jesus Came into My Heart" (1914, "What a wonderful change in my life has been wrought," Rufus H. McDaniel, B441).

Shape-note Gospel Hymnody

Following the Civil War, the impact of urban influence from the North was increasingly felt upon the rural, shape-note hymnody of the South. The seven-shape tunebooks included smaller portions of indigenous folk hymns, and larger portions of European music and music by such European-oriented

[48]Homer Rodeheaver, *Twenty Years with Billy Sunday* (Nashville: Cokesbury Press, 1936), 78.

composers as Mason, Hastings, and Bradbury, together with a southern type of gospel hymn. One 19th-century southern gospel hymn tune which has survived is the setting of "Footsteps of Jesus" (1871, text by Massachusetts school teacher Mary B. C. Slade, first line: "Sweetly, Lord, have we heard Thee calling," B483) by the Virginian (and European-trained) Asa B. Everett (1828-75). This hymn tune, while embodying the slow harmonic rhythm and limited harmonic vocabulary of a gospel hymn, is a quasi-pentatonic[49] melody, a reflection of the earlier folk hymn tradition. "Leaning on the Everlasting Arms" (1887, first line: "What a fellowship, what a joy divine," Elisa A. Hoffman, B333, M133) was set to music by Anthony J. Showalter (1858-1924), a Virginian who established in 1884 at Dalton, Georgia, the A. J. Showalter Music Company. His tune, SHOWALTER, has a hexatonic melody, omitting the fourth degree of the scale. "Victory in Jesus" (1939, first line: "I heard an old, old story," B426, M370) was both written and composed by Eugene M. Bartlett (1885-1941), president of the Hartford (Arkansas) Music Company (1918-35), who was later associated with the leading shape-note publishing firm, the Stamps-Baxter Music Company,[50] Dallas, Texas, and the James D. Vaughan Music Company, Lawrenceburg, Tennessee.[51] Shape-note gospel hymns have found a firm place in the churches of several Southern denominations, including the Church of God, Cleveland, Tennessee. In contrast to northern gospel hymnody, the environment of Southern shape-note gospel hymnody has been largely rural or small town. Its context has been the singing school and the singing convention rather than mass revivalism. More recently this tradition has been dominated by professional concert and recording artists in the gospel music field.[52] Although some congregational singing remains in current shape-note gospel singing, it has generally taken second place to professional performance.

Recent Gospel Hymnody

Mass urban revivalism declined after the early decades of this century; however, gospel hymns have continued to be written, published, and widely sung. These hymns have gained a substantial place in the congregational singing of fundamentalist churches, as well as in a number of America's evan-

[49]The seventh of the major scale is missing and the fourth occurs only once.
[50]Now under northern ownership, this firm is known as Stamps-Baxter Music of the Zondervan Corporation. For a study of the texts and music of shape-note gospel hymnody based on Stamps-Baxter publications, see Shirley Beary, "Stylistic Traits of Southern Shape-Note Gospel Songs," *The Hymn* 30 (January 1979): 26-33, 35.
[51]This firm, no longer owned by the Vaughan family, is now located at Cleveland, Tennessee.
[52]The primary organization that serves the interest of the gospel music industry is the Gospel Music Association, 1205 Division Street, Nashville, Tennessee, 37203.

gelical denominations, such as Assemblies of God, Southern Baptists, Churches of Christ, Churches of the Nazarene, Seventh-Day Adventists, Churches of God, and various Pentecostal bodies.

The leading gospel hymn writer-composer among Southern Baptists was Louisianian B. B. McKinney (1886-1952), who edited the popular *Broadman Hymnal* (Nashville: Broadman Press, 1940). He is represented by more than a dozen hymns in *The Baptist Hymnal*, 1991, including "Have faith in God" (1934, MUSKOGEE, No. 405) and "Wherever he leads I'll go" (1936, first line: "Take up thy cross and follow Me," FALLS CREEK, No. 285).

"Great is Thy faithfulness" (B54, M140, P276), one of the few gospel hymns addressed to God rather than to other persons, was written in 1923 by the Methodist minister Thomas O. Chisholm (1866-1960). It was set to music by another Methodist minister and music editor for Hope Publishing Company who for many years was associated with the Moody Bible Institute, William M. Runyan (1870-1957). The words and music to "He Lives" (First line: "I serve a risen Savior," B533, M310) were written in 1933 by the Presbyterian minister Alfred H. Ackley (1887-1960),[53] who was associated with the Rodeheaver Publishing Company as a compiler and editor. This exuberant gospel hymn incorporates an expanded harmonic vocabulary and vocal range.

A third representative newer gospel hymn is "Surely Goodness and Mercy" (first line: "A pilgrim was I, and a wand'ring," B422), whose text and tune were jointly written in 1958 by John W. Peterson (b. 1921) and Alfred B. Smith (b. 1916), both active gospel hymn composers and editors. This gospel hymn, an expression of the Christian pilgrimage based on Psalm 23, incorporates a florid style and an expanded form that includes a coda. Smith, the first song leader for Billy Graham, established in 1941 the music publishing firm of Singspiration, which he sold to the Zondervan Publishing House, Grand Rapids, Michigan, in 1962. A prolific hymn writer and composer, Peterson has published more than 1,000 songs.

Another recent gospel hymn, written in 1971, is "Because He Lives" (first line: "God sent his Son, they called him Jesus," B407). An Indiana couple, Gloria (b. 1942) and William J. Gaither (b. 1936), wrote the text; William J. Gaither composed the music. "Because He Lives," which shares a similar theme with Ackley's "He Lives," also has something else in common with this earlier gospel hymn—an expanded range and harmonic vocabulary.

[53]His brother, Bentley D. Ackley (1872-1958), also a hymn writer, was pianist for many years in the Sunday-Rodeheaver meetings.

The Gaithers are widely known in America as performers, recording artists, and publishers of gospel music.

Black (African-American) Gospel Hymnody

Black gospel hymnody is based on elements of the spiritual and the blues, as well as the White gospel hymn, but its style of performance is distinctively Black. Important factors in its performance are its improvised melodies and rhythmic piano accompaniments, which since the 1940s have been combined with the Hammond electronic organ. In Black holiness churches, various percussion instruments are also used. Although Black gospel hymnody is a 20th-century development, its roots lie in a much older tradition of preaching, singing (including a continuing tradition of lining-out[54]), shouting, and clapping. African-American gospel music is known to Whites primarily through professional performers, such as Mahalia Jackson (1911-1972) and Andraé Crouch (b. 1945) and the Disciples. The distinction between congregation and choir (or ensembles or soloists) is blurred in Black worship; the congregation often sings along with the choir and expresses its joy or affirmation in terms of hand-clapping, "hallelujahs," or "amens."

Two representative composers of Black gospel hymnody are Charles A. Tindley (1851-1933) and Thomas A. Dorsey (1899-1993). Tindley, pastor of the Tindley Temple Methodist Church in Philadelphia from 1902 until his death, wrote both words and music to "We'll Understand It Better By and By" (1905, first line: "We are tossed and driven on the restless sea of time"[55]; M525; altered version: "Trials dark on ev'ry hand, and we cannot understand," B522) and "Stand By Me" (1905, first line: "When the storms of life are raging, stand by me," M512[56]). Both of these hymns reflect the life of poverty and discrimination experienced by many Black Americans. Note, for example, the second stanza of "We'll Understand It Better By and By":

> "We are often destitute of the things that life demands,
>> Want of food and want of shelter, thirsty hills and barren lands;
> We are trusting in the Lord, and according to God's word,
>> We will understand it better by and by."

[54]Ben E. Bailey, "The Lined-Hymn Tradition in Black Mississippi Churches," *The Black Perspective in Music* (Spring 1978): 3-17.
[55]*The New National Baptist Hymnal* (Hereafter: N) (Nashville: National Baptist Publishing Board, 1977), No. 325; *A.M.E. Hymnal* (Hereafter: A) (N. P.: A.M.E. Sunday School Union, 1954), No. 542.
[56]A287, N500.

Dorsey, a native of Georgia who lived in Chicago throughout his adult life, composed both blues and gospel in his early years, but since 1929 devoted himself exclusively to gospel music. Two of his best-known hymns for which he wrote or arranged both words and music are "Precious Lord, take my hand" (1932, B456, M474),[57] and "There'll be peace in the valley for me" (1939, first line: "I am tired and weary, but I must toil on"). These hymns, like those of Tindley, offer encouragement and hope to the discouraged and weary. To understand the significance of Black gospel hymnody and Black church music in general, it is necessary to go beyond the pages of a hymnal to experience these hymns amid the enthusiastic mood of traditional Black worship. Black church music, and Black gospel hymnody in particular, cannot be adequately studied from a printed page; the musical score provides only a skeleton which, when clothed through embellishments and other variations in performance, assumes a form that has an expressive character of its own.

Summary

Gospel hymnody, forged in the setting of the urban Sunday School and mass revivalism, reflects the same freedom of personal expression found in the earlier rural hymns and Negro spirituals. The more artistic gospel hymns have survived and can be found in many hymnals, especially those of revivalistic churches. Gospel hymnody has not been limited to America and Britain. Through the work of missionaries and evangelists, this hymnody has been translated into many languages and has spread to every continent. It is of interest to note, for example, that some gospel hymns which are no longer in current use in this country still survive in Spanish, Portuguese, Chinese, Korean, and Japanese hymnals. Gospel hymnody has not remained static in musical style or language; it has continued a process of development for more than a century. A gospel hymn of Sankey's day, for example, will be recognizably different from most gospel hymns of Peterson or Gaither. Furthermore, offshoots of gospel hymnody, such as shape-note gospel hymnody (based on folk hymnody) and Black gospel hymnody (based on the spiritual), have also developed from the older traditions.

---

[57]N446. Dorsey's tune PRECIOUS LORD is an adaptation of the tune MAITLAND by George N. Allen (1812-1877), a setting for the hymn "Must Jesus bear the cross alone" (B475, M424). For a detailed study of Dorsey, see Michael W. Harris, *The Rise of the Gospel Blues: The Music of Thomas Andrew Dorsey in the Urban Church* (New York: Oxford University Press, 1992).

HYMNOLOGY IN AMERICA

Many major American hymnals now have companions or handbooks which provide background information on each of their hymns and tunes and biographical sketches of their authors and composers. Behind these companion volumes lies a wealth of hymnological scholarship dating back to the 19th century. Two American hymnologists who contributed to Julian's *A Dictionary of Hymnology* (1892) are Philip Schaff (1819-1893) and Louis F. Benson (1855-1930). Schaff, a Reformed Church minister born in Switzerland and obtaining university training in Germany, came to Pennsylvania at the age of 24 to teach theology. His hymnological works include an important Julian *Dictionary* article on "German Hymnody."[58] Benson, a Presbyterian minister who is recognized as America's greatest hymnologist, was also a hymnal editor and hymn writer. Benson's *The English Hymn* (1915) continues to be the most definitive history of the hymn in English.[59]

Whereas Schaff and Benson were concerned mainly with the texts of hymns, two other American hymnologists dealt with the *music* of congregational song. Waldo Selden Pratt (1857-1939), a musicologist who taught church music and hymnology at Hartford Theological Seminary, wrote two works dealing with the music of metrical psalmody: *The Music of the Pilgrims* (1921) and *The Music of the French Psalter of 1562* (1939).[60] Robert Guy McCutchan (1877- 1958) was a college music teacher and administrator who edited *The Methodist Hymnal* (1935) and authored its companion, *Our Hymnody* (1937), the first hymnal companion of significance to be published in America.[61]

Hymnology in America has advanced significantly through the work of the Hymn Society in the United States and Canada (formerly known as the Hymn Society of America), an interdenominational organization founded in 1922. In addition to its activities encouraging the writing of new hymns and tunes and giving impetus to congregational singing in general, it has published a series of scholarly papers (from 1930 on) and numerous hymnological studies in its quarterly, *The Hymn* (from 1949 on).

The Dictionary of American Hymnology Project (DAH) is a mammoth endeavor of the Society to produce an American equivalent of Julian, *Dictionary of Hymnology*. The DAH, which grew out of efforts to update the American sections of Julian, was first under the editorship of Henry Wilder

---

[58]Richard G. Appel, "Philip Schaff, Pioneer American Hymnologist," *The Hymn* 14 (January 1963): 5-7.
[59]Morgan Phelphs Noyes, *Louis F. Benson, Hymnologist*, Paper XIX of the Hymn Society of America, 1955.
[60]"Waldo Selden Pratt," *The Hymn* 6, 2 (April 1955), 38. See also Pratt's *The Significance of the Old French Psalter*, Paper IV of the Hymn Society of America, 1933.
[61]Helen Cowles McCutchan, *Born to Music*, Paper XXVIII of the Hymn Society of America, 1973.

Foote[62] in the early 1950s and from 1955 to 1984 was edited by Leonard Ellinwood.[63] Two parts of the DAH files have been published in microform: *Bibliography of American Hymnals*, compiled from the *Files of the Dictionary of American Hymnology* (microfiche, 1983) and *Dictionary of American Hymnology: First Line Index* (microfilm, 1984).[64] Work on the DAH is continuing in its headquarters at the Oberlin College Library under the leadership of librarian/coordinator Mary Louise VanDyke. It is anticipated that the DAH first-line index will eventually be available on a computerized data base and that its essays will also be published.

20TH-CENTURY CHURCHLY HYMNODY
Hymns in Ecumenical Use

Eight American hymn texts of this century have found a place in most major hymnals issued in this country in recent years. Five of the eight hymn texts were written before World War I. One of the two earliest, a favorite hymn for children as well as adults, is "This is my Father's world" (TERRA PATRIS or TERRA BEATA, B43, L554, M144, P293, MERCER STREET, by Malcolm Williamson,[65] E651), written in 1901 by Presbyterian minister Maltbie D. Babcock (1858-1901) and set to music in 1915 by his friend Franklin L. Sheppard (1852-1930). Also written in 1901 but not appearing often in hymnals until recently was "Lift every voice and sing" (B627, E599, L562, M519, P563). Sometimes known as the African-American "National Anthem," this hymn reflecting the struggles of Blacks for freedom was written by James Weldon Johnson (1871-1938) and set to music by his brother, J. Rosamond Johnson (1873-1954).

In 1907 "Joyful, joyful, we adore Thee" (B7, E376, L551, M89, P464) was written (to fit the famous melody from Beethoven's Ninth Symphony, HYMN TO JOY) by the Presbyterian minister and professor of English literature, Henry van Dyke (1852-1933). Van Dyke's exuberant hymn, together with Beethoven's joyful melody, is a fine example of unity in text and tune. Three Presbyterian hymn writers of the early 20th century served at one time as pastors of New York City's historic Brick Presbyterian Church: Van Dyke from 1883-99, Babcock from 1899-1901, and William P. Merrill from 1911-38.[66]

[62]See Arthur Foote, 2nd, *Henry Wilder Foote, Hymnologist*, Paper XXVI of the Hymn Society of America, 1965.
[63]Leonard Ellinwood, "The Dictionary of American Hymnology Project," *The Hymn* 19 (January 1968): 19-22.
[64]Both published for the Hymn Society by University Music Editions, New York City.
[65]See Chapter 7, "British Traditions," 173.
[66]See Edith Holden and George Litch Knight, "Brick Church's Role in American Hymnody," *The Hymn* 3, 3 (July 1952): 73-78.

"God of grace and God of glory" (B395, E594, 595, L415, M577, P420) was written for the dedication of the Riverside Church in New York City in 1930 by its prominent minister, Harry Emerson Fosdick (1878-1969). Fosdick, a Baptist, sought to make the Riverside Church an ecumenical congregation, serving the needs of all classes of people. This hymn, his prayer for wisdom and courage, has become a prayer of worshiping groups throughout America.[67]

The most recent American hymn to gain general use in major hymnals is "God, who stretched the spangled heavens" (B47, E580, L463, M150, P268), written in 1965 by Catherine Cameron (b. 1927).

Hymns of Wide Acceptance

In addition to these hymns of ecumenical acceptance in 20th-century America, more than two dozen other hymn texts and several hymn tunes are frequently found in current hymnals.[68] Four of these hymns appeared before 1920.

The earliest, "O sing a song of Bethlehem" (B120, M179, P308) by hymnologist Louis F. Benson (1855-1930), actually was first published in a Presbyterian Sunday School hymnal in 1899, but did not begin to appear in hymnals of other denominations until the second decade of the 20th century. Written for children, this is one of the relatively few hymns dealing with the boyhood and ministry of Jesus. In 1903 appeared "Where cross the crowded ways of life" (E609, L429, M427, P408), written by the Methodist minister Frank Mason North (1850-1935). North, who from 1892 to 1912 edited *The Christian City*, incorporated his concern for reaching the urban masses with the Christian message into this hymn, which has become the classic American hymn on the city.

A third hymn of this period is "O holy city, seen of John" (E582, 583, M726, P453), written in 1910 by Walter Russell Bowie (1882-1969), a distinguished Episcopal clergyman and seminary professor. Bowie's text, set to the early American melody MORNING SONG, deals powerfully with the need to apply the gospel to dealing with injustice. The fourth pre-World War I hymn of wide acceptance is "Rise up, O men (ye saints) of God" (B400, E551, M576), written in 1911 by Presbyterian minister William P. Merrill (1867-1954). This hymn emphasizes brotherhood and was original-

[67]See Linda Clark, "God of Grace and God of Glory: A Very Urgent Personal Prayer," *The Hymn* 29 (October 1978): 206-210, 213.
[68]Texts or tunes were considered to be of wide acceptance if they appeared in three or four of our key hymnals, or if they appeared in 1977 or later and were published in two of the four key hymnals after the *Lutheran Book of Worship* of 1978.

ly written for men's meetings. Merrill's hymn has become problematical to many because it has been used in worship services including women even though Merrill intended it for men's services.

One of the following three hymns was written in the 1920s, and two were written in the 1930s. Louis F. Benson wrote the communion hymn "For the bread which thou hast (you have) broken" (E340, L200, M614, 615, P508, 509) in 1924. Both hymns from the 1930s were written by Episcopal minister F. Bland Tucker (1895-1984). "All praise to thee, for thou, O King divine" (B229, E477, M166,) is Tucker's paraphrase of Philippians 2:5-11. "Our Father (Parent) by whose name" (E587, L357, M447), a prayer for families, was written in 1939.[69] No American hymns of wide acceptance were written during the 1940s.

Three widely accepted American hymns were written in the 1950s. "Hope of the world, thou Christ of great compassion" (E472, L493, M178, P360) was written in 1954 for the Second Assembly of the World Council of Churches at Evanston, Illinois, by the Methodist minister and theologian Georgia Harkness (1891-1974). This hymn, a fervent prayer like Fosdick's earlier hymn, affirms Christ as "Hope of the world" and ends with a strong assertion of God's victory.[70] "Hope of the world" was the winning hymn of a competition sponsored in 1954 by the Hymn Society. A second hymn from this decade, also the result of one of the Hymn Society's "searches," is "O Jesus Christ, may grateful hymns be rising" (E590, L427, P424), written by United Methodist minister Bradford Gray Webster (1898-1991) and published in Five New Hymns on the City (The Hymn Society, 1954). A third hymn from this decade, also written by a United Methodist minister, is William W. Reid, Jr.'s "O God of every nation" (E607, M435, P289), a strong prayer for a world of love and peace.

The first of three widely accepted American hymns of the next decade is Presbyterian minister Frank von Christierson's "As men (those) of old their firstfruits brought" (B639, E705, P414), a winning hymn on stewardship in a search for new hymns conducted by the Hymn Society in 1960. The second hymn, written by Lutheran minister Herbert Brokering (b. 1926) for the 90th anniversary of St. Olaf College in 1964, is "Earth and all stars" (E412, L558, P458). Brokering's text, which calls for a new song of praise to the Lord in the circumstances of daily living, was provided an expansive tune in 1968 by David N. Johnson (1922-1987).

[69]This hymn is quoted in Chapter 13, "The Hymn in Ministry," 304.
[70]See Deborah C. Loftis, "The Hymns of Georgia Harkness," The Hymn 28 (October 1977): 186-91.

The third hymn, in a free form that may be seen as stream of consciousness hymnody,[71] is Lutheran minister Jaroslav Vajda's (b. 1919) text of 1968 depicting the movements of worship, "Now the Silence," (NOW, E333, L205, M619). It is set to an equally captivating tune by the Lutheran composer Carl Schalk (b. 1929). In 1983 Vajda and Schalk produced another text and tune which have gained wide acceptance: "God of the sparrow" (ROEDER, M122, P272). Also a stream of consciousness type hymn, Vajda's text expresses simple yet profound biblical truths set by Schalk to a unison tune of folk-like simplicity.[72]

A significant worship phenomenon of recent decades, the development of the charismatic movement among mainline denominations, both Protestant and Catholic, has produced new hymnody, including the following examples. The first of several widely accepted American hymns of the 1970s, Karen Lafferty's "Seek ye first," (B478, E711, M405, P333) is an example of the popular Scripture songs originating in charismatic congregations. A setting of Matthew 6:33 and 7:7, Lafferty's simple tune is provided guitar chords in some hymnals. A second hymn of charismatic origin from this decade is "Alleluia, alleluia! Give thanks to the risen Lord" (B170, E178, M162). Its text and tune of 1973 were written by Donald Fishel (b. 1950), a member of The Word of God, a Roman Catholic community in Washtenaw County, Michigan.

Several other composers have produced hymn tunes of wide acceptance in the 1970s and 1980s. In some cases, as with VINEYARD HAVEN ("Rejoice, ye pure in heart," E557, M161, P146), tunes have been composed for an established older text. Composed by Richard Dirksen (b. 1921) of Washington (Episcopal) Cathedral, VINEYARD HAVEN has also been used with Watts's "Come, we that love the Lord" (E392). Dirksen's tune has been described by Schulz-Widmar as "a modern hymn of the grand kind, embracing fully the 19th-century notion of the inherent powers of functional chromaticism."[73]

Another Episcopal composer, David Hurd (b. 1950), represented by nine tunes in The Hymnal 1982, has two tunes that also appear in another key hymnal. Hurd is particularly known for song-like melodies with accompaniments, as in JULION (1983, E268, M197), his setting for "Ye who claim the faith of

[71]Russell Schulz-Widmar, "Hymnody in the United States Since 1950," Companion to The Hymnal 1982, Vol. 1 (New York: Church Hymnal Corporation, 1991), 605-7.
[72]For more hymns of Vajda, see Now the Joyful Celebration: Hymns, Carols, and Songs by Jaroslav J.Vajda (St. Louis: Morning Star Music Publishers, 1987) and So Much to Sing About: Hymns, Carols, and Songs (St. Louis: Morning Star Music Publishers, 1991).
[73]Schulz-Widmar, "Hymnody," 621.

Jesus." JULION begins with a four-bar introduction which also functions as interludes between the stanzas and as a postlude. Also noteworthy are JULION's syncopated pedal points which support half of the tune. Hurd's tune MIGHTY SAVIOR (E35, M684) for the Mozarabic hymn "Christ, mighty Savior," is regarded as "one of the treasures of twentieth-century hymnody," by Schutz-Widmar, who characterizes it as "at once both simple and lavish, consisting essentially of a natural melody floating over a gentle, rocking bass… the space between [filled] with delicious sonority."[74]

Two United Methodist composers who have contributed one hymn tune each to two recent hymnals are Jane Manton Marshall (b. 1924) and Carlton R. Young (b. 1926). Marshall, widely known as a composer of anthems, composed the tune JACOB (1984; E466, P340) for Christopher Idle's paraphrase of a prayer by Alcuin (c. 735-804).[75] The four symmetrical phrases of JACOB have a balance of $\frac{6}{4}$ and $\frac{5}{4}$ meter; its melody and harmony achieve innovative sounds chiefly through the lowered seventh tone. Young, editor of the United Methodist hymnals of 1966 and 1989, composed the tune BEGINNINGS for Brian Wren's communion hymn, "This is a day of new beginnings" (B370, M383). Young's unison tune closes stanzas 1-4 with a half cadence, reserving the full cadence for the final stanza. Also notable is Young's skillful use of syncopation and altered ninth chords to enhance the singing of this text.

With the acceptance of the common lectionary in many churches, both Catholic and Protestant, there has been a need for new hymns based on these Scripture readings. In response to this need, a collection of 52 new hymn texts and tunes for year B of the three-year lectionary entitled *New Hymns for the Lectionary: To Glorify the Maker's Name* (Oxford University Press) was published by the poet-composer team of Thomas H. Troeger (b. 1945) and Carol Doran (b. 1936) in 1986. Troeger, a Presbyterian clergyman, and Doran, an Episcopal church musician, served then on a theological seminary faculty in Rochester, New York. The hymn for Pentecost, entitled "Wind who makes all winds that blow," addresses the Holy Spirit as Wind, Light, Power, Might, and Strength. One key hymnal (M538) uses Doran's FALCONE, a through-composed unison tune peppered with a good supply of dissonant harmony, while the other (P131) uses the 19th-century Welsh tune ABERYSTWYTH.

---

[74]Ibid, 618.
[75]JACOB also serves as the musical setting for William Bright's "How oft, O Lord, thy face hath shown" (E242).

Two more widely accepted hymns of this decade were written by Jeffery W. Rowthorn (b. 1934), an Anglican priest from Wales who taught worship at Yale University's Divinity School and Institute of Sacred Music and since 1987 has been Episcopal bishop suffragan of Connecticut. "Creating God, your fingers trace" (E394, 395, M109), a paraphrase of Psalm 148 written in 1974, was published in *The Hymn* (April 1979) after it was selected as a winning hymn in the Hymn Society's "New Psalms for Today" competition. This hymn was followed in 1978 by Rowthorn's hymn on the church's mission, "Lord, you give the great commission" (E528, M584).

A Roman Catholic contribution of wide acceptance is GIFT OF FINEST WHEAT ("You satisfy the hungry heart," M629, P521), the official hymn of the 41st International Eucharistic Congress, held in Philadelphia in 1976. Its author, Omer Westendorf (b. 1916), founded the World Library of Sacred Music in 1950 and compiled a widely used hymnal, *The Peoples Mass Book* (Cincinnati, 1964, later eds., 1966, 1970, 1976, 1984). The tune GIFT OF FINEST WHEAT, which alternates smoothly between $\frac{4}{4}$ and $\frac{3}{4}$, was composed by Robert E. Kreutz (b. 1922), who has set other Westendorf hymns to music. "You Satisfy the Hungry Heart" has become a popular hymn for communion.

In contrast to earlier decades in this century, there is a much larger group of American hymns of wide acceptance in the 1980s. These hymns, which appeared after the selection of hymns for the 1978 *Lutheran Book of Worship*, are found in at least two of the other four key American hymnals used with this text.

Three of these new hymns are texts of Carl P. Daw, Jr. (b. 1944), a professor of English literature who became an Episcopal clergyman. The first, "Like the murmur of the dove's song" (E513, M544, P314), is a prayer to the Holy Spirit written in 1981 to fit Peter Cutts' tune BRIDEGROOM. The second, "O day of peace that dimly shines" (E597, M729, P450), was written in 1982 to fit Charles Hubert H. Parry's expansive tune of 1916, JERUSALEM. The third, "God the Spirit, guide and guardian," (1987, M648, P523), is a hymn for ordination.[76]

Two more Americans have written texts of wide acceptance in the 1980s: Russell Schulz-Widmar (b. 1944) and Gracia Grindal (b. 1943). Schulz-Widmar, a Lutheran who teaches in an Episcopal seminary and directs music at a United Methodist Church in Austin, Texas, has written a fine wedding hymn, "Your love, O God, has called us here" (1982; B509, E353, M647), a hymn

---

[76]Additional hymns of Carl P. Daw, Jr. are found in his collected hymns, *A Year of Grace: Hymns for the Church Year* (Carol Stream, IL: Hope Publishing Company, 1990).

that is a prayer not only for those being married, but also for every husband and wife. Grindal, a Lutheran on the faculty of Luther Northwestern Theological Seminary in St. Paul, is a teacher of writing who has contributed to recent discussions on the language of hymnody.[77] A widely accepted contribution of hers is a narration of the angel Gabriel's annunciation to the virgin Mary, "To a maid engaged to Joseph" (1984; M215, P19). Grindal's hymn is provided a traditional folk-like tune, ANNUNCIATION, composed in 1983 by the Lutheran minister Rusty (Howard M. III) Edwards (b. 1955).[78]

Summary

Twentieth-century American hymn texts in the churchly stream which have achieved broad acceptance are few; even fewer American hymn tunes of this tradition are widely used. In contrast to those of England, no single American hymnist of this century has written a significant number of widely accepted hymns. Several themes are recognizable in 20th-century American hymns:

1. Brotherhood is a prominent emphasis, exemplified by "Joyful, joyful, we adore thee" and "Rise up, O men of God."

2. No longer strictly rural in their context, hymns also recognize the needs of urban Americans. The classic American hymn on the city is "Where cross the crowded ways of life."[79]

3. There is an increasing emphasis on justice and social responsibility. These related themes are especially prominent in "God of grace and God of glory," and "O holy city, seen of John."

4. America's experience in the wars of this century is reflected in hymns emphasizing the tragedy of strife and the need for peace (for example, "Hope of the world").[80]

5. Many recent hymns are occasional, having been written for specific events. "God of grace and God of glory" was written for the dedication of the Riverside Church in 1930. "Hope of the world" was written for the Second Assembly of the World Council of Churches in 1954. Hymns written for competitions sponsored by

[77]See, for example, Gracia Grindal's "Where We Are Now," The Hymn 38, 4 (Oct. 1987): 22-26.
[78]See Howard M. (Rusty) Edwards, III, The Yes of the Heart: Faith, Hope and Love Songs (Carol Stream, IL: Hope Publishing Co., 1993).
[79]Other city-oriented American hymns include "O Jesus Christ, may grateful hymns be rising" (E590, L247, P590), "Stir your church, O God our Father" (B392), "The voice of God is calling" (M436), and "Where restless crowds are thronging" (L430). See Chapter 13, "The Hymn in Minstry," 300-301.
[80]Other American hymns reflecting these themes include "O day of peace that dimly shines" (E597, M729, P450), "O God, empower us" (L422), and "O God of every nation" (E607, L416, M435, P287).

the Hymn Society include "Hope of the world," "As men (those) of old their firstfruits brought," "O God of every nation," "Creating God, your fingers trace," and "O Jesus Christ, may grateful hymns be rising."

Most American denominations have issued revised hymnals in recent years, each compiled to meet the needs of its own constituency. Thus, each hymnal is distinctive, mirroring a particular heritage which in turn reflects a history of theological beliefs and musical tastes. In some cases several denominations, especially those of similar background, have combined their efforts to produce a single hymnal. The *Lutheran Book of Worship* (1978), for example, was compiled by several cooperating Lutheran bodies in this country. Some have also sought to encourage ecumenism in hymnody. The Consultation on Ecumenical Hymnody[81] has published lists of hymns and tunes recommended for ecumenical use. But in spite of ecumenical influences, each denomination's hymnal still tends to embody much of its own heritage. Practically all recent major American hymnals have incorporated a greater representation of early American folk hymnody (including Negro spirituals) than in the past. These recent hymnals are also admitting hymns from the Third World cultures of Africa and the Orient.[82] America's pluralistic society is reflected in the great variety of its religious denominations. This pluralism is accurately pictured in the wide diversity of its hymnals and in its varied congregational singing practices.

RECENT CANADIAN HYMNODY

Hymn writing has flourished in Canada since the middle of this century. In *The Hymn Book* (1971), a joint project of the Anglican Church of Canada and the United Church of Canada,[83] there are no fewer than 45 Canadian authors represented, 24 of whom had not contributed hymns to any previous hymnal.[84] Among an earlier generation of this century's Canadian hymnists represented in American hymnals are Robert B. Y. Scott (b. 1899-1987) and Moir A. J. Waters (1906-80). Scott, a United Church minister

---

[81]See Ford Lewis Battles and Morgan Simmons, "The Consultation on Ecumenical Hymnody," *The Hymn* 28 (April 1977): 67-68,87; "Hymns and Tunes Recommended for Ecumenical Use," *The Hymn* 28 (October 1977): 192-209; and Robert J. Batastini, Donald P. Hustad, Austin C. Lovelace, and Cyril V. Taylor, "The CEH List: Four Diverse Appraisals." *The Hymn* 29 (April 1978): 83-90.
[82]See examples in Chapter 9, "Cultural Perspectives."
[83]The United Church of Canada is a union of Congregational, Methodist, Presbyterian, and United Brethren bodies.
[84]Stanley L. Osborne, "Recent Canadian Hymnody," *The Hymn* 29, 3 (July 1978): 135. This article is an excellent survey of recent Canadian hymn texts.

and former theological seminary professor, is best known for his hymn of judgment, "O day of God, draw nigh" (1939, ST. MICHAEL, B623, E601, M730, P452; BELLWOODS, E600). Waters, also of the United Church of Canada, wrote in 1968 a hymn on John the Baptist as the herald of Jesus, "Herald, sound the note of judgment" (NEW MALDEN, E70, L556).

A third hymnist, United Church of Canada clergyman, church historian, and theological professor, John Webster Grant (1919-1994), has contributed to hymnody through his masterful translations of Medieval Latin hymns into 20th-century English. All four of his translations from the Latin in *The Hymn Book* (1971) were selected for inclusion in *The Hymnal 1982* of the Episcopal Church: "O Holy Spirit, by whose breath" (*Veni Creator Spiritus*, E501, 502), "Holy Spirit, font of light" (*Veni, sancte Spiritus*, E228), "The flaming banners of our King" (*Vexilla Regis prodeunt*, E161), and "King of the martyrs' noble band" (*Rex gloriose martyrum*, E236).

E. Margaret Clarkson (b. 1915), a Presbyterian who was a school teacher for many years in Toronto, writes hymn texts with an evangelical emphasis. Her best known text, a missionary hymn, is "So send I you," a hymn of 1938 which she rewrote in 1962 to provide a stronger biblical basis; it was set to music in 1954 by the American gospel-hymn composer, John W. Peterson. The full first line of the rewritten version is "So send I you, by grace made strong to triumph" (B565, TORONTO). Other recently published texts by her include "Burn in me, Fire of God" (1938, 1986, B496), "Our cities cry to you, O God" (1981, P437), and "We gather here to bid farewell" (1987, P444).[85]

A leading Anglican Church of Canada hymnist is T. Herbert O'Driscoll (b. 1928), who came to Canada from his native Ireland about 1954. His longest post was as dean of Christ Church Cathedral, Vancouver, 1968-82. He was a member of the committee that compiled *The Hymn Book* (1971), two of his texts being included: "God who has caused to be written thy word for our learning"[86] and "From the slave pens of the Delta." The latter hymn was included in *The United Methodist Hymnal* with its original line four as the first line, "Let my people seek their freedom" (EBENEZER, M586). O'Driscoll's text effectively retells the great

---

[85] A collection of more than 130 of her hymns is *A Singing Heart* (Carol Stream, IL: Hope Publishing Co., 1987).

[86] This text and "Who are we who stand and sing" were published in *More Hymns for Today: A Second Supplement to Hymns Ancient and Modern* (London and Great Yarmouth: William Clowes & Sons, 1980), Nos. 134 and 196.

Hebrew exodus and applies it to the mission of the church in today's world.[87]

Another hymnist who emigrated to Canada is Barrie Cabena (b. 1933). Originally from Melbourne, Australia, he completed his musical studies in England and came to Canada in 1957. Active as organist, composer, and teacher, since 1970 he has taught at Waterloo Lutheran University (now Wilfrid Laurier University). In addition to two contributions in *The Hymn Book*,[88] Cabena composed the tune ATKINSON for "O God of light, your Word, a lamp unfailing" (1978, L237), an expansive, majestic setting which requires the congregation to stretch its range to an octave and a fourth.

A vital part of the renaissance of hymn writing in Canada is Walter H. Farquharson (b. 1936), a United Church pastor at Saltcoats, Saskatchewan, who was elected moderator of his denomination in 1990. "God who gives to life its goodness" (1969, ABBOT'S LEIGH) is one of his four hymns in the 1971 *Anglican-United Hymn Book*. The first four lines of Farquaharson's stanzas proclaim the works of God; the latter lines constitute a prayer of human response to God's loving initiative:

> "God who gives to life its goodness,
>   God creator of all joy,
> God who gives to us our freedom,
>   God who blesses tool and toy;
> teach us now to laugh and praise you,
>   deep within your praises sing,
> till the whole creation dances
>   for the goodness of its King."
> "God who fills the earth with beauty,
>   God who binds each friend to friend,
> God who names us co-creators,
>   God who wills that chaos end:
> grant us now creative spirits,
>   minds responsive to your mind,
> hearts and wills your rule extending,
>   all our acts by Love refined."[89]

---

[87]A collection of O'Driscoll's hymns is *Alleluia! 20 New Hymns by Herbert O'Driscoll with 10 New Tunes and Arrangements by Patrick Wedd* (Toronto: Anglican Book Centre, 1979).

[88]These are the tune PIER PAUL to "O Lord of love, who gives this sign to be" (312) and the harmonization of JESUS AHATONHIA to "'Twas in the moon of winter time" (412).

[89]Copyright © 1970 by Walter Henry Farquharson. Used by permission.* Farquharson's "Would you bless our homes and families" (1974) is in B507.

A hymn from the 1971 hymnal which has been published in both England and in the United States is "Let there be light" (1968, CONCORD, M440) by Frances Wheeler Davis (1936-76), a teacher. Set in the unusual 4.7.7.6 meter, her text is a simple but strong prayer for peace set to music of equal simplicity by the distinguished Canadian composer, Robert J. B. Fleming (1921-76).

The most recent contributions from Canada in this survey are the texts of Sylvia Dunstan (1954-93), a United Church minister whose hymns were written in the 1980s and early 1990s. Her hymns were collected and published in 1991 as *In Search of Hope & Grace: 40 Hymns and Gospel Songs*.[90] Among her hymns, the one which has received the most attention is "Christus Paradox," which was chosen as a theme hymn for the 1984 General Council. With "You, the everlasting instant" as a unifying phrase in the next to last line of each stanza, "Christus Paradox" is replete with paradoxes. Note, for example, stanza three:

> "You, who walk each day beside us,
>   sit in power at God's side.
> You, who preach a way that's narrow,
>   have a love that reaches wide.
> You, the everlasting instant;
>   You, who are our pilgrim guide."[91]

Canada's renaissance of hymn writing is thus continuing more than three decades since the 1971 *Hymn Book*. In the 1990s, several Canadian denominations are scheduled to release new hymnals, including Anglicans, Presbyterians, Roman Catholics, and the United Church of Canada. With the release of these new hymnals, the work of Canadian hymnists will undoubtedly become better known, and Canadian hymns will be more often published and sung in the United States of America.

[90]G.I.A. Publications, Chicago.
[91]© Copyright 1991. G.I.A. Publications. Used by permission.*

9

CULTURAL PERSPECTIVES

CULTURAL DIVERSITY IN CONGREGATIONAL SONG

The typical hymnal of our time is an anthology of poetry and music representing many diverse cultures. Culture, which may be described simply as the "man-made part of the environment,"[1] includes to some extent what we eat and drink, what we wear, what we read, and what we sing. A hymn is man-made and therefore is a work of culture reflecting a particular heritage.

The cultural diversity of current hymnals may be described in various ways. Hymns in most American hymnals primarily come from Great Britain and the United States, with a lesser proportion from Continental Europe and a much smaller number from other continents. Cultural diversity is also evident in the many languages in which hymns have been written. Beginning with the Greek and Latin tongues of Medieval Christianity, hymns have been written in each of the major modern languages of Europe (with an especially large number in German and English). With the spread of Christianity to Africa, Asia, Australia, and the Americas, hymns are found in the various native tongues of these continents. Today hymnals may be seen in every country where there are Christian churches. Although these hymnals typically contain a large number of hymns from Europe and/or North America (the traditional 19th and 20th century missionary-sending areas), hymnals in Third World countries are evidencing the development of congregational song in the language and musical idiom of each culture.

The cultural diversity of congregational song exists not only in reference to different continents and nations, but is also found within a single nation. In the United States, for example, a large number of religious denominations exists, each with its own heritage of hymns. Although some different

---

[1]Melville J. Herskovits, *Cultural Anthropology* (New York: Alfred A. Knopf, 1958), 305. Note that this definition of culture as used by anthropologists differs considerably from the elitist sense which signifies that some people have culture and others do not.

denominations have similar enough heritages to enable them to use the same hymnal, most religious bodies have one or more hymnals, compiled specifically for their own use. Sub-cultural diversity also exists in congregational song among regions of a nation. For example, the southern part of the United States in particular developed a large body of folk hymnody, including expressions of song from both White and Black communities.

Diversity in congregational song also exists in congregations of the same community and denomination. Among denominations that have no official hymnal, it is not uncommon for some of its churches in the same city to use different hymnals. Even when congregations use the same hymnal, their preferences may vary, depending on their cultural backgrounds.

Cultural diversity in hymns and hymn singing may also be viewed on an individual level. Why do you prefer the hymns of a particular type? If you have a favorite hymn, why is it your favorite? The answers to these questions must involve an examination of one's own cultural background, including experiences with congregational song from the time of childhood to the adult years.

Since the New Testament times, Christianity has been a singing faith, a faith which broke out of the bonds of a narrow provincialism to spread to every inhabited continent. The message of Christianity is expressed in hymns which parallel to some extent the cultural diversity among nations and continents, language groups and races, religious denominations, regions, local congregations, and individuals.

UNDERSTANDING HYMNIC DIVERSITY

To understand the diversity of congregational song from a cultural perspective, one views the hymn as human expression of religious thought reflecting a particular people or peoples from which it originated. The study of the origin of a hymn may help us to understand why the author wrote the hymn, why the composer wrote the hymn tune, and why each is written in a particular style.

Each hymn originates within a particular cultural setting: a human environment shaped by numerous factors, such as geography, race, language, economic status, religion, family life, and social customs. A cultural understanding of a hymn involves examination of its setting, including both the circumstance of its origin and its continuing use.

In addition to a consideration of its human context, the hymn must be studied in regard to how it functions within its setting. Does the hymn function as an expression of formal worship within a liturgical service? Does the hymn function as a tool of evangelism within an informal revival service? Does the hymn function in a very personal way to comfort an individual or family in a time of sorrow? Questions such as these involve a study of the hymn beyond its existence as words and music printed in a hymnal. From this perspective one views the hymn as it again comes alive in human experience, functioning in a certain way in a particular cultural context.

TRADITIONS ILLUSTRATING CULTURAL DIVERSITY

The cultural diversity of congregational song can be illustrated by many Christian traditions. Several of these will be briefly described in this section, with a focus first on several traditions of the United States of America and then on one tradition each of Europe, Africa, and Asia.[2]

Early New England: Lining-out

This first example illustrates conflict between those who wanted to sing in an established tradition and those who wanted to replace it with another tradition of congregational music. Early 18th-century New England congregations were lining-out their psalms, following a practice brought over from England. It originated because the people either could not read or did not have hymnbooks.

In lining-out, the minister or deacon would read or sing the metrical psalm (or hymn) line by line before it was sung by the congregation. In time, the psalm tunes used in early New England became considerably altered, so much that one of their ministers observed that in their congregations it was "hard to find two that sing exactly alike"; he further observed concerning their singing that "Your usual way of singing is handed down by tradition only, and whatsoever is only so conveyed down to us, it is a thousand to one if it be not miserably corrupted, in three or four-score years' time."[3] Several of these New England ministers had studied music at Harvard and became greatly concerned for the state of their congregational singing, which one of them viewed as "something so hideous and disorderly as is beyond Expression bad."[4]

[2]For information on additional hymnic traditions, including Spanish-language and American hymnody, see Chapter 14, "Trends and Issues in Hymnody," page 318.
[3]Thomas Symmes, *The Reasonableness of Regular Singing, or Singing by Note* (Boston, 1720); Quoted in Gilbert Chase, *America's Music* 3rd ed. rev. (Urbana and Chicago: University of Illinois Press, 1987), 22.
[4]Thomas Walter, *The Grounds and Rules of Musik Explained, or An Introduction to the Art of Singing by Note* (Boston: Printed by J. Franklin, 1721); quoted in Chase, 20.

Singing schools to teach music reading eventually brought the practice of lining-out and its accompanying style of singing to an end in early New England. In spite of widespread ridicule, lining-out has survived in some Primitive Baptist and in certain Black Baptist congregations.[5]

Although one may take the view that lining-out was simply an inferior type of congregational singing practiced only by the uneducated, Gilbert Chase has made a strong case for regarding it as an "Early New England Folk Style" with the same call-and-response pattern and traits of oral tradition found in the African-American spiritual and in certain other bodies of folk song.[6]

To come to an appreciation of what lining-out meant and still means to those who practice it, it is important for us to suspend temporarily our own cultural conditioning and to seek with imagination and empathy to adopt the perspective of those who carry on this tradition. When one adopts this perspective—an attitude and an approach known as cultural relativism[7] and practiced by anthropologists—we can gain new insight into the meaning of congregational song to persons in societies that are different from our own.

Old Order Amish

This Swiss-American denomination, stemming from the Anabaptist-Mennonite branch of the Reformation, has sought to maintain its cultural heritage through its religious faith, its strong family ties, its use of the Pennsylvania Dutch (German) dialect in their homes, and through its separation from the world by rejecting many elements of present-day American culture. These conservative people are largely farmers or carpenters by trade. They are well-known for conflicts with governmental authorities over their objection to having their children attend school beyond the elementary grades, for they believe that modern high school education destroys their agricultural way of life.

The Old Order Amish do not build church buildings but meet in homes where worship services are conducted in the standard German of their European forefathers.[8] Their singing is from the Anabaptist *Ausbund* (1564), a

[5]See Terry W. York, "Lining-Out in Congregational Singing," *The Hymn* 28, 3 (July, 1977): 110-117, and Nicholas Temperley, "The Old Way of Singing: Its Origins and Development," *Journal of the American Musicological Society* (34, 1981): 512.

[6]Chase, 33. For an interesting and provocative description and interpretation of this early New England cultural conflict, see Chase's chapter, "New England Reformers," 2nd ed. rev., 22-40. Lining-out has also survived in Gaelic congregational singing in certain isolated areas of Scotland. See the recording, *Gaelic Psalms from Lewis*, recorded and documented by the School of Scottish Studies, University of Edinburgh. Tangent Records TNGM 120 (52 Shaftesbury Avenue, London WIV 7DE).

[7]See David Biley, "Culture: Cultural Relativism," in *International Encyclopedia of the Social Sciences*, edited by David L. Silles, Vol. 3 (New York: The Macmillan Co., and The Free Press, 1968), 543.

[8]For an interesting introduction to Amish culture, see John A. Hostetler, *Amish Life* (Scottsdale, PA: Herald Press, 1952, 1959).

German words-only hymnal whose content has been little changed since the 16th century.[9] The Amish do not use musical instruments in worship and have refused to notate their music. They have developed a style of embellished singing which may not be far from that associated with lining-out in early New England. Scholars who have transcribed the hymn singing of the Amish and eliminated notes considered to be embellishments have discovered both secular and sacred melodies from the 16th century,[10] preserved in oral tradition by the Amish and their forefathers for more than 400 years! Although their embellished singing of these old melodies may sound strange to an outsider, these hymns have a deep significance to the Old Order Amish which can be appreciated by adopting a cultural perspective of hymnody.[11]

Southern Shape-note

This tradition of hymnody, in general use in singing schools and churches of the South and Midwest in the mid-19th century, takes its name from a system of notation in which the solmization syllables are represented by different shaped noteheads designed to simplify music reading.[12] In spite of the rejection of shape notes by leading music educators and the devastation of southern culture by the Civil War, this system has survived and today has two bodies of hymnody associated with it: (1) the older folk hymnody stemming from the pre-Civil War period, represented mainly in singings using the famous tunebooks[13] *Southern Harmony* (1835) and *The Sacred Harp* (1844); (2) the post-Civil War gospel hymn tradition combining traits of the northern gospel hymn and the southern folk hymn, represented in gospel singing using paperback songbooks. This shape-note gospel hymnody is still alive, but is confined chiefly to singing conventions in the South.[14]

[9]A reprint of the first American printing of the *Ausbund* was made in 1975 by the Lancaster Press, Inc., Lancaster, Pennsylvania. Copies can be ordered from Gordonville Bookstore, Gordonville, PA 17529. See Martin E. Ressler, "Hymnbooks Used by the Old Order Amish," *The Hymn* 28 (January 1977): 11-16.

[10]Paul M. Yoder, "The Ausbund" in *Four Hundred Years with the Ausbund* (Scottsdale, PA: Herald Press, 1964), 7-10. For an extensive study of Old Order Amish hymnody, see Rupert Karl Hohmann, "The Church Music of the Old Order Amish of the United States" (Ph.D. dissertation, Northwestern University, 1959).

[11]In addition to the Old Order Amish, other religious bodies in America who have maintained distinctive traditions of hymnody which have particular cultural interest include the Mennonites, the Moravians, the Seventh-Day Baptists of Ephrata, Pennsylvania, and the Shakers. See "Dissenters and Minority Sects," Chapter 3 of Chase, *America's Music*, 38-54.

[12]See Chapter 4, "Shape-Note Hymnody," for the two most common systems of shape notation.

[13]Two other pre-Civil War shape-note tunebooks still in use are Joseph Funk's *New Harmonia Sacra* (originally entitled *Genuine Church Music*, 1832) used mainly by Mennonites of the Shenandoah Valley, and M. L. Swan's *New Harp of Columbia* (1867; reprint, Knoxville: The University of Tennessee Press, 1978), used mainly in the mountains of eastern Tennessee.

[14]See Shirley Beary, "Stylistic Traits of Southern Shape-Note Gospel Songs," *The Hymn* 30, 1 (January 1979). For additional treatment, see Chapter 8, "Shape-note Gospel Hymnody."

The older folk hymn tradition of four-shape-note hymnody has become increasingly evident in major church hymnals in recent years. Included are such tunes as NETTLETON (B15, E686, L499, M400, P355, "Come, thou fount of every blessing"), FOUNDATION (B338, E636, L507, M529, P361, "How firm a foundation"), and MORNING SONG (E583, M726, P453, "O holy city, seen of John"). The harmonies of these shape-note tunes have been generally changed in order to accommodate them to the styles of harmony common to hymns of today.[15] This change of harmonies illustrates how folk music undergoes a transformation when it passes from its home in one society to find a new home in a different one.

African-American

As its name implies, African-American music is a syncretism, made up of both African and American elements. African-American music in turn owes much of its character to the European musical heritage. In the Black churches of America, particularly those which hold closely to older traditions, congregational singing reflects this African-American heritage.

While this heritage of congregational song is too extensive a subject to be treated in depth, we can point out two important aspects of Black African music that are prominent in Black church music of today: melodic embellishment (or improvisation on a basic melody) and rhythmic prominence.[16] When a Black congregation sings an old hymn such as "Amazing Grace," they will normally sing it in a much slower tempo than that common to most White churches. The slow tempo allows the time needed for embellishments on the melody. Although this folk hymn is of White origin, its manner of performance in Black worship is clearly African-American. This freedom of embellishment is in keeping with the freedom of expression found in traditional Black worship, ranging from singing and improvising accompaniment to spontaneous "amens," clapping, body movement, and shouting, as well as preaching which intensifies into a song-like speech. The rhythmic emphasis of the African heritage is evident in the drive and syncopation of many Black spirituals, such as "Every time I feel the Spirit" (M404, P315), "Somebody's knocking at your door" (P382), and "We are climbing Jacob's ladder" (B474, M418) and in the perfor-

[15]See the original and altered harmonizations of "Amazing Grace" in Chapter 2, "The Hymn and Music."
[16]For a fuller description of elements of this African heritage in relation to American music, see Chase, *America's Music*, 3rd ed. rev., Chapter 4, "The African Presence," 55-71; and Eileen Southern, Chapter 1, "The African Heritage," in *The Music of Black Americans, A History*, 2nd ed. (New York: W. W. Norton, 1983), 3-24.

mance of the more recent gospel music.[17]

Black spirituals have appeared in increasing numbers in the hymnals and in hymnal supplements[18] of predominantly White denominations in recent years. The singing of these spirituals by White congregations can express meaningful worship, but their performance by Whites will inevitably be adapted to fit a different culture. A basic reason for the existence of separate Black and White churches is a desire on the part of both to perform their worship music in their own cultural contexts.[19]

Welsh

Perhaps no society has given a greater place to hymn singing than the Welsh. The people of the little country of Wales, a beautiful land of mountains and valleys to the west of England, speak a Celtic language which was used in Britain at the time of the ancient Romans. Although nearly all the Welsh now speak English rather than Welsh, there is an increased effort to preserve the country's language which is so closely bound up with its national heritage.

Wales holds a special interest to Americans because large numbers of the Welsh emigrated to the United States. Pennsylvania and Ohio have substantial Welsh-American populations.

Hymn singing in Wales, in contrast to that of the United States, is a much more conspicuous activity, for it is not limited to regular church services. Welsh hymn singing today finds its expression in the *Gymanfa Ganu* (pronounced *Ga mon' va Gon' ee*), meaning an "assembly or festival of sacred song."[20] David G. Jenkins has described the cultural setting in which this hymn-singing activity originated in the 19th century: "The beginnings of the Gymanfa Ganu were humble: it began in the little chapels and churches which dot the hills and valleys of Wales. After the religious service was over the congregation would remain for an hour of song. Unaccompanied by any instrument—for the Puritan spirit was never stronger in New England than in Old Wales—led by a leader who sounded the pitch, the congregation would be

[17]For a personal and perceptive view of Black worship with an emphasis on music, see Charles G. Adams, "Some Aspects of Black Worship," *Andover Newton Quarterly* ii (January 1971): 124-138; *Music Ministry* 5 (September 1972): 2-9; *Journal of Church Music* 15 (February 1973): 2-9, 16.
[18]Three African-American supplementary hymnals issued in the 1980s respectively for Episcopal, Roman Catholic, and United Methodist use are: *Lift Every Voice and Sing: A Collection of Afro-American Spirituals and Other Songs* (New York: The Church Hymnal Corporation, 1981), *Lead Me, Guide Me: The African American Catholic Hymnal* (Chicago: G.I.A. Publications, 1987), and *Songs of Zion: Supplemental Worship Resources 12* (Nashville: Abingdon Press, 1981).
[19]See additional treatment of the African-American spiritual in Chapter 8, "American Traditions."
[20]Frank C. Isaacs, "The Gymanfa Ganu in America," *The Hymn* 14, 2 (April 1963): 47.

drilled for the forthcoming Gymanfa. For months a few selected hymns and an anthem or two would be rehearsed; then in a common meeting place congregations of one neighborhood or denomination would unitedly render the selections so prepared, under a conductor specially qualified and chosen."[21]

The present-day Gymanfa Ganu is similar to that described here, except that piano and organ accompaniment are generally used and its purpose is usually not to bring into use new material for congregational worship but rather the singing of a limited number of old favorites.

Part of the prominence of hymn singing in Welsh culture is due to its having been secularized. Welsh hymnody received its biggest thrust from the Calvinistic Methodist movement and other revivals of the 18th and 19th centuries which produced William Williams, author of "Guide me, O thou (ever) great Jehovah (Redeemer)" (B56, E690, L343, M127, P281), this nation's greatest hymnist. The puritanical character of this movement almost brought about the death of the old secular folk songs. In the course of time this cultural vacuum came to be filled by hymns, causing them to serve in places where other cultures would use secular songs. As Robert R. Williams has observed of the Welsh, "Today wherever they congregate in small or large groups, on the football field or during the meetings of the National Eisteddfod (singing competition), the hymns of the church are sung with fervor to popular tunes such as CWM RHONDDA, ABERYSTWYTH, and CRUGYBAR."[22]

Although Welsh hymns and tunes have increasingly appeared in English language hymnals, certain distinctive traits have prevented their being used to a great extent outside their own cultural setting. Welsh poetry has certain features which cannot be easily transferred to our language, such as their predilection for unusual meters, their preference for repetition of words, and the fact that many words in Welsh hymnody have an unaccented penultimate short syllable.[23] Furthermore, Welsh hymnody gives a central place to the atonement, often expressed in a way which is not in favor in much present-day preaching and theological expression.[24]

---

[21] David G. Jenkins, "The Gymanfa Ganu" in *Favorite Welsh and English Hymns and Melodies* (Warren, OH: printed for the National Gymanfa Ganu Association of the United States and Canada by Printing Service, Inc., n.d.), 92. Quoted in Isaacs, "The Gymanfa Ganu," 47-78.
[22] Robert R. Williams, "Some Aspects of Welsh Hymnody," *The Hymn* 4, 1 (January 1953): 6.
[23] Alan Luff, "Welsh Hymn Melodies: Their Present and Future Use in English Hymn Books," *Bulletin*, The Hymn Society of Great Britain and Ireland, 4 (Spring 1970): 76-77. The most comprehensive work in English on Welsh hymnody is Alan Luff, *Welsh Hymns and Their Tunes* (Carol Stream, IL: Hope Publishing Co.; London: Stainer & Bell, 1990).
[24] Isaacs, "The Gymanfa Ganu," 50.

Nevertheless, the Welsh have produced a few hymns and tunes which have transcended cultural barriers to achieve wide acceptance among English-speaking congregations in both Great Britain and America, such as "Guide me, O Thou (ever) great Jehovah (Redeemer)" to CWM RHONDDA (B56, E690, L343, M127, P281), and the tunes ABERYSTWYTH ("Jesus, lover of my soul," E699, M479, P303; "Holy Spirit, Lord of love," E349; "Savior, when in dust to you," L91; "Watchman, tell us of the night," E640, P20; "Wind who makes all winds that blow," P131; "Wild and lone the prophet's voice," P409), EBENEZER or TON-Y-BOTEL ("God hath spoken by the prophets," M108; "Let my people seek their freedom," M586; "Thy strong word did cleave the darkness," E381, L233; "Singing songs of expectation," E527; "Through the night of doubt and sorrow," L355), HYFRYDOL ("Come, thou long-expected Jesus," B77, M196, P2; "God the Spirit, guide and guardian," M648; "Praise the Lord! ye heavens adore him," B36; "Alleluia! sing to Jesus," E460, L158, P144; "Love divine, all loves excelling," E657, L315, P376; "Hear us now, our God and Father," L288; "Lord of glory, you have bought us," L424), LLANFAIR ("Hail the day that sees him rise," E214, M312; "Christ the Lord Is Risen Today; Alleluia!" L128; " 'Christ the Lord is risen today!' " P113), LLANGLOFFAN ("Rejoice! rejoice, believers," E68, P15; "O God of every nation," E607, M435, P289; "O God of earth and altar," P291; "Lead on, O King eternal," P448; "O crucified Redeemer," M425; "Where restless crowds are thronging," L430; RHOSYMEDRE ("My song is love unknown," L94; "The grace of life is theirs," P534; "Our Father (Parent), by whose Name," E587, L357, M447), RHUDDLAN ("Light's abode, celestial Salem," E621; "Judge eternal, throned in splendor," L418), and ST. DENIO ("Immortal, invisible, God only wise," B6, E423, L526, M103, P263).

Black African

Until relatively recent times, nearly all of the hymns sung by Black African Christians were imported from Europe or America and translated into African languages. Although African Christians accept these hymns as a part of the Christian faith, the hymns do not express their faith in a way which is natural to them. As Weman has observed, in the African's church and school he "does his best to sing the stipulated tunes, but since these are—almost without exception—European, it is seldom that song succeeds in loosening his tongue. He is moving in an alien world, and if his heart fails to beat in time with the music, that is only to be expected."[25]

---

[25]Henry Weman, *African Music and the Church in Africa* (Uppsala, Sweden: Ab Lundequistska Bokhandeln, 1960), 9.

The music of Black Africa contrasts with Euro-American music in numerous ways, but especially in regard to its rhythmic freedom—a characteristic "which lies far above the conformity of the Westerner to fixed groupings according to simple rhythmic schemes."[26] Thus the rhythmic simplicity of imported Christian hymns lacks the rhythmic expressiveness inherent in African song. Furthermore, hymns which modulate are unsuitable for the African because a basic rule of African melody is that "there is no key change in the course of the tune."[27] Thus the climactic modulation from F major to C major in the following score of NUN DANKET ("Now thank we all our God"):

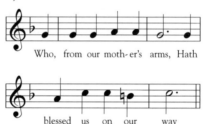

was observed by Weman in his visits to South Africa, Rhodesia, and Tanzania to be sung as follows:

This chorale melody is sung by the African in the way which fits his musical tradition, but the climax, so expressive of joy and thanksgiving to Western ears, is taken away by this change.

These rhythmic and melodic contrasts between Euro-American and African music focus on the problems found in the use of imported music by African Christians. The tradition of Western sacred music has become so strong among Christians of Africa that they often come to regard their own musical heritage as inferior.[28]

---

[26]Ibid., 62.

[27]Ibid., 46.

[28]Two collections of African hymns in English translation are Howard S. Olson, *Lead Us, Lord* (Minneapolis: Augsburg Publishing House) and Tom Colvin, *Fill Us with Your Love* (Carol Stream, IL: Agape, 1983. See also *The Hymn* (July 1979): 159-66.

"Jesus, we want to meet" (M661), one of the few[29] African hymns which has appeared in American hymnals, has several traits of African music: rhythmic freedom (note the frequent shifts in rhythmic patterns and accents—see page 230), a pentatonic melody which remains in one key, and optional drumbeat patterns. In addition to the two optional drumbeat patterns given with this hymn in the hymnals, a third and fourth have been added to further exemplify the great rhythmic variety and expressiveness of African music.[30]

The text of "Jesus, we want to meet" has the element of repetition ("On this thy holy day"), another important feature of African song. This hymn also lends itself to the typical call and response pattern often found in African music:

> *Leader*: "Jesus, we want to meet"
> *Congregation*: "On this thy holy day."

Chinese

China, one of the world's oldest cultures, has a long and complex history because organized civilizations have lived continuously on her mainland since at least 3000 B.C. As in Black Africa, music in China has occupied a prominent place in everyday life and continues to do so. In China, "There is hardly any phase of the life of the people in which music does not function, whether it be social, recreational, business and professional, or religious."[31]

Chinese music is distinctively different from Western music. The following traits are characteristic of Chinese vocal music:

1. Duple time is usual, with little use of triple time.
2. Modal endings to phrases are frequent.
3. The pentatonic scale is common, but the seven-tone scale is also used. The most characteristic trait of Chinese melody is that it never proceeds upward by a half step, but it may proceed downward by a half step.
4. Chinese melodies often sound out of tune to Western ears because they do not use the tempered scale.
5. There is no concise combination of tones (harmony) in vocal music.

[29]Other hymns from Africa in recent American hymnals include "Christ the worker" (E611), "Jesu, Jesu, fill us with your love" (B501, E602, M432, P367), and "That boy-child of Mary" (B110, M241, P55).
[30]These rhythms have been suggested by Dr. Mary Oyer of the Music Department, Goshen College, Goshen, Indiana, who is both a hymnologist and a specialist in African music. (The first two drumbeat patterns were dictated by the translator in 1962 to Austin C. Lovelace and Carlton R. Young.)
[31]Bliss Wiant, *The Music of China* (Hong Kong: Chung Chi Publications, 1965), 95.

Jesus, We Want to Meet

1. Je - sus, we want— to meet On this— Thy ho - ly day;
2. We kneel in awe— and fear On this— Thy ho - ly day;
3. Thy bless - ing, Lord,— we seek On this— Thy ho - ly day;
4. Our minds we ded - i - cate On this— Thy ho - ly day;

We gath - er round— Thy throne On this— Thy ho - ly day.
Pray God to teach— us here On this— Thy ho - ly day;
Give joy of Thy vic - to - ry On this— Thy ho - ly day.
Heart and soul con - se - crate On this— Thy ho - ly day.

Thou— art— our heav'n - ly Friend, Hear our prayers as they as - cend;
Save— us— and cleanse our hearts, Lead and guide our acts of praise,
Through - grace a - lone are we saved; In Thy flock may we be found;
Ho - ly Spir - it, make us whole; Bless the ser - mon in this place;

Look in - to our hearts and minds to - day, On this— Thy ho - ly day.
And our faith from seed to flow - er raise, On this— Thy ho - ly day.
Let the mind of Christ a - bide in us On this— Thy ho - ly day.
And— as we go,— lead us Lord; We shall be Thine ev - er - more.

Optional drumbeat patterns:

Trans. and versification © 1964 by Abingdon Press. Used by permission.

Words and music by A. T. Olajide Olude, Nigeria. Translated by Biodun Adebesin. Versed by Austin C. Lovelace. Trans. and versification copyright © 1964 by Abingdon Press. Used by permission.*

Sing with Understanding

230

6. Melodies associated with poetry have been influenced by poetic
structure and poetic form has been influenced by music.[32]

These traits of Chinese music seldom appeared in the hymns of Chinese
Christians before the 1930s because both Roman Catholic and Protestant
missionary efforts had produced a church that was largely foreign in form and
in control.[33]

In the early 1930s, six Chinese Protestant bodies united their efforts to
produce the first hymnal to include a significant number of Chinese texts
and tunes. This epoch-making hymnal, *Hymns of Universal Praise* (Shanghai, 1936), contains, alongside Western hymns, 62 original Chinese hymn
texts. Seventy-two of its hymn tunes originated in China; these include 14
of relatively ancient origin and 57 new compositions, including 23 tunes "by
foreign missionaries who, having lived in China for a considerable length of
time, have learned to think in characteristically Chinese music idioms," and
34 tunes by Chinese.[34]

One Chinese hymn from *Hymns of Universal Praise* which illustrates several traits of Chinese music is SHENG EN ("The (O) bread of life, for all is
(sinners) broken," E342, M633). The melody of this Chinese hymn is pentatonic. SHENG EN is harmonized as an accommodation to Western practice; Chinese tradition would require that it be sung in unison.

The rhythm of this Chinese melody is atypical, for rather than falling
strictly into groups of two, its rhythm consists of groups of two and three. In
Hymns of Universal Praise, the time signature of this hymn tune is $\frac{5}{4}$. Here
no time signature is listed and bar lines occur only at the ends of phrases.

In accordance with Chinese practice, this melody does not ascend by
half step (nor does it in this case descend by a half step). Furthermore,
SHENG EN'S phrase endings are modal, the final notes being approached
from above or below by a minor third. The melodic form also conforms to
Chinese practice in that it is free, having no repeated phrases.

---

[32]Summarized from ibid., 3-4.
[33]In 1928 Latourette reported: "With occasional splendid exceptions, throughout China and among both
Roman Catholics and Protestants, the Church was still dependent on the foreigner for ideas, leadership,
and financial support. Little first-class Christian literature had yet appeared from Chinese pens. No outstanding apologia, no great work of devotion had yet been written by a Chinese." Kenneth Scott
Latourette, *A History of Christian Missions in China* (New York: The Macmillan Co., 1929), 833.
[34]*Hymns of Universal Praise* (Shanghai, 1936), 10-11. A revised Chinese edition was released in 1977 and
an English edition in 1981, both published by the Chinese Christian Literature Council, 57 Peking Road,
2nd Floor, Kowloon, Hong Kong. Eighteen hymns in Mandarin Chinese are found in the hymnal, *Sound
the Bamboo*, ed. I-to Loh (Manila: Asian Institute for Liturgy and Music and the Christian Conference of
Asia, 1990).

The Bread of Life for All Is Broken

Unison

1. The bread of life for all is bro - ken! Christ drank the
1. *Jiu shi zhi shen, wei zhong- sheng bo - kai, Zai Gu - lou*
2. With god - ly fear we seek Thy pres - ence, our hearts dis -
3. O Lord, we pray, come Thou a - mong us, light - en our

cup on Gol - go - tha. God's grace we trust, and spread with
di, tong in ku - bei; Meng en xin - zhong, feng ming chang
tressed by peo - ple's grief. Thy ho - ly face is stained with
eyes, bright - ly ap - pear! Em - man - u - el, heaven's joy un -

rev - erence this ho - ly feast, and thus re - mem - ber.
ji - nian, Jing she sheng - yan, zhui - i dang nian.
bit - ter tears; our hu - man pain still bear - est Thou with us.
end - ing, our life with Thine for - ev - er blend - ing.

WORDS: Timothy Tingfang Lew, 1936; trans. by Walter Reginald Oxenham Taylor, 1943;
  phonetic transcription from the Chinese by I-to Loh, 1988
MUSIC: Su Yin-Lan, 1934; harm. by Robert C. Bennett, 1988

SHENG EN
98.98

Sing with Understanding

Other examples of Chinese-Christian hymns which have appeared in American hymnals include "Great are your mercies, O my Maker" (SONG OF THE HOE, P352), "May the Lord, mighty God" (WEN-TI, P596), "Praise our God above" (HSUAN P'ING, P480), and "Rise to greet the sun" LE P'ING, M678).

CANTATE DOMINO: UNITY IN DIVERSITY

Through the foregoing examples of hymn-singing cultures we have seen something of the diversity of Christian hymnody.

Although each hymnal reflects the cultural heritage(s) of its constituency, there has been in recent decades a growing trend in American collections to be inclusive of representative hymns from Third World countries.

By far the most internationally inclusive hymnal of its time is *Cantate Domino* (CD), whose title is taken from the Latin of Psalm 96:1, "*Cantate Domino canticum novum*" ("Sing unto the Lord a new song"). This unique multilanguage hymnal, first published in 1924 by the World Student Federation, was published in its fourth edition under sponsorship of the World Council of Churches in 1974.[35]

The purpose of CD has been described by Erik Routley, the spokesman for its editorial board: "At an early stage it was agreed that the purpose of the book was to serve the church at its 'growing points.' The Church is at present growing, we believe, through the meeting of cultures and races, as well as through experiments in text-writing, music and liturgy; an international hymn book with an experimental emphasis was clearly called for, and we have sought to include in the book material of many styles. Not only hymns of the familiar kind will be found here, but also antiphonal canticles and folk songs. We hope to make available not only the hymnody of the west to the east, and of the north to the south, as did the older missionary enterprises, but some of the new and vital hymnody of the southern hemisphere to the north, and of the east to the west."[36]

In accord with its purpose, CD contains a fascinating array of hymns representing many cultures. These hymns are given in their original languages in

---

[35]*Cantate Domino*, New edition. Published on behalf of the World Council of Churches (Kassel, Germany: Bärenreiter-Verlag, 1974).

[36]Ibid., "Editor's Introduction" by Erik Routley, xiii-xiv. In the 1990s, several international, ecumenical hymals were published, including: *In Spirit and in Truth: Hymns and Responses*, ed. Terry MacArthur (Geneva: World Council of Churches, 1991), *World Praise*, comp. David Peacock and Geoff Weaver (London: Marshall Pickering, 1993), and *Thuma Mina: Singing with Our Partner Churches, International Ecumenical Hymnbook*, ed. Dieter Trautwein (Basel: Basileia Verlag and Munich-Berlin: Strube Verlag, 1995).

addition to English and other languages which communicate their thoughts best, often including French and German. Furthermore, CD is an ecumenical hymnal, for its preparation involved active participation by Orthodox, Roman Catholic, and Protestant Christians.

The following citations from CD will give an idea of the varied multicultural scope of this unique hymnal. African hymns include the melody of a Malawi wedding song to Psalm 148, "O praise the King of Heaven" (18), and a Yoruba tune to the text "Blessed Word of God" (104). Contributions from the Americas include the Black spiritual "He is King of Kings" (85), the Jamaican folk song melody to "Take the dark strength of our nights" (31), and the Argentine hymn "Christ is risen, Christ is living" (89). East Asian hymns include, in addition to Chinese hymns, a Thai traditional melody to Psalm 1, "Happy is he who walks in God's wise way" (7), an old Japanese melody with Japanese text, "In this world abound" (106), and a melody of Philippine origin to "Father in heaven" (121). Hymns in CD from other parts of Asia include an Indian text and tune, "God is love!" (70) and a Persian text and tune, "Spread the news!" (90).[37]

In the 1980s and 1990s, most new American hymnals have been more culturally inclusive than their predecessors. Particularly inclusive of many cultures are *The United Methodist Hymnal: Book of United Methodist Worship* (1989) and *Hymnal: A Worship Book: Prepared by Churches in the Believers Church Tradition* (1992).[38]

These collections of church songs from many cultures are thus repositories of words and music demonstrating the unity in diversity which characterizes Christianity at its best. Christians express their faith in song in ways which are natural to them, whether they are from Europe, Asia, Africa, Australia, or the Americas. At the same time, however, they may sing one another's hymns in the realization that:

"In Christ there is no East or West,
   In him no South or North,

---

[37]See also the following nations or cultures represented by hymns in *Ecumenical Praise*: Chinese (53), Ghana (58, 77), Hungarian (66), Irish (23), and Shaker (45). See also C. Michael Hawn (ed.) *For the Living of These Days* (Macon: Smyth and Helwys, 1995).
[38]Carlton R. Young (ed.), *The United Methodist Hymnal: Book of United Methodist Worship* (Nashville: United Methodist Publishing House, 1989) and Rebecca Slough and Kenneth Nafziger (eds.), *Hymnal: A Worship Book: Prepared by Churches in the Believers Church Tradition* (Elgin, IL: Brethren Press; Newton, KS: Faith and Life Press; and Scottdale, PA: Mennonite Publishing House, 1992). The latter hymnal was prepared by representatives of the following churches: Church of the Brethren, General Conference Mennonite Church, Mennonite Church, Churches of God, and Mennonite Brethren.

But one great fellowship of love
Thro'out the whole wide earth."[39]

QUESTIONS FOR THOUGHT AND DISCUSSION

1. What cultural conditions have exercised a strong influence on your views of hymns and hymn singing?

2. To what extent can one accept the validity of a hymn text or tune which evidently expresses the religious experience of another Christian but not one's own?

3. Can one accept someone of another cultural background and have genuine respect for his hymn preferences, though they are different?

4. To what extent in hymn singing is cultural unity feasible or desirable?

5. How many cultural traditions are represented in your congregation's hymn singing? How fully do these traditions represent the backgrounds of these people?

6. To what extent is your congregation able to worship through hymns set to music of unfamiliar cultural traditions? To what extent is this desirable?

---

[39]This hymn of Oxenham (B385, E529, L359, M548, P439, 440) so expressive of Christian unity has been in CD since its first edition of 1924. Words used by permission of Desmond Dunkerley, Portsmouth, Hampshire, England.*

PART III:
THE HYMN IN PRACTICE

10
THE HYMN IN PROCLAMATION

Hymns function in the mission of the church in several ways. In **proclamation** the hymn functions as a vehicle for sharing the good news. In **worship** the hymn is an instrument of corporate devotion. In **education** the hymn is a means for Christian instruction. And in **ministry** the hymn functions as an inspiration for social service. Some hymns relate to several of these functions; other hymns focus primarily on one. Persons who bear leadership responsibility for congregational singing can profit greatly from an awareness of the potential use of hymns in fulfilling the church's mission and their specific application in accomplishing the tasks of proclamation, worship, education, and ministry.

THE MEANING OF PROCLAMATION

A proclamation is a public declaration. In the context of the church, proclamation is the public declaration of the gospel of salvation in Jesus Christ and of its day-to-day application in people's lives. Proclamation of the gospel may take place within a worship service, in an evangelistic meeting, or in a conversational setting. The manner in which this proclamation occurs varies according to the particular heritage and theology of each congregation. Proclaiming the gospel at a church gathering may be done formally in a variety of ways: through the preaching of a sermon, the reading of Scripture, the recitation of a creed, or the singing of a hymn.

Three important terms describing aspects of proclamation are **evangelism, witness,** and **missions.** *Evangelism* (or evangelization), which comes from New Testament Greek words meaning to "bring good news," refers to the public preaching and dissemination of the gospel. Among the hymns which encourage evangelism are "Lift high the cross" (B594, E473, L377, M159, P371), "There's a spirit in the air," (B393, M192, P433), and "Go, tell it on the mountain" (B95, E99, L70, M251, P29).

Witness as an aspect of proclamation signifies the activity in which individual Christians share their experience of faith with others. Hymns of witness recount Christian experiences, giving personal testimony in hymnic form to the love of Christ, as in "My hope is built on nothing less" (SOLID ROCK, B406, L293, 294, M368, P379), "I Know Whom I Have Believed" (EL NATHAN; first line: "I know not why God's wondrous grace," B337, M714), "My song is love unknown" (LOVE UNKNOWN, E458, P76; RHOSYMEDRE, L94), and "I heard the voice of Jesus say" (THIRD MODE MELODY, E692, L497; VOX DILECTI, B551). In addition to hymns of witness to others, there are hymns of prayer for the one who bears witness, such as "Lord, speak to me (us), that I (we) may speak" (CANONBURY, B568, L403, M463, P426) and "O Master, let me walk with thee (you)" (2nd stanza, MARYTON, B279, E659, 660, L492, M430, P357).

When evangelism is pursued across national and cultural lines, it is considered more particularly *missions* (from the Latin, meaning "let go" or "send"). Hymns also express the concerns of missions: "We've a story to tell to the nations" (MESSAGE, B586, M569), "O Zion, haste, thy mission high fulfilling" (TIDINGS, B583, M573; ANGELIC SONGS, L397), and "God, whose almighty word" (ITALIAN HYMN, L400).

Biblical Basis

Music and proclamation of the gospel have a considerable history of close association in the Scriptures. In the Old Testament the psalmist calls on worshipers to proclaim God's salvation with singing:

> "Sing a new song to the Lord!
>   Sing to the Lord, all the world!
> Sing to the Lord, and praise him!
>   Proclaim every day the good news
> that he has saved us.
>   Proclaim his glory to the nations,
> his mighty deeds to all peoples" (Psa. 96:1-3, TEV).

"A new song" testifies to the mercy and compassion of God in Psalm 40:1-3, 9-10 (TEV):

> "I waited patiently for the Lord's help;
>   then he listened to me and heard my cry.
> He pulled me out of a dangerous pit,
>   out of the deadly quicksand.

He set me safely on a rock
and made me secure.
He taught me to sing a new song,
a song of praise to our God.
Many who see this will take warning
and will put their trust in the Lord.
In the assembly of your people, Lord,
I told the good news that you save us.
You know that I will never stop telling it.
I have not kept the news of salvation to myself;
I have always spoken of your faithfulness and help.
In the assembly of all your people
I have not been silent about your loyalty and constant love."

In the New Testament, the Gospel of Luke describes how the proclamation of the birth of Jesus was accompanied by song: "Suddenly a great army of heaven's angels appeared with the angel, singing praises to God: 'Glory to God in the highest heaven, and peace on earth to those with whom he is pleased!' " (Luke 2:13-14, TEV).

Singing the good news is associated with one of the most dramatic conversions recorded in the New Testament. As the apostle Paul and his associate Silas sang during their imprisonment in a Philippian jail, an earthquake occurred; the jailer and his household were converted (Acts 16:25-31). In Colossians 3:16, Paul exhorted the churches to make known the Word of Christ through singing; the Pauline hymn fragments in 1 Timothy 3:16b and Ephesians 5:14 also sound the note of proclamation.[1]

Historical Use

Through much of Christian history, the hymn has been an effective vehicle for proclaiming the gospel. In the 13th century, Francis of Assisi gave impetus to the creation of *laudi spirituali*, popular hymns in the language of the Italian people.[2] The Protestant Reformation gained momentum partly from Luther's chorales and Calvin's metrical psalms. These songs permeated the homes, schools, and churches of Germany, Switzerland, and other coun-

---

[1]See "New Testament Song" in Chapter 5, "Early Church and Pre-Reformation Traditions," pages 78-80.
[2]His own "All creatures of our God and King," although a poem of praise, contains a word of proclamation urging forgiveness toward others and the casting of one's cares on God (LASST UNS ERFREUEN, B27, st. 3; L527, M62, st. 5).

tries where they were used. The effectiveness of congregational song for communicating the good news has been underscored by other spiritual awakenings, such as the Wesleyan revival of 18th-century England, the frontier camp meeting revivals of early 19th-century America, and the British and American urban revivals which were led by Moody and Sankey during the last three decades of the 19th century.[3]

USING HYMNS IN PROCLAMATION

For a hymn to proclaim the gospel in its New Testament sense, it must incorporate the good news of salvation in Jesus Christ. Hymns which proclaim the good news are not limited to any single century, culture, or style. For example, note the diversity of sources for the following stanzas which proclaim the good news:

From the Scottish-English Moravian James Montgomery's hymn of 1824, "Stand up and bless the Lord," stanza 4 (OLD 134TH, B30, M662, CARLISLE, P491):

"God is our strength and song,
    And his salvation ours;
Then be his love in Christ proclaimed
    With all our ransomed pow'rs."

From an anonymous Latin hymn of about the 8th century, stanzas 1 and 2 (LOBT GOTT, IHR CHRISTEN, L300):

"O Christ, our hope, our hearts' desire,
    Creation's mighty Lord,
Redeemer of the fallen world,
    By holy love outpoured,
How vast your mercy to accept
    The burden of our sin,
And bow your head in cruel death
    To make us clean within."

From the anonymous Negro spiritual, "There is a balm in Gilead" (B269, E676, M375, P394):

[3]Hymns written during these awakenings are treated in the historical chapters of this book.

"If you can't preach like Peter,
    If you can't pray like Paul,
Just tell the love of Jesus,
    And say he died for all."

Refrain:
"There is a balm in Gilead
    to make the wounded whole;
There is a balm in Gilead
    to heal the sin-sick soul."

And from Fanny Crosby's gospel hymn of 1882, "Redeemed, how I love to proclaim it" (B544):

"Redeemed, how I love to proclaim it!
    Redeemed by the blood of the lamb;
Redeemed through his infinite mercy,
    His child, and forever, I am."

Good News Hymns

The heading "Good News Hymns" is chosen here rather than "Gospel Hymns" to convey more clearly that many kinds of hymns proclaim the gospel. The types of hymns used to proclaim the gospel differ according to the liturgical heritage and cultural outlook of particular congregations and their leadership. Two contrasting approaches to proclaiming the gospel— each with its traditions of good news hymnody—are the Christian calendar and revivalism.

The Christian calendar is generally known by its major festivals of Christmas, Easter, and Pentecost—festivals which are widely observed. The calendar is biblically based, proclaiming in an annual cycle God's mighty acts in the birth, life, death, and resurrection of Jesus Christ, the coming of the Holy Spirit on Pentecost, and the nature of the triune God on Trinity Sunday.[4] The good news of salvation in Jesus Christ is found in hymns written for use in the various seasons of the Christian calendar. The following excerpts from hymns for Advent, Christmas, Holy Week, Easter, and Pentecost are representative of those used to proclaim the good news.

---

[4]Additional treatment of the Christian calendar is given in Chapter 11, "The Hymn in Worship," pages 253-5.

Advent

"Come, thou long-expected Jesus,
  Born to set thy people free;
From our fears and sins release us;
  Let us find our rest in thee....
Born thy people to deliver,
  Born a child, and yet a King,
Born to reign in us forever,
  Now thy gracious kingdom bring."
(HYFRYDOL, B77, M196; JEFFERSON, L30)

Christmas

"How silently, how silently
  The wondrous gift is giv'n!
So God imparts to human hearts
  The blessings of his heav'n.
No ear may hear his coming,
  But in this world of sin,
Where meek souls will receive him, still
  The dear Christ enters in.
(stanza 3, "O little town of Bethlehem," ST. LOUIS, B86, E79,
  L41, M230, P44; FOREST GREEN, E78, P43)

Holy Week

"There is a green hill far away,
  Outside a city wall,
Where our (the) dear Lord was crucified,
  Who died to save us all."
(HORSLEY, E167; WINDSOR, L114,)

Easter

"The three sad days have quickly sped,
  He rises glorious from the dead;
All glory to our risen head:
  Alleluia!
Lord, by the stripes which wounded you (thee),
  From death's (dread) sting free your servants too,
That we my live and sing to you (thee).

Alleluia!"
("The strife is o'er, the battle done," VICTORY, B172, E208,
L135, stanzas 3, 5; M306, stanzas 3, 4)

Pentecost
"Come, Holy Ghost, our souls inspire,
  And lighten with celestial fire;
Thou the anointing Spirit art,
  Who dost thy seven-fold gifts impart."
(VENI, CREATOR SPIRITUS, E503, 504, L472, M651, P125)

The revivalism of the 19th century in particular played a significant role in the development of American Christianity and continues to function as a means of proclaiming the good news in a number of church bodies and nondenominational evangelistic organizations. In contrast to the annual cycle of the Christian calendar, revivalism focuses on shorter periods of intensive effort, such as a weekend, half a week, or a week or more of daily evangelistic meetings. Hymns associated with revivalism tend to be more person-centered than those of the Christian calendar, focusing to a greater extent on the experiences and emotions of the individual singers. The personal pronouns *I*, *me*, and *my* abound in the hymns of revivalism. Furthermore, most hymns of revivalism emphasize personal testimony, sometimes even to the extent of excluding an explicit statement of God's work in Jesus Christ. Much revivalistic hymnody emphasizes "what Jesus means to me" rather than what He has done for the salvation of the world.

On the other hand, revivalistic hymns in their simplistic language and musical style bring the message of the gospel to persons who find it difficult to relate to more sophisticated styles of hymnody. The following themes and the hymns which illustrate them are representative of revivalistic hymnody that has found a firm place not only in revival meetings but also in the weekly (especially Sunday evening) services of a significant number of America's churches.

The Love of Jesus
"I stand amazed in the presence
  Of Jesus the Nazarene,
And wonder how he could love me,
  A sinner, condemned, unclean."

Refrain:
"How marvelous! how wonderful!
   And my song shall ever be;
How marvelous! how wonderful!
   Is my Savior's love for me!"
(MY SAVIOR'S LOVE, B547,M371)

The Atonement

" 'Man of sorrows!' what a name
   For the Son of God who came
Ruined sinners to reclaim!
   Hallelujah, what a Savior!
Guilty, vile, and helpless we,
   Spotless Lamb of God was he;
Full atonement! can it be?
   Hallelujah, what a Savior!"
(HALLELUJAH, WHAT A SAVIOR! B175, M165)

The Resurrection

"Death cannot keep its (his) prey,
   Jesus my Savior!
He tore the bars away,
   Jesus my Lord!"

Refrain:
"Up from the grave he arose,
   With a mighty triumph o'er his foes;
He arose a victor from the dark domain,
   And he lives forever with his saints to reign.
He arose! He arose! Hallelujah! Christ arose!"
(St. 3, "Low in the grave he lay," CHRIST AROSE, B160, M322)

Testimony of Salvation

"My sin, oh, the bliss of this glorious thought!
   My sin, not in part but the whole,
Is nailed to the cross, and I bear it no more,
   Praise the Lord, praise the Lord, O my soul!"

Refrain:
"It is well with my soul,
  It is well, it is well with my soul."
(St. 3, "It Is Well with My Soul," VILLE DU HAVRE, B410,
  M377)

As we have already noted, the proclamation of the gospel is not limited to any single tradition of hymnody. Both the Christian calendar and revivalism have proved to be effective means of proclaiming the good news. Churches observing the Christian calendar make greater use of hymnody designed to present the good news in the context of its seasonal emphases. Churches with a revivalistic heritage sing more hymns giving emphasis to personal testimony.

Balance is a key to evaluating proclamation hymnody. There is **objective** truth to be proclaimed: God's mighty acts which have bought salvation through the Jesus of history. There is also **subjective** experience: one's response to salvation history and how one feels about the experience of knowing God's love in Jesus Christ. Both objective and subjective expressions are valid when a balance is maintained. However, for use in congregational singing, subjective hymns present a particular difficulty. Since the subjective focuses on individual feelings, these feelings may not be valid for the entire congregation. The emotions and experiences which hymns express need to convey the sentiments of the congregation as a group of Christians.

Hymns of Call, Hymns of Response

When the gospel has been proclaimed (whether in the spoken word or in song), those who hear are called upon to respond. This response to the proclamation of the good news is often expressed in hymns. In many congregations individuals are invited to make public decisions in response to the Gospel of Christ during the singing of a hymn following the sermon. Hymns calling for a response to the proclamation of the gospel often emphasize the *call* of Christ or urge persons to *come* to the Savior:

- "Jesus *calls* us o'er the tumult" (GALILEE, B293, E549, 550, L494, M398)
- "Softly and tenderly Jesus is *calling*" (THOMPSON, B312, M348)
- "Today your mercy *calls* us" (ANTHES, L304)

- "*Come*, ev'ry soul by sin oppressed" (STOCKTON, B317, M337)
- " 'Come, follow me,' the Savior spake" (MACH'S MIT MIR, GOTT, L455)
- "*Come*, sinners, to the gospel feast" (HURSLEY, M339)
- "*Come*, ye disconsolate" (CONSOLATOR, B67, M510)
- "*Come*, ye sinners, poor and needy" (RESTORATION, B323; PLEADING SAVIOR, M340)

In other congregations a hymn of individual commitment is sung, but without any similar public decision being called for. Hymns of response to the gospel may be prayers which involve acts of repentance, faith, dedication, and a sense of joy and peace. One of the most frequently sung hymns of response is "Just as I am, without one plea" (WOODWORTH, B307, E693, L296, M357, P370). This hymn expresses the confession of a person in spiritual need and how fears and conflicts are resolved in Christ, concluding with the response, "O Lamb of God, I come." A Christian hymn of the 5th century which is also a positive response to the gospel is "Lord Jesus, think on me" (SOUTHWELL, L309, E641):

> "Lord Jesus, think on me
>   And purge away my sin;
> From selfish passions set me free
>   And make me pure within."

Although this chapter has focused on proclamation, it is important to recognize that proclamation is inseparable from worship in the mission of the church. As stated by Davies, "Personal commitment, worship, daily life, proclamation or witness are all parts of our response to Christ: to separate them is to distort."[5] Furthermore, many of the procedures for the use of evangelistic hymns are similar to those employed with hymns of worship. In the next chapter, many of the practical points concerning hymns in worship are also valid for employing hymns in proclamation.

---

[5] J. G. Davies, *Worship and Mission* (New York: Association Press, 1967), 71.

QUESTIONS FOR DISCUSSION/PROJECTS FOR ACTION

1. Using an order of worship in your church bulletin and/or book of worship for a recent Sunday, list those actions which involve proclamation of the gospel. List all the spoken and sung parts of the service which proclaim the message of God's love in Jesus Christ.

2. Evaluate your church's hymnal in terms of hymns encouraging witnessing, evangelism, and missions. Are the sections containing these hymns adequate in number or in encouragement to evangelism? Are there other hymns encouraging proclamation and missions which you would add?

3. Cite some instances in which music has been associated with proclamation in the Scriptures and in Christian history.

4. Contrast and evaluate the Christian calendar and revivalism as approaches to proclaiming the good news and the traditions of hymnody associated with each.

5. Citing appropriate examples, describe how hymns can express an invitation to Christian discipleship and an individual's response to the proclamation of the good news.

6. Plan a hymn service which proclaims the good news, using hymns and Scripture passages taken from festivals and seasons of the Christian calendar.

7. Using revivalistic hymns, plan a hymn service designed to proclaim the good news and to show how hymnody has developed in association with great spiritual awakenings.

11

THE HYMN IN WORSHIP

T he setting most natural to the function of the hymn is the service of public worship. A hymn's worship function cannot be explained apart from some understanding of the nature of corporate devotion. Public worship is a multifaceted phenomenon subject to consideration from many perspectives. One of the most fruitful is to think of it in terms of drama.

WORSHIP AS DRAMA

In a real sense worship is dramatic action. The principal actors in the drama of corporate worship are the people of the congregation who are aided and equipped for their role by the leaders of worship—the prompters from the wings, so to speak. The drama, often scripted, has a structure and sequence based upon the nature of God's dialogical encounter with God's people. A general pattern of progress in the worshiping action emerges from that dialogue. The Bible contains the record of that dramatic encounter. Though encapsulated by the time and space limits of formal worship each Lord's day, the drama actually continues in the daily lives of the individual worshipers through the week.

The Danish religious thinker Sören Kierkegaard (1813-55) has suggested the above well-known analogy.[1] Worship is indeed drama—a real-life drama because all of life is on the stage. The people of the congregation are the actors—the active participants in the work (the service) of worship. The principal audience then is God. God hears and accepts the prayers and praise offered by the congregation. God looks in the hearts and lives of the performers, discerning the motives behind their worship and their service.

The pastor, the minister of music, the choir members, the organist, and/or other instrumentalists are the prompters. They are the enablers of worship,

---

[1]Sören Kierkegaard, *Purity of Heart*. Tr. Douglas V. Steere (New York: Harper and Brothers, Torchbooks, 1956), 177-84.

seeking to help guide the congregation to do its work of worship well in the presence of God before whom they also stand as participants in the dramatic action.

The drama continues in daily life where the liturgy—the service of the people of God (Rom. 12:1)—is carried out while the church is dispersed. The word *liturgy* has differing connotations according to the church tradition of those using it. In essence, "liturgy" (as used above) simply means the service rendered by human beings to God.[2] It carries the meaning of worship as work; it also applies equally to the activity of the people of God whether they are assembled for worshipful acts or scattered for their everyday work in the world. Its form is not necessarily fixed or ecclesiastically prescribed; however, when its texts are written out as the agreed-upon order for doing things together, it may be considered the script for the drama of worship.[3]

A DIALOGICAL MODEL—ISAIAH'S VISION IN THE TEMPLE

Within the Scriptures may be found many worship experiences whose natural components can be analyzed and, by the grace of God, relived in the experience of today's worshipers. The experience of the prophet Isaiah, when he received and responded to the call of the Lord in the temple, has often been cited as one model for the structuring of the drama of worship. The structure is that of dramatic dialogue in which God speaks first, revealing Godself in mystery, majesty, and power.

I. Initiating Grace (Isa. 6:1-4)

God always takes the initiative in worship. As prime mover, God requires a response. The first movement of the worship dialogue therefore is downward and inward from God to the worshiper. By God's grace the worshiper sees God revealed in transcendent power and holiness.

II. Confession of Sin (Isa. 6:5)

Upon seeing God in majesty and holiness, Isaiah by painful contrast saw himself as sinful and in need of forgiveness. His feeling of contrition and repentance was both individual and social; as the dialogue continues, the upward and outward moving response is confession of unworthiness and sin.

---

[2]Liturgy is from the Greek, *leitourgia*, a compound word from *laos*—people and *ergon*—work. Its basic meaning then is "the work of the people." The New Testament uses it frequently (Acts 13:2; Heb. 8:6). See Paul W. Hoon, *The Integrity of Worship* (New York: Abingdon Press, 1971), 30-33.

[3]Erik Routley treated the subject of worship as drama in *Music Leadership in the Church* (Nashville: Abingdon Press, 1967), 106-120; and in *Words, Music, and the Church* (Nashville: Abingdon Press, 1968), 129-199.

III. Pardon and Renewal (Isa. 6:6-7)

Again the dramatic flow reverses, with God's response providing cleansing, forgiveness, and relief. Then God issues the call to service.

IV. Dedication of Life (Isa. 6:8)

After experiencing spiritual renewal and a new sensitivity to the voice of God, Isaiah finally responds with the commitment of his life to God's purposes. Authentic worship ends with the offering of self as the climax of the dramatic action.

Since this structure is universal, deriving from the nature of God's dramatic dealings with persons, it can be discerned in the Christian liturgies which have developed over the years, as well as in great pieces of devotional literature. Although God's Spirit cannot be limited to liturgical formulas, a service of true worship is seldom haphazard or unstructured. In fact, spontaneity often comes because of, rather than in spite of, structure.

To sum up, a service of worship is a two-way conversation between God and God's people with a given pattern and sequence. The dramatic sequence outlined above is a channel through which the Spirit of God has been pleased to act throughout history. Thus, ideally, a service of worship reflects something of this structural unity (that is, a general form and movement in which each part is logically related to the whole). Whether its tradition is "liturgical" or "free," a service of true worship constitutes a devotional whole.

THE FUNCTION OF HYMNS IN THE DRAMA OF WORSHIP

Taking into account this concept of public worship as dramatic dialogical action, the place of the hymn becomes clear. Hymns are not just an important part of the sacred script of the worship drama, but they can also be instruments of congregational action at every point in the dramatic sequence. Since the worship leaders are the prompters of that action, they can utilize hymns as precision instruments selected accurately, intelligently, and sensitively to help the people say what they want to, or should, say at specific places in the dramatic sequence.

The people need to be made aware of the place and purpose of their singing in worship. Hymns are never to be regarded as "musical breaks" for physical or mental relaxation, nor to relieve boredom, nor to cover awkward pauses, nor to function as traveling music for the ministers as they move from one part of the sanctuary to another. Rather, to express another biblical idea, hymn singing is the offering of a sacrifice of praise requiring the commitment of mind, body, spirit, and will (Psa. 107:22).

In order to grasp this view of the hymn's function, the congregation may need both patience and guidance. The participation of congregational representatives in the planning and doing of the worship may be required.[4] But the purpose of the worship planners should be clearly understood as they select hymns for the people to sing. After all, the actors must not only know the meaning of every part of the play, they must also be enlisted in a teamwork of endeavor with the "playwrights," the prompters, and all the others who are committed to bringing off the performance.

Hymns and the Dialogical Pattern of Worship

As in Isaiah's vision, worship may begin with the singing of hymns depicting the holiness, power, and majesty of God. Selections like the following enable the people to express their recognition of the divine object of their worship, as well as their adoring response:

- "Holy, Holy, Holy" (B2, E362, L165, M64, P138)
- "Immortal, invisible, God only wise" (B6, E423, L526, M103, P263)
- "All hail the power of Jesus' name" (B201, E450, L328, M155, P142)

If hymns are then used to give corporate response (that is, recognizing human weakness and sin as well as asking for forgiveness), selections of penitence and confession might be:

- "Beneath the cross of Jesus" (B291, E498, L107, M297, P92)
- "Savior, like a shepherd lead us" (B61, E708, L481, M381, P387)
- "When I survey the wondrous cross" (B144, E474, L482, M298, P100)

The dramatic word of God in forgiveness and renewal comes most specifically in the actual words of Scripture. Yet the worship leader who knows the hymnbook's resources well, and who is concerned that hymns function as worship tools, can find those which appropriately express God's forgiving and saving action:

[4]See Wilfred M. Bailey, *Awakened Worship: Involving Laymen in Creative Worship* (Nashville: Abingdon Press, 1972).

- "I heard the voice of Jesus say" (B551, E692)
- " 'Forgive our sins as we forgive' " (E674, L307, M390, P347)
- "There's a wideness in God's mercy" (B25, E469, L290, M121, P298)

Finally, hymns giving utterance to commitment and dedication of life at the climax of the drama will be imaginatively chosen:

- "O Jesus, I have promised" (B276, E655, L503, P388)
- "O Master, let me walk with thee (you)" (B279, E659, 660, L492, M430, P357)
- "Take my life and let it be (that I may be) consecrated" (B277, E707, L406, M399, P391)

It is obvious from the content of the hymns suggested here that a dimension of experience beyond Isaiah's vision is assumed in the context of Christian worship, namely the life, redeeming death, and resurrection of Jesus Christ. All Christian worship is, as it must be, in and through Christ.

Hymns in the Larger Drama of the Christian Year

For historical and ecclesiastical reasons, some Protestants have been denied the powerful dramatic aid that the observance of the church year (beyond that of Christmas and Easter) provides for Christian worship. In a manner more extended than any single worship service, the Christian year is essentially the dramatic proclamation of the mighty acts of God in Christ and in His body, the church. The gradual return of many of the free churches to an acknowledgment of the seasons of preparation for the high festival days (Advent in preparation for Christmas, and Lent in preparation for Easter) is beginning to restore a greater sense of the drama of salvation to their corporate worship.

This renewal of church year observances can also increase and enrich the knowledge and use not only of contemporary hymns, but of the great hymnic heritage bequeathed us from earlier centuries. Hymns, if known and carefully chosen, can help reinforce the theme of a given season and underline the special teaching of a particular Lord's day or festival day, thus reenacting God's dramatic acts in the redemption of humankind. For example:

• Hymns for Easter would not be used indiscriminately during the first days of Holy Week. (Nor would Christmas carols be used during Advent.) Instead, hymns would be sensitively selected for the logical sequential rehearsal of the events in the last days of Jesus's earthly life.

• For Palm Sunday, hymns such as "All glory, laud, and honor" (B126, E154, L108, M280, P88), "Hosanna, loud hosanna" (B130, M278, P89), and "Ride on, ride on in majesty" (E156, L121, P90, 91) would be sung to celebrate the triumphal entry into Jerusalem.

• For the observance of the Lord's Supper on Maundy Thursday, communion hymns would be sung: "I come with joy to meet my Lord" (B371, E304, M617, P507), "Come, risen Lord" (E305, L209, P503), "Let us break bread together on our knees" (B366, E325, L212, M618, P513).

• For Good Friday worship, hymns like "Ah, holy Jesus" (E158, L123, M289, P93), "O sacred head, sore (now) wounded" (B137, E169, L116, 117, M286, P98), and "What wondrous love is this" (B143, E439, L385, M292, P85) would be used to recall the suffering of Christ on the cross.

• Not until Easter Sunday and during Eastertide would joyous hymns of the resurrection be sung: "Christ the Lord is risen today" (B159, L130, M302, P113), "The day of resurrection" (B164, E210, L141, M303, P118), "The strife is o'er" (B172, E208, L135, M306, P119).

These are obvious examples of the kinds of choices which can be made when considering worship planning for other seasons and days of the Christian year. There are also hymns appropriate for Ascension, Pentecost, and Trinitytide.[5] Hymns which are not in a congregation's hymnal could be printed in its worship folder (if not under copyright) and sung to familiar tunes. The precise use of hymns for observing the Christian Year is one way of helping ensure that all of God's mighty acts are declared in the dramatic course of worship during each 12-month period.[6]

---

[5]See Hymns for the Church Year in the *Lutheran Book of Worship*, 929-31; Index of Topics and Categories: Christian Year in *The United Methodist Hymnal*, 937-8; the Table of Contents: The Church Year in *The Hymnal 1982*, 4; and Organization of the Hymnal: Christian Year in *The Presbyterian Hymnal*, 5.
[6]This use of hymns in accordance with the Christian calendar is also discussed on pages 242-4.

The Congregational Nature of the Hymn

It is sometimes forgotten that hymns are the offering of the entire congregation, not merely of the clergy and choir. In the worship of almost all Christian groups (even those with a prescribed liturgy) hymns are preeminently the part of corporate worship in which the congregation has assumed the largest and most direct part. In the current stress on the role of the laity in the work of the church, full involvement of the congregation in hymn singing should therefore be accentuated.

Indeed, congregational singing is presupposed if the church as the body of Christ is in actuality engaged in the action of worship. "The hymn... *is* the church singing corporately in praise of God, and not just the worshipper 'taking part' in the service over against what the priest or preacher may do."[7] Every person—young and old, homemaker, teacher, storekeeper, business executive—is included in the work of singing praise. As John Wesley exhorted in the third of his famous directions for singing: "Sing *all*. See that you join with the congregation as frequently as you can. Let not a slight degree of weakness or weariness hinder you. If it is a cross to you, take it up, and you will find it a blessing."[8]

In order for hymns to qualify for use by the entire congregation, they must be within the comprehension of the majority of the people. After all, hymns are designed for the use of "plain folk." The church is a voluntary body in which the "foolish" are of no less account than the "wise." In both thought and expression, hymn texts must be easily grasped and free from elaborate or involved structure. Their basic message must be succinct, direct, and understandable upon first encounter.

Models of such directness and clarity are Isaac Watts's "O God, our help in ages past," James Montgomery's "Stand up and bless the Lord," and Georgia Harkness's "Hope of the world." Hymns like these, when put to singable tunes, are best calculated to formulate a meaningful and useful script for the people as they enter the drama of worship.

SOME PRACTICAL SUGGESTIONS FOR WORSHIPFUL SINGING

The members of an average congregation participate in hymn singing to the extent that they know and enjoy the tunes. When a hymn is mentioned to most churchgoers, they usually respond with reference to the music they

[7]Cecil Northcott, *Hymns in Christian Worship* (Richmond: John Knox Press, 1964), 33.
[8]Preface to *Select Hymns*, 1761, quoted by James T. Lightwood, *The Music of the Methodist Hymn Book* (London: The Epworth Press, 1935), xix-xx, and to be found in numerous other places. See *The United Methodist Hymnal*, vii.

recall. Consequently, in much of the hymn singing which takes place, the mouths are open and loud noises are made, but the sentiment and thoughts of the texts are largely overlooked. Such thoughtless singing is often lethal to genuine worship. Following are some suggestions for helping solve this persistent problem.

Use of the Worship Folder

One way to aid in making the words of hymns meaningful to worshipers is to utilize worship folders (also known as service bulletins) in various helpful ways. Hymns used at particular points in public worship can be labeled by type or predominant mood or theme. For example:

- Hymn of Praise: "Praise the Lord! ye (o) heavens, adore him" (B36, E373, L540)
- Hymn of Penitence: "I lay my sins on Jesus" (B272, L305)
- Hymn of Proclamation: "Jesus shall reign (B587, E544, L530, M157, P423)
- Hymn of Commitment: "Make me a captive, Lord" (B278, M421, P378)

When not overused, this practice can draw the people's attention to the basic mood or function of a particular hymn and aid them in singing it more meaningfully.

Since the meaning of hymns is often obscured by the arrangement of the texts between the staves of musical notation on the hymnal page, printing the words as poems in the worship folder can enhance the meaning even of familiar hymns.[9] Those arriving early for worship can be encouraged to read and meditate on the words in the folder in preparation for the singing soon to follow in the service.

If not overdone, hymnological information can also be helpful when included in the printed order of service. If sources of hymns are indicated, the name of the author (the devotional poet) should not be overlooked. The tune name and its composer or source could also be supplied. For example:

- "Savior, again to thy dear name"... John Ellerton, ELLERS, Edward J. Hopkins

[9]See Erik Routley, "On the Display of Hymn Texts," *The Hymn*, 30 (January 1979): 16-20.

- "Father of mercies, in your Word,"... Anne Steele, DETROIT, from *The Sacred Harp*

Some hymnals also supply dates of composition or give the vital statistics of the author and composer. However, this can become excess baggage unless care is taken on occasion to explain the significance of the names, the sources, tune title, abbreviations, and other information which may be listed.

Verbal Introduction of Hymns

Intelligent participation of the congregation in hymn singing can be solicited by the manner in which hymns are announced. Since hymns are primarily expressive in mood and purpose, they often can be placed in the worship order as responses to that which precedes them. In a thoughtfully planned order of service, they can grow out of conditions or feeling which may have been brought about through other items or movements of worship.

In "free" services, where no fixed order exists, a few words of ascription or scriptural reminder could appropriately lead to the opening hymn of praise in order to give the people an obvious reason for singing it. For example:

- O that all would praise the Lord "for his steadfast love, for his wonderful works to humankind" (Ps. 107:8, NRSV)—after which the instrumentalist would introduce the tune of (for example) "Praise to (ye) the Lord, the Almighty" (B14, E390, L543, M139, P482).

- "Great is the Lord, and greatly to be praised" (Ps. 48:1, NASB)— followed by an instrumental introduction to "Come, Christians, join to sing" (B231, M158, P150).

Because hymns are often considered a kind of background activity or filler, many worshipers have little idea why they are singing a particular hymn at a given moment. An occasional hymn commentary by the worship leader can focus the people's attention on some reasons they may have for singing a particular hymn. For example:

- " 'Had I a thousand tongues, I would praise God with them all!' Thus exclaimed Peter Böhler, the Moravian preacher who was influential in the conversion of Charles Wesley. In 1739, near the anniversary of that conversion, Charles recalled Böhler's enthusiastic words and exclaimed: 'O for a thousand tongues to sing My great Redeemer's praise, The glories of my God and King, The triumphs of his grace!' This is one of the most exuberant of all our praise songs; it helps us recall the joy of *our* salvation. Lacking a thousand tongues, let us freely use the one tongue we do have to 'sing our great Redeemer's praise!' " ("O for a thousand tongues to sing," B216, E493, L559, M57, P46).

"Spoken modulations" are also quite effective. They can serve as verbal bridges, uninterruptedly carrying the people's thought from item to item in the flow of worship. For example, following prayer, an imaginative and creative leader will sense ways to move appropriately into the hymn which follows, such as: "Let us continue in the spirit of prayer as we speak to God in the words of the hymn, "Jesus, thou joy of loving hearts."

After Scripture reading, the simple quoting of the opening line or two of the hymn to follow will help the congregation regard it as their response to the Word of God read and shared. Hymns must be carefully selected for use as "spoken modulations" if this device is to be of maximum value.

Although the tunes selected must be familiar and acceptable to those who sing them, hymn singing can and should be much more than a mere pleasant musical pastime. Hymns have no real reason for being if they are regarded simply as *libretti* for the music. It is the opportunity and sacred responsibility of worship leaders, by whatever means they can command in introducing hymns, to focus the congregation's attention on the words of prayer, affirmation, adoration, and so forth, for which the music is the effective medium.

Instrumental Introduction and Interpretation

Meaningful verbal introduction of hymns will be ineffectual without the sensitive introduction and interpretation of the hymn tunes by the organist, pianist, or other instrumentalist. In accompanied hymn singing, instrumentalists are the real leaders of the congregation. A worthy goal of instrumentalists is to play in ways which encourage people to sing with purpose and enthusiasm. This means that while playing, they should give particular attention to the texts sung by the congregation.

It is fundamentally important that instrumentalists perform notes and rhythms accurately as well as impregnate their hymn playing with musical feeling and vitality. There must be an imaginative interpretation of the mood of hymns, with thought given to matters of tempo, tone color (organ), articulation, volume, and phrasing. Whether organists sing with the people or not, they should play as if they were singing in order to help the congregation phrase together and sing intelligently the words of the individual stanzas. Though they must avoid sudden or unexpected changes in registration or volume, organists aware of variations in textual sentiment should vary their playing accordingly.

For example, the familiar Christmas hymns "Joy to the world" (ANTI-OCH, B87, E100, L39, M246, P40) and "O little town of Bethlehem" (ST. LOUIS, B86; E78, 79; L41; M230; P44) would certainly be introduced and interpreted through contrasting kinds of registration, tempo, and volume. Moreover, the third stanza of the latter hymn, beginning "How silently, how silently the wondrous gift is given," would be treated by the imaginative organist in somewhat more subdued fashion than the other stanzas. Following the text closely in either of these hymns will also shield the player from the embarrassment of beginning to perform a fifth stanza where none exists!

There are many other details of hymn playing—treatment of ritards, modulations, free accompaniments, handling the beginnings and endings of phrases, acoustical matters, and so forth—which are beyond the purpose of this text.[10] Suffice it to say that a good instrumentalist will interpret the texts of hymns in such a manner that the people will be motivated to sing with both spirit and understanding.

Hymns as Service Music: "Liturgical Epigrams"

One writer on the subject of hymn usages in worship has commented on "a certain decorative zeal" that many churches yield to "in adding interesting non-liturgical bits"[11] to the service. Indeed, as already noted, all too often hymns are interpolated with no defined purpose. They appear to be "bric-a-brac" placed there to serve some non-worship function such as affording musical pleasure to a certain segment of the choir or congregation, or taking up time that could otherwise be profitably given over to silence.

Yet there is a legitimate place at certain points in worship for the use of short hymns or single stanzas of hymns as "liturgical epigrams." Soloists, choirs, and other vocal ensembles should not be allowed to usurp the prerogatives of the congregation in the singing of responses and other service music.

[10]See the bibliography for suggested sources dealing with hymn playing.
[11]Northcott, *Hymns in Christian Worship*, 40.

If the climax of worship is the commitment of life in dedication, how can this be better symbolized than in the offering? And if music is to accompany the self-offering at the moment of the presentation of the gifts, how can it be better done than by the singing participation of the entire worshiping group (congregation aided by the choir and others)?

The hymnal contains a mine of "liturgical" responses for the congregation. First stanzas from hymns of consecration and/or stewardship can be employed appropriately as *offertory responses*:

- "As men (saints, those) of old their firstfruits brought" (B639, E705, L404, P414)
- "As with gladness men of old" (stanza 3) (B117, E119, P63)
- "Lord of all good, our gifts we bring you now" (L411)
- "Savior, thy dying love thou gavest me" (B607)
- "We give thee but thine own" (B609, L410, P428)
- "What does the Lord require" (E605, M441, P405)

Congregational *calls to worship* may be found in abundance:

- "All people that on earth do dwell" (B5; E377, 378; L245; M75; P220, 221)
- "Come, we that love the Lord" (B524, 525; E392; M732, 733)
- "God himself is (present) with us" (E475, L249)
- "God is here!" (M660, P461)
- "Ye (You) servants of God" (B589, E535, L252, M181, P477)

Some hymns are very suitable as *invocations*:

- "Blessed Jesus, at thy (your) word" (E440, M596, P454)
- "Come, Holy Ghost (Spirit), our souls inspire (E503, 504; L472, 473; M651, P125)
- "Come, thou almighty king" (B247, E365, L522, M61, P139)
- "Come, thou fount of every blessing" (B15, 18; E686; L499; M400; P356)
- "Lord Jesus Christ, be present now" (L253)
- "Open now thy gates of beauty" (L250, P489)

There are numerous first stanzas of certain hymns which can serve as *calls* (or *responses*) *to Scripture*:

- "Break thou (now) the bread of life" (B263, L235, M599, P329)
- "Father of mercies, in your Word" (L240)
- "God has (hath) spoken by the (his) prophets" (L238, M108)
- "Lord, keep us steadfast in your Word" (L230)
- "Thanks to God whose word was spoken (written)" (E630, P331)

First stanzas of many prayer hymns are appropriate as *calls* (or *responses*) *to prayer*:

- "I need thee every hour" (B450, M397)
- "I to the hills will lift my (mine) eyes" (E668, P234)
- "Lord, teach us how to pray aright" (L438)
- "Out of the depths I cry to you (to thee I raise) (E666, L295, P240)
- "What a friend we have in Jesus" (B182, L439, M526, P403)

Some hymns can be used as *benedictions* or *responses* to closing prayers:

- "Blest be the tie that binds" (B387, L370, M557, P438)
- "God be with you till we meet again" (M672, 673; P540)
- "Lord, dismiss us with your (thy) blessing" (E344, L259, M671, P538)
- "May the grace of Christ our Savior" (B661)
- "Savior, again to thy (your) dear name" (E345, L262, M663, P539)

The term "liturgical epigram" may more appropriately apply to *portions* of stanzas of hymns which may be used as interludes or responses in moving to and from the various elements of worship. For example, following the pastoral prayer:

- "O come to my heart, Lord Jesus, There is room in my heart for thee." ("Thou didst leave thy throne," B121)
- "Here's my heart, O (Lord) take and seal it, Seal it for thy courts above." ("Come, thou fount of every blessing," B15, 18; E686; L499; M400; P356)
- "Take my life and let it be Consecrated, Lord, to thee;" ("Take my

life and let it be consecrated," B277, 283; E707; L406; M399; P391)
- "O come to us, abide with us, Our Lord Emmanuel!" ("O little town of Bethlehem," B86; E78, 79; L41; M230; P44)

In litanies, parts of hymns may be sung instead of spoken sentences of prayer or thanksgiving:

> Our Father, for Your holy Word by which we can live useful lives to
> glorify Your name...
> *"Lord of all, to thee we raise This our hymn of grateful praise."*
> ("For the beauty of the earth," B44, E416, L561, M92, P473)

> For Your great love for all the world made known in Your Son, Jesus
> Christ, through whom we have eternal life...
> *"Lord of all to thee we raise This our sacrifice of praise."*

> For the church which teaches Your truth throughout the world and
> ministers to its great heart hunger and spiritual need...
> *"Lord of all to thee we raise This our sacrifice of praise."*

> For the privilege of serving in Your kingdom and of reaching out, by
> Your grace, to help one another and all humankind...
> *"Lord of all to thee we raise This our sacrifice of praise."* Amen.

Following the benediction, some fragment of a hymn used previously in the service or in keeping with the theme of the season or sermon could be used:

- "Rejoice, rejoice, rejoice, Give thanks and sing!" ("Rejoice, ye (you) pure in heart," B39, E556, 557; L553, M160, 161; P145, 146)
- "O give me grace to follow My master and my friend." ("O Jesus, I have promised," B276, E655, L503, M396, P388, 389)
- "Take from our souls the strain and stress, And let our ordered lives confess The beauty of thy peace."
  ("Dear Lord and Father of mankind," B267; E652, 653; L506; M358; P345)

The fact that hymns belong to the people should never be forgotten. Through them is voiced the people's prayer and praise—their eternal faith and hope. Memorable snatches of hymnic expression can be carried by the people to help and to bless as they depart from the worship service, inwardly singing.

Alternation Practices

A gentle but often effective stimulus to a greater involvement of the congregation in hymn singing is the use of the old principle of alternation (*alternatim*). Alternation singing is an ancient practice extending back to the Levitical choir's performance of the Hebrew psalms in temple worship. The parallel structure of psalm verses made antiphonal chanting a natural mode of performance. The term *alternatim* was applied as early as the 12th century to alternating plain chant (performed by the entire clerical choir) and polyphony (by a group of more skilled soloists).[12]

Alternation practices among choirs, soloists, congregation, organ, and other instruments in 16th- and 17th-century Germany served the practical purpose of singing meaningfully through the many stanzas found in numerous Lutheran chorales. Presently the alternation principle can be applied to various practices which aim to bring zest, variety, and inspiration to the normal *tutti* singing of hymns.

There are at least two categories of alternation. One kind—the more usual and traditional—pertains to the various performers in hymn singing. The other kind refers to the manner or medium of hymn performance.

Alternation by Performing Groups

Under this category the stanzas of hymns may be alternately performed in the following ways:

> 1. *Congregation versus organ alone*
>
>   This gives the congregational voices a recurring breather, relieving constant singing but keeping the flow and continuity of the hymn, provided the organist "plays the words" skillfully. For the organist who possesses the skill of improvisation, this is an opportunity for the interpretation of the texts. For those organists without these skills, well-written hymn "preludes" and chorale improvisations are available in publication.[13]

[12]See "Alternation Practice" in Carl Schalk (ed.), *Key Words in Church Music* (St. Louis: Concordia Publishing House, 1978), 15-17.
[13]Consult the bibliography for selected published collections.

2. Congregation with choir versus choir alone

When a congregation is singing a familiar hymn or has gained confidence in singing an unfamiliar one, it could well function alone in alternation with the choir. Singing *with* the congregation rather than *for* them is to be considered the first responsibility of the choir.

3. Choir versus choir versus congregation

If more than one choir is present, there can be antiphonal singing between them or between soloists and *tutti*. However, lest the congregation become mere auditor, a three-way alternation (Choir A—congregation, Choir B—congregation, and so forth) could be arranged.

4. Parts of a congregation in antiphony

A congregation can be divided into two (or more) units in a number of different ways: men versus women; those on one side of the sanctuary versus those on the other side; lower congregation (downstairs) versus upper congregation (balconies); adults versus youth/children; combined (massed) choirs versus congregation, and so forth.

Many hymns and gospel songs by their poetic structure lend themselves suitably to alternation singing in one or more of the ways suggested:

1. *Question-answer hymns may be sung antiphonally:*
- " 'Are ye able' " (M530)
- "Ask ye what great thing I know" (B538, M163)
- "Watchman, tell us of the night" (E640, P20)
- "What child is this" (E115, L40, M219, P53)
- "Who is he in yonder stall" (B124, M190)

2. *Gospel songs, refrain-type hymns, and those provided with antiphons are all suitable for responsorial or antiphonal singing:*
- "All creatures of our God and king" (B27, E400, L527, M62, P455)
- "Come, Christians, join to sing" (B231, M158, P150)
- "Let all the world in every corner sing" (B28; E402, 403; M93; P468)

- "When morning gilds the skies" (B221, E427, L545, M185, P487)
- "Wonderful Words of Life" (B261, M600)

3. *Contemporary psalm settings with their antiphons lend themselves to this treatment naturally. The verses of the psalm can be either sung or said in alternation with the antiphon:*
- "My shepherd is the Lord" (Psalm 23—Gelineau) (M754, 137; P173)
- "My soul is thirsting for the Lord" (Psalm 42—Gelineau) (P190)
- "How lovely is your dwelling place" (Psalm 84—Murray) (P208)

Alternation by Manner and Medium

As already indicated in the case of psalm singing, the other kind of alternation results when the principle is extended in application to the mode or medium of performance. Used with imagination, this can lead to varied methods of congregational participation:

1. *Alternation of Scripture verses with hymn stanzas*
     This is particularly effective with metrical psalms, in which the original verse(s) for each stanza can be read preceding its singing. For example: "Unto the hills around do I lift up" (L445) or "I to the hills will lift my eyes" (P234):

Reading:	Psalm 121:1, 2
Singing:	Stanza 1
Reading:	Psalm 121:3, 4
Singing:	Stanza 2
Reading:	Psalm 121:5, 6
Singing:	Stanza 3
Reading:	Psalm 121:7, 8
Singing:	Stanza 4

2. *Alternation by singing and speaking stanzas*
     A three- or five-stanza hymn usually works best in this method. For example: "Dear Lord and Father of mankind" (B267[14]; E652, 653; L506; M358; P345) or "Nature with open volume stands" (E434):

---

[14]B267 has only four stanzas, but a fifth could be supplied from other hymnals.

Stanza 1:	sung
Stanza 2:	spoken
Stanza 3:	sung
Stanza 4:	spoken
Stanza 5:	sung

"We believe in one true God" (M85) or "We all believe in one true God" (L374, P137):

Stanza 1:	sung
Stanza 2:	spoken
Stanza 3:	sung

3. *Alternating unison with singing in harmony*

Not to be overlooked are the reasons for *alternatim*—simple congregational unison (even unaccompanied at times) and the harmonized version (by the choir). For example: "Jesus, priceless treasure" (L457, 458; M532) or "Jesus, all my gladness" (E701):

Stanza 1:	unison
Stanza 2:	harmony
Stanza 3:	unison

"Stand up and bless the Lord" (B30, M662, P491):

Stanza 1:	unison
Stanza 2:	harmony
Stanza 3:	unison
Stanza 4:	harmony
Stanza 5:	unison

Some hymnals provide for this kind of treatment in their notation and arrangement of music for the individual stanzas. For example: "For all the saints" (E287, L174, M711, P526)[15]:

Stanza 1, 2, 3:	unison
Stanza 4, 5, 6:	harmony
Stanza 7, 8:	unison

[15]The plan varies in the hymnals depending on the number of stanzas included.

4. *Alternation of modes*

Change from major to minor or vice versa is not to be done capriciously, but it can be used when the text may be illumined by this kind of alternation. For example: "Come, Holy Spirit, heavenly Dove" (P126):

Stanza 1:	major
Stanza 2, 3:	minor
Stanza 4:	major

"Amazing grace! how sweet the sound" (B330, E671, L448, M378, P280):

Stanzas 1, 2:	major
Stanzas 3, (4):	minor
Last stanza:	major

5. *Alternation of tunes*

If thoughtfully planned, there can be an alternation of hymn tunes in the progress of singing the stanzas of a hymn. For example: "How firm a foundation" (B338; E636, 637; L507, M529; P361):

Stanza 1:	ADESTE FIDELES or LYONS
Stanza 2:	FOUNDATION
Stanza 3:	ADESTE FIDELES or LYONS
Stanza 4:	FOUNDATION

"To God be the glory" (B4, M98, P485):

Stanza 1:	TO GOD BE THE GLORY
Stanza 2:	ST. DENIO
Stanza 3:	TO GOD BE THE GLORY

"My hope is built on nothing less" (B406; L293, 294; M368, P379):

Stanza 1:	SOLID ROCK
Stanza 2, 3:	MELITA
Stanza 4:	SOLID ROCK

The last example illustrates the fact that there can be textual reasons for selecting certain tunes for particular stanzas. MELITA was originally set by its composer, J. B. Dykes, to William Whiting's "Almighty Father, strong to save"—the Navy hymn. For many people this tune usually calls to mind the sea, along with concern for those who may be in peril upon it. It is thus particularly appropriate for the middle two stanzas of "My hope is built" with their references to "high and stormy gale" and "raging flood." Moreover, MELITA is a very expressive setting for the words of the chorus with its sturdy rising chromatic line for "On Christ the solid rock I stand" and the falling melodic line to the low tonic with the words "all other ground is sinking sand."[16] Here also is an example of alternation of keys. The two keys work together well, with C as the common tone for both tunes (the dominant of F major—SOLID ROCK—and the tonic of C major—MELITA).

6. *Alternation of hymns*

Using stanzas of different hymns to the same tune is rare and not to be encouraged where the unity of thought of a hymn may be disturbed. However, sometimes a medley of hymns on one tune can be used if their "message" can logically fit a common theme. For example:

Theme: "Praise the God of our Salvation"
Tune: HYFRYDOL
           "Come, thou long-expected Jesus"
           (B77, M196, P2)
           "Praise the Lord! ye heavens adore
           him" (B36, stanza 2)
           "I will sing the wondrous story" (B535)
           "Jesus! what a friend for sinners" (B185)

7. *Alternation of hymn stanzas with praise chorus*

The contemporary practice of singing short praise choruses, while musically often of questionable consequence, is bringing a welcome objectivity to the informal worship of many congregations. The exclusive use of such choruses, however, tends to

---

[16]These affinities in text and tune could have been some of the reasons for the choice of MELITA as a second tune for "My hope is built on nothing less" at L294.

make public worship one-sided and theologically threadbare.[17] In the conviction that, despite their positive values for certain worshipers, praise choruses should never replace the rich cognitive texts of classic hymnody, they may be used as "antiphons" in alternation with standard hymn stanzas. For example:

- "Alas and did my Savior bleed" (B145, L98, M294, P78), and "O how he loves you and me" (B146)

- "Come, Thou almighty king" (B247, E365, L522, M61, P139), and "Father, I adore you" (B256)

- "Great is thy faithfulness" (B54, M140, P276), and "God is so good" (B23)

8. Alternation using a descant

The use of a descant is a variation in the unison-harmony alternation. This high-soaring countermelody works well—the high voices (and/or solo instruments) singing against the unison of the congregation and choir on the principal melody. Care must be taken to train the congregation to continue singing on those stanzas to which the descant is added. Without such training, individuals in the congregation will tone down or even stop their own singing in order to listen to the descant. The purpose of the descant is to bring zest and vitality to the singing of all, not to entertain the congregation. The device, however, should be employed in moderation. Its use may best be reserved for especially festive and celebrative occasions.

Special Services

The hymn can be an effective vehicle of ministry in certain special times of worship, such as weddings and funerals. Both these occasions are services of public worship, even though this may sometimes be difficult to grasp for families who are intimately involved in such services. Some tend to look on these services as private affairs rather than as worship to the Lord in company with the larger Christian family.

---

[17]For a full discussion of praise and worship choruses, see Donald Hustad, *Jubilate II* (Carol Stream: Hope Publishing Company, 1993), 285 ff.

1. *The Christian Wedding Service* should be directed toward God in Christ rather than toward the bride or others in the wedding party. The object of attention in a Christian wedding is God in Christ whose presence blesses it. Although other types of music may be appropriately performed at weddings, the hymns directed toward God (sung by the wedding party as well as by the congregation) can also be a simple, beautiful expression of loving support for the couple being married. Hymns of praise are suitable, such as:

- "Love divine, all loves excelling" (B208, E657, L315, M384, P376)
- "Now thank we all our God" (B638; E396, 397; L533, 534)
- "Praise, my soul, the king of heaven" (B32, E410, L549, M66, P478)

These, as well as other majestic hymns, are sometimes played for the processional and recessional rather than marchlike (sometimes secular in association) music. Hymns like:

- "Joyful, joyful, we adore thee" (B7, E376, L551, M89, P464),
- "Praise the Lord! ye (O) heavens, adore him" (B36, E373, L540), or
- "Praise to (ye) the Lord, the almighty" (B14, E390, L543, M139, P482),

are far more desirable than certain secular solo selections which are often sensuous and sentimental. The wedding should not be a spectacle to be witnessed by the congregation primarily as audience. Rather, it is a drama of worship in which all the people, even for a brief time, are joining in singing God's praises. Praise is an appropriate expression of the joy and thanksgiving which is engendered by such occasions.

2. *The Christian Funeral* can also be a service of divine worship, not simply a mournful surrender to death. The role of the hymn in the funeral service is to strengthen faith and express the good news of resurrection. The declaration of confidence and trust expressed in the singing of great hymns can be an eloquent Christian testimony to those attending who may be unbelievers. In general, the favorite hymns of the deceased or of a relative should be used only if they contain strong positive expressions of Christian faith. The hymns for the funeral can function in several ways:

1. To express thanks and adoration to God
- "For all the saints" (B355, E287, L174, M711, P526)
- "Guide me, O thou great Jehovah" (B56, E690, L343, M127, P281)
- "Immortal, invisible, God only wise" (B6, E423, L526, M103, P263)

2. To comfort the living:
- "A mighty fortress is our God" (B8; E687, 688; L228, 229; M110; P260)
- "If you will only let (thou but trust in) God (to) guide you (thee)" (B57, E635, L453, M142, P282)
- "My faith looks up to thee (you) (B416, E691, L479, M452, P383)

3. To strengthen resolve for continued living:
- "God of grace and God of glory" (B395; E594, 595; L415; M577; P420)
- "O (Our) God, our help in ages past" (B74, E680, L320, M117, P210)
- "O Master, let me walk with thee (you) (B279; E659, 660; M430; P357)

While it is true that the death of a loved one is a saddening occasion and a sobering reminder of one's mortality, it must be remembered that Christians view death as the door to eternal life made possible by Christ's victory over death. The hymns sung and played in the Christian memorial service should therefore be those reflecting Easter and the resurrection.[18]

Hymn Services

Many of the goals for selecting hymns thoughtfully and using them meaningfully in corporate worship may be achieved in the context of the hymn service—a worship service designed primarily for congregational participation in hymn singing. It may involve choirs and/or other performing individuals or groups, but the focus is upon the congregation as performers.

The hymn service may sometimes be designated as a hymn festival—a term usually implying the involvement of more than one congregation and

[18]Consult the bibliography for materials containing suggestions for the selection and use of hymns in the wedding and funeral.

of a celebrative or commemorative nature. Hymn festivals are greatly encouraged, particularly those observing some great church or hymnic anniversary or honoring some outstanding figure in church or hymnic history. The ecumenicity of the hymnal can be dramatized by festivals which are planned to transcend denominational, cultural, and racial barriers. The cause of Christian neighborliness has been greatly strengthened in such endeavors.

However, community-wide festivals should not displace nor lessen the emphasis on more modest hymn services planned for local congregational worship. Such services can be infinite in variety of content. As to type they may be classified in at least three ways:[19]

1. Topical—A service arranged according to some hymnic classification not necessarily unified in theme. This could be a service in which the hymns bear a common relationship such as those of one author or composer (commemorative anniversary services for James Montgomery, Ralph Vaughan Williams, John G. Whittier, Lowell Mason); those from one nation or ethnic group (British hymns, African-American hymns); those translated from one language (Greek hymns, German hymns); those of one sect or denomination (Methodist hymns, Anglican hymns); those of certain periods of general or Christian history (Reformation hymns, 17th-century hymns), or those unified by some characteristic of their authors/composers (hymns by women, tunes by famous composers); or those of certain tune types (metrical psalm tunes, carols). These are a few suggestions for topical hymn services.[20]

2. Thematic—A service with a unifying devotional theme often based either on some religious teaching or concept, or some liturgical form, piece of devotional literature, or holy Scripture. Either classic or contemporary hymns may be used for structuring thematic hymn services. Some examples follow:

Theological Concept or Christian Virtue
1. The Cosmic Christ
2. The Christian Life
3. The Trinity

[19]See Austin C. Lovelace, "Hymn Festivals" Paper XXXI of the Hymn Society (Fort Worth: Texas Christian University, 1979).
[20]See the bibliography for sources having numerous practical suggestions for planning hymn services.

4. The Cross
5. The Church
6. Faith, Hope, Love
7. Discipleship and Service
8. The Christian Year

Scriptural Form or Passage
1. The Lord's Prayer
2. The Ten Commandments
3. The Beatitudes
4. Isaiah 6:1-8
5. Psalm 23
6. Galatians 5:22-23
7. John 3:16
8. Colossians 3:16-17

Traditional Worship Form or Theological (Liturgical) Formulation
1. The Apostle's Creed
2. The Gloria in Excelsis
3. Prayer of Francis of Assisi
4. The Church Covenant
5. Prayer of Richard of Chichester

Hymns (that line by line or stanza by stanza may be used to structure thematic services)
• "God is here!" (M660, P461)
• "God of grace and God of glory" (B395; E594, 595; L415; M577; P420)
• "Go to dark Gethsemane" (B150, E171, L109, M290, P97)
• "O sing a song of Bethlehem" (B120, M179, P308)
• "O sons and daughters, let us sing" (E203, 206; L139; M317; P116, 117)
• "One day" (B193)
• "When in our music God is glorified"(B435, E420, L555, M68, P264)
• "Who is he in yonder stall" (B124, M190)

The thematic type of service lends itself more readily than the topical kind to the use of hymns in a devotional sequence for the purpose of interpreting and expressing worship moods. However, the topical service can also be a time of divine worship if the planners are careful to give the congregation legitimate reason for its hymnic expressions of prayer and praise in ways already discussed.

It is also possible to have a hymn service which combines the topical and thematic elements.[21] For example:

1. *Tractarian Hymnody and the Christian Year*
   The topic: Hymns written by those connected with the Tractarian (Oxford, High Church) Movement in 19th-century England
   The theme: The Christian (church, liturgical) Year

2. *Baptist Hymns and the Church Covenant*
   The topic: Hymns by Baptists
   The theme: The Church Covenant

3. *Luther's Hymns and Christian Doctrine*
   The topic: The Hymns of Martin Luther
   The theme: Hymns as Vehicles of Christian Doctrine

4. *Wesleyan Hymns and the Lord's Prayer*
   The topic: Hymns by the Wesleys
   The theme: The Model Prayer of our Lord

3. Demonstrative—A service with more didactic intentions. It may be conceived as a kind of hymn study session or congregational rehearsal in which the leader assumes a more informal role as instructor and encourager rather than worship leader. The purposes are to give more direct attention to the practical matters of improving congregational singing and to promote fellowship through singing. It can have either topical or thematic aspects, but it would ordinarily be more flexible and spontaneous than the topical or thematic types. Often the demonstrative type might be

---

[21]See "Appendix 1" for a hymn service based on the worship pattern as found in the experience of the prophet Isaiah (Isa. 6:1-8) and using the hymns of Isaac Watts. This service also illustrates the *alternatim* principle in a variety of ways.

called a Hymn Sing.[22]

A hymn sing could be gathered about such themes or topics as the following:

- Hymn Meters
- Hymn Patterns (either literary or musical)
- Hymn Tune Names
- *Alternatim praxis* (Alternation practice)
- Hymn Interpretations
- Psalms and Hymns
- Favorite Hymns of the Congregation
- John Wesley's Directions for Singing

The last suggestion is a reminder of Wesley's final direction for singing which aptly sums up the major concern of this chapter:

> Above all, *sing spiritually*. Have an eye to God in every word you sing. Aim at pleasing him more than yourself, or any other creature. In order to do this, attend strictly to the sense of what you sing, and see that your heart is not carried away with the sound, but offered to God continually; so shall your singing be such as the Lord will approve here, and reward you when he cometh in the clouds of heaven.[23]

[22]See the discussion of hymn sings in Chapter 12, "The Hymn in Education," pages 290-1.
[23]Austin C. Lovelace and William C. Rice, *Music and Worship in the Church* (Nashville: Abingdon Press, 1960; revised and enlarged edition, 1976), 157, but easily found in other places. See *The United Methodist Hymnal*, vii.

QUESTIONS FOR DISCUSSION/PROJECTS FOR ACTION

1. Looking at the Topical Index in your hymnal, you would find hymns appropriate for the dialogical pattern of worship under what headings? List other hymns for each of the following aspects of that pattern:
- God's greatness, holiness, and power
- Human sinfulness and repentance
- God's mercy and forgiveness
- God's call to discipleship
- Personal commitment and dedication

2. If you worship in a tradition which does not give particular observance to the church year, consult a hymnal such as the *Lutheran Book of Worship* to study the index entitled "Hymns for the Church Year" (929-31) in order to make a list of hymns appropriate for Advent, Lent, and Pentecost.[24]

3. Make a file of service bulletins from various churches to discover:
- the number of hymns sung in a service.
- the kinds of hymns chosen.
- the ways hymns are labeled (if at all).
- the unusual manner in which hymns are used (if any).

4. Make a list of ways you could aid a congregation to sing hymns as genuine expressions of prayer and praise.

5. Think of three ways in which parts of these hymns (a stanza or phrase) may be used as "liturgical epigrams":
- "Lead on, O king eternal" (B621; E555; L495; M580; P447, 448)
- "Open my eyes, that I may see" (B502, M454, P324)
- "O come, O come, emmanuel" (B76, E56, L34, M211, P9)
- "This is the threefold truth" (B408)

6. Sketch one possible *alternation* treatment for each of these hymns:
- "Jesu, Jesu, fill us with your love" (B501, E602, M432, P367)
- "Rock of ages, cleft for me" (B342, E685, L327, M361)
- "The Lord will come and not be slow" (E462, L318)
- "When peace, like a river" (B410, L346, M377)

7. Think of one suitable integrating subject for each of the three kinds of hymn services treated in this chapter: Topical, Thematic, and Demonstrative. Select at least five hymns which could appropriately be used in each.

8. Sketch in detail a one-hour hymn service using one of the integrating subjects chosen above.

---

[24]Another source for hymn selection is the Index of Topics and Categories: Christian Year in *The United Methodist Hymnal* (937-938). The bibliography contains other sources on the meanings of the church season.

12

THE HYMN IN EDUCATION

SOME VALUES IN THE TEACHING OF HYMNS

"If a hymn is worth singing, it is worth studying seriously in concert or privately."[1]

While much of the church's attention has been focused upon teaching the Bible (and rightly so), teaching the hymnal has yet to become a significant part of the educational program of most congregations. Why should a church teach hymns?

One basic reason is that hymns are a means of communicating the message of the church. Some hymns are paraphrases of Scripture and others are based on specific Scripture verses.[2] Hymns also effectively convey the church's theology.[3] While listening to a sermon can be a passive experience, hymn singing is meant always to involve the congregation actively. Furthermore, hymns sung over and over again, year after year effectively teach through repetition. Their melodies tend to linger long in the memory, carrying the thoughts connected with them into the mind and heart.

Hymns should also be taught for their value in helping a congregation or an individual to worship. Sometimes when worshipers lack words to express their feelings, they find them expressed meaningfully in the words of a hymn. In celebrating the birth of Christ or His resurrection, they are helped to express their worship through joyful hymns and carols. In the somber meditations upon the sufferings of Christ on the cross, one finds hymns which communicate these sacred events with poignant power.

For example, those who are at a loss for words to utter their profound wonder concerning Christ's sacrifice may find their feelings expressed in certain hymns. A medieval poet's reaction to the crucifixion is embodied in "O

[1]David Hugh Jones, "Comments of a Hymnal Editor," *The Hymn* 29, 4 (October 1978): 227.
[2]See Chapter 3, "The Hymn and Scripture," pages 49-62.
[3]See Chapter 4, "The Hymn and Theology," pages 63-75.

sacred head, now wounded" (B137, E168, 169, L116, 117, M286, P98):

"What language shall I borrow
    To thank thee, dearest Friend,
For this thy dying sorrow,
    Thy pity without end?
O make me thine forever,
    And should I fainting be,
Lord, let me never, never
    Outlive my love to thee."

The pioneer English hymnist Isaac Watts expressed his feelings concerning the death of Christ in "When I survey the wondrous cross" (B144, E474, L482, M298, 299, P100, 101):

"See, from his head, his hands, his feet,
    Sorrow and love flow mingled down;
Did e'er such love and sorrow meet,
    Or thorns compose so rich a crown?

Were the whole realm of nature mine,
    That were a present far too small;
Love so amazing, so divine,
    Demands my soul, my life, my all."

An anonymous African-American reacted to the cross of Christ with the following words (B156, E172, L92, M288, P102):

"Were you there when they crucified my Lord?
    Were you there when they crucified my Lord?
Oh! Sometimes it causes me to tremble, tremble, tremble.
    Were you there when they crucified my Lord?"

Hymns have value in providing instruction in Christian living. The Baptist, Methodist, and Lutheran hymnals have major headings related to Christian Living: "Christian Life" in *The Baptist Hymnal*, 1991, "Sanctifying and Perfecting Grace" in *The United Methodist Hymnal*, and "The Life of Faith" in the *Lutheran Book of Worship*. For example, hymns can effectively teach that the Christian life involves a commitment to active service. Notice the action words in these hymn titles: "O Master, let me walk with thee (you)" (B279, E660, L492, M430, P357), "Rescue the perishing" (B559, M591), and "Go, tell it on the mountain" (B95, E99, L70, M251, P29).[4]

The teaching of hymns is an avenue for passing on the heritage of the church. One cannot study hymnody without encountering such giants in the history of the Christian church as Ambrose of Milan, John of Damascus, Francis of Assisi, Martin Luther, John Calvin, John Wesley, John Mason Neale, and Harry Emerson Fosdick. In addition to Christian biography and the general sweep of church history, one learns a significant portion of the church's devotional poetry through hymnody. Through a study of hymns one can also learn about poetic form and style, including meter, rhyme, and the various poetic devices.[5] Much of the musical heritage of the church is encountered in hymnology (the practical study of and about hymns). Such forms as plainsong, chorale, psalm tune, and gospel hymn relate to interesting segments of the church's heritage.[6] Furthermore, a knowledge of hymnody illuminates the larger forms of church music related to hymns. To take just one example, a knowledge of Luther's Easter hymn *Christ lag in Todesbanden* ("Christ Jesus lay in death's strong bands," E185, 186, L134, M319) greatly enhances the meaning one finds in Bach's Easter cantata (BWV 4) based on this hymn.

Thus through hymn instruction one is able to teach the message of the church, to help persons worship, to provide guidance in Christian living, and to present the vast heritage of the church, including knowledge of outstanding leaders in its history and a significant portion of its devotional literature and music.

HYMNS IN THE CHURCH'S EDUCATIONAL PROGRAM
Where Hymns Are Used

Hymn singing in most churches is not limited to the central worship services. This activity also takes place in many of the church's organizations. Church organizations that can make good use of hymns include the Sunday School, graded choirs, mission study and action groups, and senior citizen groups. In addition, special educational courses, such as church membership or catechetical classes and Vacation Bible Schools, can make effective use of

[4]See Harry Eskew, "Hymns in the Church's Teaching Ministry," *The Theological Educator*, 8, 2 (Spring 1978): 86-97.
[5]See Chapter 1, "The Hymn and Literature," pages 14-28.
[6]See Chapter 2, "The Hymn and Music," pages 38-46.

hymns. Each of the church organizations whose programs can allow for hymn singing provide excellent opportunities for the church music leader to enhance the effectiveness of this experience educationally.

Hymns in the Curriculum

The curriculum of each of the church's educational organizations can be effectively supported by appropriate hymns. For example, a Sunday School lesson dealing with Psalm 72 could make use of "Jesus shall reign" (B587, E544, L530, M157, P423). The fullest opportunity for singing hymns and teaching hymnology, however, is provided through the graded choir program.

The importance of children's learning good hymns has often been emphasized. The favorite hymns of adults are frequently those they learned when they were young. Children, because they can do so with ease, should be encouraged to memorize hymns. The following suggestions for establishing a hymn memorization program are given in Mary Nelson Keithahn's *Our Heritage of Hymns*:

> 1. Make a list of all the hymns that children in your congregation should know.
>
> 2. Choose a theme that can serve as the framework for teaching a group of hymns during your program year.
>
> 3. Decide how many hymns children should be challenged to learn in your program year.
>
> 4. After you have decided on a theme and chosen the hymns that children will study, assemble the resources you will need for teaching and using these hymns during the year.
>
> 5. Introduce the program to the children and their families, emphasizing that it is a *program*, not a competitive contest.
>
> 6. When the children feel they have a hymn memorized, encourage them to sing it for one another to make sure it is learned well enough to pass inspection.
>
> 7. Decide how you will record and recognize the children's progress in the program.
>
> 8. Interpret the Hymn Memorization Program to the congregation.[7]

---

[7]Mary Nelson Keithahn, *Our Heritage of Hymns* (Garland, TX: Choristers Guild, 1986), 67-69. Used by permission. This volume and the same publisher's *Exploring the Hymnal* (1986), by Mary Nelson Keithahn and Mary Louise VanDyke, are excellent resources for use in teaching hymns to children.

Hymns and hymn tunes should be included in every church's graded choir curriculum. Kindergarten children can be prepared to learn hymns through exposure to hymn tunes, such as TERRA PATRIS (BEATA) ("This is my Father's world," B43, L554, M144, P293), DUKE STREET ("Jesus shall reign where'er the sun," B587, E544, L530, M157, P423), and TALLIS' CANON ("All praise to thee (you), my God, this night," B449, E43, L278, M682, P542). Children in grades one, two, and three can learn to sing "Praise God, from whom all blessings flow" (B253, E43, L564, M95, P591), "Holy, holy, holy! Lord God Almighty!" (B2, E362, L165, M64, P138), and "Fairest Lord Jesus" (B176, E383, 384, M189, P306; "Beautiful Savior," L518).

Children in these early grades can begin to use the hymnal and to learn about authors and composers of hymns and hymn tunes. Children in choirs for grades four, five, and six can learn more hymnology and additional hymns, such as "Now thank we all our God" (B638, E396, 397, L533, 534, M102, P555), "All creatures of our God and King" (B27, E400, L527, M62, P455), and "For the beauty of the earth" (B44, E416, L561, M92, P473). One plan that involves the systematic integration of hymns into the children's choir curriculum consists of two three-year hymn cycles—one three-year cycle for grades one through three, and another for grades four through six.[8]

100 Hymns for Children and Youth

The following list of 100 hymns is suggestive of the hymnic wealth available for the Christian education of children and youth. This list is not meant to be a "canon," for there are many other excellent hymns which may be used in the church's teaching ministry.

Although this list is divided into three age groupings, these divisions are not rigid. For example, some hymns in the second group (for fourth, fifth, and sixth graders) may be quite appropriate for third graders. Children in the early grades can be taught "Holy, holy, holy! Lord God Almighty!" and other hymns of similar complexity, but it is often wise for them to learn one stanza rather than attempting to master the entire hymn. Children need not understand the full meaning of a hymn in order to benefit from it. As they grow, they will grow in their understanding of the hymns they have been taught.

[8]This plan is being followed by the Music Department of the Southern Baptist Sunday School Board (127 Ninth Ave., N., Nashville, TN 37234) and is incorporated in their periodicals: *Music Makers* (grades 1-3), *Young Musicians* (grades 4-6), *The Children's Choir* (grades 1-6), and *The Music Leader* (for leaders of children's choirs).

20 Hymns for Grades 1-3 (ages 6-8)

- "All glory, laud, and honor" (ST. THEODULPH, B126, E154, L108, M280, P88)
- "All praise to thee (you), my God, this night" (TALLIS' CANON, B449, E43, L278, M682, P542)
- "All things bright and beautiful" (SPOHR, B46; ROYAL OAK, E405, M147, P267)
- "Awake, my soul, and with the sun" (MORNING HYMN, E11, L269, P456)
- "Away in a manger" (MUELLER, B103, M217, P25; CRADLE SONG, E101, P24)
- "Come, Christians, join to sing" (MADRID, B231, P150; SPAN-ISH HYMN, M158)
- "Come, thou long-expected Jesus" (HYFRYDOL, B77, M196, P2; JEFFERSON, L30; STUTTGART, P1)
- "Fairest Lord Jesus" (CRUSADERS' HYMN or ST. ELIZABETH or SSCHÖNSTE HERR JESU, B176, E383, 384, M189, P306; "Beau-tiful Savior," L518)
- "From all that dwell below the skies" (DUKE STREET, B13, M101; OLD 100TH, E380, L550; LASST UNS ERFREUEN, P229)
- "Go, tell it on the mountain" (GO TELL IT, B95, E99, L70, M251, P29)
- "God of the sparrow" (ROEDER, M122, P272)
- "Holy, holy, holy! Lord God Almighty!" (NICAEA, B2, E362, L165, M64, P580)
- "Joy to the world" (ANTIOCH, B87, E100, L39, M246, P40)
- "O come, all ye faithful" (ADESTE FIDELES, B89, E83, L45, M234, P41)
- "O little town of Bethlehem" (ST. LOUIS, B86, E79, L41, M230, P44; FOREST GREEN, E78, P43)
- "O sing a song of Bethlehem" (KINGSFOLD, B120, M179, P308)
- "Praise God, from whom all blessings flow" (OLD 100TH, B253, E380, L564, 565, M95, P591, 592, 593)
- "Savior, like a shepherd lead us" (BRADBURY, B61, M381, P387; HER VIL TIES, L481; SICILIAN MARINERS, E708)
- "Take my life and let it (that I may) be consecrated" (HENDON, B277, P391; PATMOS, L406; MESSIAH, M399)
- "This is my Father's world" (TERRA PATRIS or TERRA BEATA,

B43, L554, M144, P293; MERCER STREET, E651)

40 Hymns for Grades 4-6 (ages 9-11)
- "A mighty fortress is our God" (EIN' FESTE BURG, B8, E687, 688, L228, 229, M110, P259, 260)
- "All creatures of our God and King" (LASST UNS ERFREUEN, B27, E400, L527, M62, P455)
- "As with gladness men of old" (DIX, B117, E119, L82, P63)
- "Christ the Lord is risen today" (EASTER HYMN, B159, M302; RESURREXIT, E189; ORIENTIS PARTIBUS, L130; LLANFAIR, P113)
- "Come, thou almighty King" (ITALIAN HYMN, B247, E365, L522, M61, P139)
- "Come, ye (you) thankful people come" (ST. GEORGE'S WINDSOR, B637, E290, L407, M694, P551)
- "Faith of our fathers" (ST. CATHERINE, B352, E558, L500, M710)
- "For the beauty of the earth" (DIX, B44, E416, L561, M92, P473)
- "God moves (O God) in a mysterious way" (ST. ANNE, B73; LONDON NEW, E677; BANGOR, L483; DUNDEE, P270)
- "God of our fathers (the ages)" (NATIONAL HYMN, B629, E718, L567, M698, P262)
- "God, who stretched the spangled heavens" (HYMN TO JOY, B47; HOLY MANNA, E580, L463, M150, P268)
- "Good Christian friends (men), rejoice" (IN DULCI JUBILO, B96, E107, L55, M224, P28)
- "Hark! the herald angels sing" (MENDELSSOHN, B88, E87, L60, M240, P31, 32)
- "Hosanna, loud hosanna" (ELLACOMBE, B130, M278)
- "How firm a foundation" (FOUNDATION, B338, E636, L507, M529, P361)
- "I sing a song of the saints of God" (GRANDE ISLE, E293, M712, P364)
- "I sing the almighty (mighty) power of God" (FOREST GREEN, B42, E398, M152)
- "In Christ there is no east or west" (ST. PETER, B385, P439; MCKEE, E529, L359, M548, P440)
- "Jesus shall reign" (DUKE STREET, B587, E544, L530, M157, P423)

- "Joyful, joyful, we adore thee" (HYMN TO JOY, B7, E376, L551, M89, P464)
- "Let all the world in every corner sing" (ALL THE WORLD, B28, AUGUSTINE, E402, M93, P468; MACDOUGALL, E403)
- "Let us break bread together" (BREAK BREAD, B366, E325, L212, M618, P513)
- "Let us with a gladsome mind" (MONKLAND, E389, P244; WILLIAMS BAY, L521)
- "Lord, I want to be a Christian" (I WANT TO BE A CHRISTIAN, B489, M402, P372)
- "Now thank we all our God" (NUN DANKET, B638, E396, 397, L533, 534, M102, P555)
- "O beautiful for spacious skies" (MATERNA, B630, E719, M696, P564)
- "O come, O come, Emmanuel" (VENI EMMANUEL, B76, E56, L34, M211, P9)
- "Praise the Lord! Ye (O) heavens adore him" (HYFRYDOL, B36; DANIEL'S TUNE, E373; AUSTRIA, L540)
- "Praise to (ye) the Lord, the Almighty" (LOBE DEN HERREN, B14, E390, L543, M139, P482)
- "Rejoice the Lord is King" (DARWALL, B197, P155; GOPSAL, E481, M716; LAUS REGIS, L171)
- "Sing praise to God who reigns above (the highest good)" (MIT FREUDEN ZART, B20, E408, M126, P483; LOBT GOTT DEN HERREN, IHR, L542)
- "Sing we now of Christmas" (FRENCH CAROL, B111, M237)
- "Stand up, stand up for Jesus" (WEBB, B485, L389, M514; MORNING LIGHT, E561)
- "The church's one foundation" (AURELIA, B350, E525, L369, M545, 546, P442)
- "The day of resurrection" (LANCASHIRE, B164, M303, P118; HERZLICH TUT MICH ERFREUEN, L141; ELLACOMBE, E210)
- "The God of Abraham praise (Praise to the living God)" (LEONI or YIGDAL, B34, E401, L544, M116, P488)
- "The Lord's my shepherd, I'll not want" (CRIMOND, M136, P170; BROTHER JAMES' AIR, L451)
- "We've a story to tell to the nations" (MESSAGE, B586, M569)
- "When morning gilds the skies" (LAUDES DOMINI, B221, L546,

M185, P487; O SEIGNEUR, L545)

• "While shepherds watched their flocks by night" (WINCHESTER OLD, E94, M236, P58; CHRISTMAS, M236, P59)

40 Hymns for Youth (ages 12 up)

• "Ah, holy Jesus, how hast thou offended" (HERZLIEBSTER JESU, E158, L123, M289, P93)

• "All hail the power of Jesus' name" (CORONATION, B202, E450, L328, M154, P142)

• "Amazing grace! how sweet the sound" (AMAZING GRACE or NEW BRITAIN, B330, E671, L448, M378, P280)

• "Be thou my vision" (SLANE, B60, M451, P339)

• "Breathe on me, Breath of God" (TRENTHAM, B241, M420, P316; DURHAM, L488)

• "Built on the Rock (a rock) the church shall (doth) stand" (KIRKEN or KIRKEN DEN ER ET GAMMELT HUS, B351, L365)

• "Christ is alive" (TRURO, B173, E182, M318, P108)

• "Come, ye (you) faithful, raise the strain" (GAUDEAMUS PARITER or AVE VIRGO VIRGINUM, E200, L132, P114; ST. KEVIN, E199, M315, P115)

• "Crown him with many crowns" (DIADEMATA, B161, E494, L170, M327, P151)

• "For all the saints" (SINE NOMINE, B355, E287, L174, M711, P526)

• "God of grace and God of glory" (CWM RHONDDA, B395, E594, L415, M577, P420)

• "Great is thy faithfulness" (FAITHFULNESS, B54, M140, P276)

• "Guide me, O thou (ever) great Jehovah (Redeemer)" (CWM RHONDDA, B56, E690, L343, M127, P281)

• "Hope of the world" (DONNE SECOURS, E472, L493, P360; VICAR, M178)

• "I know not why God's wondrous grace" (EL NATHAN, B337, M714)

• "If you (thou) will only let (but suffer, but trust in) God (to) guide you" (NEUMARK or WER NUR DEN LIEBEN GOTT, B57, E635, L453, M142, P282)

• "Immortal, invisible, God only wise" (ST. DENIO, B6, E423, L526, M103, P263)

- "Jesu, Jesu, fill us with your love" (CHEREPONI, B501, E602, M432, P367)
- "Jesus, thou (O Jesus) joy of loving hearts" (DICKINSON COLLEGE, E649; WALTON, L356; QUEBEC, P510; JESU DULCIS MEMORIA, P511)
- "Jesus, thy boundless love to me" (ST. CATHERINE, B123, M183, P366; RYBURN, L336)
- "Lead on, O King Eternal" (LANCASHIRE, B621, E555, L495, M580, P447)
- "Lo, how a rose (e're blooming) is growing" (ES IST EIN' ROS', B78, E81, L58, M216, P48)
- "Love divine, all loves excelling" (BEECHER, B208, M384; HYFRYDOL, E657, L315, P376)
- "Many and great, O God, are thy works" (LACQUIPARLE, B49, E385, M148, P271)
- "My hope is built on nothing less" (SOLID ROCK, B406, L293, M368, P379; MELITA, L294)
- "O day of God, draw nigh" (ST. MICHAEL, B623, E601, M730; BELLWOODS, E600)
- "O for a thousand tongues to sing" (AZMON, B216, E493, L559, M57, P466)
- "O (Our) God, our help in ages past" (ST. ANNE, B74, E680, L320, M117, P210)
- "O Master, let me walk with thee (you)" (MARYTON, B279, E660, L492, M430, P357)
- "O worship the King" (LYONS, B16, M73, P476; HANOVER, E388, L548)
- "O sacred Head, now (sore) wounded" (PASSION CHORALE or HERZLICH TUT MICH VERLANGEN, B137, E168, 169, L116, 117, M286, P98)
- "Of the Father's love begotten" (DIVINUM MYSTERIUM, B251, E82, L42, P309)
- "Our Father (Parent) by whose name" (RHOSYMEDRE, E587, L357, M447)
- "Tell out, my soul, the greatness of the Lord" (WOODLANDS, B81, E438, M200; BIRMINGHAM, E437)
- "The (O) bread of life for all men (sinners) broken" (SHENG EN, E342, M633)

- "Though I may speak" (GIFT OF LOVE or O WALY WALY, B423, M408, P335)
- "Were you there when they crucified my Lord?" (WERE YOU THERE, B156, E172, L92, M288, P102)
- "What wondrous love is this" (WONDROUS LOVE, B143, E439, L385, M292, P85)
- "When I survey the wondrous cross" (HAMBURG, B144, M298, P101; ROCKINGHAM, E474, L482, M299, P100)
- "When in our music God is glorified" (ENGLEBERG, B435, E420, M68, P264; FREDERICKTOWN, L555)

TEACHING UNFAMILIAR HYMNS

Teaching hymns to a congregation requires a certain knowledge of their hymn-singing repertory: which hymns they know and sing well. A list of hymns the congregation knows may be compiled in several ways: (1) utilizing a hymn survey form, (2) surveying old church bulletins, or (3) interviewing persons who have been longtime members of the church. This list should serve as a starting point for planning hymns to be used in worship and for introducing unfamiliar hymns.

How a Hymn Is Learned

The trained musician who takes music reading for granted may forget that most people in a typical congregation cannot read music. Most worshipers learn hymns by rote: hearing their melodies over and over again. Giving the congregation ample opportunities to hear a new hymn sung or played is important in helping create a readiness to learn it. Most people are not automatically ready to learn new hymns. In fact, most individuals in our churches probably prefer to sing hymns they already know and with which they are comfortable.

Arousing Interest

Through church bulletins, newsletters, and posters, as well as the spoken word, the music leader or pastor can help create a readiness to learn new hymns. Arousing interest in learning a hymn may be accomplished in several ways:

> *1. Relate an unfamiliar hymn to a particular theme of worship.* For example, a service of worship emphasizing the Bible

would be an ideal occasion to introduce hymns on the Scriptures, such as "O Word of God (Christ, the Word), incarnate" (MUNICH, E632, L231, M598, P327).

2. Emphasize the central message of the hymn text and how it relates to the beliefs and aspirations of the congregation. For example, the central message of Georgia Harkness' "Hope of the world" (DONNE SECOURS, E472, L493, P360; VICAR, M178) is that Christians place their hope in Christ, who is the hope of all humanity.

3. Stress the scriptural integrity of the hymn. Some hymnals have an index of scriptural bases of hymns.[9] Some hymnals also list related scripture verses above each hymn.[10] A helpful resource is Donald A. Spencer's *Hymn and Scripture Selection Guide*, rev. ed. (Grand Rapids: Baker Book House, 1993). When a congregation is aware, for example, that the servant poem of Philippians 2 is the basis of F. Bland Tucker's "All praise to thee, for thou, O King divine" (SINE NOMINE, B229, M166; ENGELBERG, E477), they will probably have more interest in learning this hymn.

4. Recall an interesting fact concerning the hymn's origin. The story of John Wesley's contacts with German-speaking Moravians on his transatlantic voyage to Georgia will help to arouse interest in his hymn translation from the German of Paul Gerhardt, "Jesus (Jesu), thy boundless love to me" (ST. CATHERINE, B123, M183, P366; RYBURN, L336).

A Positive Experience

Learning a new hymn should be a positive experience, an experience so pleasant that the congregation will want to repeat it. Careful preparation is important for a good hymn-learning experience. The instrumentalists and choirs should be thoroughly familiarized with the hymn to be introduced. The sureness of the choir in singing the hymn helps to erase the uncertainties felt by the congregation and bolsters the congregation's confidence in setting out into new territory.

The suggestions for introducing new hymns given in this chapter can be

[9]See *The Baptist Hymnal*, 1991, 737; *The United Methodist Hymnal*, 1989, 923; and *The Presbyterian Hymnal*, 1990, 687.
[10]See *The Baptist Hymnal*, 1991, and *The Worshiping Church: A Hymnal*, ed. Donald P. Hustad (Carol Stream, IL: Hope Publishing Co., 1990).

adapted to formal or informal gatherings. If handled with care and dignity, learning new hymns can be an integral part of the major weekly worship service when the largest number of people are present.

The Value of Repetition

Since most people learn hymns by rote, they must have opportunity to hear a melody before they can be expected to sing it with a reasonable degree of confidence. The instrumental introduction to a new hymn should include the entire hymn tune and should be played in such a way as to emphasize the melody. Beyond this, another opportunity to hear the tune can be provided by having the choir sing the first stanza in unison; the congregation can then join the choir on the remaining stanzas. The new hymn can also be presented instrumentally and chorally. The organist, pianist, and other instrumentalists may perform a piece based on the hymn tune as a prelude, offertory, or postlude. The choir can sing an anthem, a call to worship, or an introit based on the hymn tune while it is being taught to the congregation.

Once a new hymn has been introduced and sung by the congregation, it needs to be repeated before it is forgotten. It is unrealistic to expect worshipers to sing a new hymn once and then to sing it again with ease six months or a year later. Keeping records is invaluable in determining when a particular hymn has been sung and in planning for its repetition. Through repeated use, a hymn once unknown and unsung can become a vital vehicle for worship.

Hymn Rehearsals and Sings

For most congregations, learning new hymns takes place during regularly scheduled worship services. Because of the limited time available and the desire not to use service time for hymn learning, some leaders prefer to schedule rehearsal time immediately before the beginning of worship or at a separate gathering, such as on a Sunday evening or at a midweek service.

Many of the same methods used in teaching music in choir rehearsals can be used effectively for teaching new hymns to a congregation. Although shorter hymns may be taught by playing and singing them over once, many longer hymn tunes need a line-by-line method. In teaching a hymn like "At the name of Jesus" to the tune KING'S WESTON (E435, L179, M168, P148), one can first call attention to the scriptural basis found in the servant poem of Philippians 2:5-11. The entire hymn melody could be played, perhaps without the harmony. Although all four lines of Ralph Vaughan Williams's tune are different, it might be helpful to point out that the rhythms of the first three lines are practically identical and that their melodic lines begin low and rise. After singing these lines for the people, demonstrate the contrast of the final line in which the rhythm is different and the melody begins high and falls. Because each line of KING'S WESTON is different (including different initial pitches), it is important to learn each one separately. When the individual lines are learned, the entire first stanza can be sung, with the accompanist playing only the melody in unison or octaves. Then the remaining stanzas can be sung, reinforcing the learning of the melody through repetition.[11]

While a hymn rehearsal may be devoted entirely to learning one or more unfamiliar hymns, a hymn sing provides an opportunity to introduce some new hymns sandwiched between old favorites. One church music leader used a quarterly (fifth Sunday) hymn sing to teach new hymns by devoting each hymn sing to a particular topic, such as "Consecration and Dedication Hymns," "Hymns of the Great Revivals," and "A Survey of Hymns in their Historical Progression."[12] During a hymn sing on "The Christian Hope," for example, the relatively new hymn "Hope of the world" (DONNE SECOURS, E472, L493, P360; VICAR, M178) can be sandwiched between two more familiar hymns and related to Scripture as follows:

1. "Let thy steadfast love, O Lord, be upon us, even as we hope in thee" (Ps. 33:22, RSV)

"O God, our help in ages past" (ST. ANNE)

2. "God so loved the world that he gave his only Son, that whoever believes in him should not perish but have eternal life." (John. 3:16, RSV)

"Hope of the world" (DONNE SECOURS, VICAR)

3. "For they drank from the supernatural Rock which followed them, and the Rock was Christ" (1 Cor. 10:4, RSV)

"My hope is built on nothing less" (SOLID ROCK, MELITA)

Hymn-of-the-Month Plan

The most widely used scheme for learning new hymns is the Hymn-of-the-Month Plan. Under this plan a congregation is exposed to a particular

[11]See James R. Sydnor, *Introducing a New Hymnal: How to Improve Congregational Singing* (Chicago: GIA Publications, 1989), for additional teaching plans, "Examples of New Hymn Introduction," 44-61.
[12]See Paul M. Hall, "Hymn Rehearsals and Public Worship," *The Church Musician* 16, 6 (June 1965).

hymn through varied means several times during a month. For example, a hymn could be presented in four successive Sundays: (Sunday 1) use it as an organ prelude,[13] (Sunday 2) use it as a choral selection, (Sunday 3) use it as a congregational hymn with the choir singing the first stanza, (Sunday 4) sing it entirely in normal fashion by the congregation. In addition to its use in formal worship, the hymn-of-the-month can be used in the graded choir program and in the Sunday School. Background and interpretative information on the hymns-of-the-month can be included in the church newsletter or as an insert in the church bulletin.[14]

For some denominations, the hymn-of-the-month can be selected from hymns recommended for that particular season in the Christian calendar. Suitable hymns for all of the services of the Book of Common Prayer are listed in *A Liturgical Index to The Hymnal 1982*,[15] the *Lutheran Book of Worship* provides a list of "Hymns for the Church Year" (929-31) which relates to the three-year common lectionary.

Hymn Study Classes

One of the most effective ways of teaching unfamiliar hymns is through a special class in hymnology. During the several hours of time normally available in such a class, one is able to give more detailed attention to individual hymns and perhaps to study enough hymns to illustrate the entire history of hymnody from the early church to the present century.

A hymn study class also offers time to engage in a careful study of the hymnal, including its organization and various indexes. A class meeting in the weeks before Christmas could concentrate on hymns for Advent and Christmas. Class sessions might be devoted to hymns related to a church's own denominational heritage. Some denominations provide textbooks and other materials suitable for hymn study classes. A hymn study text commissioned by the Hymn Society and by the American Guild of Organists and suitable for ecumenical use is James Rawlings Sydnor's *Hymns: A Congregational Study*.[16]

---

[13]Two general reference works listing organ music based on hymn tunes are Jean Slater Edson, *Organ Preludes*, 2 vols. (Metuchen, NJ: Scarecrow Press, 1970; Supplement, 1974) and Joy E. Lawrence, *The Organist's Shortcut to Service Music* (Cleveland: Ludwig Music Publishing Co., 1986; Supplement I, 1988). Similar information for the current Episcopal hymnal is found in Dennis Schmidt, *An Organist's Guide to Resources for The Hymnal 1982* (New York: The Church Hymnal Corporation, 1987).
[14]See Austin C. Lovelace, *Hymn Notes for Church Bulletins* (Chicago: G.I.A. Publications, 1987).
[15]Compiled by Marion J. Hatchett (New York: Church Hymnal Corporation, 1986) (*Hymnal Studies Five*).
[16]Carol Stream, IL: Agape, 1983.

Hymns in the Home

In the days of Luther and Calvin, the hymnal figured prominently in the homes and daily lives of Christian families. Although this is still the case with some Evangelicals of Latin America and in some other areas, the hymnal unfortunately for most American churchgoers is only a part of the church furniture to be used only when at church. Consequently, "As regards hymnody the congregation is very much where it would be in knowledge of scripture if there were no Bibles except those in the pulpit or the lectern."[17]

How can the families of the church be encouraged to sing hymns in their homes? First of all, family members old enough to read could have their own hymnals. The hymns learned in church could also be a part of family worship. Devotional materials for family worship could suggest appropriate hymns for singing at home. Although some families will be fortunate enough to have a member who can accompany them on the piano, organ, guitar, or autoharp, good hymn singing can be done without accompaniment. Excellent recordings are available to assist families in singing hymns.

Several suggestions for encouraging family hymn singing have been made by James R. Sydnor:[18]

1. The church office can keep a supply of hymnals to be sold to members.

2. A list of suggested uses of hymns in the home can be published in the church bulletin.

3. Children can be provided music appreciation and training (for example, recordings, private music study, and membership in a children's choir) which will result in improved hymn singing.

4. Parents may request piano teachers to include hymn playing in the private music studies of their children.

5. A hymn stanza frequently can be used as a table grace (for example, the Doxology, "For the beauty of the earth," "Now thank we all our God").

6. Parents can use an evening hymn as they tuck their children into bed.

7. Families can enjoy informal hymn singing, either by themselves or with invited friends.

[17]Louis F. Benson, *The Hymnody of the Christian Church*. Reprint of the original 1927 edition (Richmond: John Knox Press, 1956), 275.
[18]*The Hymn and Congregational Singing*, 139. This helpful book is unfortunately out of print.

The congregation whose families sing hymns at home will realize a greater vitality of singing in Sunday worship. Furthermore, family hymn singing will be a unifying force in helping build a stronger family life.

QUESTIONS FOR DISCUSSION/PROJECTS FOR ACTION

1. Why do people retain more theology from the hymns they sing than through the sermons they hear?

2. Name some specific ways in which hymns provide instruction in Christian living and cite specific hymns which do this.

3. What aspects of the church's heritage can be learned through the teaching of hymns and their backgrounds?

4. Which organizations in your church make use of hymns? In what ways can the use of hymns in these organizations be made more effective? Are there additional church organizations which could be making more effective use of hymns? Formulate a plan for an effective use of hymn singing in one of your church's organizations.

5. At what ages should children learn hymns and hymn tunes? Develop a hymn curriculum for children of one age group in your congregation.

6. What resources are available for teaching hymns and hymn tunes to children? Cite some appropriate hymns for (1) younger elementary grade children, (2) older elementary grade children, and (3) youth.

7. How do most people learn hymns? What does this imply for teaching new hymns?

8. What are some ways of arousing interest in learning new hymns?

9. Can hymns be effectively taught without distracting from the dignity of a formal worship service? Why or why not?

10. Why is it important to keep a record of hymns sung?

11. What methods could be used to teach the following hymns?
   - "Of the Father's love begotten" (DIVINUM MYSTERIUM, B251, E82, L42, M184, P309)
   - "What wondrous love is this, O my soul, O my soul" (WONDROUS LOVE, B143, E439, L385, M292, P85)
   - "When in our music God is glorified" (ENGLEBERG, B435, E420, M68, P264; FREDERICKTOWN, L555)

12. Is the Hymn-of-the-Month or some plan being used to teach new hymns systematically to your congregation? Evaluate the effectiveness of hymn learning in your church.

13. In what ways can you encourage hymn singing within families of the church? Formulate a plan for encouraging hymn singing within the families of your

Continued on next page

congregation during Advent, Lent, or another season observed as a time of spiritual emphasis by your congregation.

13
THE HYMN IN MINISTRY

Ministry, however defined, carries the basic meaning of service. The Christian enters into a distinctive ministry—the ministry of Jesus Christ. The nature of Christian ministry has been determined by Christ's "life, death, and resurrection and by the work of his Spirit in the shaping of the apostolic ministry."[1] Thus, there is a biblical basis for ministry that is applicable to every Christian and is not restricted to the vocational ministry. In this sense, Christian ministry may be interpreted as an active, positive response to the gospel of Jesus Christ by serving human needs: food for the hungry, companionship for the lonely, hope for the depressed, and assurance for the anxious, all given in the name of Christ. Ministry, by nature including a "minister" and the one "ministered to," involves responsive concern for the individual in all domains of life.

In one sense, the hymn functions in ministry whenever it is used. Thus, the last three chapters dealing with the hymn in proclamation, worship, and education are dealing with forms of ministry. In this chapter, however, the focus will be on the hymn as it relates to Christian social service.

HYMNS ENCOURAGE MINISTRY

Hymns serve as a stimulus to ministry, exhorting us to minister and urging us beyond ourselves. As expressed in a recent hymn of Milburn Price,

"Believers all, our common task
   Is service in His name
As we, in word and song and deed,
   God's saving grace proclaim.

[1]James D. Smart, *The Rebirth of Ministry* (Philadelphia: The Westminster Press, 1960), 20.

Yet, ministry has broader aims,
  So we pursue the goal
Of meeting persons' fuller needs
  Of body, mind, and soul. " (Stanza 2, B399)[2]

Love of God and serving Christ through serving others are inextricably tied together in Jesus' teachings: " 'Whenever you did this for one of the least important of these brothers of mine, you did it for me!' " (Matt. 25:40, TEV).

Godfrey Thring's prayer for caring concern toward all persons in "O God of mercy, God of light" (L425) is based on the tenet that love of God finds expression in one's relationship to other persons:

"Teach us the lesson Jesus taught:
  To feel for those his blood has bought,
That ev'ry deed and word and thought
  May work a work for you."

"For all are kindred, far and wide,
  Since Jesus Christ for all has died;
Grant us the will, and grace provide
  To love them all in you."

"In sickness, sorrow, want or care,
  Each other's burdens help us share;
May we, where help is needed, there
  Give help as though to you." (Stanzas 3-5)

Fred Pratt Green's "When the church of Jesus" (B396, M592) acknowledges the tendency to allow the loftiness of worship to prevent the church from seeing the need for ministry to others:

"When the church of Jesus
  Shuts its outer door,
Lest the roar of traffic
  Drown the voice of prayer:
May our prayers, Lord, make us
  Ten times more aware

That the world we banish
Is our Christian care."

"If our hearts are lifted
Where devotion soars
High above this hungry
Suff'ring world of ours:
Lest our hymns should drug us
To forget its needs,
Forge our Christian worship
Into Christian deeds."

"Lest the gifts we offer,
Money, talents, time,
Serve to salve our conscience
To our secret shame:
Lord, reprove, inspire us
By the way You give;
Teach us, dying Savior,
How true Christians live."[3]

HYMNS EXPRESS SPECIFIC MINISTRY

Hymns explore and define areas of ministry. They plant seeds which may germinate in active ministry. Hymns sometimes spring from the writer's response to a need and the ensuing recognition that the task requires more than one person's labors.

"Rescue the perishing" (B559, M591) grew out of Fanny Crosby's involvement with the homeless in New York City. The immediacy of their needs is communicated by ungarnished imperatives: "Rescue the perishing," "Care for the dying," and "Lift up the fallen." The urgency of human need requires ministry that is compassionate and timely.

Specific needs pointed out in hymns are those of the sick, the handicapped (blind, deaf, and lame), the homeless, the lonely, the adolescent, and the aged. Frequently a number of these human conditions are grouped together. Albert F. Bayly's "Lord, whose love in (through) humble service" (E610, L423, M581, P427) holds up Christ's example of ministry and enumerates the opportunities for active response—response that is an outgrowth of worship:

"Lord, whose love in humble service
　　Bore the weight of human need,
Who upon the cross, forsaken,
　　Worked your mercy's perfect deed:
We, your servants, bring the worship
　　Not of voice alone, but heart;
Consecrating to your purpose
　　Ev'ry gift which you impart."

"Still your children wander homeless;
　　Still the hungry cry for bread;
Still the captives long for freedom;
　　Still in grief we mourn our dead.
As you, Lord, in deep compassion
　　Healed the sick and freed the soul,
By your Spirit send your power
　　To our world to make it whole."

"As we worship, grant us vision,
　　Till your love's revealing light
In its height and depth and greatness
　　Dawns upon our quickened sight,
Making known the needs and burdens
　　Your compassion bids us bear,
Stirring us to ardent service,
　　Your abundant life to share."[4]

Fred Pratt Green focuses on the poor in the second stanza of "The church of Christ, in every age" (B402, L433, M589, P421):

"Across the world, across the street,
　　The victims of injustice cry
For shelter and for bread to eat,
　　And never live before (until) they die."[5]

---

[4]Copyright © Oxford University Press. Used by permission.*
[5]Copyright © 1971 by Hope Publishing Co., Carol Stream, IL 60188. All rights reserved. Used by permission.*

Hymns are sometimes very specific in enumerating the ills of humankind. Edward H. Plumptre's "Thine arm (Your hand), O Lord, in days of old" (E567, L431) cites some of the human conditions to which Jesus ministered and prays for those presently in need of healing, and as well as for those engaged in the ministry of healing:

"Your hand, O Lord, in days of old
    Was strong to heal and save;
It triumphed o'er disease and death,
    O'er darkness and the grave.
To you they came, the blind, the dumb,
    The palsied and the lame,
The lepers in their misery,
    The sick with fevered frame."

"And lo, your touch brought life and health,
    Gave speech and strength and sight;
And youth renewed and frenzy calmed
    Revealed you, Lord of light.
And now, O Lord, be near to bless,
    Almighty as before,
In crowded street, by beds of pain,
    As by Gennes'ret's shore."

"Oh, be our great deliv'rer still,
    The Lord of life and death;
Restore and quicken, soothe and bless,
    With your life-giving breath.
To hands that work and eyes that see
    Give wisdom's healing pow'r,
That whole and sick and weak and strong
    May praise you evermore."

A recent hymn of Dorothy Diemer Hendry, set in *The Presbyterian Hymnal*, 1990, (348) to Emma Lou Diemer's tune HUNTSVILLE, asks us to open our ears and eyes to the cries of those in need of ministry, concluding each stanza with a response of Christian commitment.

"Christian women, Christian men,
    Have we ears to hear
The crying of a homeless child
    Hungry and in fear?
In the name of Jesus, yes,
    We have ears to hear!
In the name of Jesus, yes,
    We hear! We hear!"

"Down a grimy city street
    Have we eyes to see
The faces of the aged and ill
    Lost in poverty?
In the name of Jesus, yes,
    We have eyes to see!
In the name of Jesus, yes,
    We see! We see!"

"When Satanic gloom assails,
    Have we strength to hold
The fortress of our living faith
    Till God's day dawns gold?
In the name of Jesus, yes,
    We have strength to hold!
In the name of Jesus, yes,
    We hold! We hold!"

"Christian women, Christian men,
    Have we hearts to love
Our neighbors as we love ourselves,
    Serving God above?
In the name of Jesus, yes,
    We have hearts to love!
In the name of Jesus, yes,
    We love! We love!"[6]

Other hymns encourage ministry or point out places of ministry. The compassion of Christ who wept over the city of Jerusalem is the basis for the prayer Frank Mason North voices in "Where cross the crowded ways of life" (E609, L429, M427, P408). The second stanza describes the plight of a city in need of ministry:

> "In haunts of wretchedness and need,
>   On shadow'd thresholds dark with fears,
> From paths where hide the lures of greed,
>   We catch the vision of thy tears." (Stanza 2)

A number of places in the city where opportunities for Christian ministry may be found are given in Thomas C. Clark's "Where restless crowds are thronging" (L430): "along the city ways," "homes where kindness falters," "in busy streets of barter," and "in lonely thoroughfare." In addition to the city, Edward M. Blumenfeld's "The Son of God, our Christ" (L434) mentions "in town" and "on the soil." Other hymns of recent decades mention the inner city, the suburbs, the ghetto, the prison, the slum, the mine, the field, and the marketplace.

HYMNS SPEAK TO PERSONS IN NEED

Hymns not only proclaim the necessity of ministry in the lives of Christians and illustrate specific needs in specific places, but hymns also minister by communicating to people in need. Just as Scripture verses speak to particular human circumstances, hymns can communicate to varied life situations. This is reflected in some of the categories used in topical indexes of hymnals: Assurance, Calmness, Consolation, Courage, Faith, Hope, Humility, Joy, and so forth. Stories abound in which hymns have played significant roles in the lives of people, and have been a source of strength in times of need.

During the dark days after America entered World War I, President Woodrow Wilson found strength in the singing of a hymn. His biographer has described how Wilson, while cruising on the Potomac on a Sunday afternoon in June of 1917 with a Princeton classmate, suggested that they sing a favorite hymn of their undergraduate days:

> "When peace, like a river, attendeth my way,
>   When sorrows like sea billows roll;

Whatever my lot, thou hast taught me to say,
It is well, it is well with my soul." (Stanza 1, B410, L346, M377)[7]

Not only in time of war but also when facing death, hymns have provided a note of joy and victory in anticipation of eternal life. At the age of 88 and near death, John Wesley, the founder of Methodism, sang from his deathbed Watts's "I'll praise my Maker while I've breath" (B35, E429, M60, P253) to those in his sickroom. In the following stanza of "What wondrous love is this" (B143, E439, L385, M292, P85), the anonymous hymn writer vows to sing on, even after death:

"And when from death I'm free, I'll sing on, I'll sing on;
And when from death I'm free, I'll sing on.
And when from death I'm free I'll sing and joyful be;
And through eternity I'll sing on, I'll sing on;
And through eternity I'll sing on." (Stanza 4)

The positive declarations found in the following stanza of Lyte's "Abide with me" (B63—this stanza omitted, E662, L272, M700, P543) contribute to the frequent use of this hymn in times of death:

"I fear no foe, with thee at hand to bless;
Ills have no weight, and tears no bitterness.
Where is death's sting? Where, grave, thy victory?
I triumph still, if thou abide with me." (Stanza 3)

Hymns can provide messages of comfort to the bereaved. Note the words addressed to the grieving, offering assurance of God's loving presence in the third stanza of Johann J. Schütz's "Sei Lob und Ehr' dem Höchsten Gut" ("Sing praise to God who reigns above," B20, E408—this stanza omitted, M126, P483; L542—a different translation):

"The Lord is never far away,
But, through all grief distressing,
An ever present help and stay,
Our peace and joy and blessing;
As with a mother's tender hand

---

[7]Arthur Walworth, *Woodrow Wilson* 2nd ed., rev. vol 2 (Boston: Houghton Mifflin Co., 1965), 123.

He leads His own, His chosen band:
To God all praise and glory!" (Stanza 3)

A hymn which offers consolation in all four of its stanzas is Charles Wesley's "Thou hidden source of calm repose" (M153). Note the emphasis on the all-sufficiency of God in Wesley's first stanza:

"Thou hidden source of calm repose,
Thou all-sufficient love divine,
My help and refuge from my foes,
Secure I am if thou art mine;
And lo! from sin and grief and shame
I hide me, Jesus, in thy name."

Jesus was poor in terms of material possessions and spent His ministry largely among the poor—the supreme example that worth is not to be measured in terms of wealth. It is no surprise, then, that Christian hymns contain messages of encouragement and hope to those who live in poverty. God's providence is underscored in Civilla D. Martin's gospel hymn "God will take care of you" (B64, M130):

"Be not dismayed whate'er betide,
God will take care of you;
Beneath his wings of love abide,
God will take care of you." (Stanza 1)

Refrain:
"God will take care of you,
Through ev'ry day, o'er all the way;
He will take care of you,
God will take care of you."

John Newton's "Amazing grace" (B330, E671, L448, M378, P280, stanzas 1, 3, 4) has stepped outside the limits of the church service to minister to people of many stations, ages, races, and lands. This hymn of personal experience speaks of hope and security.

"Amazing grace! how sweet the sound,
   That saved a wretch like me!
I once was lost, but now am found,
   Was blind but now I see."

"Through many dangers, toils, and snares,
   I have already come;
'Tis grace hath brought me safe thus far,
   And grace will lead me home."
"The Lord has promised good to me,
   His word my hope secures;
He will my shield and portion be
   As long as life endures."

Hymns can minister to children, youth, and adults. Their importance in the Christian nurture of children and youth and in family life has been emphasized in Chapter 12.[8] Parents, especially during the years of rearing a family, will find encouragement in certain hymn texts. Most hymnals have a group of hymns dealing with the family, as well as others which speak to parenting. One of the finest hymns on the family is F. Bland Tucker's "Our Father (Parent), by whose name" (E587, L357, M447), a prayer to Father, Son, and Holy Spirit:

"Our Father, by whose name
   All parenthood is known:
In love divine you claim
   Each fam'ly as your own.
Bless mothers, fathers, guarding well,
   With constant love as sentinel,
The homes in which your people dwell."

"O Christ, yourself a child
   Within an earthly home,
With heart still undefiled
   To full adulthood come:
Our children bless in ev'ry place
   That they may all behold your face
And knowing you may grow in grace."

[8]See Chapter 12, the list of "100 Hymns for Children and Youth," 281-87, and "Hymns in the Home," 292-93.

"O Holy Spirit, bind
    Our hearts in unity
And teach us how to find
    The love from self set free;
In all our hearts such love increase
    That ev'ry home, by this release,
May be the dwelling-place of peace."[9]

The elderly increasingly are a significant percentage of the American population. Many senior citizens face conditions previously mentioned: poverty, sickness, and loneliness. Hymns related to these circumstances can provide a needed ministry for them. In 1976 a group of 10 hymns celebrating the later years of life and the meaning of aging was published. It included "O Lord our God, whom all through life we praise"[10] by Frances Winters (1908-93), then a retired college teacher in Hattiesburg, Mississippi. The third stanza of her hymn refers to the problems of fear, doubt, bereavement, and illness commonly faced by senior adults. These problems, however, are overshadowed by praise (stanza 1), thankfulness (stanza 2), and hope (stanza 4):

"O Lord our God, whom all through life we praise,
    As year by year days add to numbered days,
With each we prove the wonder of Thy ways,
    While still adoring, each new song we raise."

"With thankful hearts Thy goodness we confess,
    Our Guide and Help in gladness and distress.
For life, light, love, Thy holy name we bless;
    Accept the gratitude our hearts express."

"O God, be near in loneliness and need;
    From fear and doubting may our minds be freed.
When losses come, Thy consolation speed;
    For strength and healing love, O Lord, we plead."

"Our hope is founded in Thy saving grace.
    New hope abides to share love every place;

[9]Copyright © 1940 The Church Hymnal Corporation. Used by permission.*
[10]10 New Hymns on Aging and the Later Years (Springfield, OH: The Hymn Society of America; Washington, D.C.: National Retired Teachers Association and American Association of Retired Persons, 1976), 12.

And hope to serve yet spurs our slowing pace,
Till, hope fulfilled, we see Thee face to face."[11]

SOME FORMS OF MINISTRY INVOLVING HYMNS

In addition to regular worship services, the Sunday School, and other church programs which minister to the congregation in general, there are other forms of ministry in which hymns can be effective. The activities mentioned in this section are illustrative of the numerous types of ministry[12] in which a creative leader can find fruitful ways to utilize hymns.

In Special Worship Services

In addition to the usual worship services, many churches conduct worship in hospitals, nursing homes, prisons, and in missions for the homeless. In some instances, worship in these places is conducted by a chaplain. The collection *Hymns of Hope and Healing (A Chapel Hymnal)*, compiled and edited by Barbara E. Goward, R.M.T., is an interdenominational Protestant hymnal for use in hospitals. Because of its unusual ministry, this hymnal has an introductory word which explains why certain hymns were omitted:

> "Today, religious thinkers realize that the old threatening aspects of religion can often be destructive to the spirit. We have omitted the emphasis on man's unworthiness, God's fearful vengeance, and happiness to be found only in heaven. There is, however, allowance for the confession of error, necessarily followed by the assurance of Divine forgiveness and understanding.
>
> "Generally speaking, we here offer a service hymnal in which every selection will be in accord with the efforts of the minister and the hospital staff toward constructive support of the spirit and a positive approach to rehabilitation."[13]

Joe Pinson, a music therapist in Texas, has written hymns specifically to fit a particular group of persons. He has written hymns for a choir of persons with developmental difficulties in a language and musical style suited to their capabilities. These hymns are used in the chapel services at the facility where these persons reside.

[11]Copyright © 1976 The Hymn Society in the United States and Canada. Used by permission.*
[12]Many forms of recent Christian ministry are discussed in William M. Pinson, Jr., *The Local Church in Ministry* (Nashville: Broadman Press, 1973).
[13]Cincinnati: The Willis Music Company, 1960, iv.

From 1975 through 1991, Pinson edited *New Songs for God's People*, a quarterly offering new music for institutional use. The following is a text from one of the hymns Pinson has written for special people:

Refrain:
"Blessed be the name of the Lord.
   Blessed be the name of the Lord.
Blessed be the name; blessed be the name.
   Blessed be the name of the Lord."

1. "Jesus is all we need, all we ever need.
   Jesus is all we need, all we ever need."
(Repeat *Refrain*)

2. "Jesus is Lord of all, Lord of everything.
   Jesus is Lord of all, Lord of everything."
(Repeat *Refrain*)

3. "Jesus will come again, come to take us home.
   Jesus will come again, come to take us home."[14]
(Repeat *Refrain*)

Some of the best examples of the hymns and songs of Joe Pinson can be found in his collection, *Make a Joyful Noise*.[15] These have been effective in special ministry because they contain simple, straightforward concepts of faith and because there is much repetition of text and melodic ideas.

Other settings for worship conducted away from the church for particular groups include those in resort areas, summer camps, retreats, and some designed for migrant workers. In certain areas churches sponsor worship and Sunday School for nonnative English-speakers in their native language. In each case, hymns appropriate to the group can provide a significant ministry.

In Forms for the Deaf and Blind

Those who are handicapped in hearing or seeing can experience hymns through special means of communication. The deaf can visually hear the texts of hymns through sign language rendered simultaneously during con-

[14]Copyright © 1988 by Joe Pinson. Used by permission.*
[15]Pacific, MO: Cathedral Music Press, 1988.

gregational singing. Two hymnals with adaptation in language for signing are *Sing Praises*,[16] and *Sing unto the Lord—A Hymnal for the Deaf*.[17]

For those who are visually handicapped but can read large print, large-print editions of some hymnals are available, such as *The Baptist Hymnal, 1991*. For the blind, many hymnals have been published in Braille,[18] including the *Lutheran Book of Worship* and *The Hymnal 1982*.[19] Hymns are also widely available on recordings which can be used by the blind, including long-playing phonodiscs, compact discs, and cassette tapes. The convenience of cassette tapes has opened up other possibilities for ministry involving the use of hymns.

On Cassette Tape

For members of a congregation who are homebound, church services, including hymns, can be provided on cassette tapes. This same ministry can be provided for a congregation's military personnel and college students away from home. Cassette tapes of hymns can also be useful for ministry to a nursing home or prison when an accompanist and/or musical instrument is unavailable. Sometimes a group of hymns on cassette tape can be tailor-made to fit a particular person or set of circumstances.

Homebound individuals, for example, can be provided a cassette tape of some of their favorite hymns. A bereaved person can find help in a group of hymns of faith, hope, and consolation. Cassette tapes of hymns and other worship materials can be used to assist families in worship in the home.

Hymns for Devotional Use

Just as the individual reading of Scripture is an important source for personal worship, hymns can be read for their devotional value. Hymns can be read more easily when they are printed as poetry. The Hymn Society in the United States and Canada has prepared for individual worship such a resource as, *Amazing Grace: Hymn Texts for Devotional Use*.[20]

[16]Nashville: Broadman Press, 1976.
[17]By E. Theo Delaney and Clark Bailey. St. Louis: Commission on Worship and Board for Missions, The Lutheran Church, Missouri Synod, 1969.
[18]J. Vincent Higginson, "Hymns for the Blind," *The Hymn* 3, 4 (October 1952): 116-18.
[19]These are among the hymnals in Braille or large print available on a two-month loan from the Music Section, National Library Service for the Blind and Physically Handicapped, The Library of Congress, Washington, D.C. 20542. (A list of hymnals available for loan may be requested from this address.)
[20]Edited by Bert Polman, Marilyn Kay Stulken and James R. Sydnor (Philadelphia: The Westminster Press, 1994).

Hymn Singing Events

In addition to the congregational hymn sing[21] and the third type of hymn service,[22] hymns can function in informal ways in other contexts. One event which can involve music and hymn singing is an arts festival, an event in which artists from within and without a church are invited to show their work. Such a festival may include paintings, sculpture, crafts, drama, and other creative arts. Hymns written by members of the church or community can be sung.

Many churches now have clubs for senior adults which sponsor various activities involving fellowship, service, and recreation. Hymn singing, especially of selections which are well known, can be meaningful to senior citizens' organizations.

Christmas Carol Sings

In the weeks before Christmas, hymns on the birth of Christ are heard on radio, television, and in shopping centers. Although the public may be saturated with Christmas music through the media, churches have an opportunity to provide a ministry by means of live music at this season. In New Orleans in the mid-1970s, for example, the local federation of churches established a ministry in which numerous church and school choirs and instrumentalists sang carols during the noon hour in lobbies of downtown office buildings for several days during the week before Christmas. In many suburban shopping malls, live Christmas music is welcomed. Even though the motivation of the management may be primarily commercial, the opportunity to minister through songs of the season is nonetheless available. The custom of informal caroling by church groups, especially of children and youth, is widespread. Caroling often provides a ministry to the homebound. It can be done informally by neighbors who attend different churches and provides a bond of fellowship in sharing the good news of Christmas.

In this chapter and in the three preceding ones, the hymn has been treated in relation to the church's ministry in terms of social service and in the related tasks of proclamation, worship, and education. The potential of hymnody in the mission of the church needs to be more widely recognized. Intelligence, imagination, sensitivity, and skill in the use of hymns in the church contribute to the fulfillment of its mission. The resolve of

[21]See Chapter 12, "The Hymn in Education," pages 290-91.
[22]See Chapter 11, "The Hymn in Worship," page 275.

the apostle Paul remains an appropriate resolution for today's hymn singers: "I will sing with the spirit, and I will sing with the understanding also" (1 Cor. 14:15).

QUESTIONS FOR DISCUSSION/PROJECTS FOR ACTION

1. List some hymns which encourage ministry in general. How well are these hymns known to your congregation?

2. Cite hymns which encourage Christians to minister to the following categories of persons in need: the poor, the sick and handicapped, the lonely, the sorrowful.

3. What hymns do deeply troubled persons request most frequently? Plan a survey and rank the top five. Why do you think they choose those hymns? What reasons do the patients give

4. Plan a worship service using hymns based on ministry to deeply troubled people. Call a psychiatric hospital volunteer service or chaplain department for possibilities about leading such a service.

5. In what ways are hymns made available to the handicapped of sight and hearing?

6. List hymns which might speak to you in times of depression. What difficulties would a therapist encounter in selecting hymns for healing?

7. As a class project, list all the hymns pertaining to ministry within your denominational hymnal. Are there any generalizations which can be drawn concerning their origins? How adequate is this hymnal in terms of hymns on the subject of Christian ministry? What hymns pertaining to ministry would you like to see added?

8. Plan a worship service using hymns based on ministry.

9. Prepare a two-minute informal talk on hymns that have ministered to you or someone you know.

10. Make a cassette or tape of hymns for a person experiencing grief in the death of a family member.

11. Plan a Thanksgiving hymn celebration for use in a shopping mall.

PART IV:
EPILOGUE

14
TRENDS AND ISSUES
IN HYMNODY

Explosive changes have characterized the making and singing of hymns in the closing decades of the 20th century. Recent trends have not only been ecumenical, but worldwide in their influence.

RENEWAL IN WORSHIP

The latter years of the 20th century have seen a renewal in worship for Christians of many different traditions. A large number of new books, guides, and resources on the subject of worship have been published. Many denominations have adopted a three-year common lectionary cycle of Scripture readings related to the seasons of the church year and have issued new editions of their worship books, including new hymnals. In one three-year period, 1989-1991, three major American denominational hymnals were issued: *The United Methodist Hymnal* (1989), *The Presbyterian Hymnal* (Presbyterian Church. U.S.A., 1990), and *The Baptist Hymnal* (Southern Baptist, 1991). Many other new hymnals in the United States, Great Britian, and Canada were issued in the 1980s and 1990s.[1]

Roman Catholics

For Roman Catholics, the decisive event for the renewal of worship was the Second Vatican Council, 1962-65. Two major changes in Catholic worship resulting from this Council were the move from the liturgy in Latin to the vernacular languages of the people, and the strong emphasis on active participation in worship, including congregational singing.[2] For

[1]In 1995, three USA denominations issued new hymnals: *Chalice Hymnal* (St. Louis: Chalice Press) [The Christian Church/Disciples of Christ], *Moravian Book of Worship* (Bethlehem, PA and Winston-Salem, NC: Moravian Church in America), and *The New Century Hymnal* (Cleveland: The Pilgrim Press) [United Church of Christ].
[2]For information on the Council's teachings concerning worship, see the "Constitution on the Sacred Liturgy" in *The Documents of Vatican II*, eds. Walter M. Abbott and Joseph Gallagher (New York: The America Press, 1966), 138-178.

Catholics, the years since Vatican II have been a time of experimentation with congregational song in English—ranging from Gregorian chant to hymns of Protestant origin, as well as new hymns by Catholics and spanning styles from formal hymnody to folklike songs designed to be sung to guitar accompaniment. Perhaps the most comprehensive American Catholic hymnal is *Worship*.[3] A collection of the more folklike songs popular among many Catholics culled from several informal paperback songbooks is *Gather*.[4] These two volumes are complementary, each representing a different musical outlook.[5]

Charismatic Renewal

Many denominations, both Protestant and Catholic, have been affected by charismatic renewal. From the standpoint of congregational song, the charismatic focus has been upon miniature hymns characterized by brevity and simplicity; these hymns evoke both emotional and physical responses from singers. Singing is often accompanied by physical gestures, particularly uplifted or extended hands. This style of congregational singing favors Scripture songs and choruses and has come to be known as "Praise and Worship." "Praise and Worship" music originated in New Zealand in 1968 with brief scripture settings by David and Gale Garratt.[6] Among the more ecumenically accepted hymns arising from this charismatic-inspired style is Karen Lafferty's 1972 Scripture setting of Matthew 6:33, "Seek ye first" (B478, E711, M405, P333).

Quite prominent in British youth music circles during the final decade of the 20th century has been the work of Graham Kendrick (b. 1950). Born the son of a Baptist minister, Kendrick has produced lyrics and music for outdoor "Marches for Jesus" which have captured the enthusiastic attention of youth and those in the charismatic movement throughout the evangelical and Anglican world. His music is upbeat and appealing, and his texts are theologically more substantive than those of many of his contemporaries in the charismatic renewal movement.

Particularly notable from his scores of songs are "Meekness and Majesty," "The Servant King," and "Led, like a Lamb" ("You're Alive") which are to be

[3]3rd edition. (Chicago: G.I.A. Publications, Inc., 1986).
[4](Chicago: G.I.A. Publications; Phoenix: North American Liturgy Resources, 1988). North American Liturgy Resources is the publisher of another widely used folk-oriented Catholic hymnal, *Glory and Praise* (1984).
[5]George Black, "Gather & Worship: One Concept in Two Books and Many Editions," *The Hymn* 42, 2 (April 1991): 12-15.
[6]Donald P. Hustad, *Jubilate II: Church Music in Worship and Renewal*, rev. ed. of *Jubilate: Church Music in the Evangelical Tradition* (Carol Stream, IL: Hope Publishing Company, 1993), 463.

found, among others, in recently published standard hymnals in England such as *Baptist Praise and Worship,* 1991, and *Rejoice and Sing* (United Reform Church), 1991. The only song to find its way as yet into American collections is "Lord, the light of your love" ("Shine, Jesus, Shine") (B579).[7]

"Praise and Worship" indicates more than a music-text style. As observed by Hustad, "it includes the concept of a protracted period of singing led by a 'worship team'—a group of microphone-holding singers, accompanied by piano (or, more recently, synthesizer), guitars, theater drums, and other instruments as available."[8] Use of Scripture choruses varies greatly among the churches. Some sing them with the objective of increasing the emotional fervor of worship to a point of ecstasy, often climaxed by shouted hallelujahs or speaking in tongues. Others take a more restrained approach, singing choruses no more than twice, with perhaps no more excitement than when singing standard hymns or gospel songs. Often churches which have embraced "Praise and Worship" music make little or no use of hymnals or traditional hymnic forms, thus neglecting the treasury of many centuries of Christian hymnody.

The congregational song repertory of charismatic renewal music is not yet standardized. The 20 popular examples of praise songs used in "Praise and Worship" music listed in 1987 by Wohlgemuth[9] include "Seek ye first" plus five found in both *The United Methodist Hymnal,* 1989, and *The Baptist Hymnal,* 1991: Jerry Sinclair's "Alleluia" (B223, M186), Marvin V. Frey's "He is Lord" (B178, M177), Jack Hayford's "Majesty, worship his majesty" (B215, M176), Les Garrett's "This is the day, this is the day that the Lord hath made" (B359, M657), and Andraé Crouch's "To God be the glory" (B153, M99).[10]

Language Issues

Changes in the language of worship have continued to impact congregational song in the last decades of the century. With the widespread acceptance of new translations of the Bible in modern English, old English pronouns such as "thee" and "thou" are used less in worship. Although most

[7]This popular song with its prevailing image of light and emphasis on the transcendence of God has been sung during youth conferences of the Baptist World Alliance and in Billy Graham crusades. Among other American hymnals it may be found in Hope Publishing Company's *The Worshipping Church* (721).
[8]Hustad, *Jubilate II,* 463.
[9]Paul W. Wohlgemuth, "Praise Singing," *The Hymn* 38, 1 (January 1987): 23. Several other articles in this issue deal with music of charismatic worship.
[10]A thoughtful presentation concerning praise choruses and related popular hymnic idioms is given by Milburn Price, "The Impact of Popular Culture on Congregational Song," *The Hymn* 44, 1 (January 1993): 11-17.

hymnal committees have not sought to replace archaic language in classic hymnody, one major British hymnal—*Hymns for Today's Church*—has modernized the language of all its hymns, believing that "to leave them unrevised... is to create a verbal and cultural gulf which cannot be to the long term advantage of Christians at worship."[11]

Concern for inclusive language has resulted in the revision of many hymn texts whose references to persons were exclusively masculine. Hymnal committees have especially favored "invisible mending": altering hymn texts in such a way that the alterations are largely unnoticed.[12] Hymnal committees and organizations sponsoring hymn-writing competitions have generally insisted that new hymns be written in inclusive language.

While they have revised language referring to persons to be less gender specific in many hymns, hymnal committees have been more divided concerning changes in God language. A leading proponent of changing God language to avoid male-dominated terminology is the hymnist Brian Wren, whose book, *What Language Shall I Borrow? God-Talk in Worship*[13] is an important contribution to continuing discussion of this issue. While acknowledging that God has no gender, the elimination of male and female images for God has been rejected by many as making God impersonal. A new approach has been taken by a number of hymn writers who have pointed out that the Bible contains feminine as well as masculine images for God, as in Isaiah 66:13, where God is referred to as a mother comforting her children. These hymnists seek to provide both masculine and feminine images for God, as in Brian Wren's "God of many names" (M105), C. Eric Lincoln's "How like a gentle spirit deep within" (M115), and Thomas H. Troeger's "Source and Sovereign, Rock and Cloud" (M113).

Yet another area of concern impacting hymnic language is the use of military imagery. A number of theologians have held that the militant language found in many hymns—even though derived from New Testament passages which speak of Christian warfare against the forces of evil (such as

---

[11]*Hymns for Today's Church* (London: Hodder and Stoughton, 1982), 8-9.

[12]A representative example of invisible mending to provide inclusive language is in the third stanza of John Oxenham's "In Christ there is no East or West." Compare the original third stanza with that in *The Baptist Hymnal*, 1991, (B385). **Original:** "Join hands, then, brothers of the faith, Whate'er your race may be: Who serves my Father as a son Is surely kin to me." ***TBH*, 1991:** "Join hands, then, children of the faith, Whate'er your race may be; Who serves my Father as a child Is surely kin to me." (*Words used by permission of Desmond Dunkerley.**) Michael Perry has taken Oxenham's opening line, "In Christ there is no East or West," and written a new hymn on Christian unity. See *The Worshipping Church: A Hymnal* (Carol Stream, IL: Hope Publishing Co., 1990), 695.

[13]*What Language Shall I Borrow? God-Talk in Worship: A Male Response to Feminist Theology* (New York: Crossroad Publishing Company, 1989).

Ephesians 6)—is not appropriate to describe Christians who have been called to be peacemakers. Hymns which have been criticized include "Onward, Christian soldiers," which was at first dropped from those selected for the 1989 hymnal of United Methodists; it was restored following widespread protests from Methodist congregations.[14]

Concern for the handicapped and people of color has made itself felt in recent hymns. For example, stanza 6 of Charles Wesley's "O for a thousand tongues to sing" in *The United Methodist Hymnal* (57) reads:

> "Hear him, ye deaf; his praise, ye dumb,
>   your loosened tongues employ;
> Ye blind, behold your Savior come,
>   and leap, ye lame, for joy."

An asterisk before this stanza refers to a note below, "May be omitted"; in the hymnal companion it reads, "In deference to perceived discriminatory language congregations may omit stanza 6."[15] Although James Nicholson and William G. Fisher's gospel hymn, "Lord Jesus, I long to be perfectly whole," was formerly sung by African-American congregations, its refrain is now seen in the context of race and color, making this hymn no longer acceptable for their use:

> "Whiter than snow, yes whiter than snow,
>   Now wash me and I shall be whiter than snow."[16]

TRENDS TOWARD THE TRADITIONAL AND TOWARD CULTURAL INCLUSIVENESS

The late 20th century has not only been a time for the spread of new hymnody; it has been a time of recovery of older traditions and the incorporation of materials from non-European cultures into American hymnals. In general, American hymnals since the 1980s have reflected an increasing cultural diversity. This is especially apparent in *The United Methodist Hymnal* of 1989.

---

[14]"Onward, Christian soldiers" has been omitted from the 1990 *Presbyterian Hymnal*. For articles espousing opposing viewpoints of military imagery in hymns, see Anastasia Van Burkalow, "A Call for Battle Symbolism in Hymns," *The Hymn* 38, 2 (April 1987): 14-17, and Brian Wren, "Onward, Christian Rambos? The Case Against Battle Symbolism in Hymns," *The Hymn* 38, 3 (July 1987): 13-15.
[15]Carlton R. Young, *Companion to the United Methodist Hymnal*, 511.
[16]This hymn is included in the African-American *Baptist Standard Hymnal with Responsive Readings*, ed. Mrs. A. M. Townsend (Nashville: Sunday School Publishing Board, National Baptist Convention, U.S.A., 1924) but is omitted from *The New National Baptist Hymnal* (Nashville: National Baptist Publishing Board, 1977).

A revival of psalm singing, including metrical psalmody, has characterized many hymnals issued in recent decades. In addition to denominations which use the entire psalter, such as The Christian Reformed Church in its *Psalter Hymnal* (1987), others provide a partial psalter within their hymnals. For example, *The Presbyterian Hymnal* (1990) includes a psalter with either full or partial versions of over 80 of the 150 Psalms, most of them in meter, but some to be sung to psalm tones. Several of the psalms in this hymnal have multiple metrical versions. For example, Psalm 23 has five metrical versions in addition to Joseph Gelineau's psalm-tone setting. *The United Methodist Hymnal* (1989) includes a liturgical psalter with 100 psalms (M738-862) based on the *New Revised Standard Version*. They may be either chanted to psalm tones or read with sung responses. Thus while some denominations have not chosen to provide a complete metrical psalter, they have nevertheless given congregations a rich repertory of metrical and prose psalmody for use in worship.[17] The increase of psalmody may be seen as part of a general trend toward the inclusion of more biblical hymns in recent hymnals.

Another tradition which has seen a continuing revival as new hymnals have appeared is American folk hymnody. Recent American hymnals, such as the *Lutheran Book of Worship* (1978) and *The Hymnal 1982* of the Episcopal Church, show a marked increase of early American folk hymns compared to previous hymnals. Several of these folk hymns, such as "Amazing Grace! How Sweet the Sound" (B330, E671, L448, M378, P280) and "What wondrous love is this" (B143, E439, L385, M292, P85), have gained almost universal acceptance. The observance of the American bicentennial in the 1970s stimulated a renewed interest in the nation's musical heritage, including its folk hymnody. A number of sturdy tunes (for example, BEACH SPRING and HOLY MANNA) for American folk hymns have found a new life as settings for 20th-century hymn texts.

Practically every American hymnal of recent decades has included a larger number of African-American hymns. In addition, several African-American hymnal supplements have been issued. These include the Episcopalian *Lift Every Voice and Sing: A Collection of Afro-American Spirituals and Other Songs* (1981)[18] and the United Methodist *Songs of Zion*

---

[17]Further information is given in C. Michael Hawn's "Current Trends in Hymnody: Psalm Singing," *The Hymn* 43, 2 (April 1992): 31-42.
[18](New York: The Church Hymnal Corporation). This collection includes an essay by Irene V. Jackson, "Music Among Blacks in the Episcopal Church: Some Preliminary Considerations," xvii-xxviii.

(1981).[19] A full sized African-American Roman Catholic hymnal is *Lead Me, Guide Me* (1987).[20] Several African-American spirituals such as "Go, tell it on the mountain" (B95, E99, L70, M251, P29), "Let us break bread together on our knees" (B366, E325, L212, M618, P513), and "Were you there when they crucified my Lord" (B156, E172, L92, M288, P102) have been broadly accepted.[21]

Spanish-language hymnody has until recently found little or no place in English-language hymnals published in the United States. In the *United Methodist Hymnal*, however, 18 selections in both Spanish and English were included in the interest of broadening the repertory. One hymn of 1987 from Spain appearing in both *The United Methodist Hymnal* and *The Presbyterian Hymnal* is Cesareo Gabaraín's text and tune depicting the call of Jesus for disciples, "*Tú has venido a la orilla*" ("Lord, you have come to the lakeshore," M344, P377). Both the United Methodist and Presbyterian hymnals are multilingual in that they include a few hymns in more than one language for people of different cultures to sing together.[22] In *The Baptist Hymnal*, 1991, are several Spanish hymns translated to English, such as Mexican Juan M. Isáis's "*Te vengo a decir*" (Translated by Frank Sawyer as "I've come to tell," B222).

American hymnals have also begun to include native American hymns. The first major American hymnal to include an Amerindian hymn was *The Methodist Hymnal* of 1966, which published "Many and great, O God" (B49, E385, M148, P271), a Dakota hymn by Joseph R. Renville dating from 1842. Several American hymnals have included "'Twas in the moon of wintertime" (E114, L72, M244, P61). This was the first native American Christmas carol from the Canadian Huron Indians with words written down by the Jesuit missionary, Jean de Brébeuf (c. 1641) and set to a French carol melody, UNE JEUNE PUCELLE. This Huron carol is the earliest Canadian carol known to be in existence.

---

[19]*Supplemental Worship Resources 12*, eds. J. Jefferson Cleveland and Verolga Nix (Nashville: Abingdon). Essays included deal with performance practice and the historical development of the Negro spiritual and of Black gospel.

[20](Chicago: G.I.A. Publications, Inc.). This volume includes prefatory essays by Sister Thea Bowman, "The Gift of African American Sacred Song," and by Rev. J. Glenn Murray, "The Liturgy of the Roman Rite and African American Worship."

[21]For more information on African-American hymnody in recent hymnals, see C. Michael Hawn, "A Survey of Trends in Recent Protestant Hymnals: African-American Spirituals, Hymns, and Gospel Songs," *The Hymn* 43, 1 (January 1992): 21-28.

[22]For example, both hymnals give the first stanza of "Amazing grace, how sweet the sound" in five native American languages: Choctaw, Cherokee, Creek, Kiowa, and Navajo. *The United Methodist Hymnal* provides all seven of its stanzas of "O for a thousand tongues to sing" in Spanish (M57, 59). *The Presbyterian Hymnal* provides its two stanzas of "What a friend we have in Jesus" in Korean (P403). Neither hymnal includes an index of its hymns by language.

Other cultures represented in recent American hymnals include those from Asian nations, such as China, Japan, and Korea. *Hymns from the Four Winds* is a collection of over 100 Asian-American hymns.[23] One of its hymns, the Japanese "Here, O Lord, your servants gather," has been published in recent American hymnals (B179, M552, P465). Recent American hymnals have included representative hymns from African nations such as Ghana and Nigeria. *Fill Us with Your Love and Other Hymns from Africa*[24] includes 34 hymns from that continent. Its title hymn from Ghana, "Jesu, Jesu, fill us with your love," has found a place in several recent American hymnals (B501, E602, M432, P367).

Particularly influential for certain kinds of less formal congregational singing have been the songs, hymns, chants, and responses produced by two spiritual communities which came into being near the same time at the beginning of World War II in Europe: Iona and Taizé.

The Iona Community was founded by an inner city minister, George McLeod. Having its locale in the small remote island of Iona, off the west coast of Scotland, this ecumenical community of craftsmen and clergy is now scattered throughout the world. The main tenets of this group are world peace and justice for those members of society who are economically, racially, socially, and religiously oppressed.

Within this general movement during the 1980s, a small group of hymn writers became active in producing songs which have an immediacy of appeal in both texts and tunes. Led by John L. Bell (b. 1949), minister of the Church of Scotland, along with Graham A. Maule (b. 1958), the group has produced three collections of 150 songs and other chants and responses which reflect a Celtic spirituality and a rugged honesty in a variety of popular folk styles.[25]

More recently, in a search for openness and reciprocity in the use of indigenous devotional expressions from the world over, The Wild Goose Worship Group has issued two more collections of songs from Latin America, Africa, the Orient, and other parts of the world.[26] The singing of these

---

[23]*Supplemental Worship Resources 13* (Nashville: Abingdon Press, 1983).

[24](Carol Stream, IL: Agape, 1983). Additional information is found in C. Michael Hawn, "A Survey of Trends in Recent Protestant Hymnals: International Hymnody," *The Hymn* 42, 4 (October 1991): 24-32.

[25]The titles of the collections, all produced by John Bell and Graham Maule with The Wild Goose Music Group (The wild goose is a Celtic symbol of The Holy Spirit.), and published in Glasgow by Wild Goose Publications are: *Heaven Shall Not Wait: Wild Goose Songs Vol. 1* (1987, 1989), *Enemy of Apathy: Wild Goose Songs Vol. 2* (1988, 1989), and *Love from Below* (1989). For a comprehensive review of these collections, see Kenneth Hull, "New Sounds from Iona: A Review of The Wild Goose Song Books," *The Hymn* 43, 2 (April, 1992): 22-30.

[26]*Many and Great: Songs of the World Church Vol. 1* (Glasgow: Wild Goose Publications, 1990) and *Sent by the Lord: Songs of the World Church Vol. 2* (1991).

songs, coming mainly from oppressed peoples, is encouraged as both an instrument of solidarity and a means of intercession.

None of the songs of Bell, Maule, and other Iona Community members have as yet found a place in American hymnals until 1995[27], with the exception of those of Tom Colvin (b. 1925). He is a clergyman of the Church of Scotland and The United Reformed Church in Great Britain who served for many years as a missionary in Africa. Colvin encouraged the use of indigenous song by the folk among whom he ministered. As a member of The Iona Community, he collected and published privately these African hymns in two books: *Free to Serve* (1968) and *Leap, My Soul* (1976). Many of these songs became more widely known in 1983 with the publication in the United States of *Fill Us with Your Love and Other Hymns from Africa*.[28]

Taizé, a tiny village in eastern France not far from the famous town of Cluny, is the home of an ecumenical spiritual community founded in 1940. Today, Taizé, like Iona, is a place of pilgrimage for prayer and reflection and the seat of an appealing style of singing. Taizé's leading musician was Jacques Berthier (1923-1994), composer and organist at St. Ignatius Church, Paris, one of the European centers of liturgical renewal.

From 1975, Berthier and others were engaged in developing a new repertoire based on repetitive structures: short musical phrases (ostinato responses, canons, litanies, chants) having singable melodic units which are readily memorized.[29] Like Iona, Taizé has worldwide connections and influence. This is evidenced by the appearance of these popular musical selections in recent hymnals: "Gloria, Gloria" (LS734,[30] M72, P576), "Prepare the way of the Lord" (M207), "Jesus, remember me" (LS740, M488, P599), and "Eat this bread" (LS772, M628).

CHALLENGES OF THE HYMNIC EXPLOSION

While recent decades have witnessed a growing diversity of cultures represented in new hymnals in America, there has also been a search to find a common core of hymnody suitable for ecumenical use. The hymnal *Cantate*

[27]John Bell is represented in two American hymnals released in 1995: *Chalice Hymnal* (St. Louis: Chalice Press) for the Christian Church (Disciples of Christ) and *The New Century Hymnal* (Cleveland: The Pilgrim Press) for the United Church of Christ.
[28](Carol Stream, IL: Agape). Among other songs to be found in current hymnals, Colvin's "Jesu, Jesu, fill us with your love" (B501, LS803,* M432, P367) is the most popular. *See note 28.
[29]The music of Taizé is most readily available to Americans in the various editions (vocal, instrumental, congregational) of Jacques Berthier, *Music from Taizé: Responses, Litanies, Acclamations, Canons* (Chicago: G. I. A. Publications, 1978, 1980, 1981).
[30]LS refers to *Hymnal Supplement*, 1991, Robert J. Batastini and John Ferguson, eds. (Chicago: GIA Publications, Inc., 1991), a supplement to the *Lutheran Book of Worship* (1978).

Domino, already described in Chapter 9, "Cultural Perspectives," bears the subtitle "An Ecumenical Hymn Book." This multilingual hymnal was envisioned for use at international gatherings of Christians from many cultures or as a supplement to a parish hymnal.[31] In the 1970s, a group of persons representing about a dozen American denominations formed a Consultation on Ecumenical Hymnody (CEH) and selected 227 hymn texts with tunes recommended for ecumenical use. This CEH list was published in 1977 in *The Hymn*.[32] In the *Lutheran Book of Worship*, hymns included from the CEH list are marked with an asterisk in the first-line index. Although no revision has yet been published, The Hymn Society in the United States and Canada is revising this list of core hymnic repertory for the 1990s.

One modification of the CEH list would certainly be the inclusion of the most widely accepted hymns from the renaissance of new hymn writing from about 1970 in Britain, Canada, and in the United States. One challenge of this large number of new hymn texts has been to find suitable, singable tunes. In many cases an established tune from an earlier era has been used, as with Fred Pratt Green's "When in our music God is glorified," set in most hymnals to Charles V. Stanford's tune ENGELBERG (B435, E420, M68, P264).[33] In some cases, writers of new hymn texts have collaborated with composers, as with Brian Wren and Peter Cutts, Thomas Troeger and Carol Doran, and Jaroslav Vajda and Carl Schalk.[34] More often than not, tunes composed for recent mainstream hymnody are intended for unison singing. For Fred Kaan's "Help us accept each other," for example, both of its tunes—ACCEPTANCE by John Ness Beck (M560) and BARONITA by Doreen Potter (P358)—are intended for unison singing.

Yet another challenge of the explosion of new hymnody and the publica-

---

[31]Erik Routley, "Editor's Introduction," *Cantate Domino* New edition (Oxford: Published on behalf of the World Council of Churches by Oxford University Press, 1980), xii.

[32]28, 4 (October 1977): 192-209. See also "The CEH List: Four Diverse Appraisals," *The Hymn*, 29, 2 (April 1978): 83-90.

[33]L555 provides a new tune by the American composer Charles R. Anders, FREDERICKTOWN, for Pratt Green's text. For an interesting discussion of five different tunes associated with this hymn, see Austin C. Lovelace's "Which Is the Right Tune?," *The Hymn*, 44, 3 (October 1993): 10-14.

[34]See *Faith looking Forward: The Hymns & Songs of Brian Wren with many Tunes by Peter Cutts* (Carol Stream, IL: Hope Publishing Co., 1983). More recently Wren has published his texts with settings by a number of different composers, as in *Praising a Mystery: 30 New Hymns by Brian Wren* (Carol Stream, IL: Hope Publishing Co. 1986), *Bring Many Names: 35 New Hymns by Brian Wren* (Carol Stream, IL: Hope Publishing Co., 1989), and *New Beginnings* (Carol Stream, IL: Hope Publishing Co., 1993). For Troeger and Doran, see *New Hymns for the Lectionary: To Glorify the Maker's Name* (New York and Oxford: Oxford University Press, 1986) and *New Hymns for the Life of the Church: To Make Our Prayer and Music One* (New York: Oxford University Press, 1992). Seven settings by Carl Schalk to texts by Jaroslav Vajda are in *The Carl Schalk Hymnary* (Chicago: G.I.A. Publications, Inc., 1989), and 10 for Vajda texts are in *The Carl Schalk Hymnary Supplement* (Chicago: G.I.A. Publications, Inc., 1991).

tion of new hymnals has been to encourage and provide support for vital and meaningful congregational singing. Practical books for those responsible for developing congregational singing have been published in recent decades, such as James R. Sydnor's two books: *Hymns and Their Uses* (Agape, 1982) and *Introducing a New Hymnal: How to Improve Congregational Singing* (G.I.A., 1989). Sydnor has also provided a textbook for members of congregations to engage in a study of hymns: *Hymns: A Congregational Study* (Agape, 1983).

Help for organists in hymn playing has been provided in such texts as Austin C. Lovelace's *The Organist and Hymn Playing* (Agape, rev. ed., 1989), in book and cassette tape publications of the American Guild of Organists,[35] and in periodicals such as *The American Organist* and *Pedalpoint*.[36]

Increased concern for a good acoustical environment for congregational singing has manifested itself in recent decades. Acoustics was the theme of several articles in the July 1990 issue of *The Hymn*.[37] In 1986, Concordia published Scott R. Riedel's booklet, *Acoustics in the Worship Space*.

Increasingly, major new hymnals are being provided with handbooks or companions that include information concerning the background of the hymnal, its texts and tunes, and its authors and composers. Such volumes have been published for all five of the key hymnals referenced in this book. In addition to companions for hymnals, other practical volumes related to hymnals have appeared in the 1990s. For the hymnal *The Worshipping Church* (1990), Hope Publishing Company has provided a "Worship Leaders' Edition"; its wider-than-tall format includes the hymns in their normal size plus a commentary for the use of worship leaders beside each hymn. The commentary includes information on scriptural background, history, and suggestions for using each hymn.[38] In addition to the large *Companion to The United Methodist Hymnal* by Carlton R. Young (Abingdon, 1993), a smaller quick-reference volume was provided in *The Hymns of the United Methodist Hymnal* edited by Diana Sanchez (Abingdon, 1989). A small practical book with paragraphs of information on familiar hymns to be disseminated to congregations is Austin C. Lovelace's *Hymn Notes for Church Bulletins* (G.I.A., 1987).

[35]Two workbook and cassette publications of the AGO are Margot Ann G. Woolard's *A Mini-Course in Hymn Playing* (Fundamentals of hymn playing) and John A. Ferguson's *A Mini-Course in Creative Hymn Playing* (Advanced level hymn playing).
[36]*Pedalpoint* (Product No. 1306) is published quarterly by the Music Department of the Baptist Sunday School Board, 127 Ninth Avenue, North, Nashville, TN 37234.
[37]Republished as *Acoustics for Liturgy* (Chicago: Liturgy Training Publications, 1991).
[38]Also available is *Concordance to The Worshipping Church: A Hymnal* by Kenneth Wilson (Carol Stream, IL: Hope Publishing Co., 1991).

Of particular significance for the support of congregational singing in North America has been the revitalization of the Hymn Society with its publications, annual conferences, and workshops. Strong congregational singing has been a major focus of the Hymn Society's convocations; many persons responsible for the leadership of hymnody in local parishes have been encouraged and inspired by the rich and meaningful singing encountered in these sessions. Workshops sponsored by the Hymn Society have included courses for writers of hymn texts, composers of hymn tunes, and organists in hymn playing. Books and recordings related to hymnody that are available for purchase are listed in the Hymn Society's Book Service and published each quarter in *The Hymn*.

Yet another challenge in an age of much new hymnody is the choosing of appropriate hymns for worshiping congregations. One aspect of choosing hymns is finding those which fit a particular place in worship—a specific liturgical context. Users of the *Lutheran Book of Worship* are provided with "Hymns for the Church Year" (929-931), giving at least three suggested hymns for each Sunday plus hymns for the days of holy Week. Episcopalians are provided assistance in their choice of hymns for the liturgy in Marion J. Hatchett's separate volume, *A Liturgical Index to The Hymnal 1982* (Church Hymnal Corporation, 1986). *The United Methodist Hymnal* has within its "Index of Topics and Categories" a section on the Christian Year, and *The Presbyterian Hymnal* has its first section of hymns arranged according to the Christian Year. Scriptural indexes for hymns are given in *The Baptist Hymnal*, *The United Methodist Hymnal*, and *The Presbyterian Hymnal*.[39]

Yet another aspect of choosing appropriate hymns for congregational singing is the interpretation of their theological content. In addition to theological information found in hymnal companions, hymn text interpretations have been published regularly in *The Hymn*. Furthermore, writers of new hymn texts (for example, Brian Wren, Fred Pratt Green, Carl Daw, and Timothy Dudley-Smith) have frequently provided helpful background information concerning origins and theological content in collections of their hymns. One theologian's contribution to interpreting the theological significance of hymnody is S. Paul Schilling's *The Faith We Sing* (Westminster, 1983).

[39]One particularly intriguing scriptural arrangement of hymns within a hymnal is that given by Erik Routley for *Rejoice in the Lord: A Hymn Companion to the Scriptures* (Grand Rapids: Wm. B. Eerdmans Publishing Co., 1985). This hymnal for the Reformed Church in America is structured according to the following four main headings: Part I: The God of Abraham Praise, Part II: Behold the Lamb of God, Part III: Spirit of Truth, Spirit of Power, and Part IV: The Hope of Glory.

Beyond an understanding of the liturgical context and theology of hymns, the person choosing hymns must understand the congregation that will be expected to sing what is chosen. This understanding encompasses their educational level, their musical training, and their cultural orientation. With an informed sensitivity to where a congregation is in their practice of hymn singing, leaders can choose hymns which the people can already sing, and gradually lead them to incorporate new hymns into their repertory.

Since major new hymnals are revised infrequently, it has become more common in recent decades to go beyond a single hymnal to expand a congregation's repertory. One approach has been the purchase of a smaller supplementary hymnal focusing on newer hymnody.[40] Another approach—one which requires much effort on the part of a local parish—is the compilation and publication of its own supplementary hymnal. Yet another approach to using newer repertory is a congregation's belonging to a copyright permission service, such as Christian Copyright Licensing, Inc. (CCLI), an organization that represents more than 200 publishers.[41]

GROWTH OF HYMNOLOGICAL SCHOLARSHIP

Hymnological scholarship has grown considerably in recent years. Much of the support for hymnology is found in the growth of hymn societies. The Hymn Society of America, founded in 1922 as a strictly national organization, is now international. In recognition of its sizable number of Canadian members, its name was changed in 1989 to The Hymn Society in the United States and Canada. The *International Arbeitsgemeinschaft für Hymnologie* (IAH—International Fellowship for Research in Hymnology) was founded in (West) Germany in 1959. Although the IAH is primarily German language in its orientation, in 1981 it joined the Hymn Society of America and the Hymn Society of Great Britain and Ireland in holding an International Conference on Hymnody for the first time on English soil—at Oxford. The conference in England was followed by one in Budapest, Hungary, the first in that then Communist-controlled country. The three societies again joined forces in 1985 to have their first joint Conference on Hymnody across the Atlantic, meeting at the historic Moravian community of Bethlehem, Pennsylvania. Thus, hymnological organizations repre-

[40]In addition to a number of denominational hymnal supplements, Hope Publishing Company has published two collections for general use that include a good selection of recent mainstream hymnody: *Hymnal Supplement* (Agape, 1984) and *Hymnal Supplement II* (Agape, 1987).
[41]CCLI, 7031 NE Halsey Street, Portland, OR 97213-6359. (1-800-234-2446).

senting three geographical areas came together in the 80s in the interest of promoting a greater international understanding of hymnody.

This international cooperation bodes well for facing the hymnic challenges of a new century. George Herbert's centuries-old admonition remains remarkably appropriate: "Let all the world in every corner sing: my God and King!"

APPENDIX I

A SERVICE OF WORSHIP IN SONG
Featuring the Hymns of Isaac Watts, 1674-1748
(Planned for congregation, organ, and choir with optional trumpet)

One aspect of this hymn service requires a bit of explanation. A modulation in music is a smooth and logical transition from one key to another. Just so, a **spoken modulation** in a hymn service is a prepared statement—it may be several sentences in length—that leads the thought of the worshipers appropriately from the singing of one hymn to the next. Thus, a verbal modulation may include or consist entirely of a passage of Scripture, the quotatiuon of a poem or parts of a hymn, or it may give some word of explanation as to the purpose in singing the hymn to follow.

For example, in this "Service of Worship in Song," the hymn stanza quoted as the spoken call to worship functions as a **spoken modulation** from the worship leader's preludical commentary, "An Appreciation of Isaac Watts, Hymn Writer," to the sung call to worship, "Lord of the worlds above." This is followed by the reading of the Scripture, Psalm 90: 1-2, which is a **spoken modulation** to the singing of the hymn, "O God, Our Help in Ages Past."

The worship leader is encouraged to use her/his own imagination and creativity to formulate the other spoken modulations indicated. See Chapter 11, "The Hymn in Worship," concerning "Verbal Introduction of Hymns," 259.

THE ORDER OF SERVICE
Organ Voluntary: Prelude on HAMBURG...Paul Bunjes

Congregational Rehearsal of the Hymns

Prelude to Worship: "An Appreciation of Isaac Watts, Hymn Writer"
           (by the Pastor or other worship leader)

THE SERVICE OF WORSHIP
Contemplating God and God's Mighty Works
Call to Worship:
        Spoken: "Let all our powers be joined
                His glorious name to raise;
                Pleasure and love fill every mind
                And every voice be praise."

Sung to the DARWALL tune:
> "Lord of the worlds above,
>> How pleasant and how fair
> The dwellings of thy love,
>> Thine earthly temples are!
> To Thine abode my heart aspires
>> With warm desires to see my God."

Scriptural Modulation: Psalm 90:1-2

Hymn: "O God, Our Help in Ages Past".ST. ANNE
(Congregation will rise with choir to sing)
Stanza 1:   Sung by congregation and choir
Stanza 2:   Spoken by congregation alone
Stanza 3:   Sung by congregation and choir
Stanza 4:   Sung by choir alone
Stanza 5:   Sung in unison by choir and congregation
(with optional trumpet descant)

Sensing Our Humanity and Confessing Our Sins
Spoken Modulation

Prayer Hymn: "Come, Holy Spirit, Heavenly Dove"...................... ST. AGNES
(Congregation will remain seated)
Stanza 1:   Sung by congregation and choir
Stanza 2:   Sung by choir alone in minor
Stanza 3:   Sung by congregation and choir in minor
Stanza 4:   Sung by congregation and choir in major

Receiving Power and Comfort from God's Word
Spoken Modulation

Antiphonal Scripture Reading:
"God the Ruler of the World" ....Psalm 98: 1-4, 7-9, TEV
(Congregation will read bold-italicized words)

> "Sing a new song to the Lord; he has done wonderful things!
> ***By his own power and holy strength he has won the victory.***
> The Lord announced his victory;
> ***he made his saving power known to the nations.***
> He kept his promise to the people of Israel with loyalty and constant love for them.
> ***All people everywhere have seen the victory of our God.***
> Sing for joy to the Lord, all the earth;

praise him with songs and shouts of joy!
   Roar, sea, and every creature in you; sing, earth, and all who live on you!
Clap your hands, you rivers; you hills, sing together with joy before the Lord,
   because he comes to rule the earth.
He will rule the peoples of the world with justice and fairness."

Spoken Modulation

   Hymn: "Joy to the World! The Lord Is Come!" ....ANTIOCH
            (Congregation will rise with choir to sing)

   Introduction: Sung by choir alone
      Stanza 1: Sung by congregation and choir
      Stanza 2: Spoken by choir alone
      Stanza 3: Spoken by congregation and choir
      Stanza 4: Sung by congregation in unison *(Descant by the choir)*

Rededicating Our Lips to God's Praise; Our Lives to God's Work
Spoken Modulation

   Hymn: "When I Survey the Wondrous Cross" ....HAMBURG
            (Congregation will remain seated)

      Stanza 1: Sung by Congregation and choir
      Stanza 2: Sung by congregation and choir
      Stanza 3: Solo sung in minor
      Stanza 4: Sung by congregation and choir in major

Spoken Modulation

Antiphonal Hymn:
"From All That Dwell Below the Skies" ....LASST UNS ERFREUEN
            (Congregation will rise with choir to sing italicized words)

Benediction and Ascription of Praise ....Pastor

Organ Postlude: Fugue on ST. ANNE...J. S. Bach

Hymn Analysis Checklist*

I. Literary Structure
A. Meter (e.g., C.M.; 87.87.)
B. Poetic Feet (e.g., iambic tetrameter)
C. Rhyme Scheme (e.g., abab)
D. Poetic Devices and Figures of Speech (See pp. 20-24; and
   Lovelace, *The Anatomy of Hymnody*, Chapter 6, "Modulations and
   Poetic Devices")
E. Organization (e.g., literary patterns; e.g., itemization) (See pp. 24-26.)

II. Thought Content
A. Scriptural Background (If applicable, give scriptural references.)
B. Theological Teaching (Relate specific phrases to doctrines expressed.)
C. Direction (Godward; inward; toward people)
D. Prose Summary (In a few sentences, give a summary or prose paraphrase of
   the main ideas.) (See Chapter 4 above.)
E. Organization (e.g., thought patterns; e.g., paradox) (See pp. 69-73.)

III. Musical Characteristics
A. Phrase Structure (repetitions; through-composed)
B. Melodic Movement (step or skip; up or down; types of intervals)
C. Harmony (basic chords; altered chords; modulations; harmonic rhythm)
D. Meter (e.g., simple; compound)
E. Rhythm (e.g., straightforward; dotted; syncopated)
F. Counterpoint (e.g., relation of bass line to melodic line)
G. Form (e.g., AAB, pp. 36-37)

IV. Evaluative Questions
A. Words
   1. Are the thoughts expressed theologically sound?
   2. Does the hymn dwell on thoughts of God, or on the mood of the singer?
   3. Are the ideas expressed within the understanding of the average
      member of your congregation?
   4. What words, terms, names, phrases, if any, might need explanation?
   5. Does the poetry possess simplicity and beauty?
   6. Do the thoughts express spiritual reality? Would they apply to your
      congregation as a whole?
   7. Are the thoughts expressed relevant? Do they avoid well-worn hymnic
      clichés?

B. Music
1. Does it enhance the significance of the text?
2. Would it be within the capability of those who must sing it? (e.g., range; tessitura; melodic leaps; rhythmic contrasts).

C. Usage
1. For what occasions would it be appropriate? (e.g., formal worship; church school; evangelistic service)
2. With what age groups would it be suitable? (e.g., elementary school; middle school; high school; adults)
3. If unfamiliar to your congregation, how could it be introduced? (e.g., method of presentation; connection with a particular occasion)
4. If already familiar, how could you bring fresh meaning and excitement to its use?

* For study suggestions in further depth, see Nancy White Thomas, "A Guide to Hymn Study," *The Hymn* 15 (July 1964): 69-82.

SELECTED BIBLIOGRAPHY

GENERAL WORKS

Benson, Louis F. *The English Hymn.* New York: George H. Doran Co., 1915; reprint, Richmond: John Knox Press, 1962.

_____. *The Hymnody of the Christian Church.* New York: George H. Doran Co., 1927; reprint, Richmond: John Knox Press, 1956.

Blume, Friedrich, ed. *Protestant Church Music: A History.* New York: W. W. Norton & Co., 1974.

Davidson, James R. *A Dictionary of Protestant Church Music.* Metuchen, NJ: The Scarecrow Press, 1975.

Diehl, Katherine S. *Hymns and Tunes-An Index.* Metuchen, NJ: The Scarecrow Press, 1966.

Douglas, Winfred. *Church Music in History and Practice: Studies in the Praise of God.* Revised with additional material by Leonard Ellinwood. New York: Charles Scribner's Sons, 1961.

Julian, John. *A Dictionary of Hymnology.* 2nd. ed. rev., London: John Murray, 1907; reprint in 2 vols. Grand Rapids, MI: Kregel Publications, 1985.

Patrick, Millar. *The Story of the Church's Song.* Revised ed. by James R. Syndor. Richmond: John Knox Press, 1962.

Reynolds, William J. and Milburn Price. *A Survey of Christian Hymnody.* 3rd ed. Carol Stream, IL: Hope Publishing Co., 1987.

Routley, Erik. *A Panorama of Christian Hymnody.* Collegeville, MN: The Liturgical Press, 1979.

_____. *An English-Speaking Hymnal Guide.* Collegeville, MN: The Liturgical Press, 1979.

_____. *Christian Hymns Observed.* Princeton: Prestige Publications, 1982.

_____. *Hymns and Human Life.* London: John Murray, 1952.

_____. *The Music of Christian Hymns.* Chicago: G.I.A. Publications, 1981.

Schalk, Carl, ed. *Church Music 66/1* "The Hymn in Christian Worship." St. Louis: Concordia Publishing House, 1966.

_____. *Key Words in Church Music.* St. Louis: Concordia Publishing House, 1978.

Studwell, William E. *Christmas Carols: A Reference Guide.* Indexes by David Hamilton. New York: Garland, 1985.

Wicker, Vernon, Editor-in-Chief, *Hymnology Annual:* An International Forum on the Hymn and Worship. Vols. 1-4. Berrien Springs, MI: 1991-1995. [Vol. 4 is published by Selch Publishing Co., Kingston, NY.]

THE HYMN AND LITERATURE

Baker, Frank. *Charles Wesley's Verse.* London: The Epworth Press, 1964.

_____. ed. *Representative Verse of Charles Wesley.* Nashville: Abingdon Press, 1962.

Bayly, Albert F. "Writing Hymns for our Times," *The Hymn* 20, 1 (January 1969): 22-27.

Benson, Louis F. "The Relation of the Hymn to Literature," Lecture III in *The Hymnody of the Christian Church*. New York: George H. Doran Co. 1927; reprint, Richmond, VA: John Knox Press, 1956, 99-138.

Bett, Henry. "The Methodist Hymns and English Literature," Chapter I in *The Hymns of Methodism*. 3rd edition, rev. and enlarged. London: The Epworth Press, 1945, 9-12.

Briggs, George Wallace. "The Making of a Hymn. *The Hymn* 7, 2 (April 1956): 53-57.

Caird, V. M. "The Hymn as a Literary Form," *Bulletin of the Hymn Society of Great Britain and Ireland* 38 (January 1974): 1-9.

Clarkson, Margaret. "Helps for Aspiring Hymn Writers," *The Hymn* 42, 3 (July 1991): 26-28.

_____. "The Making of a Hymn," in *A Singing Heart*. Carol Stream, IL: Hope Publishing Co., 1987, 11-22.

Dearmer, Percy. "Introduction," *Songs of Praise Discussed: A Handbook to the Best-known Hymns and to Others Recently Introduced*. London: Oxford University Press, 1952: ix-xxv.

Flew, R. Newton. *The Hymns of Charles Wesley: A Study of their Structure*. London: The Epworth Press, 1953.

Green, Fred Pratt. "Poet and Hymn Writer," in *Later Hymns and Ballads and Fifty Poems*. Carol Stream: Hope Publishing Co., 1989, xiii-xxiv.

Gregory, A. S. *Praises with Understanding*. London: Epworth Press, 1936; 2nd ed. rev., 1949.

Grindal, Gracia. "Language: A Lost Craft Among Hymn Writers," *The Hymn* 27, 2 (April 1976): 43-48.

_____. *Lessons in Hymn Writing*. Fort Worth: The Hymn Society in the United States and Canada, 1991.

Haas, Alfred B. "American Poets as Hymn Writers," *The Hymn* 2, 1 (January 1951): 13-18.

Hewlett, Michael. "Thoughts About Words," *Bulletin of the Hymn Society of Great Britain and Ireland* 115 (Spring 1969): 11-14. Reprinted in *The Hymn* 20, 3 (July 1969): 89-92.

Holmes, John Haynes. "What Makes a Good Hymn?" *Christian Century* 59 (June 10, 1942): 755-757.

Huber, Jane Parker. "Introduction: How Do You Write a Hymn?" in *A Singing Faith*. Philadelphia: The Westminster Press, 1987.

Lovelace, Austin C. *The Anatomy of Hymnody*. Nashville: Abingdon Press, 1965; reprint, Chicago: G.I.A. Publications, 1982.

Manning, Bernard. *The Hymns of Wesley and Watts*. London: Epworth Press, 1942.

Merryweather, Frank B. "Poetry and Hymns," *The Hymn* 5, 4 (October 1954): 111-115.

Nicolson, Norman. "Bad Poetry or Good Light Verse?" *Bulletin of the Hymn Society of Great Britain and Ireland* 101 (Autumn 1964): 220-224.

Osborne, William. "Hymns for Today," *The Hymn* 20, 4 (October 1969): 115-118, 123.

Quinn, James S. J. "The Ministry of the Hymn-Writer," *Bulletin of the Society of Great Britain and Ireland* 181 (October 1989): 141-146.

Reeves, Jeremiah B. *The Hymn in History and Literature*. New York: The Century Company, 1924.

Routley, Erik R. "What Remains for the Modern Hymn Writer to Do?" *Bulletin of the Hymn Society of Great Britain and Ireland* 66 (January 1954): 148-153.

Smith, Timothy Dudley. "Hymns and Poetry-A Personal Reflection" in *Lift Every Heart*. Carol Stream: Hope Publishing Co., 1984.

_____. "What Makes a Good Hymn Text?" *The Hymn* 36, 1 (January 1985): 14-18.

Thomas, Nancy White. *A Guide to Hymn Study*. Springfield, OH: The Hymn Society of America, 1964.

Vajda, Jaroslav J. "Reflections on Hymn Writing" in *Now - The Joyful Celebration*. St. Louis: Morningstar, 1987, 5-10.

Wren, Brian. "Making Your Own Hymn," in

Faith Looking Forward. Carol Stream: Hope Publishing Co., 1983, n.p.

Zimmermann, Heinz Werner. "Word and Tone in Modern Hymnody," *The Hymn* 24, 2 (April 1973): 44-55.

THE HYMN AND MUSIC

Best, Harold M. "Hymn Tune Writing," *The Hymn* 28, 4 (October 1977): 183-85.

Bristol, Lee Hastings, Jr. "Sullivan, Hymn Tune Composer," *The Hymn* 18, 4 (October 1967): 101-103.

Brown, Ray Francis. "Appraising 20th Century Hymn Tunes," *The Hymn* 3, 2 (April 1952): 37-44, 63.

Calhoun, Philo C. "Selection of Hymn Tunes - One More Word," *The Hymn* 3, 3 (July 1952): 79-80, 94.

Carter, Philip L. "Samuel Wesley's Hymn Tunes," *Hymn Society of Great Britain and Ireland* Bulletin 170 (January 1988): 13-15.

Downey, Michael. "Writing Music for Hymns," *The Hymn Society of Great Britain and Irland Bulletin* 10/3 No. 155 (October 1982): 66-69.

Finlay, Kenneth G. "A Scot Considers the English Hymn Tune, 1900-1950," *The Hymn* 6, 4 (October 1955): 117-123.

Frost, Maurice. *English and Scottish Psalm and Hymn-tunes*. London: S.P.C.K., 1953; New York: Oxford University Press, 1953.

_____. *Historical Companion to Hymns Ancient and Modern*. London: William Clowes and Sons, Ltd., 1962.

Horn, Henry E. "The Hymn and Its Tunes," in *O Sing unto the Lord*. (Philadelphia: The Muhlenberg Press, 1956): 54-66.

Hutchings, Arthur J. B. "Dykes's Tunes," *The Hymn* 12, 3 (July 1961): 69-76.

Kroeger, Karl. "William Billings and the Hymn Tune," *The Hymn* 37, 3 (July 1986): 19-26.

Leaver, Robin A. "Dykes' NICAEA: An Original Tune or the Re-working of Another?" *The Hymn* 38, 2 (April 1987): 21-24.

Liemohn, Edwin. *The Chorale through Four Hundred Years of Musical Development as a Congregational Hymn*. Philadelphia: The Muhlenberg Press, 1953.

Lovelace, Austin C. "A Survey of Tunes," *Companion to the Hymnal*, a Handbook to the 1964 Methodist Hymnal, ed., Emory Stevens Bucke. (Nashville: Abingdon Press, 1970), 41-51.

_____. "Which is the Right Tune?" *The Hymn* 44, 4 (October 1993): 10-14.

Massey, Bernard S. "William Henry Monk 1823-89," *The Hymn Society of Great Britain and Ireland* Bulletin 163 (April 1989): 98-99.

McCutchan, Robert G. *Hymn Tune Names*. Nashville: Abingdon Press, 1957.

Patrick, Millar. *Four Centuries of Scottish Psalmody*. London: Oxford University Press, 1949.

_____. "Music in Hymnody," Occasional Paper No. 3 of the Hymn Society of Great Britain and Ireland, July, 1945.

Pocknee, C. E. *The French Diocesan Melodies*, London: Faith Press, 1954.

Pratt, Waldo Selden, *The Music of the French Psalter of 1562*. New York: Columbia University Press, 1939.

Riedel, Johannes. *The Lutheran Chorale: Its Basic Traditions*. Minneapolis: Augsburg Press, 1967.

Routley, Erik. *Hymn Tunes: An Historical Outline*. Study Notes, No. 5. Croydon: The Royal School of Church Music, n.d.

_____. *The English Carol*. London: Herbert Jenkins, 1958; New York: Oxford University Press, 1959.

_____. *The Music of Christian Hymns*. Chicago: G.I.A. Publications, 1981.

Schalk, Carl, ed. *Key Words in Church Music*. St. Louis: Concordia Publishing House, 1978. See especially Cantional, Cantional Style; Carol; Chant, Anglican; Chant, Gregorian; Chorale; Gospel Song; Hymnody.

Stevens, Denis. *Plainsong Hymns and Sequences*. Study Notes, No. 12. Croydon: The Royal School of Church Music, n.d.

Stulken, Marilyn. "Contemporary Hymn

Tunes: A Look at Some New Tunes in the Lutheran Book of Worship," *Journal of Church Music* 20, 2 (February 1978): 7-11.

Webster, Donald. *Our Hymn Tunes: Their Choice and Performance*. Glasgow: The Saint Andrew Press, 1985.

Wilson, John W. "Handel and the Hymn Tune," *The Hymn* 36, 4 (October 1985): 18-23; 37, 1 (January 1986): 25-31.

_____. *Looking at Hymn Tunes: The Objective Factors*. Croydon, England: The Hymn Society, n.d. Also published in *Duty and Delight: Routley Remembered*. Ed. Robin A. Leaver, James H. Litton, and Carlton R. Young. Norwich: Canterbury Press; Carol Stream, IL: Hope Publishing Co., 1985, 123-152.

_____. "The Evolution of the Tune 'ANTIOCH'" *The Hymn Society of Great Britain and Ireland Bulletin* 11, 5 No. 166 (January 1986): 107-114.

_____. "The Hymn Tune LASST UNS ERFREUEN as We Know It," *The Hymn Society of Great Britain and Ireland Bulletin* 9/10 No. 150 (January 1981): 194-200.

THE HYMN AND SCRIPTURE

Bailey, Albert E. *The Gospel in Hymns*. New York: Charles Scribner's Sons, 1950.

Benson, Louis F. "The Relation of the Hymn to Holy Scripture," Lecture II in *The Hymnody of the Christian Church*. Richmond: John Knox Press, 1956, 57-95.

Bett, Henry. "The Hymns and the Scriptures," Chapter VI in *The Hymns of Methodism*. London: The Epworth Press, 3rd rev.ed., 1945, 71-97.

Bushong, Ann Brooke. *A Guide to the Lectionary*. New York: The Seabury Press, 1978. Hymn List, 202-205.

Lawson, John. *The Wesley Hymns as a Guide to Scriptural Teaching*. Grand Rapids: Francis Asbury Press, 1987.

Leaver, Robin. "The Hymns and the Old Testament," *Bulletin of the Hymn Society of Great Britain and Ireland* 141 (January 1978): 14-16.

Mountain, Charles M. "The New Testament Christ-Hymn," *The Hymn* 44, 1 (January 1993): 20-28.

Routley, Erik R. *Hymns Today and Tomorrow*. Nashville: Abingdon Press, 1964.

_____. "Scriptural Resonances in Hymnody," *Reformed Liturgy and Music* XVI, 3 (Summer 1982): 120-125.

_____. "The Church Musician and His Bible" in *Music Leadership in the Church*. Carol Stream: Hope Publishing Co., 1984.

_____. "The Hymns of Philip Doddridge" in *Philip Doddridge: His Contribution to English Religion*. Edited by Geoffrey F. Nuttall. London: Independent Press, 1951.

Shero, Lucius Rogers. "Familiar hymns from the Hebrew and their Translations," *The Hymn* 13, 2 & 4 (April, October 1962): 37-44, 107-112 and 14, 2 (April 1963): 53-56.

Spencer, Donald A. *Hymn and Scripture Selection Guide*, Rev. Ed. Grand Rapids: Baker Book House, 1993.

Westerhoff, John H. *A Pilgrim People: Learning Through the Church Year*. New York: Seabury Press, 1984.

Wolfe, Janet E. "O Sing to the Lord a New Song: Biblical Texts in Music," *Reformed Liturgy and Music* 24, 4 (Fall 1990): 195-197.

THE HYMN AND THEOLOGY

Adey, Lionel. *Hymns and the Christian "Myth."* Vancouver: University of British Columbia Press, 1986.

Balleine, G. R. *Sing with Understanding, Some Hymn Problems Unravelled*. London: Independence Press, 1954.

Benson, Louis F. *The Hymnody of the Christian Church*. Richmond: John Knox Press, 1956.

Black, George. "Hymns and the Baptism of Jesus," *The Hymn* 42, 1 (January 1991): 7-12.

Braun, H. Myron. "Yes, Heresies in Hymns,"

Music Ministry 10 (September 1977): 1, 31-32.

Buszin, Walter E. "Theology and Church Music as Bearers of the *Verbum Dei*," in *The Musical Heritage of the Church VI*. edited by Theodore Hoelty-Nickel. St. Louis: Concordia Publishing House, 1963, 17-31.

Campbell, Duncan. "Introduction," to *Hymns and Hymn-Makers*. London: A. and C. Black, 1912, XV-XXVII.

Dewar, Lindsay. "Hymns and Theology," *Bulletin of the Hymn Society of Great Britain and Ireland* 30 (January 1945): 4-6.

Doran, Carol and Thomas H. Troeger. "Writing Hymns as a Theologically Informed Discipline," *The Hymn* 36, 2 (April 1985): 7-11.

Enneking, Tom. "Theology and Christmas Hymns," *Liturgy* 4 (Summer 1984): 45-51.

Foelsch, Charles B. "Let's Not Lose the 'Category of the Holy,' " *The Hymn* 24, 4 (October 1973): 109-11.

Foreman, Kenneth J. "Theology and the Hymnal," *Presbyterian Outlook* (January 26, 1953): 4-5.

Goldhawk, Norman P. *On Hymns and Hymnbooks*. London: Epworth Press, 1979.

Giles, William Brewster. "Christian Theology and Hymnody," *The Hymn* 14, 1 (January 1963): 9-12.

Grant, John Webster. "The Hymn as Theological Statement," *The Hymn* 37, 4 (October 1986): 7-10.

Gregory, A. S. "Hymns and the Faith," Chapter III in *Praises with Understanding*. Second edition (revised and enlarged). London: The Epworth Press, 1949, 57-85.

Hall, Raymond. "Hymns for This Age," *The Hymn* 27, 2 (April 1976): 62-63.

Houghton, Edward. "Poetry and Piety in Charles Wesley's Hymns," *The Hymn* 6, 3 (July 1955): 77-86.

Jones, Kenneth O. "Hymns and Theology," *The Hymn* 12, 2 (April 1961): 36.

Langford, Norman F. "Church Hymnody as a Repository of Doctrine," *Religion in Life*

25 (Summer 1956): 421-31.

Leaver, Robin A. "Hymnody and the Reality of God," *The Hymn* 44, 3 (July 1993): 16-21.

————. "The Hymnbook as a Practical Theology," *Reformed Liturgy and Music* 24, 2 (Spring 1990): 55-57.

————. "Theological Problems for Hymnology," *The Hymn* 4, 2 (April 1953): 45-51.

————. "Theological Dimensions of Mission Hymnody: The Counterpoint of Cult and Culture," *Worship* 62, 4 (July 1988): 316-331.

McElrath, Hugh T. "The Hymnbook as a Compendium of Theology," *The Review and Expositor* 87, 1 (Winter 1990): 11-31.

————. "We Proclaim our Beliefs Through Congregational Song," *The Church Musician* 16 (December 1965): 6-7.

McKim, Linda Jo. "Interpreting Atonement through Hymnody," *Reformed Liturgy and Music* 24, 1 (Winter 1990): 13-15.

Naumann, Martin J. "Hymnody: A Reflection on the Beginning, Middle, and End of Man's Destiny," in *The Musical Heritage of the Church VI* edited by Theodore Hoelty-Nickel. St. Louis: Concordia Publishing House, 1963, 32-37.

Parry, Kenneth. *Christian Hymns*. London: SCM Press, 1956.

Payne, Ernest A. "The Theology of Isaac Watts as Illustrated in His Hymns," *Bulletin of the Hymn Society of Great Britain and Ireland* 45 (October 1948): 49-58.

Pirner, Reuben G. "The Nature and Function of the Hymn in Christian Worship," *Church Music* 66, 1: 1-5.

Rattenbury, John E. *The Evangelical Doctrines of Charles Wesley's Hymns*. London: The Epworth Press, 1941-42.

Routley, Erik R. *Church Music and Theology*. Philadelphia: Muhlenberg Press, 1959.

————. *Hymns and the Faith*. Greenwich, CT: The Seabury Press, 1954.

————. *Hymns Today and Tomorrow*. New York: Abingdon Press, 1964.

_____. *Church Music and the Christian Faith*. Carol Stream, IL: Agape, 1978.

Schilling, S. Paul. *The Faith We Sing*. Philadelphia: Westminster Press, 1983.

_____. "God and Nature in Hymnody," *The Hymn* 42, 1 (January 1991): 24-28.

Spencer, Jon Michael. *Theological Music: Introduction to Theomusicology*. New York: Greenwood Press, 1991.

Stählin, Wilhelm. "The Church Hymn and Theology," *Reponse* 1 (Pentecost, 1959): 22-30.

Thomas, Nancy White. "Hymns Draw Out and Point Up Meaning," *The Hymn* 13, 1 (January 1962): 24-27.

Troeger, Thomas H. "Personal, Cultural, and Theological Influences on the Language of Hymns and Worship," *The Hymn* 88, 4 (October 1987): 7-16.

_____. "Theological Considerations for Poetic Texts Used by the Assembly," *Worship* 59, 5 (September 1985): 404-413.

EARLY CHURCH AND PRE-REFORMATION TRADITIONS

Apel, Willi. *Gregorian Chant*. Bloomington: Indiana University Press, 1958.

Binder, A. W. *Biblical Chant*. New York: Philosophical Library, 1959.

Bullough, John F. "Notker Balbulus and the Origin of the Sequence," *The Hymn* 16, 1 (January 1965): 13-16, 24.

The Catholic Encyclopedia, 1913 ed. S.v. "Hymnody and Hymnology" by Clemens Blume.

Crocker, Richard and David Hiley. *The Early Middle Ages to 1300*. Vol. 2, *The New Oxford History of Music*, 2nd ed. Oxford and New York: Oxford University Press, 1990.

Cumming, Charles G. *The Assyrian and Hebrew Hymns of Praise*. New York: Columbia University Press, 1934.

Encyclopedia of Religion and Ethics. S.v. "Hymns (Greek Christian)," by A. Baumstark.

Ferguson, John. "Hymns in the Early Church," *Bulletin of the Hymn Society of Great Britain and Ireland* 180 (July 1989): 114-123.

Higginson, J. Vincent. "A Thirteenth Century Anniversary" (The Contributions of Saint Thomas Aquinas and Saint Bonaventure to Hymnody), *The Hymn* 26, 3 (July 1975): 80-84.

Hoppin, Richard H. *Medieval Music*. New York: W. W. Norton, 1978.

The Interpreters Dictionary of the Bible, 1962 ed. S.v. "Music" by Eric Werner.

Johansen, John H. "Hymnody in the Early Church," *The Hymn* 25, 2 (April 1974): 45-53.

_____. "Te Deum Laudamus," *Journal of Church Music* 10 (April 1968): 2-3, 32.

Jones, Douglas. "The Background and Character of the Lukan Psalms," *Journal of Theological Studies*. N.S. 19 (April 1968): 19-50.

Julian, John. *A Dictionary of Hymnology* 2 vols. New York: Dover Publications, 1985. Reprint of the Second Revised Edition, 1907. Articles on "Greek Hymnody," "Latin Hymnody," "Sequence," "Carols."

Lamb, J. A. *The Psalms in Christian Worship*. London: Faith Press, 1962.

Lituack, Leon B. "The Greek Hymn Translations and Adaptations of N.F.S. Grundvig and J. M. Neale," *Bulletin of the Hymn Society of Great Britain and Ireland* 183 (April 1990): 182-187.

Massey, Bernard S. "O Quanta Qualia," *Bulletin of the Hymn Society of Great Britain and Ireland* 185 (October 1990): 230-231.

Messenger, Ruth E. *The Medieval Latin Hymn*. Washington: Capital Press, 1953.

_____. "Rabanus Maurus," *The Hymn* 16, 2 (April 1965): 44-48.

_____. "Vernacular Hymnody of the Late Middle Ages," *The Hymn* 16, 3 (July 1965): 80-86.

Moule, C. F. D. *Worship in the New Testament*. Richmond: John Knox Press, 1961.

Neale, John Mason. *Collected Hymns, Sequences, and Carols*. London: Hodder and Stoughton, 1914.

Pierik, Marie. *The Song of the Church*. New York: Longmans, Green and Co., 1947.

Pocknee, C. E. "Gloria in Excelsis," *Bulletin of the Hymn Society of Great Britain and Ireland* 6 (April 1965): 14-16.

————."Three Latin Hymns: Te Deum Laudamus, Gloria Laus et Honor, Veni Creator Spiritus," *Bulletin of the Hymn Society of Great Britain and Ireland* 6 (Spring 1970): 61-65.

————. "Veni, Veni, Emmanuel," *Bulletin of the Hymn Society of Great Britain and Ireland* 7 (Spring 1970): 65-69.

Prothero, R. E. *The Psalms in Human Life.* London: John Murray, 1904.

Raby, F. J. E. *A History of Christian-Latin Poetry from the Beginnings to the Close of the Middle Ages.* Second ed. London: Oxford University Press, 1953.

Routley, Erik. *The Church and Music.* London: Duckworth and Co., Ltd., 1950.

Sanders, J. T. *The New Testament Christological Hymns; Their Historical Religious Background.* Cambridge, England: Cambridge University Press, 1971.

Shepherd, Massey H., Jr. *The Psalms in Christian Worship.* Minneapolis: Augsburg Publishing House, 1976.

Wellesz, Egon. *A History of Byzantine Music and Hymnography.* Second ed. Oxford: Clarendon Press, 1961.

————. *Ancient and Oriental Music.* Vol. 1, *The New Oxford History of Music.* London: Oxford University Press, 1957.

Werner, Eric. *The Sacred Bridge.* New York: Columbia University Press, 1959; London: Dennis Dobson, 1960.

REFORMATION TRADITIONS
The Chorale

Arndal, Steffen. "Awakening and Singing in German Pietism and Moravianism," *The Hymn* 36, 3 (July 1985): 11-15.

Blankenburg, Walter. "The Music of the Bohemian Brethren" in *Protestant Church Music: A History* by Friedrich Blume. New York: W. W. Norton & Co., 1974, 591-607.

Blume, Friedrich. "The Age of Confession-alism," in *Protestant Church Music: A History.* New York: W. W. Norton Co., 1974, 125-315.

————. "The Period of the Reformation: (rev. by Ludwig Finscher), in *Protestant Church Music: A History,* 1-123. New York: W. W. Norton & Co., 1974.

Buszin, Walter E. "Johann Crüger: On the Tercentenary of His Death," *Response in Worship - Music - The Arts* 4 (1962): 89-97.

————. "Luther on Music," *Musical Quarterly* 32 (January 1946): 8-97.

Cantate Domino. New Edition. [4th ed.] Kassel, Germany: Published by Bärenreiter Verlag for the World Council of Churches, 1974.

Ellingsen, Svein. "An Interview with Svein Ellingsen," *The Hymn* 37, 2 (April 1986): 7-13.

Erikson, J. Irving. *Twice-Born Hymns,* Chicago: Covenant Press, 1976.

Feder, Georg. "Decline and Restoration," in *Protestant Church Music: A History* by Friedrich Blume. New York: W. W. Norton & Co., 1974, 317-404.

Frostenson, Anders (ed.) and Fred Kaan (tr.). *Songs and Hymns from Sweden.* London: Stainer & Bell, Ltd., 1976.

Gennrich, F., ed. *Troubadours, Trouveres, Minne and Meistersinger.* v. 2 of *Anthology of Music,* ed. K. G. Fellerer. Cologne, Germany: Arno Volk Verlag, 1960.

Giesler, John H. "Bicentennial of Gregor's Hymnal 1778," *The Hymn* 29, 4 (October 1978): 211-13.

————. "Musical Ministers of the Moravian Church," *The Hymn* 29, 1 (January 1978): 6-14, 28.

Hewitt, Theodore Brown. *Paul Gerhardt as a Hymn Writer and His Influence on English Hymnody.* New Haven: Yale University Press, 1918; Reprint ed. with a new afterword and updated bibliography, St. Louis: Concordia Publishing House, 1976.

Jenny, Markus. "The Hymns of Zwingli and Luther: A Comparison," In *Cantors at the Crossroads,* ed. Johannes Riedel. St.

Louis: Concordia Publishing House, 1966, 45-63.

Leupold, Ulrich S., ed. *Liturgy and Hymns.* Vol. 53 of *Luther's Works.* Philadelphia: Fortress Press, 1964.

Liemohn, Edwin. *The Chorale Through Four Hundred Years of Musical Development as a Congregational Hymn.* Philadelphia: Muhlenberg Press, 1953.

Moore, Sydney H. *Sursum Corda, Being Studies of Some German Hymn Writers.* London: Independent Press, 1956.

Petri, Theodoricus. *Piae Cantiones* (1582). Facsimile. Documenta Musicae Fennicae X. Helsinki: Edition Fazer, 1967.

Riedel, Johannes. *The Lutheran Chorale, Its Basic Traditions.* Minneapolis: Augsburg Publishing House, 1967.

Schousboe, Torben. "Protestant Church Music in Scandinavia," in *Protestant Church Music: A History* by Friedrich Blume. New York: W. W. Norton & Co., 1974, 609-636.

Selander, Inger. "Swedish Hymns from Lina Sandell to Britt G. Hallqvist," *The Hymn* 45, 1 (January 1994): 21-29.

Smith, C. Howard. *Scandinavian Hymnody from the Reformation to the Present.* Metuchen, NJ and London: American Theological Library Association and Scarecrow Press, 1987.

Teuscher, Gerhard. "A Devout Heart and Spirit: Johann Heermann (1585-1647)," *The Hymn* 37, 4 (October 1986): 16-20.

_____. "In Memorium Martin Rinkhart (1586-1649): A Poet's Song of Praise Lives On," *The Hymn* 39, 3 (July 1988): 11-13.

_____. "Joachin Neander: A Seventeeth-Century Hymnwriter Who Made a Name for Himself in Anthropological Research," *The Hymn* 44, 3 (July 1993): 33-40.

Werner, Matthias. "Zinzendorf's Hymns in the Context of His Voyage to North America," *The Hymn* 36, 3 (July 1985): 15-17.

Metrical Psalmody

Bible Songs. Due West, SC: Executive Board, Associate Reformed Presbyterian Church, 1930, 7th ed., 1975.

Blankenburg, Walter. "Church Music in Reformed Europe," in *Protestant Church Music: A History* by Frederick Blume. New York: W. W. Norton & Company, 1974, 509-590.

The Book of Psalms for Singing. Pittsburgh: Board of Education and Publication, Reformed Presbyterian Church of North America, 1973; 2nd ed., 1975.

Brink, Emily. "Metrical Psalmody in North America: A Story of Survival and Revival," *The Hymn* 44, 4 (October 1993): 20-24.

Frost, Maurice. *English and Scottish Psalm and Hymn Tunes* c. 1543-1677. London: SPCK; London, New York: Oxford University Press, 1953.

Haraszti, Zoltan, ed. *The Bay Psalm Book. A Facsimile Reprint of the First Edition of 1640.* Chicago: University of Chicago Press, n.d. [1956].

Hohmann, Walter. "The Greiter Melody and Variants," *The Hymn* 12, 2 (April 1961): 47-51.

Lowens, Irving. "The Bay Psalm Book in 17th Century New England," in *Music and Musicians in Early America.* New York: W. W. Norton, 1964, 25-38.

Mullinax, Allen B. "Musical Diversity in Reformation Strasbourg: Martin Bucer's Strasbourg Song Book," *The Hymn* 45, 1 (January 1994): 9-13.

Patrick, Millar. *Four Centuries of Scottish Psalmody.* London: Oxford University Press, 1949.

Pidoux, Pierre. *Le Psautier Huguenot du XVIe Siecle.* 2 vols. Basel: Edition Bärenreiter, 1962.

Pratt, Waldo S. *The Music of the Pilgrims.* Boston: Oliver Ditson Co., 1921. Reprint edition. New York: AMS Press, 1966.

_____. *The Music of the French Psalter of 1562.* New York: Columbia University Press, 1939; Reprint ed., New York: AMS Press, 1966.

Psalter Hymnal. Grand Rapids, MI: CRC Publications, 1987, 1988.

The Scottish Psalter. London: Oxford University Press, 1929.

Terry, Richard, ed. *Calvin's First Psalter (1539)*. London: Ernest Benn, 1932.

BRITISH TRADITIONS

Adey, Lionel. *Class and Idol in the English Hymn*. Vancouver: University of British Columbia Press, 1988.

Anglican Hymn Book. London: Church Book Room, Ltd., 1965.

Baker, Frank and George W. Williams. *John Wesley's First Hymnbook: A Collection of Psalms and Hymns*. Charleston: Dalcho Historical Society, 1964.

Baker, Frank, ed. *Representative Verse of Charles Wesley*. London: The Epworth Press, 1962. New York: Abingdon Press, 1962.

Bishop, Selma L. *Issac Watts, Hymns and Spiritual Songs*. A Study in Early Eighteenth Century Language Changes. London: The Faith Press, 1962.

Brant, Cyr de. "Chope's Christmas Carols," *The Hymn* 23, 4 (October 1972): 105-110.

Braley, Bernard. *Hymnwriters 1, 2, 3*. London: Stainer and Bell, 1987, 1989, 1990.

Brunton, Grace. "Horatius Bonar, Minister and Hymnist, 1808-1889," *The Hymn* 9, 4 (October 1958): 101-105, 125.

_____. "John Ellerton, 1826-93" *The Hymn* 12, 4 (October 1961): 101-106, 112.

_____. "Reginald Heber, Bishop of Calcutta," *The Hymn* 11, 2 (April 1960): 37-44.

Bunn, Leslie H. "Richard Baxter Speaks to Our Time," *The Hymn* 9, 3 (July 1958): 79, 82.

_____. "Hymns Ancient and Modern," *The Hymn* 12, 1 (January 1961): 5-12.

_____. "Why Julian Needs Revision," (a review of British hymnic trends in the first half of the 20th century). *The Hymn* 7, 1 (January 1956): 5-8, 17.

Cairns, William T. "Richard Baxter, Hymn Writer," *Bulletin of the Hymn Society of Great Britain and Ireland* 24 (July 1943): 1-6.

Carter, Sydney. *Songs of Sidney Carter in the Present Tense*. London: Galliard, Ltd., 1969.

Clarke, William Kemp Lowther. *A Hundred Years of Hymns Ancient and Modern*. London: William Clowes and Sons, Ltd., 1960.

Cohn, Wayne H. "Ralph Vaughan Williams and Hymnody," *The Hymn* 19, 3 (July 1968): 81-85.

Crocker, Richard and Hiley, David, eds. *Early Medieval Music up to 1300. New Oxford History of Music*, Vol. II. London: Oxford University Press, 1990.

Davis, Arthur P. *Isaac Watts*. London: Independent Press, 1943.

Dearmer, Percy, ed. *The English Hymnal with Tunes*. New ed. London: Oxford University Press, 1933.

_____. *Songs of Praise*. Enlarged ed. London: Oxford University Press, 1931.

_____. *Songs of Praise Discussed*. London: Oxford University Press, 1933.

Dearmer, Percy, Ralph Vaughan Williams and Martin Shaw. *The Oxford Book of Carols*. London: The Oxford University Press, 1964.

Dunstan, Alan. "Robert Bridge's Contribution to English Hymnody," *The Hymn Society of Great Britain and Ireland Bulletin* 9, 11 No. 151 (April 1981): 205-212.

England, Martha Winburn and John Sparrow. *Hymns Unbidden*. New York: New York Public Library, 1966.

English Praise. London: Oxford University Press, 1975.

Escott, Harry. "The Influence of Richard Baxter on English Hymnody," *The Hymn* 3, 4 (October 1952): 105-109, 118.

_____. *Isaac Watts, Hymnographer: A Study of Beginnings, Development and Philosophy of the English Hymn*. London: Independent Press, Lt., 1962.

Eskew, Harry. "Cyril V. Taylor: Composer of 'ABBOT'S LEIGH'," *Journal of Church*

Music 30, 1 (Jan. 1988), 4-9.

_____. "Fred Pratt Green: Retirement Hymnist," *Journal of Church Music* 29, 1 (Jan. 1987), 9-12.

_____. "John Wilson: Encourager of Fine Hymnody," *Journal of Church Music* 29, 6 (June 1987), 7-11.

Flanigan, Alexander. "Cecil Frances Alexander," *The Hymn* 5, 2 (April 1954): 37-42, 59.

_____. "Thomas Kelly, 1769-1855," *The Hymn* 6, 2 (April 1955): 59-64.

Flew, Newton, *The Hymns of Charles Wesley: A Study of Their Structure.* London: The Epworth Press, 1953.

Fountain, David. *Isaac Watts Remembered.* Worthing: Henry E. Walter, Ltd., 1974.

Fox, Adam. *English Hymns and Hymn Writers.* London: William Collins Sons and Co., Ltd., 1947.

Frost, Maurice. "The Tunes Associated with Hymn Singing in the Lifetime of the Wesleys," *Bulletin of the Hymn Society of Great Britain and Ireland* 4 (Winter 1957/8): 118-126.

_____. *English and Scottish Psalm and Hymn Tunes c. 1543-1677.* New York: Oxford University Press, 1953.

_____, ed. *Historical Companion to Hymns Ancient and Modern.* London: William Clowes and Sons, Ltd., 1962.

Goldhawk, Norman. "Hymns for the Use of the People Called Methodists, 1780," *The Hymn Society of Great Britain and Ireland Bulletin* 9, 9 No. 149 (September 1980): 170-175.

Herbert, George. *The Temple. Sacred Poems and Private Ejaculations.* London: n.p., 1667.

Higginson, J. Vincent. "English Carols - Survival and Revival," *The Hymn* 23, 4 (October 1972): 101-105.

_____. "William Henry Havergal, 1793-1870," *The Hymn* 20, 1 (January 1969): 9-16, 21.

_____. "Daniel Sedgwick: Pioneer of English Hymnology," *The Hymn* 4, 3 (July 1953): 77-80.

_____. "Richard Redhead: Organist and Composer, 1820-1901," *The Hymn* 21, 2 (April 1970): 37-42.

_____. "Edward Perronet," *The Hymn* 18, 4 (October 1967): 105-113.

_____. "John Keble and Hymnody," *The Hymn* 17, 3 (July 1966): 85-90.

_____. "John Mason Neale and 19th Century Hymnody, His Work and Influence," *The Hymn* 16, 4 (October 1965): 100-127.

_____. "Sir George J. Elvey, 1816-1893," *The Hymn* 18, 1 (January 1967): 5-10.

Hodges, H. A. "Williams Pantycelyn," *Bulletin of the Hymn Society of Great Britain and Ireland* 8 (February 1976): 145-152; 8 (June 1976): 161-166.

Holbrook, Arthur S. "American Associations of James Montgomery," *The Hymn* 5, 3 (July 1954): 73-78.

Horder, Garrett. *The Hymn Lover. An Account of the Rise and Growth of English Hymnody.* 3d ed., Rev. London: J. Curwen, and Sons, Ltd., 1889.

Horder, Mervyn. "George Ratcliffe Woodward," *The Hymn Society of Great Britain and Ireland Bulletin* 11, 3 No. 164 (July 1985): 50-53.

Hull, Kenneth. "New Sounds from Iona: A Review of the Wild Goose Song Books," *The Hymn* 43, 2 (April 1992): 22-30.

Hymns and Songs. London: Methodist Publishing House, 1969.

Hymns Ancient and Modern Revised. London: William Clowes and Sons, Ltd., 1950.

Jefferson, H. A. L. *Hymns in Christian Worship.* London: Rockliff, 1950.

Johansen, John H. "The Christian Psalmist," *The Hymn* 22, 2 (April 1971): 51-53.

_____. "Frances Ridley Havergal, 1836-1879: Poetess of Consecration," *The Hymn* 7, 2 (April 1956): 41-48.

_____. "John Cennick, 1718-1755 Moravian Evangelist and Hymn Writer," *The Hymn* 6, 3 (July 1955): 87-97.

Kaan, Fred. "Saturday Night and Sunday Morning," *The Hymn* 27, 4 (October 1970): 100-108.

Knight, George Litch. "Philip Doddridge's

Hymns," *The Hymn* 2, 3 (October 1951): 100-108.

_____. "William Cowper as a Hymn Writer," *The Hymn* 1, 4 (October 1950): 5-12, 20.

Leaver, Robin A. *Catherine Winkworth: The Influence of Her Translations on English Hymnody.* St. Louis: Concordia Publishing House, 1978.

_____. *'Goostly Psalmes and Spirituall Songes.'* Oxford: Clarendon Press, 1991.

Leaver, Robin A., James H. Litton, and Carlton R. Young, eds. *Duty and Delight: Routley Remembered.* Carol Stream, IL: Hope Publishing Company and Norwich, England: Canterbury Press, 1985.

Lock, William. "Six Hymns from Olney," *Journal of Church Music* 17 (November 1975): 8-10.

Luff, Alan. *Welsh Hymns and Their Tunes.* Carol Stream: Hope Publishing Company, 1990.

_____. "John Newton and Olney Hymns," *Journal of Church Music* 4, 9 (October 1962): 2-5.

Lough, A. B. *The Influence of John Mason Neale.* London: S.P.C.K., 1962.

Martin, Hugh. *Puritanism and Richard Baxter.* London: SCM Press, Ltd., 1954.

_____. *They Wrote Our Hymns.* London: SCM Press, 1961. Napierville, IL: Alec R. Allenson, Inc., 1961.

Massey, Bernard S. "The Hymn Tunes of Elgar and Holst," *The Hymn Society of Great Britain and Ireland Bulletin* 10, 8 No. 160 (May 1984): 185-188.

Messenger, Ruth E. "John Mason Neale, Translator," *The Hymn* 2, 3 (October 1951): 5-10, 24.

Micklem, Caryl. "Pilgrim Praise-A Review," *Bulletin of the Hymn Society of Great Britain and Ireland* 7 (January 1973): 235-238.

New Church Praise. Edinburgh: Saint Andrews Press, 1975.

Nuttall, Geoffrey F., ed. *Philip Doddridge 1702-51: His Contribution to English Religion.* London: Independent Press, 1951.

100 Hymns for Today. London: William Clowes and Sons, Ltd., 1969.

Parks, Edna. *The Hymns and Hymn Tunes Found in the English Metrical Psalters.* New York: Coleman-Ross Company, 1966.

_____. *Early English Hymns: An Index.* Metuchen, NJ: Scarecrow Press, 1972.

Pfatteicher, Helen E. "The Hymn Tunes of Mendelssohn," *The Hymn* 11, 4 (October 1960): 110-113.

Phillips, C. S. *Hymnody Past and Present.* New York: The Macmillan Company, 1937.

Pocknee, Cyril E. *The French Diocesan Hymns and Their Melodies.* New York: Morehouse-Gorham Co., Inc., 1954.

Praise for Today. London: Psalms and Hymns Trust, 1974.

Praise for the Lord. London: Geoffrey Chapman Publishers, 1972. Reprinted, 1973.

Purcell, William. *Onward Christian Soldier: A Life of Sabine Baring-Gould, Parson, Squire, Novelist, Antiquary, 1834-1924.* New York: Longmans, Green and Co., Inc., 1957.

Rattenbury, John E. *The Eucharistic Hymns of John and Charles Wesley.* The Epworth Press, 1948.

_____. *Wesley's Legacy to the World.* London: The Epworth Press, 1928.

Reilly, Joseph J. "The Hymns of John Henry Newman," *The Hymn* 2, 1 (January 1951): 5-10, 20.

Rogal, Samuel J. "John Bunyan and Congregational Song," *The Hymn* 28, 3 (July 1977): 118-125.

Ronander, Albert C. "Christmas Carols New and Old," *The Hymn* 21, 4 (October 1970): 103-110, 122.

Routley, Erik. "The Hymnody of Congregationalism," *The Hymn* 8, 1 (January 1957): 5-14.

_____. "Hymn Writers of the New English Renaissance," *The Hymn* 28, 1 (January 1977): 6-10.

_____. *I'll Praise My Maker.* London: Independent Press, Ltd., 1951.

_____. *The English Carol.* London: Barrie and Jenkins, 1958; New York: Oxford University Press, 1959.

_____. "James Montgomery in the

Church of Today," *Bulletin of the Hymn Society of Great Britain and Ireland* 7 (Spring 1971): 129-132.

_____. *A Short History of English Church Music.* London: Mowbray's, 1977.

_____. *The Musical Wesleys.* London: Herbert Jenkins, 1968; New York: Oxford University Press, 1968.

_____. "Percy Dearmer: 20th Century Hymnologist," *The Hymn* 19, 3 (July 1968): 74-80.

Sharpe, Eric. "Developments in English Hymnody in the Eighties," *The Hymn* 42, 2 (April 1991): 7-11.

_____. "1970-1980: The Explosive Years for Hymnody in Britain," *The Hymn Society of Great Britain and Ireland Bulletin* 10, 1 No. 153 (January 1982): 9-20.

Skrine, Peter. *Susanna and Catherine Winkworth: Clifton Manchester and the German Collection.* Croyden: University of Bristol Press, 1991.

Smith, S. E. Boyd. "The Effective Countess: Lady Huntingdon and the 1780 Edition of 'A Select Collection of Hymns,' " *The Hymn* 44, 3 (July 1993): 26-32.

Telford, John. *The Methodist Hymn-book Illustrated in History and Experience,* 7th ed. London: The Epworth Press, 1959.

Temperly, Nicholas. "The Anglican Communion Hymn," A Series of Four Articles. *The Hymn* 30 (January 1979): 7-15; (April 1979): 93-101, 105; (July 1979): 178-186; (October 1979): 243-251.

Turner, Maxine. "Joseph Addison's Five Hymns," *The Hymn* 23, 2 (April 1972): 40-41.

Wesley, John. *A Collection of Psalms and Hymns.* Charlestown: Lewis Timothy, 1737; facsimile ed. Nashville: United Methodist Publishing House, 1988.

Westermeyer, Paul. "The Hymnal Noted: Theological and Musical Intersection," *Church Music,* 73:2 [1973]: 1-9.

Williamson, Malcolm. *12 New Hymn Tunes.* London: Joseph Weinberger, Ltd., 1962.

_____. *16 Hymns and Processionals.* Carol Stream: Agape, 1975.

Wilson, John. "Handel's Tunes for Charles Wesley's Hymns," *The Hymn Society of Great Britain and Ireland Bulletin* 11, 2 No. 163 (May 1985): 32-37.

Woodward, G. R., ed. *Songs of Syon.* London: Schott and Co., 1923.

Young, Carlton R. "John Wesley's 1737 Charleston Collection of Psalms and Hymns," *The Hymn* 41, 4 (October 1990): 19-27.

Young, Robert H. "The History of Baptist Hymnody in England from 1612 to 1800," D.M.A. diss., University of Southern California, 1959.

AMERICAN TRADITIONS

Alexander, Helen C. and J. Kennedy Maclean. *Charles M. Alexander.* London: Marshall Brothers Ltd., 1920.

Allen, William Allen, Charles P. Ware, and Lucy McKim Garrison, eds. *Slave Songs of the United States.* New York, 1867. Reprint: New York: Peter Smith, 1951. Rev. ed., New York: Oak Publications, 1965.

American Hymns Old and New. 2 vols. Albert Christ-Janer, Charles W. Hughes, and Carlton Sprague Smith. *Notes on the Hymns and Biographies of the Authors and Composers* by Charles W. Hughes. New York: Columbia University Press, 1980.

Appel, Richard G. *The Music of the Bay Psalm Book 9th Edition (1698).* New York: Institute for Studies in American Music Monographs Number 5, 1975.

_____. "Philip Schaff, Pioneer American Hymnologist," *The Hymn* 14, 1 (January 1963): 5-7.

Batastini, Robert J., Donald P. Hustad, Austin C. Lovelace, and Cyril V. Taylor. "The CEH List: Four Diverse Appraisals," *The Hymn* 29, 2 (April 1978): 83-90.

Battles, Ford Lewis, and Morgan Simmons. "The Consultation on Ecumenical Hymnody," *The Hymn* 28, 2 (April 1977): 67-68, 87.

Beary, Shirley. "Stylistic Traits of Southern Shape-Note Gospel Songs," *The Hymn*

30, 1 (January 1979): 26-33, 35.

Britton, Allen Perdue, Irving Lowens, and Richard Crawford, *American Sacred Music Imprints 1698-1810: A Bibliography.*" Worcester, MA: American Antiquarian Society, 1990.

Buchanan, Anabel Morris, ed. *Folk Hymns of America.* New York: J. Fischer and Brother, 1938.

Chase, Gilbert. *America's Music: From the Pilgrims to the Present.* Rev. 2nd ed., New York: McGraw-Hill, 1966; Rev. 3rd ed., Chicago and Urbana: University of Illinois Press, 1987.

Clark, Linda. "God of Grace and God of Glory: A Very Urgent Personal Prayer," *The Hymn* 29, 4 (October 1978): 206-210, 213.

Cobb, Buell E., Jr. *The Sacred Harp: A Tradition and Its Music.* Athens: University of Georgia Press, 1978, 1989.

Crawford, Richard A. *The Core Repertory of Early American Psalmody* (Vols. 11 and 12 of *Recent Researches in American Music*). Madison: A-R Editions, 1984.

Cross, Virginia Ann. "The Development of Sunday School Hymnody in the United States of America, 1816-1869." D.M.A. diss., New Orleans Baptist Theological Seminary, 1985.

Davisson, Ananias. *Kentucky Harmony.* Harrisonburg, VA, 1816. Reprint with a new introduction by Irving Lowens. Minneapolis: Augsburg Press, 1976.

Downey, James Cecil. "The Music of American Revivalism." Ph.D. diss., Tulane University, 1969.

Ellinwood, Leonard. *The History of American Church Music.* New York: Morehouse-Gorham Co., 1968; Rev. Ed. Da Capo Press, 1970.

————. *To Praise God: The Life and Work of Charles Winfred Douglas.* Papers of The Hymn Society of America, XXIII, 1958.

Epstein, Dena J. *Sinful Tunes and Spirituals.* Urbana: University of Illinois Press, 1977.

Eskew, Harry. "Shape-Note Hymnody in the Shenandoah Valley, 1816-1860." Ph.D. diss., Tulane University, 1966.

————. "Southern Harmony and Its Era," *The Hymn* 41, 4 (October 1990): 28-34.

Fleming, Jo Lee. "James D. Vaughan, Music Publisher, Lawrenceburg, Tennessee, 1912-1964." S.M.D., diss., Union Theological Seminary, 1972.

Foote, Henry Wilder. *Recent American Hymnody.* Papers of the Hymn Society of America, XVII, 1952.

————. *Three Centuries of American Hymnody.* Cambridge, MA: Harvard University Press, 1940. Reprint ed. Hamden, CT: The Shoe String Press, 1961.

Hall, Jacob Henry. *Biography of Gospel Song and Hymn Writers.* New York: Fleming H. Revell Co., 1914. Reprint ed. New York: AMS Press, 1971.

Hammond, Paul. "The Hymnody of the Second Great Awakening," *The Hymn* 29, 1 (January 1978): 19-28.

Harris, Michael W. *The Rise of the Gospel Blues: The Music of Thomas Andrew Dorsey in the Urban Church.* New York: Oxford University Press, 1992.

Hatchett, Marion J. "Benjamin Shaw and Charles H. Spilman's *Columbian Harmony, or, Pilgrim's Musical Comparisons,*" *The Hymn* 42, 1 (January 1991): 20-23.

Higginson, J. Vincent. *Hymnody in the American Indian Missions.* Papers of The Hymn Society of America, XVIII, 1954.

Hill, Richard S. "Not So Far Away in a Manger. Forty-one Settings of an American Carol." *Notes* 2nd ser. 3 (December 1945): 12-36.

Hitchcock, H. Wiley. *Music in the United States: A Historical Introduction.* 3rd ed. Englewood Cliffs, NJ: Prentice-Hall, Inc., 1988.

Holden, Edith and George Litch Knight. "Brick Church's Role in American Hymnody." *The Hymn* 3 (July 1952): 73-78.

Horn, Dorothy D. *Sing to Me of Heaven: A Study of Folk and Early American Materials in Three Old Harp Books.* Gainesville: University of Florida Press, 1970.

Hulan, Richard Huffman. "Camp Meeting Spiritual Folksongs: Legacy of the 'Great Revival in the West.' " Ph.D. diss., University of Texas at Austin, 1978.

Hustad, Donald P. "The Explosion of Popular Hymnody," *The Hymn* 33, 3 (July 1982): 159-167.

"Hymns and Tunes Recommended for Ecumencial Use," *The Hymn* 28, 4 (October 1977): 192-209.

Jackson, George Pullen. *Another Sheaf of White Spirituals*. Gainesville: University of Florida Press, 1952.

————. *Down East Spirituals and Others*. 2nd ed. Locust Valley, N.Y.: J. J. Augustin, 1953; Da Capo Press, 1975.

————. *Spiritual Folk-Songs of Early America: Two Hundred and Fifty Tunes and Texts*. New York: J. J. Augustin, 1937. Reprint. New York: Dover Publications, 1975.

————. *White and Negro Spirituals*. New York: J. J. Augustin, 1943. Reprint ed. New York: J. J. Augustin, 1975.

————. *White Spirituals in the Southern Uplands*. Chapel Hill: University of North Carolina Press, 1933. Reprint eds. Hatboro, PA: Folklore Associates, 1964. New York: Dover Publications, 1965.

Johnson, Charles A. *The Frontier Camp Meeting: Religion's Harvest Time*. Dallas: Southern Methodist University Press, 1955.

Loftis, Deborah Carlton. "Big Singing Day in Benton, Kentucky: A Study of the History, Ethnic Identity, and Musical Style of *Southern Harmony* Singing." Ph.D. diss., University of Kentucky and University of Louisville, 1987.

————. "The Hymns of Georgia Harkness," *The Hymn* 28, 4 (October 1977): 186-191.

Lorenz, Ellen Jane. *Glory Hallelujah! The Story of the Campmeeting Spiritual*. Nashville: Abingdon, 1980.

McCurry, John G. *The Social Harp*. Hart County, GA (printed at Philadelphia, PA), 1855. Reprint edited by Daniel W.

Patterson and John F. Garst. Athens: University of Georgia Press, 1973.

McCutchan, Helen Cowles. *Born to Music. The Ministry of Robert Guy McCutchan*. Papers of the The Hymn Society of America, XXVIII, 1972.

McKay, David P. and Crawford, Richard. *William Billings of Boston*. Princeton: Princeton University Press, 1975.

McLoughlin, William G. *Billy Sunday Was His Real Name*. Chicago: University of Chicago Press, 1955.

————. *Modern Revivalism*. New York: The Roland Press Co., 1959.

Marrocco, W. Thomas and Gleason, Harold, eds. *Music in America: An Anthology from the Landing of the Pilgrims to the Close of the Civil War 1620-1865*. New York: W. W. Norton & Co., 1964.

Mason, Henry Lowell. *Hymn Tunes of Lowell Mason. A Bibliography*. Cambridge, MA: Harvard University Press, 1944.

Metcalf, Frank J. *American Writers and Compilers of Sacred Music*. Cincinnati: Abingdon Press, 1928. Reprint, 1967, Russell & Russell.

Music, David W. "William Caldwell's *Union Harmony* (1837): The First East Tennessee Tunebook," *The Hymn* 38, 3 (July 1987): 16-22.

Noyes, Morgan P. *Louis F. Benson, Hymnologist*. Papers of The Hymn Society of America, XIX, 1955.

Osborne, Stanley L. "Recent Canadian Hymnody," *The Hymn* 29, 4 (July 1978): 134-140.

Owen, Barbara. "The Bay Psalm Book and Its Era," *The Hymn* 41, 4 (October 1990): 12-19.

Pemberton, Carol A. "Praising God through Congregational Song: Lowell Mason's Contributions to Church Music," *The Hymn* 44, 2 (April 1992): 22-30.

Porter, Ellen Jane. *Two Early American Tunes: Fraternal Twins?* Papers of The Hymn Society of America, XXX, 1975.

————. "William B. Bradbury, the Campmeeting Spiritual, and the Gospel Song,"

The Hymn 34, 1 (January 1983): 34-40.

Porter, Thomas Henry. "Homer Alvan Rodeheaver (1880-1955): Evangelistic Musician and Publisher." Ed.D diss., New Orleans Baptist Theological Seminary, 1981.

Reid, William W. *Sing with Spirit and Understanding, the Story of The Hymn Society of America*. New York: Hymn Society of America, 1962.

_____. *Sing with Spirit and Understanding: The Story of The Hymn Society of America 1962-1972*. New York: The Hymn Society of America, 1972.

Reynolds, William J. "The Hymnal 1940 and Its Era," *The Hymn* 41, 4 (October 1990): 34-39.

Rodeheaver, Homer. *Twenty Years with Billy Sunday*. Winona Lake, IN: Rodeheaver Hall-Mack, 1936.

Rothenbusch, Esther Heidi. "The Role of *Gospel Hymns Nos. 1 to 6* (1875-1894) in American Revivalism." Ph.D. diss., The University of Michigan, 1991.

Ruffin, Bernard. *Fanny Crosby*. Philadelphia: United Church Press, 1976.

Sankey, Ira D., *et al. Gospel Hymns Nos. 1-6 Complete*. New York and Chicago, 1894. Reprint ed. New York: Da Capo Press, 1972.

_____. *My Life and the Story of the Gospel Hymns and of Sacred Songs and Solos*, with an introduction by Theodore L. Cuyler. Philadelphia: The Sunday School Times Co., 1907.

Scholes, Percy A. *The Puritans and Music in England and New England*. London: Oxford University Press, 1934.

Schulz-Widmar, Russell. "American Hymnody: A View of the Current Scene," *The Hymn* 33, 3 (July 1982): 134-158.

Smith, Timothy A. "Composer Attribution in Five Primary Tunebook Sources from the Antebellum South," *The Hymn* 40, 3 (July 1989): 9-11.

Stansbury, George W. "The Music of the Billy Graham Crusades 1947-1970: An Analysis and Evaluation." D.M.A. diss., South-ern Baptist Theological Seminary, 1971.

Stebbins, George C. *Reminiscences and Gospel Hymn Stories*. With an introduction by Charles H. Gabriel. New York: George H. Doran Co., 1924.

Stevenson, Robert. *Protestant Church Music in America*. New York: W. W. Norton & Co., 1966.

Swan, M. L. *The New Harp of Columbia*. Bellefonte, AL., 1867. Reprint of 1919 edition with an introduction by Dorothy D. Horn, Ron Petersen, and Candra Phillips. Knoxville: The University of Tennessee Press, 1978.

Temperly, Nicholas and Charles G. Manns. *Fuging-Tunes in the Eighteenth Century* (Detroit Studies in Music Bibliography No. 49) Detroit: Information Coordinators, 1983.

Tucker, F. Bland. "Reflections of a Hymn Writer," *The Hymn* 30, 2 (April 1979): 115-116.

Tufts, John. *An Introduction to the Singing of Psalm Tunes*. 5th ed. Boston, 1721. Reprint with an introduction by Irving Lowens. Philadelphia: Printed for Musical Americana by Albert Saifer, Publisher, 1954.

Walker, William. *The Southern Harmony*. Rev. Ed. Spartanburg, SC (printed at Philadelphia, PA), 1854. Reprint with an introduction by Glenn C. Wilcox. Lexington: The University Press of Kentucky, 1987.

Walworth, Roger William. *The Life and Hymnological Contributions of Robert Lowry (1826-1899)*. D.M.A. diss., The Southern Baptist Theological Seminary, 1994.

White, B. F. and King, E. J. *The Sacred Harp*. Bremen, GA: Sacred Harp Publishing Co., 1991. (Available from 1010 Waddell Street, Bremen, GA 30110).

_____. *The Sacred Harp*. 3rd ed. Hamilton, GA (printed at Philadelphia, PA). Reprint ed. with "The Story of the Sacred Harp 1844-1944" by George Pullen Jackson and a postscript by William J. Reynolds. Nashville: Broadman Press, 1968.

Wilhoit, Mel R. "American Holiness Hymnody: Some Questions: A Methodology," *Wesleyan Theological Journal* 25, 2 (Fall 1990): 39-63.

_____. "'Sing Me a Sankey': Ira D. Sankey and Congregational Song," *The Hymn* 42, 1 (January 1991): 13-19.

Wilhoit, Melvin Ross. *A Guide to the Principal Authors and Composers of Gospel Song in the Nineteenth Century.* D.M.A. diss., The Southern Baptist Theological Seminary, 1982.

Wyeth, John. *Wyeth's Repository of Sacred Music, Part Second.* 2nd ed. Harrisburg, PA, 1820. Reprint ed. with an introduction by Irving Lowens. New York: Da Capo Press, 1964.

Yoder, Don. *Pennsylvania Spirituals.* Lancaster, PA: Pennsylvania Folk Life Society, 1961.

York, Terry Wayne. "Charles Hutchinson Gabriel (1856-1932): Composer, Authur, and Editor in the Gospel Tradition." D.M.A. diss., New Orleans Baptist Theological Seminary, 1985.

Zellner, John F., III. "Robert Lowry: Early American Hymn Writer," *The Hymn* 26, 4 (October 1975): 117-124; 27, 1 (January 1976): 15-21.

American Denominational Hymnody

Batastini, Robert J. "Repertory in the American Catholic Parish," *The Hymn* 37, 1 (January 1986): 10-13.

Binder, A. W. "History of American Jewish Hymnody," *The Hymn* 14, 4 (October 1963): 101-107; 15 (January 1964): 23-26.

Burrage, Henry S. *Baptist Hymn Writers and Their Hymns.* Portland, ME: Brown, Thurston and Co., 1888.

Brandon, George. "The Hymnody of the Disciples of Christ in the U.S.A.," *The Hymn* 15 (January 1964): 15-22.

Cornwall, J. Spencer. *Stories of Our Mormon Hymns.* Salt Lake City: Deseret Book Co., 1961.

DeLaney, E. Theodore. "Prairie Hymnody - Lutherans: 1820-1970," *The Hymn* 23, 4 (October 1972): 119-124; 24 (January 1973): 23-28.

The Development of Lutheran Hymnody in America. Articles reprinted from *The Encyclopedia of the Lutheran Church,* edited by Julius Bodensieck, for The Lutheran World Federation. Minneapolis: Augsburg Publishing House, 1967.

Drummond, R. Paul. *A Portion for the Singers: A History of Music among Primitive Baptists since 1800.* Atwood, TN: Christian Baptist Library and Publishing Co., 1989.

Durnbaugh, Hedwig T. *The German Hymnody of the Church of the Brethren, 1720-1903.* Philadelphia: The Brethren Encyclopedia, Inc., 1986.

Dyck, Cornelius and Dennis D. Martin, eds. *The Mennonite Encyclopedia.* S.v. "Hymnology of the American Mennonites," by Harold S. Bender.

Eskew, Harry, David W. Music, and Paul A. Richardson, *Singing Baptists: Studies in Baptist Hymnody in America.* Nashville: Church Street Press, 1994.

Foote, Henry W. *Catalogue of American Unitarian Hymn Writers and Hymns.* New York: Compiled by The Hymn Society of America, 1959.

_____. *Catalogue of American Universalist Hymn Writers and Hymns.* New York: Compiled by The Hymn Society of America, 1959.

Graham, Fred Kimball. "With One Heart and One Voice: A Core Repertory of Hymn Tunes Published for Use in the Methodist Episcopal Church in the United States: 1808-1878." Ph.D. diss., Drew University, 1991.

Hall, Roger. "Shaker Hymnody," *The Hymn* 27, 1 (January 1976): 22-29.

Higginson, J. Vincent. *Handbook for American Catholic Hymnals.* Springfield, OH: The Hymn Society of America, 1976.

"The Hymnal of the Protestant Episcopal Church in the U.S.A." in *The Hymnal 1940 Companion.* 3rd, rev. ed. New York: The Church Pension Fund, 1951, xix-xxviii.

Hinks, Donald R. *Brethren Hymn Books and Hymnals, 1720-1884*. Gettysburg, PA: Brethren Heritage Press, 1986.

Holland, Harold E. "The Hymnody of the Churches of Christ," *The Hymn* 30, 4 (October 1979): 263-268.

McDonald, William J., ed. *New Catholic Encyclopedia*. S.v. "Hymnology," by J. Szövérffy.

_____. S.v. "Hymns and Hymnals," by M. M. Hueller, M. A. Bichsel, E. J. Selhorst.

Patterson, Daniel W. *The Shaker Spiritual*. Princeton, NJ: Princeton University Press, 1979.

Reynolds, William J. "Baptist Hymnody in America," in *Handbook to The Baptist Hymnal*. Nashville: Broadman Press, 1992, 30-54.

Rivard, Eugene Francis. "The Hymnody of the Christian and Missionary Alliance (1891-1978) As a Reflection of Its Theology and Development." D.M.A. diss., Southwestern Baptist Theological Seminary, 1991.

Schalk, Carl. "Hymnody, American Lutheran," in *Key Words in Church Music*, ed. Carl Schalk. St. Louis: Concordia Publishing House, 1978, 222-231.

Smith, C. Howard. "Scandinavian Free Church Hymnody in America," *The Hymn* 29, 4 (October 1978): 228-237.

Spencer, Jon Michael. "The Hymnody of the National Baptist Conventions," *The Hymn* 41, 2 (April 1990): 7-18.

Tanner, Don R. "Hymnody of the Assemblies of God," *The Hymn* 31, 4 (October 1980): 252-256, 258.

Van Burkalow, Anastasia. "Expanding Horizons: Two Hundred Years of American Methodist Hymnody," *The Hymn* 17, 3 (July 1966): 77-84, 90.

Weber, William A. "The Hymnody of the Dutch Reformed Church America," *The Hymn* 26, 2 (April 1975): 57-60.

Westendorf, Omer. "The State of Catholic Hymnody," *The Hymn* 28, 2 (April 1977): 54-60.

Westermeyer, Paul. "German Reformed Hymnody in the United States," *The Hymn* 31, 2 & 3 (April and July 1980): 89-94, 200-204, 212.

Young, Carlton R. "Hymnals of the Evangelical United Brethren Church," "Hymnals of the Methodist Church," in *Companion to the United Methodist Hymnal*. Nashville: Abingdon Press, 1993, 75-89, 91-122, 123-180.

CULTURAL PERSPECTIVES

Adams, Charles G. "Some Aspects of Black Worship," *Andover Newton Quarterly* 11 (January 1971): 124-38; *Music Ministry* 5 (September 1972): 2-9; *Journal of Church Music* 15 (February 1973): 2-9, 16.

Ahyoung, Selwyn F. "The Music of the Shouter-Baptists of Trinidad, West Indies," *The Hymn* 37, 1 (January 1986): 19-24.

Bakke, Corean. *Let the Whole World Sing*. Chicago: Cornerstone Press, 1994.

Bartel, Lee R. "The Tradition of the Amish in Music," *The Hymn* 37, 4 (October 1986): 20-26.

Breckbill, Anita. "The Hymns of the Anabaptists: An English-Language Bibliography," *The Hymn* 39, 3 (July 1988): 21-23.

Cantato Domino New Edition (4th ed.). Kassel, Germany: Published by Bärenreiter Verlag for the World Council of Churches, 1974.

Castle, Brian C. *Hymns: The Making and Shaping of a Theology for the Whole People of God: A Comparison of the Four Last Things in Some English and Zambian Hymns in Intercultural Perspective*. Frankfort am Main: Peter Lang, 1990.

Colvin, Thomas. *Fill Us With Your Love, and Other Hymns from Africa*. Carol Stream, IL: Agape, 1983.

Corbitt, J. Nathan. "Congregational Songs of the Harvest: Revival Music in East Africa," *The Hymn* 39, 2 (April 1988): 24-25.

E.A.C.C. *Hymnal*, Daniel T. Niles (general ed.) and John M. Kelly (music ed.). Tokyo:

East Asia Christian Conference, 1964. (Distributed by AVACO, 22 Midori-gaokamachi, Shibuya-ku, Tokyo, Japan.)

Funk, Joseph. *New Harmonia Sacra*. (originally entitled *Genuine Church Music*, 1832) 25th ed. Intercourse, PA: Good Books, 1993.

Herskovits, Melville J. *Cultural Anthropology*. New York: Alfred A. Knopf, 1958.

Hohmann, Rupert Earl. "The Church Music of the Old Order Amish in the United States." Ph.D. diss., Northwestern University, 1959.

Hymns of Universal Praise. Shanghai, 1936. English Edition. Hong Kong, 1981. (Available from Chinese Christian Literature Council, Ltd., 57 Peking Road, 2nd floor, Kowloon, Hong Kong).

Isaacs, Frank C. "The Gymanfa Ganu in America," *The Hymn* 14, 2 (April 1963): 47-52.

Joyner, Jane Linville. "Black Music in a White Church," *Music Ministry* 8 (February 1976): 2-5.

Laster, James H. "The Persian Tunebook: A Dream Fulfilled," *The Hymn* 30, 2 (April 1979): 78-88.

Lead Me, Guide Me: The African American Catholic Hymnal. Chicago: G.I.A. Publications, 1987.

Lift Every Voice and Sing: A Collection of Afro-American Spirituals and Other Songs. New York: The Church Hymnal Corporation, 1981.

Loh, I-to (ed.). *Hymns from the Four Winds: A Collection of Asian American Hymns*. Supplemental Worship Resources 13. Nashville: Abingdon Press, 1983.

_____. "Transmitting Cultural Traditions in Hymnody," *Church Music Workshop* 4, 3 (September-December 1994): 1-6.

Luff, Alan. *Welsh Hymns and Their Tunes*. Carol Stream, IL: Hope Publishing Company; London: Stainer & Bell, 1990.

McAlpine, Pauline Smith. "Japanese Hymnody: Its Background and Development," *The Hymn* 32, 1 (January 1981): 37-43.

McAlpine, Pauline Smith. *Japanese Hymns in English*. Nagoya, Japan: Tsubobue Sha, 1975.

McKellar, Hugh D. "The Lord's Song in a Strange Land: Music in the Ethnic Churches of Toronto," *The Hymn* 29, 4 (October 1978): 217-221.

Malm, William P. *Music Cultures of the Pacific, the Near East and Asia*. 2nd ed. Englewood Cliffs, NJ: Prentice-Hall, Inc., 1977.

Merriam, Alan P. *The Anthropology of Music*. Evanston, IL: Northwestern University Press, 1964.

Nettl, Bruno. *Folk and Traditional Music of the Western Continents*. Englewood Cliffs, NJ: Prentice-Hall, Inc. 1965.

Nketia, J. H. Kwabena. *The Music of Africa*. New York: W. W. Norton and Co., 1974.

Olson, Howard S. (comp.). *Lead Us, Lord: A Collection of African Hymns*. Minneapolis: Augsburg Publishing House, 1977.

_____. *Set Free: A Collection of African Hymns*. Minneapolis: Augsburg Fortress, 1993.

Picken, Laurence. "The Music of Far Eastern Asia. 1. China," in *New Oxford History of Music*, v. 1, *Ancient and Oriental Music*. London, New York and Toronto: Oxford University Press, 1957, 82-134.

Ressler, Martin E. "Hymnbooks Used by the Old Order Amish," *The Hymn* 28, 1 (January 1977): 11-16.

Sills, David L. and Robert King Merton, eds. *International Encyclopedia of the Social Sciences*. S.v. "Culture: Cultural Relativism," by David Bidley.

Slough, Rebecca, and Kenneth Zafziger (eds.). *Hymnal: A Worship Book: Prepared by Churches in the Believers Church Tradition*. Elgin, IL:Brethren Press; Newton, KS: Faith and Life Press; and Scottdale, PA: Mennonite Publishing House, 1992.

Songs of Zion: Supplemental Worship Resources 12. Nashville: Abingdon Press, 1981.

Southern, Eileen. *The Music of Black Americans: A History*. 2nd ed. New York: W. W. Norton and Co., 1983.

Spencer, Jon Michael. *Black Hymnody: A*

Hymnological History of the African-American Church. Minneapolis: Fortress Press, 1992.

_____. *Protest and Praise: Sacred Music of Black Religion.* Minneapolis: Fortress Press, 1990.

_____. *Sing a New Song: Liberating Black Hymnody.* Minneapolis: Fortress Press, 1995.

Swan, M. L. *New Harp of Columbia.* 1867. Reprint. Knoxville: The University of Tennessee Press, 1978.

Tamke, Susan S. *Make a Joyful Noise unto the Lord: Hymns as a Reflection of Victorian Social Attitudes.* Athens: Ohio University Press, 1978.

Temperley, Nicholas. "The Old Way of Singing: Its Origins and Development," *Journal of the American Musicological Society* 34 (Fall 1981): 511-544.

Weman, Henry. *African Music and the Church in Africa.* Uppsala, Sweden: Ab Lundequistska Bokhandeln, 1960.

Wiant, Bliss. *The Music of China.* Hong Kong: Chung Chi Publications, 1965.

Williams, Robert R. "Some Aspects of Welsh Hymnody," *The Hymn* 4, 1 (January 1953): 5-11.

Yoder, Paul M., ed. *Four Hundred Years with the Ausbund.* Scottdale, PA: Herald Press, 1964.

York, Terry W. "Lining-Out in Congregational Singing," *The Hymn* 28, 1 (July 1977): 110-113.

THE HYMN IN PROCLAMATION

Barrows, Cliff. "Musical Evangelism," *Decision* 3 (December 1962): 12-13.

Cleall, Charles. "An Interlude on Evangelism and Music," in *The Selection and Training of Mixed Choirs in Churches.* London: Independent Press Ltd., 1960, 57-73.

Davies, J. G. *Worship and Mission.* New York: Association Press, 1967.

Elmer, Richard M. "Modern Evangelism and Church Music," *The Hymn* 7, 1 (January 1956): 13-17.

Gold, Charles E. "The Gospel Song: Contemporary Opinion," *The Hymn* 9, 3 (July 1958): 69-73.

Hille, Waldemar. "Evaluating Gospel Songs," *The Hymn* 3, 1 (January 1952): 15-18.

Hull, William E. "Make a Joyful Noise unto the Lord," *The Church Musician* 28 (July 1977): 12-13, 24.

Hustad, Donald P. *Jubilate II: Church Music in Worship and Renewal.* Rev. ed. Carol Stream, IL: Hope Publishing Co., 1993.

_____. "Music and the Church's Outreach," *Review and Expositor* 69 (Spring 1972): 177-185.

Kerr, Phil. *Music in Evangelism.* 4th ed. Glendale, CA: Gospel Music Publishers, 1939, 1954.

Lacour, Lawrence. "Music in Evangelism," *Music Ministry* 4 (August 1964): 2-4, 14.

McKissick, Marvin. "The Function of Music in American Revivals Since 1875," *The Hymn* 9 (October 1958): 107-117.

Proclamation: Aids for Interpreting the Lessons of the Church Year (a series of 25 books). Philadelphia: Fortress Press, 1974.

Sallee, James. *A History of Evangelistic Hymnody.* Grand Rapids, MI: Baker Book House, 1978.

Smyth, Richard Renwick. "A Sermon in Song-The Word Proclaimed by John Wesley; The Response to This Word Confessed in Song by Charles Wesley," *The Hymn* 15, 2 (April 1964): 47-52.

Troeger, Thomas H. "The Hidden Stream that Feeds: Hymns as a Resource for the Preacher's Imagination," *The Hymn* 43, 3 (July 1992): 5-13.

Webber, F. R. "The Gospel in the Great Hymns," *Christianity Today* 4 (August 29, 1960): 6-8.

Westerman, R. Scott. "The Term 'Gospel Hymn,'" *The Hymn* 9, 2 (April 1958): 61-62.

Wilson, John F. "Music in Evangelism," in *An Introduction to Church Music.* Chicago: Moody Press, 1965, 51-64.

THE HYMN IN WORSHIP

Arnold, Corliss R. "Hymns of Advent, Christmas and Epiphany," *The Hymn* 5, 4 (October 1954): 121-127.

Babcock, Richard M. "The Liturgical Year in Six Contemporary Protestant Hymnals," *The Hymn* 12, 4 (October 1961): 113-119.

Brand, Eugene L. "Congregational Song: the Popular Music of the Church," *Church Music* 68-1: 1-10.

Brueggemann, Walter. "Praise and the Psalms: A Politics of Glad Abandonment," *The Hymn* 43, 3 & 4 (July 1992): 14-19; (October 1992): 14-18.

Buchner, John F. "Alternation in Hymn Singing," *Journal of Church Music* 18 (December 1976): 7-9.

Cammerer, Richard R. "The Congregational Hymn as the Living Voice of the Gospel," in *The Musical Heritage of the Church*, Vol. V, Theo. Hoelty-Nickel, ed. Valparaiso: Concordia Publishing House, 1959, 166-177.

Davies, Horton. *Worship and Theology in England from Watts and Wesley to Maurice, 1690-1850*. Princeton: Princeton University Press, 1961.

Dunstan, Alan. "Hymnody in Christian Worship," in *The Study of Liturgy*. New York: Oxford University Press, 1978, 454-465.

————. *These Are the Hymns*. London: Society for the Preservation of Christian Knowledge, 1973.

Egge, Mandus. "Let There Be a Surprise," *Journal of Church Music* 13 (July-August 1971): 2-6.

Gealy, Fred D. "What Shall We Sing?" *The Hymn* 14, 3 (July 1963): 80-82.

Gillman, Frederick J. "Reality in Worship," Occasional Paper #2. The Hymn Society of Great Britain and Ireland, October 1939.

Gray, G. F. S. *Hymns and Worship*. London: S. P. C. K., 1961.

Gregory, A. S. "The Hymn in Christian Liturgy," *Bulletin of the Hymn Society of Great Britain and Ireland* 7 (April 1939): 6-7.

Hatchett, Marion J. *Music for the Church Year*. New York: The Seabury Press, 1964.

Heaton, Charles Huddleston. "How About a Prelude of Hymns?" *Journal of Church Music* 19 (November 1977): 3.

Hiebert, Clarence. "The Selection and Use of the Sermon Hymn," *The Hymn* 5, 2 (April 1954): 51-53.

Hoon, Paul Waitman. *The Integrity of Worship*: Ecumenical and Pastoral Studies in Liturgical Theology. Nashville: Abingdon Press, 1971.

Horn, Henry E. *O Sing Unto the Lord*. Philadelphia: The Muhlenberg Press, 1956.

Johansen, John H. "Come, Christians, Join to Sing," *The Hymn* 21, 4 (October 1970): 116-120.

Kimbrough, S. T., Jr. "Music, Liturgy, Humanity and Faith," *The Princeton Seminary Bulletin* 12, 1 (New Series, 1991): 29-40.

Knight, George Litch. "The Creative Use of Hymns in Worship," *Union Seminary Quarterly Review* 7 (June 1952): 21-26.

Leaver, Robin A. *The Liturgy and Music*. Nottingham: Grove Books, 1976.

————. "Hymnody and the Reality of God," *The Hymn* 44, 3 (July 1993): 16-21.

Lorah, Theodore R., Jr. "The Use of Amens," *Journal of Church Music* 18 (September 1976): 5-7.

Lovelace, Austin C. *Hymn Festivals*. Papers of The Hymn Society of America, XXXI, 1979.

———— and Rice, William C. *Music and Worship in the Church*. Revised and enlarged ed. New York and Nashville: Abingdon Press, 1976.

McDormand, Thomas Bruce. "Making the Most of Hymns," in *The Art of Building Worship Services*. Nashville: Broadman Press, 1942, 25-54.

Manning, Bernard L. *The Hymns of Wesley and Watts*. London: Epworth Press, 1942.

Miller, Edward O. "Hymns in Aid of Worship," *The Hymn* 10, 3 (July 1959): 79-80.

Miller, L. David. "Do It Yourself Descants," *Journal of Church Music* 16 (November 1974): 2-7.

Moeser, James. "Why and How Do We Celebrate?" *The Hymn* 26, 3 (July 1975): 92-94.

Northcott, Cecil. *Hymns in Christian Worship*. Richmond: John Knox Press, 1964.

Messenger, Ruth E. "Hymnology: Handmaiden of Worship," *The Hymn* 6, 2 (April 1955): 64-67.

Moyer, J. Edward. *The Voice of His Praise*. Nashville: Graded Press, 1965, 64-125.

Murphy, Donald L. *The Hymn Chart Manual*. Mt. Airy, MD: Genesis Enterprises, 1977.

Noyes, Morgan Phelps. "Hymns as Aids to Devotion," *The Hymn* 5, 1 (January 1954): 5-12.

Parker, Alice. *Creative Hymn Singing*. Chapel Hill: Hinshaw Music, Inc., 1976.

Patrick, Millar. "Congregational Song," *The Hymn* 3, 1 (January 1952): 5-9.

Pirner, Reuben G. "The Nature and Function of the Hymn in Christian Worship," *Church Music* 66, 1 (1966): 1-5.

Pratt, Waldo Selden. "Hymns and Hymn-singing," in *Musical Ministries in the Church*. New York: Fleming H. Revell Co., 1902, 45-82.

Rogers, James A. "John Wesley Can Help Improve the Hymn Singing in Your Church," *Music Ministry* 8 (March 1976): 28, 31.

Routley, Erik. *Hymns Today and Tomorrow*. Nashville: Abingdon Press, 1964.

_____. "The Art of Worship," in *Music Leadership in the Church*. Nashville: Abingdon Press, 1967, 106-20.

_____. *Music, Sacred and Profane*. Occasional Writings on Music 1950-58. London: Independent Press, 1960.

_____. "On Congregational Singing— The Next Chapter," *Bulletin of the Hymn Society of Great Britain and Ireland* 120 (January 1971): 113-122.

_____. *Words, Music, and the Church*.
Nashville: Abingdon Press, 1968.

Shealy, William R. "Towards a More Transitional Hymnody," *The Hymn* 24, 4 (October 1973): 112-118.

Smith, H. Augustine. *Lyric Religion: The Romance of Immortal Hymns*. New York: D. Appleton-Century Company, 1931.

Sydnor, James Rawlings. *The Hymn and Congregational Singing*. Richmond: John Knox Press, 1960.

Westerhoff, John H. *A Pilgrim People: Learning Through the Church Year*. New York: Seabury Press, 1984.

Westermeyer, Paul. "Beyond 'Alternative' and 'Traditional' Worship," *Christian Century* 109, 10 (March 18-25, 1992): 300-302.

Whitehead, William. "Making Hymns Meaningful Experiences," *Journal of Church Music* 19 (November 1977): 2-3.

York, David. "Hymn Singing—Now," *The Hymn* 22, 2 (April 1971): 42-43.

Young, Carlton R. "The Changing Shape of Parish Music," *Church Music* 67-2 (1967): 16-24.

The Hymn and Funeral Services

A Manual for the Funeral. New York and Nashville: Abingdon Press, 1962.

Biddle, Perry H., Jr. "Music for the Christian Funeral," *Music Ministry* 8 (February 1976): 6-7.

Hustad, Donald P. "Music in Christian Funerals," in *Jubilate II: Church Music in Worship and Renewal*. Carol Stream, IL: Hope Publishing Company, 1993, 359-363.

Knight, George Litch, William W. Reid, Jr. and Gerald E. Hedges. "Symposium: The Funeral Service and Hymns," *The Hymn* 10, 2 (April 1959): 39-48.

Mulder, Robert G. "Honor the Dead Respect the Living," *Journal of Church Music* 15 (November 1973): 11-12.

Music for Church Funerals. Greenwich: The Seabury Press, 1952.

Music for Funerals. The Joint Commission on Church Music. New York: H. W. Gray Co., 1963.

Snell, Frederick A. *Music for Church Funerals and Memorial Services*. Philadelphia: Fortress Press, 1966.

The Hymn and Weddings

Braun, H. Myron. "Here Comes the Bride," *The Hymn* 24, 3 (July 1973): 85-87.

Carlson, J. Bert. "A Pastoral View of Music for a Christian Wedding," *Journal of Church Music*, 19 (June 1977): 2-5.

Contemporary Worship 3 - The Marriage Service. St. Louis: Concordia Publishing House, 1972.

Ellinwood, Leonard. "Congregational Participation for Weddings Urged," *Diapason* (July 1957): 28.

Epley, Linda Morrison and Epley, William Arnold. *Music and Your Wedding*. Nashville: The Sunday School Board of the Southern Baptist Convention, 1972.

Fryxell, Regina H. *Wedding Music*. Rock Island, IL: Augustana Press, 1961.

Goodfellow, William D. *Wedding Music: An Index to Collections*. Metuchen, NJ: The Scarecrow Press, 1992.

Handbook of Church Music for Weddings. Chicago: Office for Divine Worship, the Archdiocese of Chicago, 1977.

Halter, Carl. "Special Services," in *The Practice of Sacred Music*. St. Louis: Concordia Publishing House, 1955, 50-51.

Hustad, Donald P. "Music in Christian Weddings," in *Jubilate II: Church Music in Worship and Renewal*. Carol Stream, IL: Hope Publishing Company, 1993, 351-357.

McDonald, Robert. "Weddings," *The Church Musician* 28 (June 1977): 8-13.

Music for Church Weddings. Greenwich: The Seabury Press, 1953.

Rotermund, Donald. "The Marriage… and the Role of the Congregation," *Church Music* 74, 1 (1974): 17-19.

Schalk, Carl. *Planning the Wedding Service*. Minneapolis: Sacred Design Associates, 1963.

Hymn Playing

Anderson, Margaret Sihler. *A Guide to Effective Hymn Playing*. Minneapolis: Augsburg Publishing, 1964.

Clokey, Joseph C. "The Organist in the Small Church," "Congregational Singing in the Small Church," "Hints for the Organist" in *In Every Corner Sing*. New York: Morehouse-Gorham Co., 1945.

Gehring, Philip. "The Role of the Organist in Congregational Song," *Journal of Church Music* 12 (April 1970): 2-5.

Greenlee, Anita. "Introducing Hymns for the Service," *Journal of Church Music* 14 (November 1972): 7-13.

Halter, Carl. "The Playing of Hymns" in *The Practice of Sacred Music*. St. Louis: Concordia Publishing Co., 1955, 30-36.

Heller, David. *Manual on Hymn Playing*. Chicago: G.I.A. Publications, 1992.

Hinkle, Donald. "Practical Suggestions for Improved Hymn Playing," *Journal of Church Music* 16 (November 1974): 9-11; *Journal of Church Music* 16 (December 1974): 5-8.

Johns, Michele. *Hymn Improvisation*. Minneapolis: Augsburg Publishing House, 1987.

Jones, Joyce. *Church Service Playing*. New York: Bradley Publications, 1981.

Krapf, Gerhard. *Liturgical Organ Playing*. Minneapolis: Augsburg Publishing House, 1964.

Kirkland, Martha H. *Better Accompaniment Next Sunday*. Nashville: Church Street Press, 1995.

Leaf, Robert. "Organists: How to Improve Your Hymn Accompanying," *Journal of Church Music* 18 (April 1976): 14-16, 46.

Litterst, Richard W. "Hymn Playing," *The Hymn* 13, 2 (April 1962): 45-47, 57.

Lovelace, Austin C. "Free Harmonizations for the Organ," *Journal of Church Music* 19 (April 1977): 17-20.

_____. *The Organist and Hymn Playing*. Nashville: Abingdon Press, 1962.

Pratt, Waldo Selden. "The Organist's Relation to Hymn Tunes and Hymn Singing," *The Hymn* 6, 2 (April 1955): 41-51.

Reynolds, William J. "Tempos and Keys in Congregational Singing" and "Instrumental Accompaniment for Congregational Singing," in *Congregational Singing*. Nashville: Convention Press, 1975, 7-40.

Ripper, Theodore W. "The Organist Can Stimulate or Stifle Congregational Song," *Music Ministry* 9 (September 1976): 5-7.

Routley, Erik. *An Organist's Companion to the Worshipbook* Vol. IX (Spring 1975) issue of *Reformed Liturgy and Music*-A Journal of Discipleship and Worship.

_____. "Can We Enjoy Hymns?" *Music Ministry* 9 (April 1977): 28-29.

_____. "The Organist and the Congregation" in *Church Music and the Christian Faith*. Carol Stream, IL: Agape, 1978, 121-128.

Scofield, Constance E. "Stand Up and Bless the Lord... a Look at Hymn Tune Introductions," *Journal of Church Music* 20 (November 1978): 8-9.

Sydnor, James Rawlings. "The Playing of Hymns" in *The Hymn and Congregational Singing*. Richmond: John Knox Press, 1960, 105-124.

Turner, Sandra Chucalo. "A Guide to Hymn Playing for the Inexperienced Adult Pianist." D.M.A. diss., The Southern Baptist Theological Seminary, 1987.

Warder, Velma. "The Organist in Church," *Journal of Church Music* 16 (April 1974): 8-11.

Wetzler, Robert. "Organists - Please Read the Words!" *Journal of Church Music* 20 (April 1978): 5-7.

Hymn Introductions and Harmonizations

Beck, Theodore. *Forty-Seven Hymn Intonations*. St. Louis: Concordia Publishing House, 1971.

Bender, Jan. *Twenty Hymn Introductions*. St. Louis: Concordia Publishing House, 1974.

_____. *Twenty-four Hymn Introductions*. St. Louis: Concordia Publishing House, 1974.

Cassler, Winston. *Organ Descants for Selected Hymn Tunes*. Minneapolis: Augsburg Publishing House, 1972.

Ferguson, John. *Ten Hymn Tune Harmonizations*. Cleveland: Ludwig Music Co., 1975.

Free Organ Accompaniments to Festival Hymns. Minneapolis: Augsburg Publishing House, 1963.

Hustad, Donald. *Organ-Piano Accompaniments for Congregational Hymns*. Carol Stream, IL: Hope Publishing Co., 1974.

_____. *Organ-Piano Accompaniments for Congregational Singing*. Nashville: Broadman Press, 1975.

Johnson, David N. *Deck Thyself, My Soul, with Gladness: Organ Music for Communion and General Use*. Minneapolis: Augsburg Publishing House, 1968.

_____. *Free Harmonizations of Twelve Hymn Tunes*. Minneapolis: Augsburg Publishing House, 1964.

_____. *Free Harmonizations for Manuals, Books I and II*. Minneapolis: Augsburg Publishing House, 1966.

Manz, Paul. *Ten Short Intonations on Well-Known Hymns*. Minneapolis: Augsburg Publishing House, 1970.

Noble, T. Tertius. *Fifty Free Organ Accompaniments to Well-Known Hymn Tunes*. Glen Rock, NJ: J. Fischer, 1949.

_____. *Free Organ Accompaniments to One Hundred Well-Known Hymn Tunes*. Glen Rock, NJ: J. Fischer, 1946.

Rohlig, Harald. *55 Hymn Intonations*. New York: Abingdon Press, 1962.

Thiman, Eric. *Varied Accompaniments to Thirty-Four Well-Known Hymn Tunes for Unison Singing*. London: Oxford University Press, 1937.

_____. *Varied Harmonizations of Favorite Hymn Tunes*. Melville, NY: H. W. Gray, 1955.

Wood, Dale. *New Settings of Twenty Well-Known Hymns Tunes*. Minneapolis: Augsburg Publishing House, 1968.

Hymn Festivals and Hymn Services

Bays, Alice A. *Worship Programs in the Fine Arts*. Nashville: Abingdon-Cokesbury Press, 1940.

Coon, Zula Evelyn. *Worship Services from the Hymns*. Westwood, NJ: Fleming H. Revell Co., 1958.

_____. *O Worship the King*. Nashville: Broadman Press, 1951.

Curry, Louise H. and Chester M. Wetzel. *Worship Services Using the Arts*. Philadelphia: The Westminster Press, 1961.

Emurian, Ernest K. *Popular Programs Based on Hymn Stories*. (Reprint of *Hymn Festivals*, 1961). Grand Rapids: Baker Book House, 1972.

Heaton, Charles Huddleston. "Hymn Festivals" in *A Guidebook to Worship Services of Sacred Music*. St. Louis: The Bethany Press, 1962, 44-52.

Kruschwitz, Robert B. "The Program of Hymn Interpretation," *The Hymn* 24, 4 (October 1973): 119-121.

Lovelace, Austin C. *Hymn Festivals*. Papers of the Hymn Society of America, XXXI, Ohio, 1979.

McDormand, Thomas, Bruce. "Making the Most of Hymns" in *The Art of Building Worship Services*. Nashville: Broadman Press, 1942, 25-45.

Moen, Kathryn Ulvilden. "Hymn Festivals," in *Hymns-How to Sing Them* by Mandus A. Egge and Janet Moede. Minneapolis: Augsburg Publishing House, 1966, 25-28.

Moyer, J. Edward. "Hymn Services" in *The Voice of His Praise*. Nashville: Graded Press, 1965, 120-125.

Sanchez, Diana. *Your Ministry of Planning and Leading Hymn Festivals*. Nashville: Discipleship Resources, 1990.

Sydnor, James Rawlings. "Hymn Services and Festivals," in *Hymns and Their Uses*. Carol Stream, IL: Agape, 1982, 140-146.

Whittlesey, Federal Lee. *A Comprehensive Program of Church Music*. Philadelphia: The Westminster Press, 1957.

_____. "Some Suggested Topics for Hymn Services," *The Hymn* 9, 3 (July 1958): 83-85.

Wold, Wayne L. "Celebrate in Song in a Hymn Festival!" *Journal of Church Music* (February 1986): 4-6.

THE HYMN IN EDUCATION

Baker, Philip E. "Existential Hymn Singing," *Music Ministry* 8 (February 1976): 28-29, 31.

Benson, Louis F. *The Hymnody of the Christian Church*. New York: George H. Doran Co., 1927; reprint ed., Richmond: John Knox Press, 1956.

Boyter, Mabel Stewart. "Growing a Hymn-Loving Church: An Interview with Mable Stewart Boyter," *The Hymn* 34, 3 (July 1983): 141-146.

Braun, H. Myron. "Do We Still Teach Hymns?" *Music Ministry* 8 (September 1975): 1, 40.

_____. "The Minister of Music as Teacher," *Music Ministry* 1 (April 1969): 40.

_____. "Our Goal is Music for Worship," *New Christian Advocate* 2 (October 1958): 42-45.

Buchner, John F. "Church Music is for the Congregation, Too," *Journal of Church Music* 16 (March 1974): 5-7.

Cheesman, Virginia. "Young People Learn Church Music" *International Journal of Religious Education* 35 (December 1958): 18-20.

Clampitt, Pamela. "Some ABC's for Using Hymns with Children," *The Hymn* 44, 2 (April 1993): 42-43.

Darnell, Grace Leeds. "How to Teach a Hymn-And Why," *The Hymn* 2, 2 (April 1951): 11-13.

Edson, Jean Slater. *Organ Preludes*. 2 vols. Metuchen, NJ: Scarecrow Press, 1970; Supplement, 1974.

Egge, Mandus A. and Janet Moede. *Hymns—How to Sing Them*. Minneapolis: Augsburg Publishing House, 1966.

Eskew, Harry. "Contributions of Hymnody to Christian Spirituality," *The Theological Educator* 43 (Spring 1991): 81-90.

_____. "Hymns in the Church's Teaching Ministry," *The Theological Educator* 8 (Spring 1978): 86-97.

Hackney, Vivian and Key, Jimmy. *Hymns to Know and Sing*. Nashville: Convention Press, 1973.

Haeussler, Armin. "The Struggle for Better Hymnody," in *Cantors at the Crossroads*. St. Louis: Concordia Publishing House, 1967, 163-84.

Hall, Paul M. "Hymn Rehearsals and Public Worship," *The Church Musician* 16 (June 1965): 12-14.

Hatchett, Marion J. Hatchett. *A Liturgical Index to the Hymnal 1982*. Hymnal Studies Five. New York: Church Hymnal Corporation, 1986.

Hawn, C. Michael. "Hymnody and Christian Education: The Hymnal as a Teaching Resource for Children," *Review and Expositor* 87, 1 (Winter 1990): 43-48.

_____. "Hymnody for Children I" and "Hymnody for Children II: Teaching Hymns to Children," *The Hymn* 36, 1 & 2 (January 1985): 19-26; 36, 2 (April 1985): 20-24.

Hicks, Roger W. "A Total Concept: Choirs, Leaders, Congregations United in Music." *Music Ministry* 1 (May 1969): 2-5.

Horn, Henry E. *O Sing Unto the Lord: Music in the Lutheran Church*. Philadelphia: Muhlenberg Press, 1956.

Hunnicutt, Judy. "Using Hymns with Children's Choirs," *The Hymn* 30 (January 1979): 34-35.

Hustad, Donald P. *(ed.) The Worshiping Church: A Hymnal*. Carol Stream, IL: Hope Publishing Co., 1990.

Keiser, Marilyn J. *Hymnal Studies Three: Teaching Music in the Small Church*. New York: The Church Hymnal Corporation, 1983.

Keithahn, Mary Nelson, *Our Heritage of Hymns*. Garland, TX: Choristers Guild, 1986.

Keithahn, Mary Nelson and Mary Louise VanDyke, *Exploring the Hymnal*. Garland, TX: Choristers Guild, 1986.

Key, Glennella. "Experiences with Hymnody" in *Guiding Fours and Fives in Musical Experiences*. Nashville: Convention Press, 1972, 131-138.

Kintner, Robert J. "A New Approach to Hymn Learning," *Journal of Church Music* 13 (April 1971): 9-11.

Lawrence, Joy E. *The Organist's Shortcut to Service Music*. Cleveland: Ludwig Music Publishing Co., 1986; Supplement I, 1988.

Lovelace, Austin C. *Hymn Notes for Church Bulletins*. Chicago: G.I.A. Publications, 1987.

Milligan, Thomas. *Readability of Hymn Texts: Baptist Hymnal, 1991, Baptist Hymnal 1975*, Jefferson City, TN: Center for Church Music, Carson-Newman College, 1991.

Morsch, Vivian Sharp. *The Use of Music in Christian Education*. Philadelphia: The Westminster Press, 1956.

Moyer, J. Edward. *The Voice of His Praise: A New Appreciation of Hymnody*. Nashville: Graded Press, 1965.

Rogers, James A. "Traditional First Church and the Pre-Service Hymn Sing," *Music Ministry* 9 (December 1976): 28.

Roth, Robert N. and Nancy L. Roth (eds.). *We Sing of God: A Hymnal for Children: Teacher's Guide*. New York: The Church Hymnal Corporation, 1989.

Schmidt, Dennis. *An Organist's Guide for The Hymnal 1982*. New York: The Church Hymnal Corporation, 1987.

Sydnor, James Rawlings. *Hymns: A Congregational Study*. Carol Stream, IL: Agape, 1983.

_____. *Hymns and Their Uses*. Carol Stream, IL: Agape, 1982.

_____. *Introducing a New Hymnal: How To Improve Congregational Singing*. Chicago: G.I.A. Publications, Inc., 1989.

_____. "Teaching Hymnology," *The Hymn* 29, 3 (July 1978): 152-54, 163.

Tamper, E. E. "From Boredom to Inspiration," *Music Ministry* 9 (1977): 25.

Thomas, Edith Lovell. *Music in Christian Education*. New York and Nashville: Published for the Cooperative Publication Association by Abingdon Press, 1953.

West, Diane. "Using the Hymnal in the Confirmation Class," *Music Ministry* 8 (December 1975): 7-8.

Woodward, Betty. *The Singing Book.* Nashville: Convention Press, 1975.

Wilson, John F. "Music in Christian Education" in *An Introduction to Church Music.* Chicago: Moody Press, 1965, 39-50.

Wright, David R. "Hymn Education: A Day-Course on the Words of Hymns," *The Hymn Society of Great Britain and Ireland Bulletin* 11, 4 (October 1985): 71-74.

_____. "To Serve the Present Age: A Study Course on the Hymns of the Wesleys," *The Hymn Society of Great Britain and Ireland Bulletin* 12, 3, (July 1988): 52-54.

THE HYMN IN MINISTRY

Berger, Joy Susanne. *Music as a Catalyst for Pastoral Care within the Remembering Tasks of Grief.* D.M.A. diss., The Southern Baptist Theological Seminary, 1993.

Burns, Sharon. "In Hospice Work, Music Is Our Great Ally," *Pastoral Music,* 17, 3 (Feb.-March 1993): 11-13.

DeLaney, E. Theo. and Bailey, Clark. *Sing Unto the Lord - A Hymnal for the Deaf.* St. Louis: Commission on Worship and Board for Missions, The Lutheran Church, Missouri Synod, 1969.

Gee, H. L. *Hymns That Came to Life.* London: The Epworth Press, 1954.

Goward, Barbara E. *Hymns of Hope and Healing.* Cincinnati: The Willis Music Co., 1960.

Haas, Alfred B. "The Theraputic Value of Hymns," *Pastoral Psychology* 1 (December 1950): 39-42.

Higginson, J. Vincent. "Hymns for the Blind," *The Hymn* 3, 4 (October 1952): 116-118.

McElrath, Hugh T. "Hymns of Concern," *The Church Musician* 18 (October 1967): 4-6.

_____. "Music - the Healer." *Search* 11, 2 (Winter 1981): 42-52.

Merrill, William P. "The Religious Value of Hymns," Paper II of The Hymn Society of America. New York: The Hymn Society, 1931.

Nichols, Kathryn L. "A Bibliography of Braille Hymnals," *The Hymn* 41, 2 (April 1991): 27-30.

Pinson, Joe. "Writing Hymns for Mentally Retarded Persons," *The Hymn* 30, 1 (January 1979): 21-25.

_____. *Make a Joyful Noise: Choruses of Faith for God's Children.* Pacific, MO: Cathedral Music Press, 1988.

Pinson, William M., Jr. *The Local Church in Ministry.* Nashville: Broadman Press, 1973.

Reid, William W., Jr. "The Social Note in Christmas and Easter Hymns," *The Hymn* 19 (April 1968): 44-48.

Rice, Cathy. *Music with the Deaf.* Murfreesboro, TN: The Bill Rice Ranch, n.d.

Sing Praise, Hymnal for the Deaf. Nashville: Broadman Press, 1975.

Smart, James D. *The Rebirth of Ministry.* Philadelphia: The Westminster Press, 1960.

Stickney, Doris Brenner. "Songs in the Night," *Journal of Church Music* 14 (November 1972): 5-6.

Ten New Hymns on Aging and the Later Years. Springfield, OH: The Hymn Society of America; Washington, D.C.: National Retired Teachers Association and American Association of Retired Persons, 1976.

Tomiak, Walter M. and Calvert, Robert H. "Guidelines for a Hymn Sing in a Nursing Home," *The Hymn* 26, 2 (April 1975): 39-40.

Turnbull, Agnes Sligh. "There's Healing in Hymns," *Christian Herald* 76 (November 1953): 64-66, 70-71.

White, Emma Jane, ed. *Let's Do More with Persons with Disabilities.* Nashville: Local Church Education, Board of Discipleship of the United Methodist Church, 1973.

Sermons/Devotional Talks Based on Hymns

Balleine, G. R. *Sing with the Understanding.* London: Independent Press, Ltd., 1954.

Brown, Lavonn, compiler. *Biblical Preaching Using Great Hymns.* Nashville: Convention Press, 1990.

Chamberlain, Martha E. & Mary B. Adams. *Hymn Devotions for All Seasons*. Nashville, Abingdon Press, 1989.

Church, Ida & Leslie. *Begin with a Hymn*. A Book for Morning Devotions. London: The Epworth Press, 1957.

Clark, M. Guthrie. *Sing Them Again*. London: Henry E. Walter, Ltd. 1955.

Clark, William. *Sing With Understanding*. London: Hughes and Coleman, Ltd., 1966.

Gee, H. L. *Hymns That Came to Life*. London: Epworth Press, 1955.

Keeler, W. T. *The Romantic Origin of Some Favorite Hymns: Their Psychological Background and Modern Implications*. London: Letchworth Press, 1966.

Konkel, Wilbur. *Living Hymn Stories*. Minneapolis: Bethany House Publishers, 1982.

_____. *More Living Hymn Stories*. Chicago: Pillar of Fire Missions, 1981.

_____. *Stories of Children's Hymns*. Chicago: Pillar of Fire Press, 1976.

Robinson, James H. *Devotional Thoughts on Favorite Hymns*. Milwaukee: Northwestern Publishing House, 1984.

Tippett, H. M. *Treasured Themes from Familiar Hymns*. Washington, D.C.: Review and Herald Publishing Association, 1959.

EPILOGUE

Black, George. "*Gather* and *Worship*: One Concept in Two Books and Many Editions," *The Hymn* 42, 2 (April 1991): 12-15.

Grindal, Gracia. "Where We Are Now" [Language of Hymnody], *The Hymn* 38, 4 (October 1990): 22-26.

Hawn, C. Michael. "A Survey of Trends in Recent Protestant Hymnals: African-American Spirituals, Hymns, and Gospel Songs," *The Hymn* 43, 1 (January 1992): 21-28.

_____. "A Survey of Trends in Recent Protestant Hymnals: International Hymnody," *The Hymn* 42, 4 (October 1991): 24-32.

_____. "A Survey of Trends in Recent

Protestant Hymnals: Mainstream American, British, and Canadian Hymnody Since 1960," *The Hymn* 42, 3 (July 1991): 17-25.

_____. "Current Trends in Hymnody: Psalm Singing," *The Hymn* 43, 2 (April 1992): 31-42.

Heller, David. *Manual on Hymn Playing*. Chicago: G.I.A. Publications, 1992.

Hovda, Robert W. "The Evolving Language of Worship," *The Hymn* 38, 4 (October 1987): 16-21.

Hustad, Donald P. "The Historical Roots of Music in the Pentecostal and Neo-Pentecostal Movements," *The Hymn* 38, 1 (January 1987): 7-11.

Johansson, Calvin M. "Singing in the Spirit: The Music of the Pentecostals," *The Hymn* 38, 1 (January 1993): 25-29.

Lovelace, Austin C. "Which Is the Right Tune?" *The Hymn* 44, 4 (October 1993): 10-14.

Price, Milburn. "The Impact of Popular Culture on Congregational Song," *The Hymn* 44, 1 (January 1993): 11-19.

Reidel, Scott R. "Worship Space Acoustics: An Annotated Bibiliography," *The Hymn* 41, 3 (October 1990): 27-29.

Sosa, Pablo. "Spanish American Hymnody: A Global Perspective" in *The Hymnology Annual: An International Forum on the Hymn and Worship*. Ed. Vernon Wicker. Vol. III (1993), 57-70.

Sovik, Edward Anders, "Architecture for Hymn Singing," *The Hymn* 41, 3 (October 1990): 10-14.

Troeger, Thomas H. "Personal, Cultural and Theological Influences on the Language of Worship," *The Hymn* 38, 4 (October 1987): 7-16.

Van Burkalow, Anastasia. "A Call for Battle Symbolism in Hymns," *The Hymn* 38, 2 (April 1987): 14-17.

Wolgemuth, Paul W. "Praise Singing," *The Hymn* 38, 1 (January 1987): 18-23.

Wren, Brian. "Onward Christian Rambos? The Call Against Battle Symbolism in Hymns," *The Hymn* 38, 3 (July 1987): 13-15.

ONE AUTHOR (COMPOSER) COLLECTIONS

Anderson, Fred R. *Singing Psalms of Joy and Praise*. Philadelphia: Westminster Press, 1986.

Beall, Mary Kay and John Carter. *Hymns for a Troubled World*. Carol Stream, IL: Hope Publishing Company, 1991.

Clarkson, Margaret. *A Singing Heart*. Carol Stream, IL: Hope Publishing Company, 1987.

Colvin, Tom. *Fill Us With Your Love*. Carol Stream, IL: Hope Publishing Company, 1983.

Crosby, Fanny. *Fanny Crosby Speaks Again*. Donald P. Hustad, ed. Carol Stream, IL: Hope Publishing Company, 1977.

Damon, Dan. *Faith Will Sing*. Carol Stream, IL: Hope Publishing Company, 1994.

Daw, Carl P., Jr. *A Year of Grace: Hymns for the Church Year*. Carol Stream, IL: Hope Publishing Company, 1992.

_____. *To Sing God's Praise: 18 Metrical Canticles*. Carol Stream, IL: Hope Publishing Company, 1992.

Duck, Ruth. *Dancing in the Universe*. Chicago: G. I. A., 1992.

Dudley-Smith, Timothy. *Lift Every Heart: Collected Hymns 1961-1983 and Some Early Poems*. Carol Stream, IL: Hope Publishing Company, 1984.

_____. *Songs of Deliverance: Thirty-six New Hymns Written Between 1984 and 1987*. Carol Stream, IL: Hope Publishing Company, 1988.

_____. *A Voice of Singing: 36 New Hymns Written Between 1988 and 1992*. Carol Stream, IL: Hope Publishing Company, 1993.

Dunstan, Sylvia. *In Search of Hope and Grace: 40 Hymns and Gospel Songs*. Chicago: G. I. A. Publications, 1991.

Edwards, Howard M. (Rusty). *The Yes of the Heart: Faith, Hope, and Love Songs*. Carol Stream, IL: Hope Publishing Company, 1993.

Ellingsen, Svein. *Praises Resound!* Tr. Hedwig T. Durnbaugh. Oslo, Norway: Norsk Musikforlag A/S, 1991.

Fedak, Alfred V. *Alfred V. Fedak Hymnary*. Accord, NY: Selah Publishing Company, 1990.

Gaunt, Alan. *The Hymn Texts of Alan Gaunt*. London: Stainer & Bell, 1991.

Green, Fred Pratt. *The Hymns and Ballads of Fred Pratt Green*. Carol Stream, IL: Hope Publishing Company, 1982.

_____. *Later Hymns and Ballads and Fifty Poems*. London: Stainer and Bell; Carol Stream, IL: Hope Publishing Company, 1989.

Hampton, Calvin. *The Calvin Hampton Hymnary*. Chicago: G. I. A., 1980.

Hopp, Roy. *The Roy Hopp Hymnary*. Kingston, NY: Selah Publishing Company, 1990.

Huber, Jane Parker. *A Singing Faith*. Philadelphia: The Westminster Press, 1987.

Hurd, David. *The David Hurd Hymnary*. Chicago: G.I.A. Publications, 1985.

Kaan, Fred and Doreen Potter. *Break Not the Circle: Twenty New Hymns*. Carol Stream, IL: 1975.

Kaan, Fred. *The Hymn Texts of Fred Kaan*. London: Stainer and Bell; Carol Stream, IL: Hope Publishing Company, 1985.

_____. *Planting Trees and Sowing Seeds: 23 Hymns by Fred Kaan*. Oxford: Oxford University Press; Carol Stream, IL: Hope Publishing Company, 1989.

Marshall, Jane. *Grace Noted*. Comp. & Ed. by Rosemary Heffley. Carol Stream, IL: Hope Publishing Company, 1992.

Monohan, Carolyn Lott. *Soli Deo Gloria: A Collection of Hymn Texts*. Louisville: Douglass Boulevard Christian Church, 1992.

Mountain, Charles M. *New Testament Scriptures for Singing: 50 Hymns by Charles M. Mountain*. Lima, OH: Fairway Press, 1990.

Murray, Shirley Erena. *In Every Corner Sing: The Hymns of Shirley Erena Murray*. Carol Stream, IL: Hope Publishing Company, 1992.

O'Driscoll, Herbert. *Alleluia!: 20 New Hymns by Herbert O'Driscoll with 10 New*

Tunes and Arrangements by Patrick Wedd. Toronto: Anglican Book Centre, 1979.

Patterson, Joy F. *Come, You People of the Promise.* Carol Stream, IL: Hope Publishing Co., 1994.

Peacey, J. R. *Go Forth for God.* Carol Stream, IL: Hope Publishing Company, 1991.

Perry, Michael. *Sing to God, Hymns and Songs 1965-1995.* Carol Stream, IL: Hope Publishing Company, 1995.

Quinn, James. *Praise for All Seasons.* Kingston, NY: Selah Publishing Company, 1994.

Routley, Erik. *Our Lives Be Praise: the Hymn Tunes, Carols, and Texts of Erik Routley.* Carol Stream, IL: Hope Publishing Company, 1990.

Rowan, William. *Together Met, Together Bound: Hymn Settings by William Rowan.* Kingston, NY: Selah Publishing Company, 1994.

Schalk, Carl. *The Carl Schalk Hymnary: Forty-seven New Hymn tunes and Carols with Various Texts.* Chicago: G.I.A. Publications, 1989.

_____. *The Carl Schalk Hymnary Supplement: Sixteen New Hymn tunes and Carols with Various Texts.* Chicago: G.I.A. Publications, 1991.

Stuempfle, Herman. *The Word Goes Forth: Hymns, Songs, and Carols by Herman Stuempfle.* Chicago: G.I.A. Publications, 1994.

Troeger, Thomas H. *Borrowed Light: Hymn Texts and prayers, and poems.* New York: Oxford University Press, 1994.

Troeger, Thomas H. Carol Doran. *New Hymns for the Lectionary: To Glorify the Maker's Name.* New York/Oxford: Oxford University Press, 1986.

_____. *New Hymns for the Life of the Church: To Make Our Prayer and Music One.* New York/ Oxford: Oxford University Press, 1992.

Vajda, Jaroslav J. *Now the Joyful Celebration.* St. Louis: MorningStar Music Publishers, 1987.

_____. *So Much to Sing About: Hymns, Carols, and Songs.* St. Louis: Morning Star Music Publishers, 1991.

Von Christierson, Frank. *Make a Joyful Noise: Hymns and Verses.* Fort Bragg, CA: Q.E.D. Press, 1987.

Wren, Brian. *Bring Many Names: 35 New Hymns by Brian Wren.* Carol Stream: Hope Publishing Company, 1984.

_____. *Faith Looking Forward: The Hymns and Songs of Brian Wren with Many Tunes by Peter Cutts.* Carol Stream: Hope Publishing Company, 1983.

_____. *New Beginnings: 33 Hymn Texts for the 90's.* Carol Stream: Hope Publishing Company, 1993.

_____. *Praising a Mystery: 30 New Hymns by Brian Wren.* Carol Stream: Hope Publishing Company, 1986.

GENERAL INDEX

A

Abelard, Peter, 65, 92

Accent, 17, 34, 47-48, 91

Achtliederbuch, 99

Ackley, Alfred H., 204

Acoustics, 322

Adams, Sarah Flower, 150

Addison, Joseph, 133

Advent. See Christian calendar.

Africa(n), 215, 219, 221, 227-229, 230, 234, 319-320

African-American, 30, 59, 186-88, 205-206, 208, 222, 224-225, 272, 278, 318

African-American hymns (spirituals), 30, 45, 222, 272, 317-318

Ahnfelt, Oscar, 113

Aikin, Jesse B., 182

Ainsworth, Henry, 122

Ainsworth Psalter (1612), 122

Alexander, Cecil Frances, 71, 89, 150

Alexander, Charles M., 201-202

Alexander, James W., 190

Alford, Henry, 153

Alington, Cyril A., 164

All Saint's Day. See Christian calendar.

Allegory, 20

Allen, George N., 206

Alliteration, 20, 28

Alpha and Omega, 57

Alternation practices, 263-269, 274, 275

Ambrose of Milan, 86-87,279,

Ambrosian, 86, 89

America(n), 42, 117, 122-124, 219, 225, 244, 301

American folk hymn(s), 44-45

American folk hymnody, 180-188, 215, 317

American Guild of Organists, 291, 322

The American Singing Book (1785)

Amerindian, 318

Amish, 222-223

Anabaptist-Mennonite, 222

Anadiplosis, 20

Anaphora, 21, 28, 138

Anatolius, 84

Ancient of Days, 56

Anders, Charles R., 321

Anderson, Fred, 125

Andrew of Crete, 83

Anglican chant, 34, 38-39, 49

Anglican Church, 118, 122, 153, 171, 215, 216-218, 272

Anglican Church of Canada, 215, 216

Anglo-Genevan Psalter (1556, 1558, 1561), 118, 119, 125

Anstruther, Joyce, 164

Anthem, 152, 164, 172, 179, 181, 212,

226, 289

Anthropologists, 219, 222

Antiphonal singing, 88, 263, 264, 269

Antithesis, 22, 72-73

Apostles' Creed, 273

Apostrophe, 24, 28

Aquinas, Thomas, 93, 95

Argentine, 234

Aria, 109

Arian, 65, 86, 88

Arius, 85

Arlington, Cyril A., 164

Arminianism, 138

Ascension. See Christian calendar.

Asian, 231-234

Asian-American, 319

Assemblies of God, 204

Associated Reformed Presbyterian Church, 125

Atkins, George, 183

Atonement, 135, 226, 245

Augustine of Hippo, *ix*, 86

Ausbund, 222-223

Australia, 173, 201, 217

Austrian, 113

B

Babcock, Maltbie D., 208

Bach, Johann Sebastian, 31-32, 39, 41, 108, 110-111, 117

Bahnmaier, Jonathan Friedrich, 111

Bailey, Albert Edward, *viii*, 102

Baker, Henry Williams, 50, 153, 156

Bakewell, John, 146

Baptism, 108, 161

Baptist(s), 129, 130, 134, 143, 145, 166, 168, 191, 197, 204, 205, 209, 222

The Baptist Hymn Book (1962), 166

The Baptist Hymnal (1991), x, 204, 278, 288, 308, 312, 314, 315, 318, 323

Baptist Praise and Worship (1991), 314

Baptist Standard Hymnal, 316

Bar form, 37, 39, 100

Baring-Gould, Sabine, 154

Barlow, 123

Barnard, John, 172

Barnby, Joseph, 157

Baroque continuo, 39

Baroque solo song style, 109

Bartlett, Eugene M., 203

Basso continuo, 103, 109

Batastini, Robert J., 320

Bates, Katherine Lee, 194

Baughen, Michael, 171, 172

Baxter, Richard, 129

Bay Psalm Book (1640), 123, 124

Bayly, Albert F., 167-168, 297

The BBC Hymn Book (1951), 165

Beaumont, Geoffry, 165-166

Beck, John Ness, 321

Beecher, Henry Ward, 192

Beethoven, Ludwig van, 112, 208

Bell, John L., 319-320

Bender, Jan, 114

Benedictine, 89, 91

Bennard, George, 202

Benson, Louis F., *viii*, 191, 207, 209, 210

Bernard of Clairvaux, 92

Bernard of Cluny, 65, 93

Berthier, Jacques, 320

Béze, Theodore de, 116

Biblical images and expressions, 54-57, 62, 100

    Alpha and Omega, 57

    Ancient of Days, 56

    Lord (of) Sabaoth, 56

    Rock of Ages, 55

    Shepherd, 54

Biblical names and places, 57-59

    Eden, 58

    Jordan/Canaan, 20, 53, 58, 187

    Zion (Sion), 59

Black African, 224-229
Black Baptist, 222
Black gospel, 205, 206
Black Holiness Church, 205
Black spiritual, 186-188, 224-225, 234
Bliss, Philip P., 196, 199-200
Blues, 205, 206
Blumenfeld, Edward M., 301
Boberg, Carl, 113
Bode, John Ernest, 149
Bohemian Brethren. *See* Moravian.
Bonar, Horatius, 149
Bonhoeffer, Dietrich, 114, 169
Book of Common Prayer (1549, 1552),
    87, 91, 152, 291
Book of Praise: Anglo-Genevan Psalter
    (1972), 125
The Book of Psalms for Singing, 125
Booke of Musicke (1591), 119
Booth, General William, 139
Borthwick, Jane, 156
Bourgeois, Louis, 116
Bowie, Walter Russell, 209
Bowring, John, 22, 150
Boyce, William, 38, 40
Bradbury, William B., 32, 196-197, 203
Brady, Nicholas, 121, 122, 131
Bramley, H. R., 158
The Breach Repaired (1691), 130
Brébeuf, Jean de, 318
Brick Presbyterian Church, 208
Bridges, Matthew, 155
Bridges, Robert, 81, 101, 161
Briggs, George Wallace, 164
Bright, William, 212
Broadman Hymnal, 204
Brokering, Herbert, 210
Brooks, Phillips, 192
Brotherhood, 209, 214
Bunyan, John, 129, 163

C

Cabena, Barrie, 217
Call and response, 26, 222, 229, 260-
    261
Calvin, John, 39, 41, 115, 125, 127, 279,
    292
Calvinism, 105, 124, 144, 175
Calvinistic Methodists, 141, 226
Cameron, Catherine, 209
Camp meeting, 183, 185-186, 188, 196
Canaan, 20, 53, 58, 187
Canada, 198, 215-218, 312, 318, 321
Canadian Reformed, 125
Canon (Greek), 82-84
Cantata, 108, 279
Cantata Domino, 113, 114, 233, 320
Canticles, 40, 78-79, 233
Carden, Allen, 181
Carol, 42-43, 95, 97, 101, 158, 160
Caroling, 309
Carols for Today, 172
Carter, Sydney, 166
Caswall, Edward, 93, 96, 156
Cennick, John, 141-142
Chadwick, John W., 194
Chandler, John, 96
Chapman, J. Wilbur, 201, 202
Charismatic renewal, 211, 313-314
"Charlestown Collection," 123, 135
Chase, Gilbert, 178, 222
Chesterton, Gilbert K., 19, 20, 162
Chiasmus, 21, 138
Children, 95, 99, 132, 191, 192, 197,
    208, 209, 222, 280-287, 292, 304
Chinese, 30, 206, 229, 231-233, 234
Chisholm, Thomas O., 204
Choir, 110, 115, 154, 155, 191, 205,
    289, 291
Choosing hymns, 323-324
Chope, R. R., 158
Chorale arias, 109

Chorale(s), 32, 37, 39, 89, 98-115 ,124, 127, 161, 178, 195, 228, 264
Choruses, v, 185-186, 190, 313-314
Christian calendar (year), 61, 69, 93, 108, 147,152, 195, 242-248, 253, 254, 274-276, 289, 312
Advent, 87, 96, 99, 240, 242, 243, 252, 253276, 291
All Saint's Day, 84
Ascension, 61, 84, 254
Christmas, 82, 88, 95, 96, 99, 100, 101, 103,110, 112, 113, 122, 155, 158, 192, 195, 242, 243, 252, 253, 309
Corpus Christi, 93
Easter, 84, 90, 93, 95, 96, 99, 100, 101, 155, 162, 170, 242, 243, 253, 254, 271
Epiphany, 88, 147, 155
Good Friday, 92, 94, 254
Holy Week, 83, 90, 242, 243, 254
Lent, 83, 253, 276, 292
Maundy Thursday, 252, 254
Palm Sunday, 100, 254
Pentecost, 69, 93, 112, 155, 204, 212, 242, 244, 254, 276
St. Stephen's Day, 147
St. Thomas Sunday, 84
Trinity Sunday, 242
Trinitytide, 254
Christian Copyright Licensing, Inc. (CCLI), 324
Christian Harmony (Walker), 185
Christian living, 278
The Christian Lyre (1831), 190
The Christian Psalmist (1825), 159
Christian Reformed Church, 125, 317
Christian social service, 295 ff.
Christian year. *See* Christian calendar.
Christierson, Frank von, 210
Christmas. See Christian calendar.
Chrysostom, Bishop John, 85

Church of God (Cleveland, Tennessee), 203
Church of Scotland, 121, 164
Church year. *See* Christian calendar.
Churches of Christ, 204
Churches of God, 204
Churches of the Nazarene, 204
Cistercian, 91
Clark, Thomas C., 301
Clarkson, E. Margaret, 216
Classical meter, 81
Claudius, Matthias, 108, 109
Clement of Alexandria, 55, 65, 81-82
Clephane, Elizabeth Cecilia, 150
Climax, 24, 28, 134, 163, 228
Cluniac, 91
Coffin, Charles, 96
Coffin, Henry Sloan, 96
A Collection of Hymns for the use of the People Called Methodists (1780), 138
Collection of Psalms and Hymns (1737), 135, 139
A Collection of Tunes Set to Music as They Are Commonly Sung at the Foundry (1742), 139
Common Meter (CM), 17, 39, 47, 119, 120
Common tunes, 120
Companions. See also Handbooks.
Companion to The Hymnal, 1982, x, 211
Companion to The United Methodist Hymnal, xi, 113, 140, 322
Hymnal Companion to the Lutheran Book of Worship, xi, 99, 102, 112
The Presbyterian Hymnal Companion, xi
Concordance to The Worshipping Church, 322
Congregational Praise (1951), 164, 165, 166

Congregational singing, *ix, xi*, 38, 46, 48, 87, 98, 103, 106, 109, 128, 141, 178, 187, 189, 203, 207, 215, 220, 222, 224, 246, 272, 290, 312, 322

Congregationalist, 93, 164, 167, 190, 192, 193, 194

Consultation on Ecumenical Hymnody, 215, 321

Converse, Charles C., 198

Copeland, Aaron, 197

Copyright permission service. *See* Christian Copyright Licensing, Inc. (CCLI)

Core of German Church Song, 111

Corpus Christi. See Christian calendar.

Cosin, John, 91

Council of Trent, 93

Counter-Reformation, 93

Coverdale, Miles, 127

Cowper, William, 143, 144, 146, 149, 152

Cranmer, Archbishop Thomas, 127, 152

Creeds (creedal), 64, 79, 85, 88, 89, 96

Croft, William, 122

Croly, George, 23, 149

Crosby, Fanny, 58, 197, 198, 200, 201, 242, 297

Cross rhyme, 16

Crossman, Samuel, 129, 131

Crouch, Andraé, 205, 314

Crüger, Johann, 101, 102, 104

Cultural diversity, *xi*, 219-234

Cultural inclusiveness, 316-320

Cultural relativism, 222

Cultural setting, 220, 225, 226

Culture, 77, 84, 140, 167, 180, 215, 219-234

Cummins, Evelyn Atwater, 72

Curriculum, 280, 281, 293

Cushing, William O., 56

Cutts, Peter, 172, 213, 321

Czech Republic, 106, 108

D

Daman, William, 118, 119

Dark Ages, 89, 91

Davies, J. G., 247

Davies, Walford, 163

Davis, Frances Wheeler, 218

Davisson, Ananias, 181, 183

Daw, Carl P., Jr., 23, 121, 172, 323

Day, John, 118

Deaf, 297, 307, 308, 316

Dearmer, Percy, 89, 90, 161, 162, 163

Denmark, 100, 112

Dexter, Henry M., 82

Dialogue, 25, 249-253

Dictionary of American Hymnology Project (DAH), 207, 208

Dictionary of Hymnology (Julian), 159, 207

Die Melodien der deutsche Kirchenlieder (Zahn), 111

Diemer, Emma Lou, 299

Dirksen, Richard, 211

Distler, Hugo, 114

Divine Songs Attempted in Easy Language for the Use of Children (Watts), 132

Dix, William Chattertonm 155

Doane, William H., 197, 198

Doddridge, Philip, 133-134

Dominican, 91

Doran, Carol, 212, 321

Dorsey, Thomas A., 205, 206

Douglas, C. Winfred, 129

Doving, Carl, 56

Doxological hymns, 80

Doxology, 17, 130, 142, 292

Doxology: Greater (*Gloria in excelsis Deo*), 65, 79, 81

Doxology: Lesser (*Gloria Patri*), 65

Draper, William H., 94
Dryden, John, 91
Dudley-Smith, Timothy, 27, 79, 171, 172, 323
Duffield, George, Jr., 193
Dunblane Consultations, 167
Duncan, Mary L., 55
Dunkerly, William A. *See* John Oxenham.
Dunstan, Sylvia, 68, 217-218
Dupuy, Starke, 185
Durnbaugh, Hedwig T., 115
Dutch, 98, 117, 123, 124, 125
Dwight, Timothy, 123, 125
Dykes, John Bacchus, 157, 268

E
Easter. See Christian calendar.
The Easy Instructor (1802), 181
Ebeling, Johann George, 104
"Echo" voices, 46
Ecumenical, 165, 170, 208, 209, 215, 233, 234
Eden, 58
Edson, Lewis, 179
Edward VI, 117
Edwards, III, Howard M. (Rusty), 214
Edwards, Paul C., 172
Edwards, Rusty. *See* Howard M. Edwards, III.
Ein New Gesengbuchlen (Weisse), 107
Elderly, 305
Ellerton, John, 90, 154, 173
Ellingsen, Svein, 115
Ellinwood, Leonard, 208
Elliott, Charlotte, 16, 150
Ellor, James, 143
Emendation, 66-68
Enemy of Apathy: Wild Goose Songs 2, 319
England, 102, 117-119, 121-122, 123,

127-177, 218
English, 98, 117, 120, 124, 125, 219, 225, 313
English folk tune, 42, 43
The English Hymnal (1906), 162-163, 168
English Praise (1975), 168, 169
Enlightenment, 109
Epanadiplosis, 24
Epiphany. See Christian calendar.
Episcopalian, 125, 192-193, 211, 212, 213, 225
Epizeuxis, 24
Este, Thomas, 119
Evangelical denominations, 203-204
Evangelical hymn, 111, 140, 146, 148, 159
Evangelical revival, 135, 140, 142, 143, 145, 146, 158, 160, 226
Evangelism, 64, 185-186, 190, 196-206, 221, 238-248
Evans, David, 164
Everest, Charles W., 192
Everett, Asa B., 203
Ewing, Alexander, 157
Excell, E. O., 44

F
Faber, Frederick William, 16, 149
Family, 81, 102, 220, 222, 270, 292-293, 304, 310
Farquharson, Walter H., 217
Fawcett, John, 145
Finland, 100, 101, 112, 158
Finlay, Kenneth G., 164
Finney, Charles G., 190
Fischer, William G., 198, 316
Fishel, Donald, 211
Fleming, Robert J. B., 218
Folk, 173, 180-188
Folk songs (music/tunes), 26, 30, 42, 43,

44, 47, 64, 95, 146, 162, 222, 226, 313
Foote, Henry Wilder, *viii*, 207-208
Fortunatus, Venantius Honorius
    Clementainus, 90
Fosdick, Harry Emerson, 209, 279
France, 92, 117, 140, 320
Francis I of France, 117
Francis of Assisi, 65, 94, 95, 279
Franciscan, 91
Franck, August H., 106
Franck, Johann, 104-105
Franklin, Benjamin, 123
Franzmann, Martin, 114
Free Kirk of Scotland, 121
French, 98, 115, 116, 123
Frere, W. H., 173
Frey, Marvin V., 314
Freylinghausen, Johann A., 106, 109
Frost, Maurice, 173
Frostenson, Anders, 114
Fuging tune, 96, 179-180
Funk, Joseph, 183

G
Gabarain, Cesareo, 318
Gabriel, Charles H., 202
Gaither, Gloria, 204
Gaither, William J., 204, 206
Gannett, William C., 142
Garratt, David, 313
Garratt, Gale, 313
Garrett, Les, 314
Gastoldi, Giovanni G., 100
Geistliche Singe-Kunst (Olearius), 105
Geistreiches Gesangbuch (Freyling-
    hausen), 106
Gelineau, Joseph, 49, 317
Genevan Psalter (completed 1562), 39,
    44, 102, 104, 105, 115-118
Genuine Church Music (1832), 183
Gerhardt, Paul, 103-104, 109, 190

German, 37, 39, 98-100, 101-106, 107-
    112, 113-114, 219, 272
Germany, 98, 99, 101, 102, 104, 105,
    114, 115, 117
Geyer, John B., 161
Geystliche Lieder (1545), 100
Ghana, 234, 319
Giardini, Felice de, 142, 146
Gibbons, Orlando, 127-128
Gilmore, Joseph Henry, 51, 191
Gladden, Washington, 192
Gläser, Carl G., 189
Gloria in excelsis Deo (the Greater Dox-
    ology), 65, 79, 81
Gloria Patri (the Lesser Doxology), 65
Gnostic, 65, 81
Goethe, Johann von, 75
Golden Canon, 84
Golden Sequence, 93
Good Friday. See Christian calendar.
Good news hymns, 242-246
Goostly Psalmes and Spirituall Songes
    (1537-43), 127, 175
Gordon, Adoniram J., 191
Gospel, 238-240, 242, 244, 246, 248,
    264, 279, 295, 303
Gospel hymn(s), 26, 32, 34, 108, 125,
    196-206, 216
Gospel Hymn Series, 199
Gospel Hymns and Sacred Songs (1875),
    196, 199
Gospel song(s). See Gospel hymn(s).
Gospel Songs (1874), 196.
Goss, John, 157
Gould, J. E., 198
Graded choir program, 280, 291
Gradual hymn, 98
Graham, Billy, 113, 204
Grant, John Webster, 91, 215-216
Grant, Robert, 24, 155
Great Awakening, 123

Greater Doxology (*Gloria in Excelsis Deo*), 65, 79, 81

Greek hymnody, 81-85, 153, 272

Green, Fred Pratt, 27, 114, 161, 168-169, 170, 172, 296, 298, 321, 323

Gregor, Christian, 107

Gregorian chant. *See* Plainsong.

Gregory I (the Great), 38, 65, 84, 89, 91

Grindal, Gracia, 213-214

Gruber, Franz, 113

Grundtvig, Nicholai Frederik Severin, 56, 112

Gurney, Dorothy Frances Blomfield, 24, 155

Gymanfa Ganu (Welsh), 225, 226

H

Hammond electronic organ, 205

Handbooks

Handbook to The Baptist Hymnal, 1991, x

Handbook to the Church Hymnary Revised (1927; 1935), 174

Handel, George F., 43, 52, 140

Handicapped, 297, 307, 308, 310, 316

Hankey, Arabella Katherine, 151, 198

Harkness, Georgia, 68, 210, 255, 288

Harmony, 31-34, 173, 224, 229, 266

Hart, Joseph, 134, 184

Harwood, Basil, 161

Hassler, Hans Leo, 100

Hastings, Thomas, 32, 189-190, 191, 196

Hatch, Edwin, 149

Havergal, Frances Ridley, 23, 151, 200

Haweis, Thomas, 143, 145

Hawks, Annie S., 197

Hayford, Jack, 314

Heber, Reginald, 67, 146-147, 148

Hebrew pattern, 22, 28, 72-73, 76

Hedge, Frederick H., 57

Heermann, Johann, 101

Helmore, Thomas, 158

Hendry, Dorothy Diemer, 299-300

Henry VIII, 117

Herbert, George, 19, 75, 128, 131, 173, 325

Heresy, 85-86, 89

Herman, Nikolaus, 100

Herresthal, Harald, 115

Hewitt, Eliza E., 200-201

Hilary of Poitiers, 86

Hill, Roland, 152

Hine, Stuart W. K., 113

Historical Companion to Hymns Ancient and Modern (1962), 173

Hoffman, Elisha A., 22, 203

Holden, Oliver, 143, 179

Holy Week. See Christian calendar.

Hopkins, John, 117-118

Hopper, Edward, 56, 193

Horae Lyricae (1705), 132

Hosmer, Frederick L., 162

Hospitals, 152, 306

Housman, Laurence, 163

How, William Walsham, 154

Howe, Julia Ward, 194

Hughes, Donald W., 168

Huntingdon, Lady, 142-143, 146

Hurd, David, 211

Hus, John, 106

Hussites. *See* Moravian.

Hymn, definition, *ix-x*

Hymn-of-the-Month plan, 290-291, 293

The Hymn Book (1971), 215-217

Hymn memorization program, 280

Hymn patterns, 70-73, 275

    objective-subjective, 70-71

    paradox and contrast, 71-72

    Hebrew pattern, 72-73

Hymn playing, 258-259, 292, 322, 323

Hymn rehearsal, 289-290
Hymn sing, 275, 289-290
Hymn Society, 210, 323
Hymn Society in the United States and
  Canada, ix, 164, 168, 169, 207, 210,
  308, 321, 323, 324
Hymn Society of Great Britain and Ire-
  land, 324
Hymn study classes, 291
The Hymnal (1982), x, 211, 216, 254,
  291, 308, 317
Hymnal: A Worship Book (1992), 115,
  234
Hymnal of the Moravian Church, 107
Hymnody, definition, x
Hymnology, definition, x
Hymns Ancient and Modern, 50, 153,
  156-158, 159, 161, 165, 167, 173
Hymns and Songs of the Church (1623),
  127
Hymns and Spiritual Songs (1707), 132
Hymns in the home, 292, 304
Hymns of Universal Praise (1936), 231-
  232
Hymns: A Congregational Study, 322
Hyperbole, 22, 28

I
Iambic, 17, 18, 35, 86, 89
Idle, Christopher, 172
Iliff, David, 172
Improvisation, 45, 187, 224, 263, 264
Inclusive language, 66-67, 315
Indian, 30, 234
Innovative hymn tunes, 46
Instrumental introduction, 258-259,
  289
International Arbeitsgemeinschaft für
  Hymnologie. See International Fel-
  lowship for Research in Hymnology.
International Fellowship for Research

in Hymnology, 174, 324
Iona Community, 319, 320
Ireland, 89, 121, 136, 198, 216, 324
Ireland, John, 129
Isáis, Juan M., 318
Isometric, 39, 41, 99, 109
itemization, 25, 28

J
Jackson, George Pullen, 180, 182, 185
Jackson, Mahalia, 205
Jacopone da Todi, 94
Jamaican, 234
James D. Vaughan Music Company, 203
Japanese, 234, 319
John of Damacus, 83-84, 279
Johnson, David N., 210
Johnson, J. Rosamond, 208
Johnson, James Weldon, 208
Johnson, Samuel, 194
Johnston, Julia H., 200
Jordan. See Canaan.
Jubilate Group, 171-172
Julian, John, 159, 207
Justice, 214, 319

K
Kaan, Fred, 114, 169-170
Kanon. See Canon (Greek).
Kantional style, 103
Das katholische deutsche Kirchenlied, 111
Keach, Benjamin, 130, 131
Keble, John, 81, 153, 154, 173
Kelly, Thomas, 16, 150, 173
Ken, Thomas, 17, 130
Kendrick, Graham, 313
Kennedy, Benjamin H., 16
Kentucky Harmony (1816), 118
Kethe, William, 118
Kierkegaard, Sören, 112, 249
King Edward VI, 117

King, E. J., 181-182
Kingsley, Charles, 162
Kirkpatrick, William J., 200, 201
Kitchin, G. W., 165
Knapp, Phoebe P., 198
Knox, John, 119
Kolb, George, 183
Kreuta, Robert E., 213

L
Lafferty, Karen, 211, 313
"Lamplighting Hymn," 81
Language issues, 314-316
Large-print editions, 308
Lathbury, Mary A., 193
Latin hymnody, 85-97
Latin American, 319
Laudi spirituali, 94, 240
Layriz, Friedrich, 111
Leaver, Robin, 174-175
Leavitt, Joshua, 190
Lectionary, 61, 125, 312
Lent. See Christian calendar.
Lesser Doxology (*Gloria Patri*), 65
Lincoln, C. Eric, 315
Lindeman, Ludvig Matthias, 112
Lindemann, Johann, 100
Lining-out, 221-222, 223
Litany pattern, 26
Literary Patterns, 25-26
  Call and Response, 26
  Dialogue, 25
  Itemization, 25
  Litany, 26
Little, William, 181
Liturgy, defined, 250
Long Meter (LM), 17, 39, 86
Longfellow, Henry Wadsworth, 81, 194
Longfellow, Samuel, 15, 194
Longstaff, William D., 200
Lord (of) Sabaoth, 56

Lowell, James Russell, 194
Löwenstern, Matthäus von, 102
Lowry, Robert, 197, 199, 202
Luff, Alan, 174
Luther, Martin, 87, 98-100, 109, 115,
  127, 139, 240, 274, 279, 292
Lutheran, 38, 98-106, 108-115, 210-
  211, 213-215
The Lutheran Book of Worship (1978), x,
  112, 213, 215, 254, 276, 278, 291,
  308, 317, 320, 321, 323
Lyte, Henry Francis, 23, 150, 302

M
Macaronic carol, 95
McCormick, David W., 179
McCurry, John G., 186
McCutchan, Helen Cowles, 207
McCutchan, Robert Guy, 128, 207
McDaniel, Rufus H., 202
McGranahan, James, 108, 200
McCurry, John Gordon, 186
McKinney, B. B., 204
McLeod, George, 319
Madan, Martin, 143, 146, 152
Magnificat, 79, 171
Major scale, 29, 31, 203
Mann, Newton, 142
Manning, Bernard, 133, 138, 139
*Many and Great: Songs of the World
  Church,* 319
Mar Saba, 83
March, Daniel, 192
Marot, Clement, 116, 117
Marsh, Charles H., 202
Marshall, Jane Manton, 212
Martin, Civilla D., 303
Mason, Lowell, 32, 43, 182, 189, 190,
  191, 203, 272
Massachusetts Bay Colony, 122
Massey, Bernard, 174

Massey, Charles, Jr., *vi*
Massie, Robert, 111
Matching tune and text, 47
Matheson, George, 21, 150
Maule, Graham A., 319
Maundy Thursday. See Christian calendar.
Maurus, Rabanus, 65, 91
Mead, Stith, 185
Medieval plainsong, 38
Meistersinger, 39, 99, 100, 103
Melody, 29, 30, 31
"Memorability," 46, 47
Mendelssohn, Felix, 111, 112
Mendicant Order, 91, 94
Mennonites, 223
Merrill, William P., 208, 209
Merryweather, Frank B., 75
Messiah, 43, 52
Metaphor, 22, 23
Meter(s), 17, 18, 29, 34, 35, 39, 45, 47, 48, 86, 226, 329
  poetic, 17, 18, 47, 86, 226
  musical, 29, 34, 35
  hymn, 17, 18, 39, 86
The Methodist Hymnal, 83, 179, 207
Methodist tunes, 139, 140, 143
Methodists, 193
Metrical index of tunes, 15, 18
Metrical Patterns, 17
  Common Meter (CM), 17, 39
  Iambic foot, 17
  Iambic tetrameter, 17, 86
  Iambic trimeter, 17
  Long Meter (LM), 17, 39, 86
  Short Meter (SM), 17, 39
Metrical Psalms, 39, 41, 98, 115-126, 140, 161, 179, 207, 221, 240, 272, 273, 317
Micklem, Caryl, 166
Middle Ages, 38, 87, 88, 91, 92, 93, 95

Miles, C. Austin, 202
Military imagery, 315, 316
Miller, Edward, 120
Miller, Josiah, 159
Milman, Henry Hart, 154
Milton, John, 19, 26, 128, 129, 131
A Mini-Course in Creative Hymn Playing, 322
A Mini-Course in Hymn Playing, 322
Ministry, 64, 65, 238, 295-310
The Missionary Hymn, 147
Missionary Movement, 195
Missouri Harmony (1820), 181
Moffatt, James, 174
Mohr, Joseph, 113
Monk, William H., 156, 157
Monsell, John Samuel Bewley, 154
Montgomery, James, 23, 24, 50, 146, 147, 148, 158, 159, 241, 255, 272
Moody and Sankey, 198-199, 241
Moody Bible Institute, 200, 204
Moody, Dwight L., 198-200, 241
Moore, Thomas, 151
Moore, William, 183
Moravian(s), 106-108, 135, 136, 141, 147, 223
More Hymns for Today (1980), 168
Mozart, 112
Murray, J. Glenn, 318
Music Leadership in the Church, 250
The Music of Christian Hymnody (1957), 101
The Music of Christian Hymns (1981), 175
The Music of the French Psalter of 1562 (1939), 207
The Music of the Pilgrims (1921), 207
Music therapist, 306

N
National Eisteddfod, 226

National hymns. *See* Patriotic.
Nativity canticles, 78, 79
Neale, John Mason, 57, 83, 84, 85, 88, 92, 93, 95, 96, 101, 156, 158, 159, 279
Neander, Joachim, 105-106
Negro spiritual, 206, 215, 241, 242
Neoplatonic philosophy, 82
Netherlands Reformed Churches, 124
Neumark, Georg, 105
Neumeister, Erdmann, 108, 200
New Beginnings, 321
New Catholic Hymnal, 166
The New Century Hymnal (1995), 320
The New Church Hymnal (1976), 50
New Church Praise (1975), 168
New England, 123, 221, 222, 223, 225
New Hymns for the Lectionary, 212, 321
New Hymns for the Life of the Church, 321
A New Metrical Psalter, 125
New Songs for the Church I and II, 167
New Testament, 51, 53, 54, 57, 58, 78, 79, 80
The New National Baptist Hymnal, 205, 316
New Oxford Book of Carols, 166
A New Version of the Psalms of David, fitted to the tunes used in Churches (1696), 121, 122, 131
Newbolt, M. R., 165
Newman, John Henry, 153
Newton, John, 52, 55, 143, 144, 145, 149, 152, 303, 304
Niceta of Remesiana, 87
Nicholson, James, 316
Nicholson, Sydney H., 165
Nicolai, Philipp, 100
Noel, Caroline M., 54
Noninclusive language, 66, 67
Norsk Salmebok, 115
North, Frank Mason, 73, 209, 300, 301

Noyes, Morgan Phelps, 207
Nursing home, 306, 308
Nuttall, G. F., 134

O

Oakeley, Frederick, 96
Oatman, Johnson, Jr., 202
Objective-subjective, 70-71, 84, 85, 246
O'Driscoll, T. Herbert, 216, 217
Old Order Amish, 222, 223
Old Testament, 51, 52, 54, 55, 56, 57, 58, 59, 61, 78
Old Testament Psalter, 78
Old Version. See *Sternhold and Hopkins Psalter.*
Olearius, Johannes, 105
Olivers, Thomas, 140, 142
Olney Hymns (1779), 143, 144, 152
Oral tradition, 42, 96, 158, 160, 180, 181, 182, 222, 223
The Organist and Hymn Playing, 322
Oriental hymnody, 229, 231, 232, 233
Orthodox(y), 65, 82, 85, 87, 88, 89, 96, 234
Osborne, Stanley L., 215
Our Hymnody (1937), 207
Our Lives Be Praise (1990), 173
Our Own Hymnbook (1866), 159
Owens, Priscilla, 201
Oxenham, John, 164, 235, 315
The Oxford Book of Carols (1928), 163
Oxford Holy Club, 140
Oxford Movement, 65, 91, 102, 149, 151-160
Oxford Reformers, 65
Oyer, Mary, *iv*

P

Pace, M. M., 20
Palestrina, 88, 94
Palm Sunday. See Christian calendar.

Palmer, Ray, 22, 93, 191, 192
Palmer, Sir Roundell, 159
A Panorama of Christian Hymnody
(1979), 176
Paradox, 21, 22, 28, 218
Paradox and contrast, 71-72
Parallelism, 23, 24
Paris Antiphoner of 1681, 92
The Paris Breviary (1736), 96
Parker, Matthew, 119
Parry, Hubert H., 161, 213
Parry, Kenneth L., 66
Patrick, Millar, viii, 174
Patriotic hymns, 195
Patterson, Robert, 184
Pauline hymn fragments, 79-80, 240
Peace, 71, 214, 218, 247, 262, 276, 301,
302, 305, 316, 319
Peacock, David, 172
The Pedagogue (ca. 200), 82
Pedalpoint, 322
Penderecki, 94
Pennsylvania Dutch, 222
Pentatonic scale, 30, 44, 229
Pentecost. See Christian calendar.
Pentecostal, 204
The People's Mass Book (1964, eds. to
1976), 213
Pergolesi, 94
Perronet, Edward, 142, 143
Perry, Michael, 79, 172
Persichetti, 94
Personification, 22
Peterson, John W., 204, 206, 216
Petri, Theodoric, 101
Phelps, Sylvanus D., 191, 197
Phillips, Philip, 199
Piae Cantiones (1582), 101, 158
Pierpoint, Folliott Sandford, 26, 156
Pietism, 105, 106, 108, 109
Pilsbury, Amos, 184

Pilgrim's Musical Companion, 184
Pilgrim's Progress (1684), 129
Pilgrims, 122
Pinson, Joe, 306-307
Plainsong (or Gregorian Chant), 30, 34,
38, 49, 82, 88, 158, 161, 189, 313
Planting Trees and Sowing Seeds, 170
Playford, John, 120
Pliny the Younger, 80
Plumptre, Edward Hayes, 53, 155, 298
Poetic feet, 17, 18, 329
Poetic form and style, 19
Poetic meter, 17-18, 35
Iambic, 17-18, 35
Trochaic, 18, 35
Poetry, 14, 19-23, 27, 63, 80, 132, 219
Poitiers, 86, 89, 90
Pollard, Adelaide A., 200
Pollock, John, 143-144
Pott, Francis, 96
Potter, Doreen, 321
Poulenc, 94
Praetorius, Michael, 101
Praise and worship, 313-314
Praise for Today (1969)
Praise the Lord, 166
Praises Resound! 115
Praising a Mystery, 321
Pratt, Waldo Selden, 116, 207
Praxis pietatis melica, 104
Prentiss, Elizabeth P., 193, 198
Presbyterian, 193, 218
Presbyterian Church (U.S.A.), 125
The Presbyterian Hymnal (Presbyterian
Church U.S.A., 1990), x, 125, 254,
288, 299, 312, 316, 317, 318, 323
Price, Carl F., ix
Price, Milburn, viii, 295, 314
Primitive Baptist, 222
Pritchard, Hugh, 146
Proclamation, 238, 240-247, 295

"Proper tunes," 120
Prose hymns, 81
Protestant Reformation, 39, 98, 240
Prudentius, Aurelius Clemens, 57, 65, 88
Psalm Praise (1973), 171
A *Psalm Sampler,* 125
Psalm tunes(s), 39, 41
Psalmes (1579), 118
Psalmes (1592), 119
Psalmes (1621), 119
The Psalmist, 191
The Psalms, 49-51, 78, 87
Psalms and Hymns, 136
Psalms and Hymns in Solemn Musick, 120
Psalms for Today (1990), 172
Psalms of David Imitated in the Language of the New Testament (1719), 123, 133
Psalter Hymnal (1927), 125
Psalter Hymnal (1987), 125, 317
Psalters, 98, 115, 119, 124
  Ainsworth, 122
  Anglo-Genevan, 118, 119, 125
  Associated Reformed Presbyterian, 125
  Bay Psalm Book, 123, 124
  Calvin's, 116
  English, 39, 117, 118, 121, 122
  Este (1592), 119
  French, 116
  Genevan, 39, 115, 117, 125, 102, 104, 105, 115-118
  John Playford, 120
  Matthew Parker, 119
  Ravenscroft, 119, 123
  Scottish, 39, 50
  Sternhold's and Hopkins, 118, 119
  Strassburg, 115
  Supplement to Tate and Brady, 122
  Tate and Brady, 118, 121, 122
  United Presbyterian, 124
Purcell, 88, 140

Puritans, 122, 123, 225, 226
Pusey, Philip, 102

Q
Quaker(s), 64, 193, 194
Queen Mary, 118
"Queen of Canons," 84
Quinn, James, 79

R
Raby, E. J. E., 92
Rankin, Jeremiah E., 22
Ravenscroft Psalter, 119, 123
Redner, Lewis, 192
Rees, Timothy, 164
Reeves, Jeremiah Bascom, 14
Reformed Church in America, 125
Reformed Presbyterian Church, 125
Refrain, interlinear, 26, 186
Reid, William W., 210
Rejoice and Sing (1991), 314
Rejoice in the Lord (1958, 1985), 62, 176, 323
Renewal in worship, 312-316
Reno, Delma B., 57
Renville, Joseph R., 318
Repository of Sacred Music, Part Second, 183
Requiem Mass, 93
Revivalism, 190, 198, 203, 244
Revival(s), 45, 101, 140, 141, 152, 168, 190, 196, 226
Reynolds, William J., *viii*, 182
Rhyme, 15
Rhyme scheme(s), 15, 16, 17, 329
Rhyming couplets, 15
Rhythm and meter, 29, 34-35
Rhythmic chorale, 39
Richardson, Paul, *iv,*
Riedel, Johannes, 39, 99, 103, 104, 106, 109

Riedel, Scott R., 322
Rinkart, Martin, 102, 166
Rippon, John, 143
Robbins, Howard Chandler, 94
Roberts, Daniel C., 193
Rock of Ages, 55-56
Rodeheaver, Homer A., 201, 202
Roland (or Rowland), 146
Roman Catholic, 102, 108, 111, 115, 118, 218, 225, 231, 234, 312, 318
Romantics, 146-148
Rosenius, Carl Olof, 113
Rothenbusch, Ester Heidi, 199
Routley, Erik, v, viii, 15, 47, 62, 85, 101, 125, 128, 131, 134, 140, 142, 144, 148, 153, 158, 162, 164, 165, 167, 168, 169, 170, 172, 175-177, 233, 250, 256, 321, 323
Rowthorn, Jeffery W., 68, 213
Runyan, William M., 204
Ryden, E. E., viii

S
The Sacred Harp (1844), 179, 181, 182, 186, 223, 257
Sacred Songs and Solos, 199
St. James of Jerusalem, 82
St. Matthew Passion (1729), 110
St. Patrick, 88
St. Stephen's Day. See Christian calendar.
St. Thomas Sunday. See Christian calendar.
Sammis, John H., 200
Sanchez, Diana, 322
Sandell-Berg, Caroline Vilhelmina, 113
Sandys, William, 158
Sankey, Ira D., 196, 198-201, 206, 241
Sapphic meter, 89, 102
Sappho, 89
Saward, Michael, 172

Sawyer, Frank, 318
Scandinavian, 39, 98, 100-101, 112-115
Scarlatti, A., 94
Scarlatti, D., 94
Schaff, Philip, 207
Schalk, Carl, iv, v, viii, 211, 263, 321
Schilling, S. Paul, 323
Schmolck, Benjamin, 108
School of Watts, 133-134
Schulz-Widmar, Russell, 211, 213
Schulz, Johann A. P., 109
Schutz, Johann J., 302
Schütz, Johann Jakob, 105
Schwedler, Johaan C., 16
Schweizer, Rolf, 113, 114
Scott, Clara H., 25, 120-122
Scott, Robert B. Y., 215
Scott, Walter, Sir, 146, 147
Scottish Psalms, 119-121
Scottish Psalter (1650), 39, 50, 120, 121
Scripture, 49-62, 63, 78-80, 86, 87, 98, 114, 115, 130, 132, 135, 137, 152, 171, 211, 212, 239-240
Scripture songs, 211, 269, 313
Scriven, Joseph M., 198
Sears, Edmund H., 194
Second Vatican Council (1962-65), 312
Seddon, James E., 172
Sedgwick, Daniel, 159
A Selection of Hymns from the Best Authors (1787), 143
A Selection of Psalms and Hymn Tunes from the Best Authors (1791), 143
Sent by the Lord: Songs of the World Church, 1 & 2, 319
Sequence hymns, 93
Sequences, 93
Seventh-Day Baptists of Ephrata, PA, 223
Sexist language, 66-67

Shakers, 223

Shape-note(s), 44, 45, 181, 202, 203, 223

Sharpe, Eric, 174

Shaw, Geoffrey, 163

Shaw, Benjamin, 184

Shaw, Martin, 164

Shelley, 146

Shepherd, 54-55

Sheppard, Franklin L., 208

Shipley, Linda, *iv*

Short Meter (SM), 17, 39

A Short Story of English Church Music, 153

Showalter, Anthony J., 203

Shrubsole, William, 143

Shubert, 94

Shurtleff, Ernest W., 192

Simile, 23

Simmons, Morgan, 215

Sinclair, Jerry, 314

"Singability," 46-47

Singers and Songs of the Church (1869), 159

Singing Psalms of Joy and Praise, 125

Singing school, 178, 222

Singing school teachers, 44, 178-180

Singspiration, 204

Singstunden, 107

Sion, 59-60

Slade, Mary B. C., 203

Slave Songs of the United States, 187

Smart, Henry, 157

Smith, Alfred B., 204

Smith, S. E. Boyd, 142

Smith, Samuel F., 191

Smith, Walter Chalmers, 155

Smith, William, 181

The Social Harp, 186

Songs of Deliverance, 171

Songs of Praise (1926), 163-164

Songs of Syon (1904, 1910), 161-162

Songs of Zion (1981), 225, 317

Songs of Zion, Being Imitations of the Psalms (1822), 50

Southern Harmony (1835), 44, 181, 184-186, 223

Southern shape-note, 223

Southey, Robert, 146, 147

Spafford, Horatio G., 200

Spanish-language hymnody, 318

Sparrow, John, 140

Spencer, Donald A., 61, 288

Spener, Philipp Jakob, 105

Spilman, Charles, H., 184

Spiritual Songs for Social Worship, 190

Spirituals, 26, 45, 59, 187, 224, 225, 234

Spitta, Karl Johann Philipp, 111

Spiritual Melody (1691), 130

Spoken modulation, 326

Spurgeon, Charles Haddon, 159

Stainer, John, 157, 158

Stamps-Baxter Music Company, 203

Stanford, Charles V., 161, 321

Stanislaw, Richard J., 181

Stanton, Walter K., 165

Stanza, defined, 14

Stead, Louisa M. R., 201

Stebbins, George C., 198, 200

Steele, Anne, 134, 257

Stein, Paul, 114

Sternhold and Hopkins Psalter, 117-119, 121

Sternhold, Thomas, 117

Stevenson, Robert, *viii*

Stewart, Malcolm, 166

Stone, Samuel J., 66, 155

Stookey, Lawrence Hull, 96

The Story of the Church's Song (1927; 1962), 122, 174

Strassburg Psalter of 1539, 115

Strophic, 36

Struther, Jan, 164
Studdert-Kennedy, Geoffrey A., 164
Studium of St. John, 84
Study of hymns, *x*, 322
Sullivan, Arthur, 157
Summa Theologica, 95
Sunday, William (Billy), 202
Supplement to the Kentucky Harmony (1820), 183
Sweney, John R., 200
Sydnor, James R., 290, 292, 322
Synecdoche, 24
Synesius of Cyrene, 82, 85
Synthesis, 72-73

T
Tag line, 26
Taizé, 319-320
Tallis, Thomas, 88, 119
Tate and Brady (New Version), 121, 122
Tate, Nahum, 121, 122, 131
Tautology, 23-24
Taylor, Cyril V., 162, 165, 215
Teaching new hymns, 287-289
The Temple: Sacred Poems and Private Ejaculations (1633), 75, 128
Tennyson, Alfred Lord, 19, 27
Tersteegen, Gerhard, 106
Teschner, Melchior, 100
Tessitura, 30
Texture and form, 29, 35-37
Theodore of the Studium, 84
Theodosuis, Emperor, 85
Theodulph of Orleans, 100
Theological controversy, 65-69, 85, 96
Theology, 63-76, 238
Thesis, 72-73
Thiman, Eric H., 164
Thirty Years' War, 89, 101, 102
Thomas of Celano, 93
Thomson, Mary Ann, 24, 192

Thomson, Virgil, 94
Thompson, Will L., 200
Thring, Godfrey, 296
Thrupp, Dorothy A., 51, 151
Tindley, Charles A., 205
Tisserand, Jean, 95
Todi, Jacopone da, 94
Toplady, Augustus, 56, 68, 69, 145, 149, 152
Torrey, Reuben A., 201
Townsend, Mrs. A. M., 316
Towner, Daniel B., 200
Tractarian Movement, 153, 274. See Oxford Movement.
Trautwein, Dieter, 113, 114
Tredinnick, Noel, 172
Trinitarian, 85, 274
Trinitarian doxology, 65
Trinity Sunday. See Christian calendar.
Trinitytide. See Christian calendar.
Trochaic, 18, 35
Troeger, Thomas H., *v*, 25, 212, 315, 321
Trope, 93, 95, 101
Troubadours, 99
Trouveres, 99
Tucker, F. Bland, 54, 55, 79, 81, 82, 92, 210, 288, 304
Tufts, John, 178-179
Tunebook, 15, 181-185, 223
The Tutor, 82
Twells, Henry, 53
Twentieth-Century Church Light Music Group, 165-166
Twentieth-Century Folk Mass (or "Jazz Mass"), 165-166

U
Unitarian hymnody, 194
The United Methodist Hymnal (1989), 216, 234, 254, 276, 278, 288, 312, 314, 316, 317, 318, 323

United Presbyterian church, 124
United Presbyterian Book of Psalms, 124
United States Harmony, 185
Unitas Fratrum, 106

V

Vajda, Jaroslav, v, 211, 321
Valentinian, Emperor, 86
Van Burkalow, Anastasia, 316
Van Dyke, Henry, 67, 208
Van Dyke, Mary Louise, 208
Vatican II, 312
Vaughan, James D., 203
Vaughan Music Company, James D., 203
Vaughan Williams, Ralph, 36, 88, 90, 128, 129, 161-163, 272, 290
Verdi, 88, 94
Verse, defined, 14
Victorian part-song, 42
A Voice of Singing: Thirty-six New Hymns, 170
Vulpius, Melchior, 100

W

Wade, John Francis, 96
Walker, William, 44, 181-187
"Walking" bass line, 46
Wallin, Johan Olaf, 112
Walter, Thomas, 178
Walton, Isaak, 88, 126, 128
Waring, Anna Laetitia, 151
Warren, George W., 193
Warren, Norman, 172
Waters, Moir A. J., 215-216
Watts, Isaac, 24, 71, 72, 73, 122-124, 128, 129, 130-135, 138, 140, 144, 148, 159, 173, 191, 255, 274, 278, 302-303, 326-328
Webb, George J., 191
Webster, Bradford Gray, 210

Weisse, Michael, 107
Welsh hymnody, 141-142, 225-227
Welsh folk tune(s), 43-44
Welsh Hymns and Their Tunes (1990), 141, 226
Wesley, Charles, 20-24, 26, 57, 64, 68, 71, 137, 139, 142, 146, 169, 191, 258, 274, 303
Wesley, John, 68, 103, 106, 123, 135, 136, 137, 138, 139, 140, 153, 255, 275, 279, 288, 289
Wesleyan hymn traits, 138-139
Westendorff, Omer, 213
What Language Shall I Borrow?, 67, 315
White spirituals, 188
White, B. F., 179, 181, 182
Whitefield, George, 140, 141, 142, 145, 152
Whiting, William, 141, 226, 268
Whittier, John Greenleaf, 16, 20, 64, 74, 162, 193, 272
Whittle, Daniel W., 72, 199
The Whole Book of Psalms (Day), 118
The Whole Book of Psalms (Playford) 120
Wienandt, Elwyn, 179
Wild Goose Worship (Music) Group, 319
Williams, Robert, 226
Williams, William, 52, 141, 226
Williamson, Malcolm, 173, 208
Willis, Richard S., 192
Wilson, John W., 46, 172, 189
Wilson, Kenneth, 322
Wilson, Woodrow, 301
Winkworth, Catherine, 111, 153, 156, 166
Wither, George, 127-128, 131
Wohlgemuth, Paul W., 314
Wolcott, Samuel, 192
Wood, Charles, 162
Woodford, J. R., 95

Woodward, George R., 161
Woolard, Margot Ann G., 322
Words, Music, and the Church, 250
Wordsworth, Christopher, 155, 173
World Library of Sacred Music (1950), 213
Worship, 249-276
Worship (1986), 313
Worship and Mission, 247
Worship Leaders' Edition. *See The Worshipping Church.*
Worship renewal, 312-314
The Worshipping Church, 288, 314, 315, 322
Wren, Brian, 17, 167, 170, 171, 172, 315, 316, 321, 323
Wyeth, John, 181, 183, 184

X
Xavier, Francis, 96

Y
Yattendon Hymnal (1899), 161-162
Young, Carlton R., 167, 170, 173, 212, 322
Young, Robert H., 179
Youth Praise 1 (1966), 171
Youth Praise 2 (1969), 171

Z
Zelner, John F., III, 197
Zimmerman, Heinz Werner, 114
Zinzendorf, Nicholaus Ludwig von, 107
Zion (Sion), 59-60
Zundel, John, 192

BIBLICAL REFERENCE INDEX

Old Testament

Genesis 1 62
Genesis 2:8 57
Genesis 11:9 57
Genesis 25:26 57
Genesis 30:24 58
Genesis 32:3 57
Genesis 36:21 57

Exodus 2:10 58
Exodus 13:21 53
Exodus 15 83
Exodus 15:1-18 84
Exodus 16:4,12,18 53
Exodus 17:1 53
Exodus 20:11 53

Numbers 32:32 53
Numbers 33:50-53 57

Deuteronomy 6:4 57
Deuteronomy 8:2 53
Deuteronomy 8:14-20 53
Deuteronomy 9:29 53
Deuteronomy 34:1 58

Joshua 1:2 58
Joshua 3:8, 17 53

1 Samuel 7:12 57

1 Samuel 16:1-22 58

1 Kings 19 55

Psalm 5:8 53
Psalm 6:2 53
Psalm 8 . . . . 38, 171
Psalm 12 116
Psalm 14 118
Psalm 18:2 53
Psalm 23 . . . . 49, 50, 51, 102, 121,
    133, 265, 273, 317
Psalm 24:8 53
Psalm 27:6 53
Psalm 28:7 53
Psalm 29:5 58
Psalm 33:22 290
Psalm 34:1 53
Psalm 40:1-3 239
Psalm 40:9-10 239
Psalm 42 . . . . 105, 122, 265
Psalm 46 99
Psalm 48:1 257
Psalm 48:11 58
Psalm 67 23
Psalm 70:5 53
Psalm 72 . . . . 24, 133, 280
Psalm 78:15-16 53
Psalm 78:52 53
Psalm 82 129

Psalm 84 . . . . 119, 121, 265
Psalm 85 129
Psalm 86 129
Psalm 90 . . . . 72, 122, 133
Psalm 90:1-2 . . . . 326, 327
Psalm 91 62
Psalm 95:1-7 40
Psalm 96:1 233
Psalm 96:1-3 239
Psalm 96: 9; 13 40
Psalm 98 133
Psalm 98:1-4, 7-9 327
Psalm 100 . . . . 116, 133
Psalm 101 117
Psalm 103 . . . . 62, 124
Psalm 107:8 257
Psalm 107:22 252
Psalm 113 78
Psalm 114 78
Psalm 115 78
Psalm 116 78
Psalm 117 . . . . 78, 133
Psalm 118 . . . . 78, 133
Psalm 121:1-8 265
Psalm 130 99
Psalm 132 118
Psalm 134 . . . . 116, 118
Psalm 136 . . . . 26, 129
Psalm 137 124
Psalm 139:10 53
Psalm 144:2 53
Psalm 146 133
Psalm 146:2 53
Psalm 148 . . . . ix, 234

Ecclesiastes 50:22-24 102

Song of Solomon 2:1 58

Jeremiah 8:22 57

Isaiah 1:24 53
Isaiah 2:1-4 171
Isaiah 6:1-4 250
Isaiah 6:1-8 . . . . 52, 273
Isaiah 6:3 87
Isaiah 6:5 250
Isaiah 6:8 251
Isaiah 6:6-7 251
Isaiah 9:67 171
Isaiah 26:4 55
Isaiah 35:4 53
Isaiah 40:1-8 . . . . 52, 105
Isaiah 40:1-11 62
Isaiah 41:10 51
Isaiah 43:2 . . . . 51, 52
Isaiah 66:13 315

Daniel 7-9 56
Daniel 13 56
Daniel 22 56

Micah 4:1-4 171

Apocrypha
Ecclesiasticus 50:22-24 102

New Testament
Matthew 1:23 57
Matthew 2:1-8 57
Matthew 2:11 58
Matthew 3:13 57
Matthew 5:1-12 62
Matthew 6:33 . . . . 211, 313
Matthew 7:7 211
Matthew 7:24-27 55
Matthew 16:25 71
Matthew 20:27 71
Matthew 25:40 296
Matthew 26:36 57
Matthew 27:33 57

Mark 1:32-33 53
Mark 11:1-10 90
Mark 16:14-20 61

Luke 1:46-55. 79
Luke 1:68-79. 79
Luke 2 112
Luke 2:8-14 . . . . 53, 131
Luke 2:13-14. 240
Luke 2:14 79
Luke 2:22 58
Luke 2:29-32. 79
Luke 2:51 58
Luke 10:41 58
Luke 15:3-7 50
Luke 18:10 58
Luke 23:33 57

John 3:16 . . . . 273, 290
John 4:25 58
John 6:48-51 53
John 9:7-11 58
John 10 51
John 12:12-19. 90
John 17:22 69
John 20:19-29. 62

Acts 1:1-11 61
Acts 6:5. 58
Acts 13:2 250
Acts 14:24-31 80
Acts 16:9 58
Acts 16:25 80
Acts 16:25-31. 240

Romans 9:29 56
Romans 12:1. 250
1 Corinthians 10:4 290
1 Corinthians 13. 171
1 Corinthians 14:15i, ... 310
1 Corinthians 28:20 53

2 Corinthians 10:4 53

Galatians 5:22-23 273
Galatians 6:14 54

Ephesians 5:14 240
Ephesians 5:18-19 . . . . ix, 80
Ephesians 6 316

Philippians 2:5-11 . . . . 54, 62, 290

Colossians 3:16. 80
Colossians 3:16-17 . . . . 62, 273

1 Timothy 3:16. . . . . 79, 240

2 Timothy 1:10. 53
2 Timothy 1:12. 72
Hebrews 2:14 53
Hebrews 8:6 250
Hebrews 11:13 53
Hebrews 12:2 57

James 5:4. 56

1 Peter 1:4-19. 114

Revelation 1:4-8 80
Revelation 1:8. . . . . 57, 88
Revelation 1:11 57
Revelation 4 171
Revelation 5 171
Revelation 5:9-10 80
Revelation 5:12 54
Revelation 11: 17-18 80
Revelation 15:3-4 80
Revelation 19:1-3 80
Revelation 21:6 57
Revelation 22:1-2 53
Revelation 22:13 57

HYMN TITLE
AND
FIRST LINE INDEX

Titles are in caps and small caps; first lines in lower case type.

A

A Hymn for the Nation, 169

A hymn of glory let us sing, 61

A mighty fortress is our God, 35, 37, 47, 76, 99, 271, 283

A pilgrim was I and a wand'ring, 204

Abide with me, 36, 76, 150, 302

Adeste fidelis laeti triumphantes, 96

Adoro te devote, 95

Ah, holy Jesus, how hast thou offended, 101, 104, 161, 254, 285

Alas, and did my Savior bleed, 71, 132, 269

All beautiful the march of days, 37, 43

All creatures of our God and King, 30, 36, 65, 94, 111, 264, 281, 283

All glory, laud, and honor, 35, 90, 100, 254, 282

All hail the power of Jesus' name, 36, 48, 70, 142, 179, 252, 285

All hail to you, O blessed morn, 111, 112

All my heart today (this night) rejoices, 103, 104

All my hope is firmly grounded, 161

All my hope on God is founded, 161

All people that on earth do dwell, 31, 35, 36, 116, 118, 260

All praise to thee, for thou, O King divine, 36, 46, 54, 70, 210, 288

All praise to thee, my God, this night, 119, 130, 281, 282

All the way my Savior leads me, 198

All things bright and beautiful, 150, 282

All who love and serve your city, 167, 172

Alleluia, 314

Alleluia, alleluia! Give thanks to the risen Lord, 211

Alleluia! Alleluia! hearts to heaven, 155

Alleluia! sing to Jesus, 35, 60, 227

Almighty (eternal) Father, strong to save, 268

Alone thou goest forth, O Lord, 92

Altissimi, omnipotente, bon Signore, 94

Am I a soldier of the cross, 25, 34, 132

Amazing grace! how sweet the sound, 30, 47, 48, 144, 184, 224, 267, 285, 303, 304, 317

America, the beautiful, 18, 195, 284

And can it be that I should gain, 137

And have the bright immensities, 43

Angels from the realms of glory, 148

Angularis fundamentum, 90

Are ye able, said the Master, 264

As Jacob with travel, 59

As men (those/saints) of old their first fruits brought, 37, 43, 210, 215, 260

As pants the heart (longs the deer) for cooling streams, 122

As with gladness men of old, 155, 260, 283

Ask ye what great thing I know, 16, 25, 54, 264

At even, ere the sun was set, 53

At the cross, her station (vigil) keeping, 94

At the Lamb's high feast we sing, 110

At the name of Jesus, 30, 54, 289
Aus fremden Landen komm ich her, 99
Aus tiefer Not schrei ich zu dir, 99
Awake, awake to love and work, 164
Awake, my soul, and with the sun, 130, 282
Awake, my soul, stretch every nerve, 134
Awake, O sleeper, rise from death, 79
Away in a manger, 195, 196, 201, 282

B

Baptized in water
Be known to us in breaking bread, 118, 148
Be not dismayed whate'er be tide, 303
Be present at our table, Lord, 31, 35, 36, 116
Be thou my vision, 36, 285
Beautiful Savior, 281, 282
Because He Lives, 204
Befiehl du deine Wege, 103
Before Jehovah's awful (awesome) throne,
    31, 35, 133
Behold a broken world, 171
Believers all, our common task, 295
Beneath the cross of Jesus, 54, 150, 252
Benedicamus Domino, 95
Benedictus, 79
Bless thou the gifts our hands have brought,
    194
Blessed assurance, Jesus is mine, 34, 48, 198
Blessed be the God of Israel, 37, 43, 79
Blessed be the name of the Lord, 26, 307
Blessed Jesus, at thy (your) word, 260
Blessed word of God, 234
Blessing and honor, 54
Blessing and honor and glory and power, 149
Blest are the pure in heart, 154
Blest be the God of Israel, 37
Blest be the King whose coming, 35
Blest be the tie that binds, 145, 261
Blott en dag ett ögonblick i sänder, 113
Blow ye the trumpet, blow, 179
Bread of the world in mercy broken, 117, 147
Break forth, O beauteous heavenly light, 110
Break thou the bread of life, 193, 261
Breathe on me, breath of God, 149, 285
Brethren, we have met to worship, 183
Bright and glorious is the sky, 112

Brightest and best of the Stars (sons) of the
    morning, 62, 147
Built on the (a) Rock, the church doth stand,
    29-30, 56, 112, 285
Burn in me, fire of God, 216
By gracious powers so wonderfully sheltered,
    114, 169

C

Called as partners in Christ's service, 33
Canticle of Praise to God, 40
Canticle to the Sun, 94
Children of the heavenly father, 113
Children of the heavenly King, 142
Christ, du Beistand deiner Kreutzgemeine, 102
Christ for the world we sing, 192, 195
Christ is alive! 170, 285
Christ is made the sure foundation, 60, 65, 90
Christ is risen (Kaan tr.), 170
Christ is risen (Wren), 170
Christ is risen, Christ is living, 234
Christ is the world's true light, 164
Christ Jesus lay in death's strong bands, 99,
    110, 279
Christ lag in Todesbanden, 99
Christ, mighty Savior, 212
Christ receiveth sinful men, 108, 200
Christ the Lord is risen today! 24, 137, 227,
    254, 283
Christ the worker, 229
Christ, upon the mountain peak, 46, 171, 172
Christ, when for us you were baptized, 120
Christ whose glory fills the skies, 137
Christi Blut und Gerechttigkeit, 107
Christian, dost thou see them? 83
Christian hearts, in love united, 107
Christians, while on earth abiding, 112
Christian women, Christian men, 300
"Christus Paradox," 218
City of God, how broad and far, 194
Come, Christians, join to sing, 37, 257, 265,
    282
Come, ev'ry soul by sin oppressed, 247
Come, follow me the Savior spake, 247
Come, Holy Ghost, God and Lord, 93
Come, Holy Ghost, our hearts (souls) inspire,

41, 65, 91, 119, 244, 260

Come, Holy Spirit, Dove divine, 36
Come, Holy Spirit, heavenly Dove, 42, 73,
   132, 267, 327
Come, let us join our cheerful songs, 54, 132
Come, let us join our friends above, 37, 43
Come, let us use the grace divine, 43
Come, my Way, my Truth, my Life, 19, 34, 128
Come now, and praise the humble saint, 119
Come, O Spirit, dwell among us, 30
Come, O thou traveller unknown, 137
Come, risen Lord, 164, 254
Come, sinners to the gospel feast, 247
Come, thou almighty King, 37, 56, 145, 146,
   260, 269, 283
Come, thou Fount of every blessing, 37, 44,
   61, 184, 185, 186, 224, 260, 261
Come, thou Holy Spirit bright, 93
Come, thou long expected Jesus, 21, 35, 137,
   227, 243, 268, 282
Come to Calvary's holy mountain, 112
Come, we (ye) that love the Lord, 59, 132,
   211, 260
Come with us, O blessed Jesus, 110
Come, ye disconsolate, 151, 247
Come, ye sinners, poor and needy, 134, 184,
   247
Come, ye (you) faithful, raise the strain, 18,
   84, 285
Come ye (you) thankful people, come, 31,
   153, 283
Comfort, comfort ye (you) (now) my people,
   52, 105, 117
Corde natus ex Parentis, 88
Cradling children in his arm, 112
Creating God, your fingers trace, 213, 215
Creator God, creating still, 36
Creator of the earth and skies, 168
Creator Spirit, by whose aid, 91
Crossing the Bar, 19
Crown Him with many crowns, 18, 61, 155,
   285

D
Day by day and with each passing moment,
   113

Day is dying in the west, 52, 193
De contemptu mundi, 93
De såg ej dif blott timmermannens, 114
Dear Lord and Father of mankind, 16, 20, 64,
   194, 262, 265
Dearest Jesus, we are here, 108
Deck thyself (yourself), my soul, with glad-
   ness, 104
Deep River, 59
Dejlig er den Himmel blaa, 112
Den signede Dag, 112
Depth of mercy, can there be, 137
Det dimer nu til Julefest, 112
Die güldne Sonne voll Freud und Wonne, 104
Dies irae, 93
Draw us in the Spirit's Tether, 163
Du som fromma hjartan vaarder, 112
Du, som gaar ud, 112

E
Earth and all stars, 210
Earth has many a noble city, 88
Eat this bread, 320
Ein' feste Burg ist unser Gott, 57, 99
Eternal Father, strong to save, 156
Eternal God, whose power upholds, 37, 43
Eternal Light, shine in my heart, 172
Eternal Ruler of the ceaseless round, 194
Evening and morning, 104
Every time I feel the Spirit, 188, 224

F
Fairest Lord Jesus, 281, 282
Faith of our fathers, 34, 149, 283
Faith, while trees are still in blossom, 114
Father eternal, ruler of creation, 163
Father, I adore You, 269
Father in heaven, 234
Father of mercies, in thy (your) word, 134,
   257, 261
Father, we praise thee (you), 65, 89, 163
Father, we thank you for you planted, 82
Father, we thank you, 117
Fight the good fight with all thy might, 34,
   154
Footsteps of Jesus, 203

For all the saints, 36, 46, 154, 266, 271, 285
For the beauty of the earth, 26, 156, 262, 281, 283
For the bread which thou hast (you have) broken, 210
For the fruits of all creation, 169
Forever with the Lord, 36
Forgive our sins as we forgive, 183, 253
Forth in thy name, O Lord, I go, 34
Forward through the ages, 42
Fred til Bod for bittert Savn, 112
Friday Morning, 166
Fröhlich soll mein Herze springen, 103, 104
From all that dwell below the skies, 31, 34, 35, 133, 282, 328
From Greenland's icy mountains, 67
From heaven above to earth I come, 99
From the slave pens of the Delta, 216
From thee all skill and science flow, 162
Frölich soll mein Herze springen, 103

G
Gentle Mary laid her Child, 101
Give me that old time religion, 185
Give to our God immortal praise, 34
Give to the winds your (thy) fears, 103, 136
Gloria, Gloria, 320
Gloria in excelsis Deo (the Greater Doxology), 65, 79, 81
Gloria, laus et honor, 90, 100
Gloria Patri (the Lesser Doxology), 65, 102
Glories of your name are spoken. See Glorious things of thee are spoken.
Glorious things of thee are spoken, 52, 55, 60, 144
Glory be to God on high, 81, 85
Glory be to Jesus, 93
Glory be to God the Father, 54
Glory to God in the highest, 81
Go forth and tell! O church of God, 172
Go forth for God, 116-117
Go forward, Christian soldier, 42
Go, make of all disciples, 42
Go, tell it on the mountain, 188, 238, 279, 282, 318
Go to dark Gethsemane, 28, 148, 273

Go to the World, 68
Go with us, Lord, and guide the way, 119
God be with you till we meet again, 22, 261
God, bless your church with strength, 110
God hath (has) spoken by the (his) prophets, 30, 164, 227, 261
God himself is (present) with us, 52, 106, 260
God is here! 169, 260, 273
God is love, 234
God is love, let heaven adore him, 164
God is our refuge and our strength, 41, 119
God is so good, 269
God is working his purpose out, 46
God moves in a mysterious way, 18, 36, 120, 144, 283
God of grace and God of glory, 209, 214, 271, 273, 285
God of love and God of power, 106
God of many names, 315
God of mercy, God of grace, 23, 150
God of our fathers (the ages), whose almighty hand, 192, 195, 283
God of the sparrow, 211, 282
God, our Father, we adore Thee, 33
God, our Lord, a King remaining, 154
God sent his Son, they called him Jesus, 204
God that madest earth and heaven, 147
God the Father of your people, 144
God the Spirit, guide and guardian, 213, 227
God-who gives to life its goodness, 217
God, who stretched the spangled heavens, 35, 183, 209, 283
God, whose almighty word, 239
God will take care of you, 303
God will, when he comes to earth, 113
God's Word is our great heritage, 112
Good Christian friends (men), rejoice, 43, 95, 283
Good Christians all, rejoice and sing, 100
Good King Wenceslaus, 101
Good news from far abroad I bring, 99
Gott ist gegenwärtig, 106
Grace Greater than Our Sin, 200
Gracious Spirit, Holy Ghost, 155
Great are your mercies, O my Maker, 233

Great God, we sing that mighty hand, 134
Great is thy faithfulness, 204, 269, 285
Guds kärlek är som stranden och som gräset, 114
Guds Ord det er vort Arvegods, 112
Guide me, O thou great Jehovah (ever, great Redeemer), 20, 52, 53, 59, 141, 226, 227, 271, 285

H

Hail! Gladdining Light, 81
Hail the day that sees him rise, 137, 227
Hail Thee, Festival Day, 90
Hail, Thou Once Despised Jesus, 61, 146
Hail to the Lord's Anointed, 24, 148
Hallelujah! Jesus lives, 112
Happy is he who walks in God's wise way, 234
Happy the home when God is there, 42
Hark! A thrilling voice is sounding, 107
Hark! the glad sound! the Savior comes, 119, 134
Hark! the herald angels sing, 21, 35, 43, 112, 137, 283
Hark, the voice of Jesus calling, 52, 190, 192, 195
Have faith in God, 204
Have no fear, little flock, 114
Have thine own way, Lord, 200
He is arisen! Glorious Word, 111
He is king of kings, 234
He is Lord, 314
He is risen, he is risen, 106
He leadeth me! O blessed thought, 51, 71, 191, 195, 197
He Lives, 204
He Never Said a Mumbalin' Word, 188
He sat to watch o'er customs paid, 112
He (all) who would valiant be, 129, 163
Heal Me, Hands of Jesus, 172
Heal Us, Emmanuel, Hear our Prayer, 144
Hear the good news of salvation, 37
Hear us now, our God and Father, 35, 227
Heavenly Hosts in Ceaseless Worship, 171
Heavenly Sunlight, 70
Help us accept each other, 170, 321
Herald, sound the note of judgment, 216

Here Am I, Send Me, 52
Here, O Lord, your servants gather, 319
Here, O My Lord, I See Thee Face to Face, 149
Herren straekker ud sin Arm, 112
Herz und Herz vereint zusammen, 107
Herzliebster Jesu, was hast du verbrochen, 101
Higher Ground, 202
Holy God, we praise thy (your) name, 52, 111
Holy, holy, holy! Lord God Almighty! 31, 47, 48, 52, 147, 252, 281, 282
Holy spirit, ever living in the church's very life, 164
Holy Spirit, fount of light, 216
Holy Spirit, Lord of love, 110, 227
Holy Spirit, Truth divine, 15, 194
Hope of the world, 116, 210, 214, 215, 255, 285, 288, 290
Hosanna, loud hosanna, 254, 283
How blest are those who trust in Christ, 36
How bright appears the Morning Star, 100, 111
How can we name a Love, 36
How can we sinners know, 117
How firm a foundation, ye saints of the Lord, 44, 51, 56, 145, 183, 267, 283
How good to give thanks, 114
How great our God's majestic name! 34, 171
How great thou art, 113
How happy is each child of God, 41, 119
How like a gentle spirit deep within, 315
How lovely is your dwelling place, 265
How lovely is thy dwelling place, 121
How sweet the name of Jesus sounds, 28, 36, 144, 190
Humbly I Adore Thee, 95

I

I am thine, O Lord, 198
I am tired and weary, but I must toil on, 206
I am trusting You, Lord Jesus, 151
I bind unto myself today, 89
I come to the garden alone, 75, 202
I come with joy to greet (meet) my Lord, 170, 254
I gave my life for thee, 151, 200
I greet Thee, who my sure Redeemer art, 117

I have decided to follow Jesus, 30
I heard an old, old story, 203
I heard the voice of Jesus say, 119, 149, 239, 253
I know not where the road will lead, 72
I know not why God's wondrous grace, 72, 200, 239, 285
I know that my Redeemer lives, 34
I Know Whom I Have Believed, 72, 200, 239, 285
I lay my sins on Jesus, 42, 112, 149, 256
I love thee, Lord, but not because, 96
I love thy (your) kingdom, Lord, 18, 60, 124
I love to tell the story, 151, 198
I need thee every hour, 197, 261
I serve a risen Savior, 204
I sing a song of the saints of God, 283
I sing the almighty power of God, 37, 43, 132, 283
I stand amazed in the presence, 202, 244
I to the hills will lift my eyes, 41, 120, 261, 265
I want Jesus to walk with me, 188
I will sing of my Redeemer, 34, 200
I will sing the wondrous story, 35, 268
I will trust in the Lord, 188
If you (thou) will only let (but suffer, but trust in) God (to) guide you (thee), 105, 271, 285
I'll praise my Maker while I've breath, 116, 133, 302
I'm pressing on the upward way, 202
Immortal Love, forever full, 74, 162, 194
Immortal, invisible, God only wise, 18, 35, 43, 56, 155, 227, 252, 271, 285
In Christ there is no east or west, 36, 164, 234, 283, 315
In dir ist Freude, 100
In dulci jubilo, 95
In heavenly love abiding, 151
In the cross of Christ I glory, 22, 54, 150
In the day of need, 172
In the Garden, 75, 202
In the hour of Trial, 148
In the stillness of the evening, 115
In thee is gladness, 100
In this world abound, 234
Isaiah in a vision did of old, 52

It came upon the midnight clear, 162, 192, 194, 195, 196
It is well with my soul, 200, 246, 301-302
'It's Jesus we want,' requested the Greeks, 114
I've come to tell, 318
I've got peace like a river, 188
I've wandered far away from God, 201

J

Jerusalem, my happy home, 96, 131
Jerusalem, the Golden, 62, 65, 93
Jesu, dulcis memoria, 92
Jesu, 'geh voran, 107
Jesu meine Freude, 104
Jesu, Jesu, fill us with your love, 229, 276, 286, 319, 320
Jesus, all my gladness, 104, 266
Jesus calls us o'er the tumult, 71, 150, 246
Jesus Christ is risen today, 95
Jesus Christ, my sure defense, 104
Jesus, I my cross have taken, 150, 190
Jesus is all the world to me, 201
Jesus is all we need, all we ever need, 307
Jesus is tenderly calling thee home, 198, 200
Jesus, joy of our desiring, 110
Jesus, keep me near the cross, 71, 198
Jesus lives! The victory's won, 104
Jesus, lover of my soul, 21, 69, 137, 227
Jesus loves me, 197
Jesus, my all, to heaven is gone, 186
Jesus nimmt die Sünder an, 108
Jesus, our Mighty Lord, 55, 65, 82
Jesus, priceless treasure, 104, 105, 110, 266
Jesus, remember me, 320
Jesus, Savior, pilot me, 193, 195, 196
Jesus shall reign where'er the sun, 34, 48, 133, 256, 280, 281, 283
Jesus, still lead on, 107
Jesus, tender Shepherd, hear me, 55
Jesus, the very thought of thee, 42, 92, 119
Jesus, thou (O Jesus) joy of loving hearts, 192, 258, 286
Jesus, thou (our) divine Companion, 190
Jesus, thy (your) blood and righteousness, 107, 136

Jesus, thy boundless love to me, 34, 103, 136, 286, 288

Jesus, united by thy grace, 42

Jesus, we want to meet, 229, 230

Jesus! what a friend of sinners, 268

Joy to the world! The Lord is come! 29, 31, 34, 43, 47, 133, 189, 259, 282, 328

Joyful, joyful, we adore thee, 35, 67, 208, 214, 270, 284

Judge eternal, throned in splendor, 227

Just as I am, without one plea, 16, 48, 150, 197, 247

K

King of the martyrs' noble band, 216

Kirken den er et gammelt Hus, 112

Kommt Gott als Mensch in Dorf und Stadt, 113

Kum ba yah, 188

L

Lauda Sion, 93, 95

Lead on, O king eternal, 18, 42, 44, 192, 227, 276, 286

Leaning on the Everlasting Arms, 22, 203

Led, like a Lamb, 313

Let all mortal flesh keep silence, 82

Let all the world in every corner sing, 128, 173, 265, 284

Let all together praise our God, 100

Let every Christian pray, 42

Let my people seek their freedom, 30, 216, 227

Let saints on earth in concert sing, 41, 120

Let the whole creation cry, 52, 110

Let there be light, 218

Let thy blood in mercy poured, 104

Let us break bread together on our knees, 188, 254, 284, 318

Let us with a gladsome mind, 26, 129, 284

Liebster Jesu, wir Sind hier, 108

Life of ages, richly poured, 194

Lift every voice and sing, 208

Lift high the cross, 165, 238

Light's abode, celestial Salem, 227

Like a river glorious, 23, 151

Like the murmur of the dove's song, 23, 172, 213

Lo, He comes with clouds descending, 137, 142

Lo, how a rose e're blooming, 286

Lobe den Herren, dem mächtigen König der Ehren, 105-106

Look, ye saints, the sight is glorious, 61, 76, 150

Lord Christ, the Father's Almighty Son, 167

Lord Christ, when first thou cam'st (you came) to earth, 107

Lord, dismiss us with your blessing, 145, 261

Lord, enthroned in heavenly splendor, 62

Lord God, Your love has called us here, 17, 171

Lord, I want to be a Christian, 26, 30, 188, 284

Lord, I'm coming home, 201

Lord, it belongs not to my care, 129

Lord Jesus Christ, be present now, 260

Lord Jesus, I long to be perfectly whole, 316

Lord Jesus, think on me, 82, 85, 118, 247

Lord, keep us steadfast in your word, 261

Lord of all good, our gifts we bring you now, 117, 168, 260

Lord of all hopefulness, 37, 164

Lord of glory, you have bought us, 227

Lord of our life and God of our salvation, 102

Lord of the dance, 166

Lord of the worlds above, 326, 327

Lord, our Lord, Thy glorious name, 106

Lord, save your world, 168

Lord, speak to me that I may speak, 76, 151, 239

Lord, teach us how to pray aright, 261

Lord, the light of your love, 314

Lord, thy word abideth, 166

Lord, we have come at your own invitation, 169

Lord, who throughout these forty days, 118

Lord, whose love in (through) humble service, 168, 182, 297

Lord, with glowing heart I'd praise thee, 190

Lord, you give the great commission, 68, 213

Lord, you have come to the lakeshore, 318

Lorica, 88

Love divine, all loves excelling, 23, 28, 33, 35, 57, 68, 138, 192, 227, 270, 286

Low in the grave he lay, 245

M

Magnificat, 79, 171
Majestic sweetness sits enthroned, 190
Majesty, worship his majesty, 314
Make me a captive, Lord, 21, 28, 72, 150, 256
Make room within my heart, O God, 37, 43
'Man of sorrows!' what a name, 199-200, 245
Many and great, O God, are thy works, 286, 318
Marvelous grace of our loving Lord, 200
May the Grace of Christ, Our Savior, 144, 261
May the Lord, mighty God, 233
Meekness and Majesty, 313
Mine eyes have seen the glory of the coming of the Lord, 186, 194, 195
More about Jesus would I know, 200
More holiness give me, 200
More love to thee, O Christ, 193, 195, 198
Morning has broken, 58
Most high, omnipotent, good Lord, 94
Must Jesus bear the cross alone, 206
My country, 'tis of thee, 191, 195
My faith looks up to thee, 22, 93, 189, 191, 192, 271
My God, how wonderful thou (you) art, 35, 119, 120, 149
My God, I love thee, 41, 96, 119
My hope is built on nothing less, 197, 239, 268, 286, 291
My Jesus, I love thee, 191
My Lord, what a morning, 188
My savior first of all, 58, 201
My shepherd is the Lord, 265
My shepherd will supply my need, 133
My song is love unknown, 129, 227, 239
My soul is thirsting for the Lord, 265

N

Name of all majesty, 172
Nature with open volume stands, 132, 266
Nearer, my God, to thee, 150, 189
New every morning is the love, 154
New songs of celebration render, 117
Nocte surgentes vigilemus omnes, 89
Not for tongue of heaven's angels, 171, 172

Now Israel may say, 116
Now may your servant, Lord, 116
Now, on land and sea descending, 194
Now praise the Lord, all living saints, 36
Now thank we all our God, 102, 104, 112, 166, 228, 270, 281, 284
Now the day is over, 154
Now the silence, 211
Now yield we thanks and praise, 110
Nun danket alle Gott, 102
Nun komm der heiden Heiland, 99
Nunc dimittis, 79, 115

O

O beautiful for spacious skies, 195, 284
O Bread of life, for sinners broken, 30
O Chief of Cities, Bethlehem, 88
O Christ, our hope, our hearts' desire, 241
O Christ, the great foundation, 42
O Christ, the healer, 110, 169
O Christ, the Word Incarnate, 154
O come, all ye faithful, 43, 96, 282
O come and dwell in me, 117
O come, O come Emmanuel, 30, 38, 96, 276, 284
O crucified Redeemer, 43, 164, 227
O day full of grace, 112
O day of God, draw nigh, 117, 216, 286
O day of peace that dimly shines, 213, 214
O Day of Rest and Gladness, 52, 155
O filii et filiae, 95
O food to pilgrims given, 110
O for a closer walk with God, 73, 120, 144
O for a thousand tongues to sing, 20, 22, 26, 28, 35, 48, 64, 138, 189, 258, 286, 316
O for a world where everyone, 35
O gladsome light, O grace of God the Father's face, 81, 116
O God, empower us, 214
O God, O Lord of heav'n and earth, 114
O God of Bethel, by whose hand, 41, 120, 134
O God of earth and altar, 20, 43-44, 162, 227
O God of every nation, 43, 210, 214, 215, 227
O God of God, O Light of Light, 54
O God of Jacob, by whose hand, 36

O God of light, your Word, a lamp unfailing, 217

O God of love, enable me, 36

O God of Love, O King of Peace, 153

O God of mercy, God of light, 296

O God, our help in ages past, 28, 36, 63, 72, 122, 133, 255, 271, 286, 290, 326, 327

O God, to those who here profess, 42, 120

O God, we ask for strength to lead, 42

O God, whom neither time nor space, 120

O gracious Light, Lord Jesus Christ, 81, 119

O Happy Day, That Fixed my Choice, 134

O Haupt vol Blut und wunden, 100, 103

O holy city, seen of John, 183, 209, 214, 224

O Holy Spirit, by whose breath, 91, 216

O Holy Spirit, enter in, 111

O How He Loves You and Me, 269

O Jesu Christ, mein schönstes Licht, 103

O Jesus Christ, may grateful hymns be rising, 210, 214, 215

O Jesus, crowned with all renown, 43

O Jesus, I have promised, 112, 149, 253, 262

O Jesus, Joy of Loving Hearts, 92

O Jesus, king most wonderful, 190

O little town of Bethlehem, 37, 43, 192, 195, 243, 259, 262, 282

O Lord of love, who gives this sign to be, 217

O Lord, our God, how excellent, 41, 119

O Lord our God, whom all through life we praise, 305

O Lord, throughout these forty days, 120

O Love that wilt not let me go, 28, 150

O lux beata, Trinitas, 87

O Master, let me walk with Thee, 36, 192, 239, 253, 271, 279, 286

O Mighty God, when I behold the wonder, 113

O Morning Star, how fair and bright, 100, 110-111

O my soul, bless God the Father (your Redeemer), 124

O perfect love, all human thought transcending, 24, 155

O praise the gracious power, 25

O praise the king of heaven, 234

O quanta qualia, 92

O sacred head, now wounded, 100, 103, 110, 190, 254, 277-78, 286

O safe to the Rock that is higher than I, 56

O sing a song of Bethlehem, 43, 209, 274, 282

O sola magnarum urbium, 88

O sons and daughters, let us sing, 95, 274

O Spirit of the living God, 37, 43

O splendor of God's glory bright, 87, 161

O splendor of the Father's light, 87

O store Gud, 113

O that will be glory for me, 70, 75

O Thou, in whose presence, 73

O trinity of blessed light, 87

O what their joy and their glory must be, 60, 65, 92

O word of God (O Christ, the Word) incarnate, 112, 154, 288

O worship the King, 24, 56, 122, 155, 286

O Zion, haste, thy mission high fulfilling, 24, 60, 192, 195, 239

Of the Father's love begotten, 34, 38, 57, 65, 88, 101, 286, 293

On a hill far away stood an old rugged cross, 202

On Jordan's bank the Baptist's cry, 96, 101

On Jordan's stormy banks I stand, 45, 59, 186

On Pentecost they gathered, 112

On this day earth shall ring, 101

On this day, the first of days, 106

On what has now been sown, 144

Once again my heart rejoices, 103

Once he came in blessing, 107

Once in royal David's City, 150

Once to every man and nation, 33, 194, 196

One day when heaven was filled with his praises, 202, 274

Onward, Christian soldiers, 42, 154, 316

Open my eyes, that I may see, 25, 276

Open now thy gates of beauty, 106, 108, 260

Our cities cry to you, O God, 216

Our Father (Parent), by whose name, 210, 227, 286, 304

Our Father, Lord of heaven and earth, 110

Our God has built with living stones, 34

Our God, to whom we turn, 110

Our Savior's infant cries were heard, 42

Out of the depths I cry to thee, 99, 261

P

Pange lingua gloriosi proelium certaminus, 90

Pass me not, O gentle Savior, 70, 75, 198

Peace to soothe our bitter woes, 112

Phos Hilaron, 81

Poor wayfaring stranger, 59

Praise and thanks and adoration, 117

Praise God, from whom all blessings flow, 30, 31, 35, 36, 111, 116, 130, 281, 282

Praise God, Praise Him, 60

Praise Him! Praise Him!

Praise, My Soul, the King of Heaven, 73, 76, 150, 270

Praise our God above, 233

Praise the Lord, 114

Praise the Lord, the King of Glory

Praise the Lord through every nation, 110

Praise the Lord who reigns above, 138

Praise the Lord! ye heavens adore him, 35, 145, 152, 227, 256, 268, 270, 284

Praise to (ye) the Lord, the Almighty, 37, 106, 257, 270, 284

Prayer is the soul's sincere desire, 23, 148

Precious Lord, take my hand, 206

Prepare the way of the Lord, 320

Psalm 72, 24

R

Redeemed, how I love to proclaim it, 242

Rejoice! rejoice, believers, 43, 227

Rejoice, rejoice this happy morn, 111

Rejoice the Lord is king, 138, 211, 284

Rejoice with us in God the trinity, 172

Rejoice, ye pure in heart, 155, 262

Rescue the perishing, 37, 198, 279, 297

Ride on! ride on in majesty, 154, 254

Rise to greet the sun, 233

Rise up, O men (ye saints) of God, 209, 214

Rock of ages, cleft for me, 35, 55, 56, 68, 145, 190, 276

S

Salve, festa dies, 90

Savior, again to Thy (Your) dear name we raise, 154, 256, 261

Savior, like a shepherd lead us, 51, 112, 151, 197, 252, 282

Savior of the nations, come, 87, 99, 110

Savior, thy dying love, 191, 195, 197, 260

Savior, when in dust to you, 227

Saviour, breathe an evening blessing

See the morning sun ascending, 106

See, to us a Child is born, 171

Seek ye first, 211, 313

Sei Lob und Ehr dem höchsten Gut, 105, 302

Send the Light, 202

Shall we gather at the river, 197

Shepherd of eager youth, 81, 82

Shepherd of souls, refresh and bless, 42

Shine, Jesus, shine, 314

Silence, frenzied, unclean spirit, 46

Silent night, holy night, 34, 43, 113

Since Jesus came into my heart, 202

Sing my tongue, the glorious battle, 90

Sing praise to God who reigns above (the highest good), 105, 107, 284, 302

Sing them over again to me, 199

Sing to the Lord a new song, 114

Sing to the Lord of harvest, 154

Sing unto the Lord a new song

Sing we now of Christmas, 284

Sing with all the saints in glory, 35

Singet dem Herrn ein neues Lied, 114

Singing songs of expectation, 30, 227

Sinners Jesus (Jesus sinners) will receive, 108, 200

'Sleepers, wake!' A voice astounds us, 100, 110

So send I you, by grace made strong to triumph, 216

Softly and tenderly Jesus is calling, 201, 246

Soldiers of Christ, arise, 138

Somebody's knocking at your door, 224

Sometimes a light surprises, 144, 190

Songs of thankfulness and praise, 110, 155

Soul, adorn yourself with gladness, 104

Source and Sovereign, Rock and Cloud, 315

Spirit of God, descend upon my heart, 23, 149

Spirit of God, sent from heaven abroad, 112

Splendor paternae gloriae, 87

Spread, (O) Oh, spread, almighty (thou

mighty) Word, 106, 111
Spread the news! 234
Stabat mater dolorosa, 94
Stand By Me, 205
Stand up and bless the Lord, 117, 148, 241, 255, 266
Stand up, stand up for Jesus, 35, 191, 193, 284
Standing on the promises, 35, 36
Stille Nacht, heilige Nacht, 113
Stir your church, O God our Father, 214
Sunset and evening star, 19
Surely goodness and mercy, 204
Surrexit Christus hodie, 95
Sweet hour of prayer, 18, 62, 197
Sweetly, Lord, have we heard thee calling, 203

T
Take my life and let it be consecrated, 151, 253, 261-262, 282
Take my life, lead me, Lord, 52
Take the dark strength of our nights, 234
Take time to be holy, 200
Take up thy cross and follow me, 204
'Take up thy (your) cross,' the Savior said, 183, 192
Te Deum laudamus, 56, 65, 87-88, 102
Te vengo a decir, 318
Tell it out with gladness, 35, 68
Tell me the story of Jesus, 200
Tell out, my soul, the greatness of the Lord, 79, 171, 286
Thanks to God Whose Word Was Spoken, 261
That Boy-child of Mary, 229
That Easter Day with joy was bright, 101
The Angel Gabriel from Heaven Came, 154
The Battered, Battered Bride, 66
The bells of Christmas, 112
The bread of life, for all is (sinners) broken, 231, 232, 286
The Christ who died but rose again, 30
The church of Christ, in every age, 169, 298
The church's one foundation, 42, 66, 155, 284
The day is past and over, 84, 110

The day of resurrection, 42, 84, 254, 284
The Day Thou Gavest, Lord, Is Ended, 154
The duteous day now closeth, 110
The earth and all that dwell therein, 120
The First Day of the Week, 169
The First Nowell, 43
The flaming banners of our King, 90, 216
The Glory Song, 201
The God of Abraham praise, 35, 142, 282
The God of Heaven, 172
The grace of life is theirs, 227
The great Creator of the worlds, 119
The head that once was crowned, 16, 30, 54, 61, 150
The heavens above declare God's praise, 120
The King of love my shepherd is, 50, 153
The Lord will come and not be slow, 116, 128-129, 276
The Lord's my shepherd, I'll not want, 50, 121, 284
The love of Christ who died for me, 35
The love of God is broad like beach and meadow, 114
The Old Rugged Cross, 70, 202
The people who in darkness walked, 41, 120
The royal banners forward go, 90
The servant King, 313
The Solid Rock, 63
The Son of God goes forth to War, 147
The Son of God, our Christ, 301
The Son of Man goes forth to war
The spacious firmament on high, 133
The strife is o'er, the battle done, 96, 244, 254
The voice of God is calling, 52, 214
Thee, we adore, O hidden Savior, 95
Thee will I love, my strength, 136
There is a balm in Gilead, 188, 241
There is a fountain filled with blood, 44, 144
There is a green hill far away, 119, 150, 243
There is sunshine in my soul today, 200
There shall be showers of blessing, 200
There'll be peace in the valley for me, 206
There's a call comes ringing o'er the restless wave, 202
There's a spirit in the air, 171, 172, 238
There's a sweet, sweet Spirit in this place, 46

There's a wideness in God's mercy, 16, 33, 149, 253

They crucified my Lord, 26

They saw you as the local builder's son, 114

Thine arm (Your hand), O Lord, in days of old, 122, 299

This is a day of new beginnings, 170, 212

This is my Father's world, 36, 208, 281, 282

This is the day the Lord hath made, 34, 120, 133

This is the day, this is the day that the Lord hath made, 314

This is the Spirit's entry now, 35

This is the three-fold truth, 276

Thou didst leave Thy throne, 261

Thou hidden love of God, whose height, 106, 110, 136

Thou hidden source of calm repose, 71, 303

Thou (God), whose almighty word

Though I may speak, 287

Through the night of doubt and sorrow, 227

'Thy kingdom come!' on bended knee, 118, 162

Thy mercy and Thy truth, O Lord, 119

Thy strong word did cleave the darkness, 30, 227

Tis dawn, the lark is singing, 191

Tis so sweet to trust in Jesus, 201

To a maid engaged to Joseph, 214

To God be the glory, 198, 314

To God we lift our voices, 20

To mock your reign, O dearest Lord, 43, 119, 169

Today we are all called to be, 43

Today your mercy calls us, 246

Ton sig sträcker efter frukten, 114

Trials dark on ev'ry hand, and we cannot understand, 205

Tröstet, tröstet, meine Lieben, 105

Trust and Obey, 200

Tryggare kan ingen vara, 113

Tut mire auf die schöne Pforte, 108

Twas in the moon of wintertime, 217, 318

U

Unto the Hills Around Do I Lift Up, 265

Unto us a boy is born, 101

Urbs beata Jerusalem, 90

V

Var hälsad, sköna morgonstund, 112

Veni, Creator Spiritus, 91

Veni, redemptor gentium, 87, 99

Veni, Sancte Spiritus, 93

Verborgne Gottesliebe du, 106

Vexilla regis proderunt, 90

Vi lova dig, o store Gud, 112

Vi ville dig se, sâ grekerna bad, 114

Victimae paschali laudes, 93, 99

Victory in Jesus, 203

Von guten Mächten wunderbar geborgen, 114

Von Himmel hoch da komm ich her, 99

W

Wachet auf, ruf uns die Stimme, 100

Wake, awake, for night is flying, 100, 110

Walte, walten nah und fern, 111

Watchman, tell us of the night, 25, 150, 227, 264

We all believe in one true God, 266

We are climbing Jacob's ladder, 187, 188, 224

We are the Lord's, 111

We are tossed and driven on the restless sea of time, 205

We believe in one true God, 266

We bind ourselves in freedom's chains, 36

We gather here to bid farewell, 216

We gather together, 36

We give thee but thine own, 154, 260

We have heard the joyful sound, 201

We know that Christ is raised, 161

We meet You, O Christ, 170

We plow the fields, and scatter, 109

We praise thee (you), O God, our Redeemer, 36

We sing the glorious conquest, 112

We sing the praise of him who died, 112, 150

We stand united in the truth, 119

We thank thee, Lord, for this our food, 142

We utter our cry, 170

We walk by faith, and not by sight, 153

We welcome glad Easter, 43

We worship you, O God of might, 112

Weary of all trumpeting

Welcome, happy morning, 90

We'll Understand It Better By and By, 205

Wer nur den lieben Gott lässt walten, 105

We're not just anyone; we're not just nobodies

Were you there when they crucified my Lord, 187, 188, 278, 287, 318

We've a story to tell to the nations, 239, 284

What a fellowship, what a joy divine, 203

What a friend we have in Jesus, 45, 198, 261

What a wonderful change in my life has been wrought, 202

What child is this, 25, 43, 155, 264

What does the Lord require for praise and offering, 168, 260

What star is this, with beams so bright, 101

What wondrous love is this, 184, 254, 287, 293, 317

What wondrous love is this, O my soul, O my soul, 302

When all my labors and trials are o'er, 201-202

When all your mercies, O my God, 41, 119, 133

When Christ was lifted from the earth

When Christ who died but rose again

When I survey the wondrous cross, 18, 24, 28, 30, 37, 54, 132, 189, 252, 278, 287, 328

When in our music God is glorified, 161, 169, 274, 287, 293, 321

When in the night I meditate, 118

When Israel was in Egypt's land, 188

When Jesus left his Father's throne, 43

When morning gilds the skies, 42, 93, 116, 265, 284

When my life-work is ended, and I cross the swelling tide, 201

When peace, like a river, attendeth my way, 200, 276, 301

When Stephen, full of power and Grace

When the church of Jesus, 30, 169, 296

When the storms of life are raging, stand by me, 205

When we walk with the Lord, 200

Where charity and love prevail, 36

Where cross the crowded ways of life, 73, 209, 214, 301

Where restless crowds are thronging, 43, 214, 227, 301

Where shall my wandering soul begin? 137

Wherever he leads I'll go, 204

While shepherds watched their flocks by night, 41, 53, 119, 122, 131, 285

Who is He in yonder stall, 25, 264, 274

Who would true valour see, 129

Why are nations raging, 110

Wie schön leuchtet der Mogenstern, 100

Wild and lone the prophet's voice, 227

Wind who makes all winds that blow, 227

Wir pflügen und wir streuen, 109

Wir sind des Herrn, wir leben oder sterben, 111

Wir sind nicht irgendwer und nicht nur ungefähr, 114

With high delight let us unite, 107

Wonderful words of life, 34, 199, 265

Would You bless our homes and families, 37, 44, 217

Y

Ye holy angels bright, 129

Ye servants of God, your Master proclaim, 54, 122, 138, 260

Ye watchers and ye holy ones, 30, 111

Ye who claim the faith of Jesus, 211-212

You are the way; through you alone, 41, 120

You satisfy the hungry heart, 213

Your hand, O Lord, in days of old, 53

Your kingdom come! O Father, hear our prayer, 116

Your love, O God, has called us here, 213

Your supper, Lord, before us spread, 30, 37

You're alive, 313

Z

Zion, praise thy Saviour singing, 60, 93

Hymn Tune Index

A

ABBOT'S LEIGH, 165, 217
ABERYSTWYTH, 212, 226, 227
ACCEPTANCE, 321
ADESTE FIDELIS, 43, 96, 267, 282
ALL THE WORLD, 128, 284
AMAZING GRACE, 44, 45, 47, 285
AMERICA, 191
AMSTERDAM, 139
ANGELIC SONGS, 239
ANNUNCIATION, 214
ANTHES, 246
ANTIOCH, 29, 31, 34, 43, 47, 189, 259, 282, 328
ARLINGTON, 34, 48
ASSAM, 30
ATKINSON, 216
AUGUSTINE, 128, 173, 284
AURELIA, 42, 284
AUSTRIA, 284
AUTHORITY, 46
AVE VIRGO VIRGINUM, 285
AZMON, 35, 189, 286

B

BALM IN GILEAD, 45
BANGOR, 283
BARONITA, 321
BATTLE HYMN, 186
BEACH SPRING, 182, 317

BEECHER, 33, 48, 192, 286
BEGINNINGS, 212
BELLWOODS, 216, 286
BESANCON, 163
BETHANY, 189
BIRABUS, 172
BIRMINGHAM, 286
BLOTT EN DAG, 113
BOURBON, 183
BRADBURY, 197, 282
BREAK BREAD, 45, 284
BREAK BREAD TOGETHER, 45
BRESLAV, 112
BRIDEGROOM, 172, 213
BRISTOL, 119
BROTHER JAMES' AIR, 284

C

CAITHNESS, 120
CANNOCK, 165
CANONBURY, 239
CANTERBURY, 128
CARLISLE, 241
CAROL, 192
CARPENTER 1970, 114
CHAPMAN, 202
CHEREPONI, 286
CHESTERTON, 166
CHINA, 45, 197
CHRIST AROSE, 245

CHRIST LAG IN TODESBANDEN, 110
CHRIST WHOSE GLORY, 173
CHRISTE SANCTORUM, 90, 164
CHRISTMAS, 285
CLEANSING FOUNTAIN, 44
CONCORD, 218
CONSOLATION, 183
CONSOLATOR, 247
CONVERSE, 45
CORONATION, 32, 143, 179, 285
COVENTRY CAROL, 163
CRADLE SONG, 201, 282
CRIMOND, 284
CROSS OF JESUS, 157
CRUCIFER, 165
CRUGYBAR, 226
CRUSADER'S HYMN, 282
CWM RHONDDA, 141, 226, 227, 285

D
DANIEL'S TUNE, 284
DARWALL, 139, 284, 327
DETROIT, 183, 257
DIADEM, 36, 139, 143
DIADEMATA, 285
DICKINSON COLLEGE, 286
DIE GÜLDNE SONNE, 104
DIVINUM MYSTERIUM, 38, 88, 101, 286, 293
DIX, 157, 283
DOMINUS REGIT ME, 157
DONNE SECOURS, 116, 285, 288, 290
DOWN AMPNEY, 162-163
DU FRIENDENSFÜRST, HERR JESU CHRIST, 110
DU SOM GAAR UD, 112
DUKE STREET, 34, 139, 281, 282, 283
DUNDEE, 41, 120, 125, 283
DUNLAP'S CREEK, 184
DURHAM, 119, 285

E
EASTER HYMN, 139, 283
EBENEZER, 30, 48, 141, 216, 227
EIN' FESTE BURG, 35, 37, 39, 47, 99, 109, 283
EL NATHAN, 239, 285
ELLACOMBE, 283, 284
ELLERS, 256
ELLESDIE, 190
ENGELBERG, 161, 287, 288, 293, 321
ERHALT UNS HERR, 110
ERMUNTRE DICH, 110
ES IST EIN' ROS', 286
EVENING PRAYER, 200
EVENTIDE, 36, 157
EWING, 93, 157

F
FAITHFULNESS, 285
FALCONE, 212
FALLS CREEK, 204
FOREST GREEN, 37, 43, 162, 243, 282, 283
FORTUNATUS, 157
FOUNDATION, 44, 146, 224, 267, 283
FRED TIL BOD, 112
FREDERICKTOWN, 287, 293, 321
FRENCH CAROL, 284
FREU DICH SEHR, 105, 117
FREUEN WIR UNS ALL IN EIN, 107

G
GALILEE, 246
GARELOCHSIDE, 164
GARTAN, 164
GAUDEAMUS PARITER, 285
GELOBT SEI GOTT, 100
GENEVA 124, 116
GENEVAN 47, 116
GIFT OF FINEST WHEAT, 213
GIFT OF LOVE, 287
GLORY, 172

GO TELL IT, 282
GOPSAL, 139, 284
GORDON, 191
GOTT SEI DANK, 106
GOTT SEI DANK DURCH ALLE WELT, 106
GOTTES SOHN IST KOMMEN, 107
GRACIAS, 166
GRÄFENBERG, 104
GRANDE ISLE, 283
GREENSLEEVES, 43
GROSSER GOTT, 111
GUD SKAL ALTING MAGE, 112

H
HSUAN P'ING, 233
HALLELUJAH, 184
HALLELUJAH, WHAT A SAVIOR! 245
HAMBURG, 37, 48, 189, 287, 326, 328
HANOVER, 122, 286
HENDON, 282
HER VIL TIES, 112, 282
HERZLICH TUT MICH ERFREUEN, 284
HERZLICH TUT MICH VERLANGEN, 286
HERZLIEBSTER JESU, 101, 104, 285
HIDING PLACE, 190
HOLY MANNA, 183, 283, 317
HORSLEY, 243
HUNTSVILLE, 299
HURSLEY, 247
HYFRYDOL, 35, 141, 146, 227, 243, 268, 282, 284, 286
HYMN TO JOY, 35, 48, 208, 283, 284

I
I DE SENE TIMERS STILLHET, 115
I WANT TO BE A CHRISTIAN, 284
ICH HALTE TREULICH STILL, 110
IN DIR IST FREUDE, 100
IN DULCI JUBILO, 43, 95, 283

INTERCESSOR, 114, 161
ISTE CONFESSOR (ROUEN), 102
ITALIAN HYMN, 37, 146, 239, 283

J
JACOB, 212
JACOB'S LADDER, 45
JEFFERSON, 243, 282
JERUSALEM, 213
JESU DULCIS MEMORIA, 286
JESU, JOY OF MAN'S DESIRING, 110
JESU MEINE FREUDE, 104, 110
JESUS AHATONHIA, 216
JESUS LOVES ME, 45, 197
JESUS MEINE ZUVERSICHT, 104
JULION, 211, 212

K
KEDRON, 184
KING'S LYNN, 162
KING'S WESTON, 30, 289, 290
KINGSFOLD, 43, 162, 282
KIRKEN, 29, 285
KIRKEN DEN ERET GAMMELT HUS, 285
KREMSER, 36
KUORTANE, 164

L
LACQUIPARLE, 286
LANCASHIRE, 18, 42, 284, 286
LAND OF REST, 96
LANGHAM, 163
LASST UNS ERFREUEN, 30, 36, 94, 111, 240, 282, 328
LAUDA ANIMA, 157
LAUDES DOMINI, 42, 157, 284
LAUDS, 172
LAUS REGIS, 284
LE CANTIQUE DE SIMÉON, 116
LE CÉNACLE, 114

LE P'ING, 233
LENOX, 179-180
LEONI, 35, 281
LET US BREAK BREAD, 45
LIGHT, 190
LITTLE CORNARD, 163
LITTLE FLOCK, 114
LLANFAIR, 164, 227, 283
LLANGLOFFAN, 43, 141, 164, 227
LOBE DEN HERREN, 32, 37, 39, 284
LOBT GOTT DEN HERREN, 284
LOBT GOTT, IHR CHRISTEN, 100, 241
LONDON NEW, 120, 283
LOVE UNKNOWN, 129, 239
LYONS, 267, 286

M
MACDOUGALL, 284
MCKEE, 283, 284
MACH'S MIT MIR, GOTT, 247
MADRID, 37, 164, 282
MAITLAND, 206
MAJESTAS, 172
MANNA, 46
MARYTON, 36, 48, 239, 286
MATERNA, 284
MEINEN JESUS LASS ICH NICHT, 108
MELITA, 157, 268, 286, 290
MENDELSSOHN, 35, 43, 112, 283
MERCER STREET, 173, 208, 283
MESSAGE, 239, 285
MESSIAH, 282
MIGHTY SAVIOR, 212
MILES LANE, 143
MIT FREUDEN ZART, 107, 284
MONK'S GATE, 129
MONKLAND, 284
MOODY, 200
MORNING HYMN, 282
MORNING LIGHT, 35, 191, 284
MORNING SONG, 183, 209, 224

MOSCOW, 37, 146
MOWSLEY, 165
MUELLER, 282
MUNICH, 112, 288
MUSKOGEE, 204
MY SAVIOR'S LOVE, 245

N
NAAR MIT ÖIE, 112
NATIONAL HYMN, 193, 283
NEED, 197
NETTLETON, 37, 44, 224
NEUMARK, 109, 286
NEW BRITAIN. *See* AMAZING GRACE.
NEW MALDEN, 216
NEWTOUN, 120
NICAEA, 31, 47, 48, 157, 282
NOËL NOUVELET, 163
NOUS ALLONS, 163
NOW, 211
NUN DANKET, 104, 111, 228, 284
NUN DANKET ALL UND BRINGET EHR,
  104
NUN KOMM, DER HEIDEN HEILAND,
  110
NUNC DIMITTIS, 116
NYLAND, 164

O
O FILII ET FILIAE, 95
O QUANTA QUALIA, 92
O SEIGNEUR, 116, 285
O STORE GUD, 113
O WALY WALY, 287
O WELT, ICH MUSS DICH LASSEN, 110
OLD 100TH, 31, 35, 36, 41, 116, 118,
  282
OLD 107TH, 116
OLD 113TH, 116
OLD 124TH, 116
OLD 134TH, 48, 117, 241

OLD RUGGED CROSS, 45, 46
OLIVET, 189, 191
ORIENTIS PARTIBUS, 283
ORTONVILLE, 190

P
PASSION CHORALE, 39, 100, 110, 287
PATMOS, 282
PERSONET HODIE, 101
PICARDY, 82
PIER PAUL, 217
PILOT, 198
PLEADING SAVIOR, 190, 247
PRECIOUS LORD, 206
PROMISED LAND, 45, 186
PROMISES, 32, 33, 35, 36
PROTECTION, 183
PSALM 42, 105, 117
PUER NOBIS, 101
PUER NOBIS NASCITUR, 101, 162
PURPOSE, 46, 163

Q
QUEBEC, 286

R
RANDOLPH, 162
REGENT SQUARE, 157
RENDEZ À DIEU, 41, 117
RESCUE, 37
RESTORATION, 247
RESURREXIT, 283
RHOSYMEDRE, 227, 239, 287
RHUDDLAN, 227
RICHMOND, 139, 143
ROCKINGHAM, 287
ROEDER, 211, 282
ROYAL OAK, 163, 282
RUSTINGTON, 161
RYBURN, 286, 289

S
ST. AGNES, 42, 48, 327
ST. ANDREW OF CRETE, 83
ST. ANNE, 36, 122, 125, 283, 286, 291, 327, 328
ST. CATHERINE, 34, 283, 286, 289
ST. DENIO, 18, 35, 43, 141, 227, 268, 286
ST. DUNSTAN'S, 129
ST. ELIZABETH, 282
ST. FLAVIAN, 118
ST. GEORGE'S WINDSOR, 31, 283
ST. GERTRUDE, 42, 157
ST. KEVIN, 157, 285
ST. LOUIS, 192, 243, 259, 282
ST. MAGNUS, 30
ST. MATTHEW, 122
ST. MICHAEL, 117, 216, 286
ST. PETER, 36, 284
ST. THEODULPH, 35, 48, 100, 282
SAGINA, 139
SALVE FESTA DIES, 90
SALZBURG, 110
SAMSON, 172
SANKEY, 199
SAVANNAH, 48, 139
SCHMÜCKE DICH, 104
SHARPTHORN, 173
SHEAVES, 172
SHELDONIAN, 165
SHENG EN, 30, 231, 232, 287
SHILLINGFORD, 46, 172
SHOWALTER, 203
SICILIAN MARINERS, 282
SIMPLE GIFTS, 166
SINE NOMINE, 36, 46, 163, 285, 288
SLANE, 36, 164, 285
SOLID ROCK, 197, 268, 286, 291
SOMETHING FOR JESUS, 197
SONG 1, 128
SONG 13, 128

SONG 34, 128
SONG 67, 128
SONG OF THE HOE, 233
SOUTHWELL, 118, 247
SPANISH HYMN, 37, 282
SPOHR, 282
SSCHÖNSTE HERR JESU, 282
STILLE NACHT, 34, 43
STOCKTON, 247
STUTTGART, 282
SUTTON COMMON, 172
SWEET SPIRIT, 45-46

T
TALLIS' CANON, 119, 281, 282
TALLIS' ORDINAL, 119, 125
TEMPUS ADEST FLORIDUM, 101
TERRA BEATA, 36, 208, 281, 282
TERRA PATRIS, 36, 208, 281, 282
THE CALL, 34, 128
THE EIGHTH TUNE, 119
THE FIRST NOWELL, 43
THIRD MODE MELODY, 119, 239
THOMPSON, 246
THORNBURY, 161
TIDINGS, 239
TO GOD BE THE GLORY, 268
TON-Y-BOTEL, 227
TOPLADY, 35, 190
TORONTO, 216
TOULON, 117
TRENTHAM, 285
TRINITAS, 172
TRUMPETS, 114
TRURO, 285
TRUSTING JESUS, 199
TRYGGARE KAN INGEN VARA, 113

U
UNE JEUNE PUCELLE, 318
UNSER HERRSCHER, 106, 109

V
VALET WILL ICH DIR GEBEN, 35, 100
VATER UNSER, 110
VENI, CREATOR SPIRITUS, 244
VENI EMMANUEL, 30, 38, 284
VENI, VENI, EMMANUEL, 30
VENITE EXULTEMUS, 38, 40
VEXILLA REGIS, 90
VICAR, 286, 288, 290
VICTORY, 244
VILLE DU HAVRE, 200, 246
VINEYARD HAVEN, 211
VOX DILECTI, 157, 239

W
WACHET AUF, 110
WALDA, 83
WALTON, 286
WARRENTON, 186
WARUM SOLLT' ICH, 104
WAS FRAG' ICH NACH DER WELT, 110
WEBB, 35, 191, 193, 284
WER NUR DEN LIEBEN GOTT, 286
WERDE MUNTER, 112
WERE YOU THERE, 45, 287
WIE SCHÖN LEUCHTET, 112
WIE SCHÖN LEUCHTET DER MORGEN-
    STERN, 110
WILLIAMS BAY, 284
WINCHESTER OLD, 41, 119, 285
WINDSOR, 119, 243
WIR PLÜGEN, 109
WITTENBERG NEW, 114
WONDROUS LOVE, 287
WOODLANDS, 287
WOODWORTH, 48, 197, 247
WORDS OF LIFE, 34
WUNDERBARER KÖNIG, 106

Y
YIGDAL, 35, 284